TRENDS IN MISSION

TRENDS IN MISSION

Toward the Third Millennium

Essays in Celebration of Twenty-Five Years of SEDOS

Edited by
William Jenkinson, CSSp and Helene O'Sullivan, MM

ORBIS BOOKS

Maryknoll, New York 10545

The Catholic Foreign Mission Society of America (Maryknoll) recruits and trains people for overseas missionary service. Through Orbis Books, Maryknoll aims to foster the international dialogue that is essential to mission. The books published, however, reflect the opinions of their authors and are not meant to represent the official position of the society.

Copyright © 1991 by Orbis Books
All rights reserved
Published by Orbis Books, Maryknoll, NY 10545
Manufactured in the United States of America

Library of Congress Cataloging-in-Publication Data

Trends in mission : toward the third millennium : essays in
  celebration of twenty-five years of SEDOS / edited by William
Jenkinson and Helene O'Sullivan.
      p.   cm.
   ISBN 0-88344-766-5
   1. Catholic Church—Missions.   I. Jenkinson, William (William R.)
II. O'Sullivan, Helene.   III. SEDOS (Organization)
BV2183.T74   1991
266'.2—dc20   91-18469
                                                          CIP

CONTENTS

PART ONE
THE CONTEXT OF MISSION TODAY

LOCAL CHURCHES

POPULAR RELIGIOSITY

PART TWO
MODELS OF MISSION AND MINISTRY

MINISTRIES IN A DYNAMIC LOCAL CHURCH

JUSTICE, PEACE AND INTEGRITY OF CREATION

DIALOGUE

PART FOUR
MISSION: FROM VATICAN II INTO THE COMING DECADE

PREFACE

Robert Schreiter, CPPS

SEDOS came into being at a time marked by a real sea-change in the understanding of what constituted mission, the kind of sea-change that happens only a few times in the course of history. It was the end of the Second Vatican Council, a remarkable event that would redirect the church's sense of itself and its mission and ministry in the world. A new understanding of the church's relation to the Reign of God, of its relation to the world, to other religious traditions, and to the cause of human promotion would understandably have an impact on how mission would be conducted. There was great optimism that local churches would develop and flourish, urged on by the vision of the Council, and directed by the new frameworks that were emerging.

But it was not only the church that was changing; the world was being reshaped as well. The colonial age was coming rapidly to an end, and region after region in the Southern Hemisphere became free of imperial bondage and took on the status of nations. There was great optimism in the air about the growth of new nations as partners to the established nations of the Northern Hemisphere, and dreams of a new economic order.

A quarter of a century later, that vision of church and world has not become what many would have hoped. Change in the church, while dramatic, has not been without its problems. The mandate of the Council to renew has encouraged some to see renewal and change as a continuing process, but it has filled others with a fear that fundamental principles were being set aside and that important elements of identity were being lost. Some of the energies that the Council had released were now being diverted into intramural struggles within the church, instead of fueling the hopes that *Gaudium et Spes* had so eloquently evoked. Nor have the dreams of the young nations been realized. They soon discovered that the end of colonial rule had left them as flag democracies rather than independent nations who could direct their own futures. An economic colonialism continued, and many nations found themselves bereft of the economic and cultural resources that they needed to effect genuine change.

WHY MISSION?

In the midst of these new realities in church and world, those involved with missionary activity faced what seemed to be even more momentous change.

From the side of the church, the challenge to inculturate the gospel seemed most acute in those regions of the world farthest away from Europe and North America. The call to dialogue with other religious traditions was heard most clearly by those who found themselves in a minority among the adherents of Islam, Buddhism, and the religions of India. And the language of development often seemed too weak to address the plight of the poor and oppressed. The move away from colonialism caused a deep self-reflection for missionaries who had often allied themselves with the imperial powers and who now wished to stand more clearly with the victims of colonialism. It is not surprising, then, that for some years the question "Why mission?" overshadowed any other query about the future of missionary activity.

SEDOS (the Documentation and Research Center) has been in the forefront throughout this entire period, asking questions and suggesting possibilities. Born of the collaborative efforts of religious institutes of men and women concerned about mission, it has represented their collective wisdom and has often transcended what any one or any small group of institutes might have conceived. It is a true heir to the collaborative spirit of Vatican II. It has been willing to face courageously those difficult questions for which there are no clear answers. It has served as a meeting point for committed persons and their institutes to promote the kinds of sharing and dialogue that are so crucial to effective mission today. And it has provided services and resources to enhance the ministries of the institutes that called it into existence.

Twenty-five years is not a long time in the history of the church or the history of mission. But this last quarter-century has been a fast-paced one, both in the church and in its world context. Thus it is valuable to have a volume such as this, which not only records important insights and moments in SEDOS's years of service and provides significant documents that it has produced during that time, but which also—in the best spirit of SEDOS—keeps before us those challenges that have no easy answers and that continue to shape mission today. The four parts of this volume reflect this: the context of mission (the "where" of mission), the models of mission and ministry (the "how" of mission), the people in mission (the "who" of mission), and the challenges of mission (the "whither" of mission). These four points form, as it were, the coordinates of mission, upon which the "what" of mission comes to be situated. For that "what" of mission is not something that stands above time and history. How mission is inculturated, how the Christian message interacts with other great traditions, who bears the message, and what is envisioned as the end result of the communication of the message all become part of the message itself. Certainly that has been one of the most important things learned in these last twenty-five years.

By way of introducing this volume, then, it might be useful to reflect on each of these four coordinates, and think about how they are helping us to trace the future of mission. For this volume is more than a retrospective look at the achievements of SEDOS; it is also intended to help direct us into the next stage of mission. And it is certainly in the best tradition of SEDOS never to expect things to stand still: we must keep moving forward, trying to discern what the

God who goes before us has in mind for the mission in which we hope to participate.

THE CONTEXT OF MISSION

What, then, of the context of mission today? An important change in twenty-five years has been the extent to which we now attend to context itself. The church no longer sees itself as the perfect society, over against and independent of the world. The church and its mission, rather, are incarnated in the world. Accepting that fact helps us become more aware of how contexts can shape and direct our options in mission without ever entirely determining them.

The first part of this volume gives ample evidence of how SEDOS has struggled with context through the years. The local churches themselves, in their theologies, provide a context for mission that was often ignored in the past. Not to understand those theologies is to miss the very conversation in which we hope to engage. But other contextual forces come to bear on this conversation as well: the challenge of Enlightenment thinking (generally referred to as "modernity") and the thinking that now questions some of the Enlightenment's project (now called "post-modernity"); the enduring power of local forms of religious thinking and behavior ("popular religiosity") to shape the perceptions and expectations of communities struggling with their continued evangelization; and the concrete realities of distinct regions of the world—such as South Africa or Europe—that influence the way mission takes shape and the challenges to which it is called.

There is another dimension of context that might be added here, a dimension that is undergoing profound change at this time. In some ways this dimension has been so monumental that it remains almost beyond awareness until it begins to shift; then we cannot fail but take note of it. But we are so unaccustomed to thinking about this dimension shifting that we barely know what questions to ask.

For the first time in five hundred years, there are two major economic groups among the nations of the world who do not in some way share the Christian heritage. One set is made up of the countries of the eastern Pacific rim, especially South Korea, Japan, and Singapore. The other set is constituted by the petroleum-rich Muslim nations of the Middle East and South Asia. These players, especially Japan, provide a counter to the economic hegemony exercised by the United States and a soon-to-be-united European Economic Community. New York and London no longer set world prices alone; major markets are now open twenty-four hours a day. We are moving to a genuinely polycentric world where no one place can dominate as was once the case. Europe and North America shared common cultural and religious assumptions that do not now reach to the new centers of power. What will this mean for Christian mission? Is it coincidental that the modern form of mission had its beginning with the eclipse of Ottoman power in Europe and the economic and military rise of the Christian nations? What shape will mission take now that that era of domination is coming rapidly to an end? What will this mean for the poor nations of the world? Will they be even more oppressed as more centers exploit them? The questions tumble out faster than they can possibly be answered.

Important ideological shifts are taking place as well. The remarkable and swift events in Eastern Europe and the Soviet Union in the late 1980s dramatically changed the world context in a variety of ways. Financial aid to revolutionary causes in the poorer nations will be less forthcoming as the COMECON economies turn inward to rebuild themselves and focus their attention on aid from the world centers of wealth. Will European and American aid and investment be directed to the new and potentially lucrative markets of Eastern Europe and the Soviet Union and away from the South? The lucrative arms industry will be thrown into a crisis as East-West tensions ease and defense spending is scaled back. Will arms dealers attempt to peddle their deadly wares even more to the poor nations of the South than they now do? Will the North-South split become even more aggravated as the East-West division starts to disappear? The implications of this for North-centered mission-sending religious institutes are enormous. Marxism could well be largely replaced by anti-Northern fundamentalisms as the South reacts to Northern exploitation. Fundamentalisms such as that of the Sendero Luminoso in Peru—an essentially anti-modern fundamentalism under a veneer of Maoism—might well become the norm in desperately poor countries.

These two shifts, economic and ideological, profoundly change the context for tomorrow's mission. They may affect who may even be able to engage in mission, and will certainly affect the forces with which mission will have to contend.

MODELS OF MISSION

Models of mission and ministry have already been considerably altered in the past twenty-five years, as the selections in Part Two recount. The vision of both mission and ministry has been broadened to include more than the sacramental and homiletic dimensions of ministry. This came about partly as a new understanding of how the church developed, but partly, too, from realizing how context-bound the received models had been. Local churches are seeking to express their own call to mission in ways more adequate to the challenges as they see them. The fundamental shift in attitude about ministry—that ministry is rooted first in baptism and thus in a call to all the People of God—provides the foundation for thinking about new ways of carrying out mission.

But new values have also been held up that shape the "how" of mission. Ecumenism among the churches, dialogue with the adherents of other religious traditions, the importance of struggling for justice and working for peace, the support of the integrity of creation in all its forms, the importance of witnessing by sheer presence in the "dialogue of life"—all of these have become part and parcel of engaging in mission today.

The articles collected here attest to the struggle to understand the meaning of these values for mission. But most would admit at the same time that we are still but beginning to understand what they will mean for mission. Some fear that attending to dialogue and justice, or making the witness of life central to our activities, will dilute the purpose of mission itself: namely, the proclamation of the Good News of Jesus Christ. It is perhaps at this point that we see the struggle to develop new models of mission most clearly, for it is here that older models that took the conversion of souls or the establishment of the church as their goals have run up against their own inadequacy. Concern about dialogue or justice may have started as practical concerns, because there was no alternative for a minority religion or because human need cried out so strongly. But reflection by missionaries has brought us all to realize that these are not alternatives to evangelization but utterly constitutive of it. People look at what Christians do, not just what they say or profess. There has to be an integrity about what we do and say.

Again, we are only beginning. The implications for mission of a commitment to dialogue, justice, and witness are the most daunting challenge for the future conduct of mission. The ultimate question in dialogue may be the most profound theological issue to face the church in the twenty-first century: just what is the relation of the revelation of God in Christ to the revelation of God in other traditions? The quest of justice will become even more of a priority than it now is as economic gaps yawn open even more widely, and more and more poor countries slide into utter misery. And the question of witness raises the issue of what constitutes a genuinely Christian existence in any culture, especially when we cannot look to the support of the state to protect or sustain us.

PEOPLE IN MISSION

The discussion of people in mission has centered around two points: new relationships in mission (the inclusion of lay people in greater numbers, and more equal and mutual relations between men and women), and what is needed to sustain those new relationships. It has taken religious institutes some time to come to terms with including lay persons in their ministry as missionaries, but many are now doing it with generosity and mutual respect. The rise, too, of groups of lay missionaries operating independently of religious institutes is a welcome development in thinking about mission. Likewise, feminist thought has contributed greatly to the recasting of male-female relationships in mission.

There are three other sets of questions that increasingly influence mission thinking, implied in both the developments just sketched and in the larger environment in which mission is conducted. The first is the role of the short-term missionary—priest, lay person, religious sister or brother. This has meant the involvement of a larger number of people in the missionary activity of the church, who thereby come to experience the fundamentally missionary nature of the church. Many if not most missionaries of this kind are changed in important ways by this experience; for ideally, missionaries not only change the communities to which they are sent, but are themselves changed. Likewise, the sending church also receives the benefit of this transformation. Yet, aside from these advantages, twenty years' experience with short-term missionaries begins to raise certain questions about this as a model of missionary activity. Is short-term missionary activity to be the norm? Did it develop because of the resources that allow for easier travel than before? (Or conversely, would we have had life-term missionaries if we had had air travel earlier?) What, ultimately, is the value of the short-term missionary to a local church? Is it to help with some specific, short-term needs that a local church has? Is it primarily an opportunity to witness to the church as a communion of local churches? Or is it to provide an opportunity for a local (receiving) church to give instruction to another local (sending) church? What does the short-term say about the need to learn another way of life in a different language and culture? What are the theological reasons for this kind of missionary activity? To what extent does it reflect the vocational patterns of rich cultures that have the resources to change employment several times in a lifetime?

This questioning is not intended to be considered hostile. But the future of mission requires that any new patterns or models of mission be thoroughly and critically examined in order to assure that they are indeed new models and not just continuations of old mistakes under new guises.

A second set of questions revolves around the people in mission and the resources that support mission. Most international religious institutes now find the majority of their candidates coming from what used to be termed "mission" countries—the poorer nations of the South. The economic resources of those same institutes, however, generally remain ensconced in the North. This is already the source of conflict in many institutes, despite honest efforts in both North and South to combine evangelical witness with faithful stewardship of resources. Two major shifts, however, seem likely in the future. Unless patterns change, within two decades most members of many institutes will be from the Southern countries. What will this mean for policies set by General Chapters? What will this mean as institutes learn to think in fundamentally different, non-European ways about how they approach problems, and the human and financial resources they bring to them?

The second shift may arise out of the exacerbation of relations between North and South. Will members of international institutes in the South even be able to receive help from the North? Will hostilities between North and South bring about, not an internationalization of religious institutes, but a new regionalization?

The third set of issues has to do with the missionary activity of Southern people in the (re)evangelization of the North. Will Southern local churches have the opportunity to exercise the missionary nature of their vocation not only among other Southern peoples or minority groups in Northern cultures, but in the very heart of the dominant cultures of Europe and North America? What role do mission-sending religious institutes have in pioneering this way of thinking about mission? To this point, it has been assumed that a people or a community cannot evangelize itself in a fundamental way without some help from the outside (echoing Romans 10:14). Yet there is also an assumption that the North Atlantic countries will somehow re-evangelize themselves. More thought needs to be given to this problem, because how we answer this question bespeaks how we understand mission. Are missionaries to the North seen as guest workers or immigrant laborers, or as people bearing something we need in the North?

THE CHALLENGES OF MISSION

The challenges of mission are many today, and Michael Amaladoss sets them out clearly and superbly in Part Four of this volume. Let me close these introductory words by highlighting a few challenges that he refers to as areas as yet underexplored in thinking about mission.

First of all, Christian mission has generally been better at dealing with rural communities than with urban ones. We tend to replicate rural models in urban centers when we are forced to face the prospects of urban mission. According to statistician David Barrett, the majority of foreign missionaries today work in rural areas and in villages. But the planet is becoming urbanized at an alarming rate. To be sure, many megalopolises are ruralized by the influx of rural peoples, but only to a certain extent. Without some measure of urbanization in terms of economic development and deployment of services, these centers are likely to inch more closely to collapse. What can missionary institutes do to develop models of mission more adequate to the city and to ways of living out the gospel in the city?

Second, Amaladoss rightly points out that, for the most part, Christian mission has fared better with the outcasts in a society than with its elites. There may be good theological reasons for this, but in a desperately fragile physical environment and in a world where power is concentrated in a few centers rather than distributed more widely, should we not consider how to evangelize the powerful, while we continue our efforts on the part of the oppressed? Can we afford to bypass the powerful or continue merely with methods (such as running schools for the children of the elite) that have largely been unsuccessful in terms of evangelization?

Third, if the hypothesis sketched out above about a North–South split becomes fact, it will be important for the future of mission to develop a spirituality that deals satisfactorily with conflict and violence. Christian values center on communion and harmony; thinking about conflict is avoided when possible. Consequently, Christians historically have not been very good at dealing with conflict, even though Christian's are called to embrace the cross, an instrument of violence. Perhaps the time has come to give conflict more direct attention—both what it means to live in conflict and what might be the means of overcoming it—in order to make sustained Christian witness in such situations possible. Missionaries have much to learn from the poor who have lived in many places with overt conflict, often for long periods of time. Whatever we can learn from this should become part of any program of missionary formation.

In the later 1960s and early 1970s the question was "Why mission?" Two decades later new complexities and challenges have arisen, and questions of "how," "who," and "whither" come flooding back to us. In many ways, this is an exciting time to be part of the church's mission. SEDOS has helped shape thinking about mission as no other single institution has been able to do. This collection attests to that. May it be with us for at least another twenty-five years—for the horizons of the twenty-first century, which this volume already allows us to see dimly, will soon be upon us, with the opportunities and challenges which the God of liberation and of hope holds out to us.

INTRODUCTION

William Jenkinson, CSSp and
Helene O'Sullivan, MM

SEDOS is a study and documentation center at the service of mission societies. They all have a common aim: to make known the Good News of the gospel across boundaries of culture, race, class, and nationality. The first small group of members came together during the closing sessions of the Second Vatican Council. This year SEDOS celebrates its Silver Jubilee — twenty-five years of collaboration in carrying out a common mission.

The present volume is published on the occasion of this Silver Jubilee. It is dedicated to those first seven who followed a vision in 1966 and to all those other mission societies who, following their inspiration, have joined SEDOS through the years. SEDOS has indeed "growed like Topsy" to a membership of seventy-two societies. Their combined membership is approximately a quarter of a million. They are dedicated to mission, some totally and uniquely, some partially as part of their wider charism, but all to making known the God of love and the love of God.

The world today is characterized by increasingly rapid and far-reaching change. It is in this world that mission takes place. Missionaries must foresee and respond to this change if they are to be truly at the service of God's peoples. Hence the seminars, meetings, and other events organized, facilitated, and inspired by SEDOS.

The present volume brings together a selection of conferences delivered each year at the annual research seminars and other significant SEDOS meetings and conferences. Begun in 1982, they implement and further develop the Agenda for Future Planning, Study, and Research in Mission drawn up at the March 1981 Research Seminar. A copy of this Agenda is included in the appendix to this volume.

A word about the nature of these seminars. The topics are chosen by the SEDOS Executive Committee in consultation with the membership. They are key issues of mission today. The seminars invariably follow a methodology of creative reflection based on an experiential approach. This has five movements: getting to know one another; expressing involvement; analyzing experience; evaluating experience; charting future directions.

Resource persons come from all the continents. Participants at the seminars are themselves also rich resource persons who come from the leadership of the

SEDOS membership—superior generals, their assistants, members of their general councils or secretariates for mission. It is not unusual that a single small discussion group of nine people has in its membership a combined total of two hundred years of mission experience; nor is it unusual that participants come from more than twenty different nationalities, all continents, and thirty mission societies. Much of the work is carried out in groups. There are shared scripture reflections, prayer, and celebration of the eucharist, the latter taking place increasingly over the years in small groups.

A word about the criteria used in choosing papers for this volume. We have aimed at a balance between reflective and experiential contributions. We have chosen papers from all continents and from both women and men. Inevitably this meant that we had to omit many contributions of great merit. The papers chosen by us were written or delivered in English, French, Italian, and Spanish. We have attempted to establish a written style which, while being faithful to the original meaning and at times to the dramatic and moving experiences recounted by some speakers, nevertheless preserves a certain uniformity.

During the course of this past decade there have been momentous changes in mission. Perhaps these may be encapsulated in one significant development which is reflected in this volume. SEDOS with its seventy-two member societies, almost all of whom have their origins and the greater proportion of their membership in the Northern Hemisphere, chose Michael Amaladoss, SJ, from the Southern Hemisphere to give the keynote address at the celebration of the twenty-fifth anniversary of SEDOS in December 1989. His theme, "Mission: From Vatican II into the Coming Decade," was presented as he said by "a recipient of mission and from the underside." The theme is taken up once again by him as Part Four of this present volume.

The authors of the papers collected in this volume are a cross section of a courageous body of people. They come from North and South, East and West; they are married people, with children, or dedicated single people, sometimes dedicated through religious vows; they are priests, bishops, and even archbishops. They are monks. And they are sinners. They live lives of dialogue, of commitment to justice and liberation, they try to inculturate to heroic degrees; they preach the God of love and the love of God in universities, seminaries, city churches, and small bush chapels, and in no chapels at all. And they do pay with their lives for their dedication. We hope you will read about them and what they think and write. We are privileged to present them to you in this volume.

PART ONE

THE CONTEXT
OF MISSION TODAY

1

Emerging Trends Challenge the Churches of Asia

Felix Wilfred

Let me express, at the outset, my satisfaction over the formulation of the theme of this SEDOS seminar, "Local Church: Practices and Theologies." The organizers have rightly placed practices before theology, and thereby have set the proper methodological orientation for the seminar. Following this approach, in the first part of my paper I will present a few reflections on the present-day trends and sociocultural processes which call for an appropriate praxis on the part of local churches. Though these trends and processes are not exclusive to Asia, they are nevertheless reflected upon from an Asian perspective and on the basis of Asian experiences. The second part of the paper is devoted to the study of a suitable ecclesiology for the Asian context.

EMERGING TRENDS AND SOCIOCULTURAL PROCESSES AT THE TURN OF THE CENTURY: CHALLENGES TO ECCLESIAL PRAXIS

The last stage of the journey of the human family in this century has been marked by many momentous events and new turns. The ominous prospect of a nuclear holocaust, which not long ago seemed to hang over the human family as Damocles' sword, now seems to have vanished as a bad dream, while fresh signs of hope are emerging both at the global and local levels.

Among the significant developments are the changes in the relationship between the First and the Second Worlds and the victory of peoples' movements in many parts of the world. The political and military confrontation between the First and the Second Worlds characterized the post-war period and determined global politics has now undergone a sea-change. As for peoples' movements, they suffered heavily in the hands of the vested interests. The repression of these movements (which has not abated and leaves no room for naive and

premature optimism) made many skeptical about their ability to bring about
any effective change in the prevailing order of things. Such apprehensions are
today laid to rest as the future of peoples' movements has brightened, with
events like the Edsa revolution in the Philippines and the uprising of the people
of Eastern Europe against self-serving rulers, party chiefs and bureaucrats. The
most dramatic of all was the dethronement and execution of Ceausescu and
his wife Elena.

We who have witnessed such significant developments at the end of the 1980s
cannot but pose certain questions concerning the future. What is the shape of
things to come? In which direction might the human family be moving in the
next few decades? Is the domination and oppression of the poor and the weak
going to intensify or diminish? These are, obviously, very difficult questions to
answer. Some indications of future directions can be found if we examine some
of the trends and sociocultural processes that are beginning to emerge.

A study of the emerging trends at the turn of the century is indispensable
and crucial for the local churches in Asia and, for that matter, anywhere in the
world. It is necessary for their self-understanding, insertion and relevant praxis
in the new century that is about to dawn.

CONFLICT BETWEEN THE MACRO AND THE MICRO

One of the phenomena which we observe all over the world today is the
conflict between the macro and micro—the big trying to dominate the small
and the latter refusing to be dominated and reduced. This can be seen in almost
all areas of societal life.

At the political level, for example, we have the macro in the form of the
nation-state, a political entity of the modern world which was brought into
existence by setting aside the diverse ethnic, linguistic and regional groups at
the micro level. In most cases, the overarching structure of the nation-state
does not acknowledge the experiences and self-perceptions of the various
groups and peoples subsumed, nor respect their legitimate autonomy and differing identities. Resistance, therefore, to the macro political reality on the part
of the micro is something quite pervasive. In Asia we have such a situation, for
example, in Sri Lanka, India, Pakistan, Malaysia, Indonesia, Thailand, the Philippines, and so forth.

POLITICAL FUNDAMENTALISM

In this context I must add a word about political fundamentalism which is
emerging everywhere. It is a phenomenon which has appeared with the collapse
of macro-level realities, and has come to fill in the ideological vacuum that
exists today. Fundamentalism is an attempt on the part of one of the constituents in a society to assume the role of the macro and in this process suppress
other groups and identities.

What is happening at the political level in terms of macro and micro is but
a modern reproduction of the contrast between the "great tradition" of the
dominant groups, classes, and religious agents and the "little tradition" of the
marginalized groups in society. The macro, the great, often declares its respect

for the micro. But history and experience show that the macro, in reality, develops its own world, its own interests, and in this process seeks to absorb the micro.

CULTURE

At the level of culture we note a dangerous trend toward transforming the whole world into a monocultural zone. The politically and economically powerful First World tries to impose subtly on the rest of the world a culture, or rather a subcultural way of life, based on standardized forms of production and the same patterns of marketing and consumption of goods. It passes for macro culture and, indeed, culture. The struggle against this cultural imperialism is visible in the societies of the Third World.

SOCIAL SCIENCES

If we take the social sciences such as anthropology, the same trend is discernible. Grand social and anthropological theories are construed in relation to the situations and experiences of those at the micro level. These grand theories are applied to micro-level realities only for verification and confirmation. This approach and orientation is today being challenged. Many concrete experiences at the micro level simply break preconceived schemes and theories. The reality at the micro level presents such differences and variety that they defy classification into one general frame; they call for totally new explanations and interpretations.

NATURAL SCIENCES AND TECHNOLOGY

The conflict between the macro and the micro is also evident in the field of natural sciences and technology. One of the principal reasons for the gross disparity in economic growth in the world is the dissociation of science and technology from the social and economic base of the people at the micro level, those at the bottom. Gripped by a megalomaniac vision, science and technology proceed with giant strides to accomplish the political and economic designs of the powerful.

It is this mega or macro science which is unfortunately imported into the Third World, into Asia. Therefore there is a cleavage between the needs of a society at the micro level and the grand designs of imported science and technology. While the gap may continue with serious consequences for the poor and the marginalized, there will also develop a strong trend toward taming macro science. The demand for a science and technology with social concern and a human face will be strengthened further in the years to come. This trend will share the objectives of the ecological movement which is putting pressure on macro science to develop itself in relationship with environmental concerns. The conflict between the macro and the micro is likely to continue to the turn of the century and even beyond, leading finally to a clear choice in favor of the micro in science and technology.

RELIGIOUS INSTITUTIONS

At the religious level, the second part of the twentieth century has brought fresh awareness about the great religious traditions of humanity, in spite of, or perhaps because of, the powerful trend towards secularization. The great religions are in fact macro institutions or "great traditions." But at the turn of the century we are witnessing the trend of not letting oneself be impressed by the macro religiosity which is identified with huge institutions, power, wealth, and so forth. There is a search for salvation in the small, in the neglected and despised. It is a trend in which the mustard seed assumes importance, a trend in which what happens to people at the micro level in terms of religious experience becomes more significant and more crucial than the mighty religious institutions, their interests and concerns.

This orientation reflects the attitude of Jesus in his time. He was not impressed by the grandiose temple to which the disciples drew his attention (Mark 13:1, Matt. 24:1). On his part, he pointed rather to an insignificant widow in the same temple, highlighting the worth of her small mite (Mark 12:41–44, Luke 21:1–4). The prominent place popular religiosity is acquiring points towards the future.[1] So too, the small, micro, basic communities are clear expressions of the religious orientation and praxis of the years to come. The multiplication of sects in the past years, which is likely to continue, represents a protest against macro religious institutions, traditions which are becoming sterile and a spent force. The turn of the century may witness in the religious field, as in other fields, an intensification of the conflict between the macro and the micro.

FROM FRAGMENTATION TO INTEGRATION

In today's world we note forces of division and marginalization operative in various areas of societal life. In spite of these many tendencies toward fragmentation in today's world, we also note, on the other hand, how the process of globalization is taking place at a very fast pace. Thanks to the powerful modern communications media, the problem of one people or group does not remain isolated but is brought to international attention. This emerging global consciousness is a great sign of hope. The human family is moving today toward a unity never before achieved in history. There is a deep aspiration to get out of situations of marginalization and division and reach integration. If fragmentation is the self-destruction of humanity, the movement toward unity is the sign of its redemption.

Nobody can deny that, in spite of many hurdles, international cooperation is getting stronger today. There are many initiatives at the international level to take up jointly issues affecting humanity, such as apartheid and violation of human rights. We have, further, bodies of regional cooperation as, for example, SAARC and ASEAN in Asia.

NORTH–SOUTH RELATIONS

The effectiveness of the movement toward the unity of the human family will depend on the development of the relationship between the three blocks into which our world has been divided in the past decades. Significant and dramatic changes have occurred in the relationship between the First and Second Worlds. The concrete shape of this new interrelationship has yet to be seen. If ideology was the bone of contention between the First and Second Worlds, economic difference and imbalance continue to divide the First World from the Third World. The prospect, therefore, of the First and Third Worlds, the North and the South, meeting will be real to the extent that economic and consequently political issues are faced. In this regard we envisage in the coming decades the possibility of two parallel processes developing. On the one hand, the capitalist nations, which depend on finding new markets for their continued growth, will try to be generous towards poor nations by offering credit so that these third-world countries will in turn be able to buy their products—machinery, arms, and so forth. Even countries now relatively safe from debt will be trapped into a serious debt crisis.

On the other hand, the already existing solidarity among third-world nations on the political level will begin to express itself more and more on the economic front as well. This economic cooperation may initially take the form of trade relationships among third-world nations in particular regions. The general movement toward the unity of the human family may have to pass through these stages of conflict and tension on the one hand, and phases of partial cooperation and solidarity on the other.

A HOLISTIC PERSPECTIVE

At a more basic level, the trend toward viewing reality from a holistic and integral perspective, despite the pervasive tendency to atomize and dichotomize, is slowly gaining momentum. This orientation is supported by modern empirical sciences like physics, biology, psychology, and so forth. Modern science has passed from the mechanistic paradigm of Newton to a new paradigm of quantum physics in which the whole universe is seen as interconnected within one and the same movement and dynamism.[2] In the face of the unity of all reality, sciences like sociology, anthropology, and psychology are becoming more and more aware of their limitations. Each one of them can deal only with a fragment of reality which cannot be explained without being linked to the other dimensions. Today, interdisciplinary approaches are becoming common and even indispensable. The myth that reality can be known by atomizing it is giving way to a holistic and integral approach which can unfold the web of relationships connecting all the parts of reality.

ECOLOGICAL AND FEMINIST MOVEMENTS

Today's trend toward unity and integration includes two important movements: the ecological movement and the feminist movement.[3] They are powerful affirmations of unity and at the same time a protest against fragmentation. The ecological movement challenges the one-sided emphasis on domination and control in the relationship between humankind and nature and underscores the necessity of harmony. The feminist movement, which calls for the complementarity of woman and man, protests against a male-dominated society—a society marked by aggression, violence, and war. The concerns voiced by these two movements will set the agenda for the century that is dawning. They will help to bring about a much-needed balance in the growth of the human family.

POSITIVE RECOGNITION OF PLURALISM

The coming decades will be characterized by an ever greater recognition of pluralism in all areas of life. Centralization of every kind—political, economic, religious—will be forced to loosen its grip. Decentralization of power, wealth, and ideology will begin, thus keeping alive the dream of the unity of humanity in diversity, despite signs of division and conflict. Pluralism is going to be the strongest antidote against all domination, control and regimentation. Its language is dialogue and its attitude and praxis is participation, for pluralism is based on the recognition of the otherness of the other. The liberation of the oppressed and the quality of human life in the decades ahead will depend in great measure on our recognition and appreciation of pluralism.

I must add that the pluralism we envisage is not some kind of irenism in which each group or people is simply let be in their diversity without regard to others. Such a pluralism is not desirable, and could be even counterproductive to the true welfare of humankind whose various peoples, nations, and groups should mutually communicate, confront, and correct each other so as to grow as one family. In true pluralism the element of challenge is as important as dialogue and participation. Further, the pluralism we envisage is not without limits. The limit of pluralism means that there is no choice when there is a question of justice, a question of solidarity with the poor or a question of an unjust social, economic or political order.

THE PROCESS OF MODERNIZATION

The process of modernization is a global question which affects every society. Whether East or West, North or South, in every society we find traditional elements in varying degrees alongside the forces of modernization. But in third-world societies the impact of modernization is much more evident than elsewhere. Science, technology, industrialization, modern means of communication, urbanization, modern educational and political systems have profoundly influenced traditional cultures, institutions, and ways of life. Even more deeply, they have brought about a transformation in attitudes and values and in the consciousness of individuals and groups. These changes are immediately visible in the cities of Asia which are growing at an alarming rate through mass migration and urbanization consequent upon modernization.

I do not want to enter into the various theories regarding the process of modernization as they may take us too far afield from the focus of this paper.[4] Let me, however, make three observations which are important in understanding this process. First, modernization is not to be equated with "Westernization," which is the process by which a non-Western individual or group adopts the forms of life, ways of thinking, values, and behavioral patterns of the West.[5] Second, the expression "modernization" is value-laden. It presupposes that the characteristics of the developed world should also one day be the traits of the underdeveloped societies of today. (And that is perhaps why the temptation exists to identify modernization with Westernization.) Third, the economic developments and modernization which have taken place in the West are not, as often assumed, independent of the underdevelopment of the Third World.[6] Modernization cannot be understood without the colonial and neocolonial history of exploitation.

MODERNIZATION AND TRADITION

It is important that the question of the relationship between modernity and tradition be posed differently from the way it has been in the past few decades, especially since the 1960s. Most of the theories rested on two premises. Firstly, it was assumed that there was a dichotomy between tradition and modernity. No distinction was made between the various types of tradition.[7] Tradition, as such, was viewed as a force restraining the process of modernization. It was not recognized that there are some traditions which can block the process of modernization and others which can be a valuable resource for it. Experience shows how certain traditional cultural and religious elements, known for their immobility, become in new circumstances a strong force for change and transformation.

Secondly, it was assumed that the so-called "theory of convergence of industrialized societies" is universally valid. According to this theory, traditional societies of different kinds become more and more similar as they become industrialized and urbanized. This is a somewhat simplistic approach. It does not reflect the complexity of social change in traditional societies. The people of a particular culture perceive, approach, and handle the same issues and problems of modernization differently from other peoples because their underlying core values and perceptions are culturally influenced.[8] Therefore the responses to modernization will be different in different societies. A variety of responses in the same society is also possible. Evidently, core perceptions do change but their pace and mode of change are different from the structural and institutional changes which may result from modernization.

In practice, the encounter between traditional societies and modernity has produced a wide variety of situations. Modernization has produced dual systems in economic, political and cultural spheres. In Asian societies, for example, we find tradition juxtaposed with modernity. Asians, accustomed as they are to living with contradictions, live with one foot in modernity and the other in tradition. In some other situations we have a transference of traditional attitudes and values onto modern systems or, reversely, the superimposition of the modern onto tradition.[9] As far as Asia is concerned it is undeniable that the response of the vast majority has been a profound desire to reap the benefits of modernity without losing the identity of one's traditional culture and its long-cherished values, ideals, and core perceptions. This is the challenging task facing Asian societies at the turn of the century. How should we go about this task?

Modernization is an ambiguous process. If it contains great potential for humanization, it also contains elements of dehumanization. Economic development based on limitless growth and backed by political power has caused wealth for some at the expense of the poverty and misery of the masses. Therefore, ethical and humanistic perspectives from Asian cultural resources need to be brought into the modern process of development. This challenging task also calls for a prophetic critique of all forms of alienation and negation caused by the process of modernization. The following reflections on the centrality of culture denote responses to modernization in the future.

PROGRESSIVE CENTRALITY OF CULTURE

As a consequence of modernization, the cultural dimension of life is relegated to the background. Economy becomes the all-embracing and dominant factor in human and social life. We can observe this in the model of development set forth by the First World for third-world countries. In the so-called development decades of the 1950s and 1960s, the progress of Asian countries as well as other underdeveloped parts of the world was thought of in terms of economic growth. But slowly the realization dawned that development was not being achieved by or for the poor because economic issues were tied up with political ones.[10] In the 1970s and early 1980s we tried to come to terms with the political question—the issue of power. Today, with poverty and misery still weighing heavily on the poor in our villages and slums, attention is progressively turning to the role of culture. Today, one begins to realize the key role of culture for both economic development and the acquisition of political power by the people. Even more basic than these, culture affects their selfhood as persons, as active subjects and agents of history.

The culture of a people expresses their spirit, their collective unconscious. Like the trees of the forest which preserve the soil from erosion, the cultural roots of a people give them strength and selfhood to withstand the oppression and exploitation of the powerful. It is the living embodiment of their experiences transmitted from generation to generation; it is the unique, specific way of a people's knowing, feeling, and perceiving reality and interacting with it. How an ancient culture cannot be simply gotten rid of is exemplified by the short-lived cultural revolution in China. Culture does change, but it cannot be forcibly cast off.

ECONOMIC DEVELOPMENT AND CULTURE

For future economic development serious attention will have to be paid to the culture of a people from which stem their values, motivations, and attitudes. For example, Japan may exhibit the same traits as the industrially advanced countries of the West. And yet Japanese capitalism has a different cultural matrix from that of the West. The thesis of Max Weber concerning the relationship between capitalism and Protestantism is well known. Japanese capitalist growth, however, is based on the traditional cultural institution of *furusato* — old home village — where people were engaged collectively in rice cultivation through close bonds of relationships with each other and with nature.[11] Chinese entrepreneurship and business traits derive from Confucian philosophy and ethics.

The centrality of culture is manifested differently in the West and in the East. In the West it has begun to express itself as a quest for meaning and a search for new symbols. It expresses itself also as a virulent critique of empirical rationality which characterizes the present model of development. This model of development is often antihuman and devoid of humanizing culture. In Asia, which was dominated by colonial powers, the centrality of culture can be seen in the affirmation of the identity of a people as a group, a nation. It is also seen in the search for cultural roots to undergird modern-day economic, social, and political life. The cultural comes to the fore in our Asian societies also in the aspiration of the people to determine for themselves, on the basis of their history, tradition, and values, their own patterns of development and forms of self-government. People will no longer allow political and economic consider-ations to supplant their culture. They are becoming increasingly aware that both the political system and economic growth must bear the imprint of their culture.

Following the political independence of third-world nations from colonial rule, it was thought that political unity would automatically bring about unity among the various ethnic, cultural, and linguistic groups. This has been belied by experiences of ethnic conflict and civil war within various nation-states. Sub-sequently it was thought that the creation of a common economic system would unify peoples of different races and countries. This too is being contradicted by experience. European unity, which rests primarily on an economy base and a common market, is being eroded today with the reunification of the two Germanys, which has caused serious concern among their neighbors. Ethnic and cultural elements are again coming to the fore and breaking open economic frames. The conflicts between the Armenians and the Azerbajdzans as well as the demands of Lithuanians, Estonians, and Latvians are all indications of the central role that cultural identity is going to play in the years to come.

The assumption by the First World that it had resolved the ethnic question through a common economic system, and the assumption by the Second World that it had resolved the same problem through a common ideology, are both being proved false by these trends. The re-emergence in the First and Second Worlds of the cultural and ethnic dimensions of life should lead to the reali-zation of the limitation of the economic and the ideological dimensions. The First World and Second World, which thought that ethnic and cultural conflicts were simply a third-world phenomenon, are learning from their own experience the complex situations that third-world societies are facing and the difficulties of finding solutions in merely economic and ideological terms.

CRISIS OF SURVIVAL

The teeming millions of Asia are today caught in a deep crisis of survival. The natural resources of land, sea, and forests which were for them life-sup-porting have been taken from them and are today controlled by oppressive forces from within Asia and from abroad. Industrialization which is both capital-and resource-intensive is taking place in Asian societies. It has marginalized the masses for whom life has become unbearable in the rural areas. Impover-ished and dispossessed they are fleeing in large numbers to cities and towns to eke out their existence in abject poverty around slums and shanty towns. They

are deprived of the necessary power to decide their own destinies. The economic policies adopted by many Asian governments have suppressed the rights
of workers, peasants, and marginalized sections of society, including tribals,
women, dalits (the untouchables), and oppressed youth. The gross imbalance
in the relationship between production, distribution, and consumption has widened the gap between the affluence of a few and the abject poverty of the
dispossessed masses.

FOCUS ON THE VILLAGE

The line of economic development followed in the past few decades has
heavily favored the cities to the detriment of rural villages where the bulk of
third-world people live. This trend is likely to intensify in the years to come,
aggravating the crisis of survival for marginalized and powerless groups. A refo-
cusing on the village is imperative to overcome this crisis.

ESCALATION OF VIOLENCE AND TERRORISM

Another development in the years ahead is the unfortunate escalation of
violence and terrorism. It will be the result of economic conditions rather than
politically motivated. Colonialism in the first half of the century and the economic policies of the development decades in the second half strengthened the
already powerful and further marginalized the powerless. This situation will
reach a breaking point in the years to come. It appears that recourse to violence
and robbery in order to force the powerful and the rich to part with their wealth
will become increasingly common in India. Escalation of unrest, revolts, and
violence on economic grounds can be expected among oppressed groups of
people, especially tribals, dalits, and poor peasants. Such a development will
force structural and institutional changes—a goal that has not been achieved
by the present pattern of development.

The roots of future change can be found in both the upsurge of consciousness
about the present situation and in the conviction by the marginalized that this
situation is not to be taken as their inevitable fate but as something to be
overcome. From the general ocean of misery voices of protest are being raised.
There is a persistent demand from various quarters to transform the present
oppressive order into one in which people can grow, flourish, and blossom as
human persons. It is a struggle, first and foremost, to obtain the basic necessities
of life. Equally important is the struggle for equality by social outcasts and
marginalized peoples like the dalits, tribals, and other ethnic minorities.

The experience of past decades shows that the crisis of survival cannot be
overcome by pinning one's hope on one single approach. No single ideology,
no single political system or economic arrangement can claim to be the panacea
for the woes afflicting the oppressed. A plurality of approaches is called for,
depending on the specific situation of oppression with its unique characteristics,
history, and cultural roots. In some cases, sharp confrontations will lead to the
overcoming of long-standing oppression, whereas in other cases religion may
furnish the rallying point for the people in their struggle against unjust economic and political situations. In still other cases a fresh awareness of their

ethnic and cultural identity will prove the most effective means for establishing justice and equality.

THE ROLE OF IDEOLOGIES

What role will ideologies play in relation to the struggle of the people? All ideologies promise to get the poor and the marginalized out of their crisis of survival. But the type of ideology necessary for sociopolitical transformation cannot be dictated from above. It has to be shaped and formed from out of the experiences of the people in specific situations and contexts. People cannot simply surrender to any ideology that promises to liberate them, because ideology can be made into a myth by vested interests, party chiefs, and bureaucrats, or into a totem which the people have only to prostrate before and adore.

Recent events in Eastern Europe illustrate the consequence of turning any ideology into an idol. It would be wrong to interpret these developments in Eastern Europe as a victory for capitalism, which has little to boast about. Capitalism too has undergone and is still undergoing even more serious crises, even though it may not be so evident and dramatic as what has happened in Eastern Europe. The concentration of wealth in the hands of a few with the subsequent impoverishment of the many, racism, new forms of poverty in the so-called developed countries, the production and sale of armaments—these are the handiwork of industrial capitalism which cannot claim to help overcome the crisis of survival in which humanity is enveloped. Rather, it is the principal cause of the global crisis of survival.

It may not be easy for Asia and other third-world societies to get out of the stranglehold of advanced industrial capitalism as its tentacles spread further and further. But the direction of future development is becoming clearer to us. If the greater part of the twentieth century has been under the sign of the two mega ideologies, the emphasis in the future is going to shift from ideologies to the people as the center. Codified and institutionalized responses in the form of ideologies are inadequate to meet the challenges of poverty and survival. We can expect the emergence of fresh and creative responses on the part of the people to the questions of poverty, misery, and human survival.

RESPONSE OF THE LOCAL CHURCH

Responses at the local level to these global questions will shape the specificity of each local church. The praxis and agenda of the local church cannot be something separate from or parallel to these sociocultural processes. For the churches, to respond to the questions and challenges is to respond to the living God who is in the midst of the people and in their history. In this perspective the communion among local churches will also be a communion in praxis in which all respond to the same voice of God speaking today in a wide variety of situations—situations which more and more bear common traits and form part of convergent sociocultural processes.

ANTHROPOLOGICAL AND CULTURAL FOUNDATIONS OF ECCLESIALITY

In a recent public interview, the Deputy Prime Minister of India, Mr. Devi Lal, stated that "Christians have no business in the country and should take off to where they belonged, America, England or even Italy."[12] There is nothing new about this view. He has given a sharp and renewed expression to a deeply embedded attitude among Asians that Christians in Asia are an alien body.

Many reasons may be adduced to explain this rootlessness of Christianity in Asia: the colonial past, spiritual and material dependence on foreign resources, lack of involvement in the national scene, failure to practice inculturation, and so forth. These factors may, to some extent, account for the situation. But they do not touch the heart of the question, namely, the lack of an anthropological and cultural foundation for the very being of the church among the Asian peoples. None of the present-day ecclesiological orientations seems to meet this crucial concern of Asia.

In this second part of the paper I intend to highlight the necessity of developing an anthropologically- and culturally-based ecclesiology in Asia and to spell out some of its implications. The reflections made here, let me state clearly, are tentative and provisional. None of them is to be understood as an independent model of the church. They are rather four strands differently mixed to form concrete images of the church.

MAJOR ECCLESIOLOGICAL ORIENTATIONS

REFORMIST

This ecclesiological current originated a few decades before the Council and made its mark on Conciliar deliberations and documents. It is a ferment of thought which, in contrast to the centralizing ultramontanist ecclesiology of "the perfect society," calls for an understanding of the church as communion and highlights the aspect of mystery. It is characterized by its tendency to *resourcement* — going back to the Fathers and the tradition of the early centuries to derive fresh insights for the understanding of the nature and mission of the church. Promoting unity among all Christians through dialogue has been one of its chief concerns. It is this ecclesiology which brought the idea of local church to the fore and underlined the place of eucharist, Spirit, word of God and ministry as its constitutive elements. As a major ecclesiological orientation a large number of theologians are associated with it, among them Yves Congar, E. Lanne, H. Legrand, J. M. R. Tillard, Avery Dulles, Joseph A. Komonchak.[13]

LIBERAL

This orientation is characterized by its critical approach. It calls into question the way the church functions, its triumphalism, its mode of exercising authority, its strong centralization. Freedom of thought and expression, respect for human dignity and rights in the church, openness and flexibility in its life — these are some of the concerns of this orientation. It views critically doctrines like infallibility and primacy as they have been formulated and understood. The present is adjudged in the light of the gospel to which this orientation repeatedly draws our attention. It is concerned with making the church meaningful to people in a secularized and "adult world." Hans Küng, Leonard Swidler, J. L. McKenzie and many others represent this orientation.[14]

Both these ecclesiological strands — reformist and liberal — are today locked in a controversy with forces in the church that are trying to reassert a centralist ecclesiology through a movement of restoration and integralism. The debate relates especially to Vatican II—its reception and its significance as well as its continuity or discontinuity with earlier tradition.[15]

LIBERATIONAL

Christian unity and openness to the world were concerns very much present in the thinking of the Council. But there was another important question which, although it did not receive the attention it deserved, nevertheless was part of the original spirit of the Council. It was the imperative need to be a church of the poor. This question formed part of the vision of the initiator of the Council, Pope John XXIII, and was expressed in the speeches of a few Council fathers like Cardinal Lercaro. That the churches should be in solidarity with the poor and the suffering, in imitation of Jesus Christ, was expressed in passing in the documents of the Council, especially in *Lumen Gentium*, 8 and *Ad Gentes*, 5. These few indications, coupled with a sharp awareness of the poverty, misery and oppression of the poor in various parts of the Third World, and especially in Latin America, led to an ecclesial praxis of liberation, and consequently to the development of an innovative and fresh ecclesiology of liberation.[16] The focal point of this liberational praxis and reflection has been the basic ecclesial communities. As representatives of this trend we may cite Jon Sobrino, Leonardo Boff, and Juan Luis Segundo.[17]

INCULTURATIONAL

The post-Conciliar period has given a greater impetus to this orientation. The main task of the church in the Third World, particularly in Asia and Africa, is seen to be inculturating the church by assuming the cultural and spiritual heritage of its peoples. This process of inculturation is viewed as contributing to the realization of the catholicity of the church. This ecclesiological orientation drew inspiration from the teachings of the Council as articulated in several documents, above all in *Ad Gentes*. Inculturational ecclesiology gained momentum through the works of theologians like Karl Rahner and Walbert Bühlmann, who saw the fundamental significance of Vatican II in its transition from a Eurocentric church to a world church.[18] This perspective points out that, numerically, Christians in the Third World have overtaken those in the West; the church is becoming in fact a third-world church with its prehistory in Europe.[19]

ANTHROPOLOGY PRECEDES THEOLOGY

The above four orientations embody significant issues and concerns which affect the churches in Asia. Nevertheless, they are inadequate for Asia because, in varying ways and degrees, they let the theological precede the anthropological and the cultural. Instead, the approach to be taken is one in which ecclesiology rests on anthropological and cultural foundations in the spirit of the axiom *gratia presupponit naturam*. Rather than trying to make the church local by relating it to indigenous cultural forms, we need to perceive, understand, and reappropriate the essence of the church in terms of Asian culture, ways of life and human relationships.

Social and anthropological theories of the past which defined community as an objective social fact consisting of structures and institutions are no longer valid today. Community is seen more and more as a reality to be explained in symbolic terms.[20] Community is basically a symbolic reality, and symbols belong to the anthropological and cultural realm. Therefore, the very nature of the community of the disciples of Jesus among a people has to be reinterpreted and redefined through their world and their symbols and reconstituted by the fibers drawn from their ways of being a people and a community. If the human person is "an animal suspended in the web of significance that he or she has spun,"[21] then the nature and identity of the ecclesial community can be understood only by starting from this human and cultural web. Let us examine some of the human and cultural values in Asia and their implications for the church.

JESUS COMMUNITIES OF VARYING DEGREES AND LEVELS

Inclusivism is a characteristic Asian cultural trait which is reflected in the way any community is conceived and lived. The boundaries are not rigidly marked, structures not rigorously fixed and conditions of belonging not strictly laid down. Community exists in the people, in their attitudes, their spirit, their values, their vision, and experience. Therefore from the Asian perspective, to be in the community of Jesus cannot be a matter of belonging to a well-defined group, marked off from the rest by a clearly defined identity. The either-or way of thinking and being is quite alien to Asians.[22] Belonging to a church community in the way that we generally understand it does not exist in the Asian cultural ethos. What matters to most people is not the external religious identity but the deeper religious experience and the path one follows to attain it. Among the Hindus, for example, the *margas* or paths like *bhakti* (way of devotion), *jnana* (way of knowledge), and *karma* (way of involvement and action) characterize a person's religious leanings rather than his or her institutional membership in a religion and its ecclesia. The nomenclature "Hinduism" is relatively recent and if today there is a tendency among some Hindus to see Hinduism as a specific religious identity and system, this is seen as the result of a "semitization of Hinduism."[23]

In the Asian way of being a community, the boundaries are so fluid that one could be in the Jesus community without ceasing to be a participant in other religious experiences and expressions of community and vice versa. This explains the fact that there are millions of followers of Jesus in Asia who experience him deeply in their lives, who are enlightened by his teaching and drawn by his personality without, however, being members of any institutional church.[24] It is also a fact that they follow him much more closely than many within the boundaries of the visible church. When we speak of the church in Asia should we not direct our attention to this larger Jesus community and not primarily to the well-established and structured churches which are but replicas of Western churches with some local inculturation frills appended to them?

Such a larger Jesus community will have an Asian anthropological and cultural basis which is inclusive and open.

OPENNESS AND FLUIDITY

In Asia we must be ready today to accept various levels of ecclesial community. People can belong to the Jesus community in varying degrees. This is in keeping with the gospels in which discipleship of Jesus is presented as having a certain fluidity. Not all the followers belonged to his community in the same way. There was the larger crowd that followed him everywhere he went, fascinated by his teaching, his authority, and so forth (Matt. 4:23–25). There were the seventy-two disciples and the Twelve. And even among the Twelve some were closer to Jesus than others. The Sermon on the Mount and the Sermon on the Plain were addressed not only to the disciples but to the whole crowd as well. The content and form of the missionary instructions given to the Twelve (Luke 9:1–6) were the same as those given to the seventy-two (Luke 10:1–16), but Luke highlights the mission of the seventy-two. Nicodemus (John 19:39) and Joseph of Arimathea (Matt. 27:57) were in the circle of the followers of Jesus. There were also people like Zacchaeus who, listening to Jesus' words, declares himself ready to part with half of his riches (Luke 19:1–10) and Lazarus who was a friend of Jesus and whom Jesus visited often (John 11:1–4; 12:1–2).[25]

All these people and many others like the centurion (Matt. 8:5–13) and the people of Samaria (John 4:41–43) came under the influence of Jesus and belonged to his community in varying degrees and ways. Jesus' community was not a closed group. The Reign of God was the heart of his community and therefore it was basically an open-ended community with no barriers and limits. We know that Jesus did not want to create a group with rigid structures like that of the Essenes, nor were his twelve disciples seen by him as an elitist group replacing the people of Israel. The values of fluidity and inclusiveness which Jesus espoused correspond to the Asian understanding of community.

The truth that different kinds of people were in Jesus' company in different ways has been obscured in the history of Christianity, especially during the second millenium. Under the ideal of Christendom, there was but one form of belonging to the community of Jesus and this was membership in the Christian society, with its clear boundaries and structures. Within the Western world this ideal was later broken open by the emergence of secular societies. At the time of missionary expansion it was this ideal of Christendom that was carried to different parts of the world. It succeeded in Latin America, but not in Asia (except the Philippines), which resisted Christendom's way of belonging to a religious group. The question of Jesus community in a world of religious pluralism such as Asia has never been seriously faced in Christian history. In spite of all ecclesiological renewal, in practice, the basic model of the church which we have today is the one derived from Christendom—the church existing concretely as a well-organized and structured institution with strict conditions of entry. Even what is envisaged under *votum ecclesiae* is a matter of invisibly belonging to this same institutional church.[26] According to this perspective, the invisible and unknown church to which others belong is the same church which is visible and known to its explicit members. This is quite a different thing from the various grades and levels of belonging to the Jesus community which sees the traditional and historically-conditioned institutional form as one way of belonging.

DIVERSE FORMS OF ECCLESIAL COMMUNITY

ASHRAM

An anthropologically- and culturally-based ecclesiality in Asia will find embodiment in a wide variety of forms. The present model of the church transported from the West has as its focus the locality where the eucharist is celebrated, where the word of God is announced, and the people are served by ministers. This basic structure is reproduced everywhere with allowance for local variations. Such a form of the church is very often seen as a superimposition on a people and their culture. If the form of the church community must be an expression of the culture and genius of the people, then we should be ready to accept other ecclesial forms, different from what we are used to. In India, for example, Ashram could become an important expression of ecclesial community. Ashram is a community of God-seekers gathered around a spiritually experienced guru or master whose doors are open to peoples of all faiths and all strata of society without discrimination of any kind—male or female, higher or lower caste.[27] It is something that embodies the spirit, culture, and tradition of India and at the same time a form of community that is most congenial to the realization of Jesus' vision of humanity as a family under the Fatherhood of God. Contemplation, simplicity of life, interiority, hospitality, renunciation, and the practice of poverty as a protest against selfishness and greed are traditional Indian religiocultural values practiced in Ashram life. These values and practices make Ashram life a fruitful terrain for the blossoming of a gospel-based Jesus community. No one would see a Jesus community of Ashram as alien to or without root in Indian soil.

ACTION GROUPS

Another form of ecclesial community could be the so-called action groups and movements which are found in many parts of Asia. These are small grassroots groups involved with the people in their struggle for life, liberation, and human dignity. They are often spontaneously formed to respond to the plight of the most lowly, oppressed, and marginalized sectors in the society. In these groups one finds people of different faiths, all gripped by the same vision of a world of justice, love, fellowship, freedom, and solidarity—ideals which correspond so well to Jesus' vision of the Reign of God.[28]

The praxis of these groups reflects the criteria of belonging to the Reign of God that were given by Jesus in his discourse on the last judgment (Matt. 25:31–46). One can see in such groups and movements the community of Jesus united in fellowship for the realization of the ideals of the Reign of God. Those who do God's will are the brothers, sisters, and mother of Jesus (Mark 3:33–35). And like Joseph of Arimathea they are in close contact with the suffering body of Jesus as they seek to remove the nails and take that body—the least and lowliest—from the cross where it is today crucified. The existence of such successors to Joseph of Arimathea, united so intimately with the wounded body of Jesus, should lead us to understand that the community of Jesus is a reality with open frontiers. Here the church becomes for us truly the mystery of God which we can comprehend only by touching his wounds, by mystical contemplation, and by experience.

There could be many such forms of ecclesial communities in Asia reflecting the Reign of God in different ways, and at the same time expressive of the human and cultural background of the people. The communion of churches could also be interpreted as communion among these various forms of communities—Ashrams, action groups, and so forth. Each one may have a particular focus. For example, the Ashram community will emphasize the *bhakti marga* and *jnana marga*. They would thus enrich and complement each other. Obviously, this is a different type of communion of churches.

THE ROLE OF TRADITION

The anthropological and cultural foundations and forms suggested here may raise the question: how does all this fit into the centuries-old tradition of Christianity? Yves Congar states that Christianity does not begin every time from zero.[29] He is perfectly right. We cannot, obviously, deny the significance of Christian heritage for Asia. But the point to be examined is whether the Christian heritage and tradition need have the same importance and application in Asia as in their places of origin and growth. The present-day Asian cultural situation with its religious pluralism was certainly not foreseen as the environment of a Jesus community when certain institutional structures evolved in Christian tradition. The present Asian situation with its religious pluralism is quite unique and it may not be right to expect ready-made answers from the past for today's problems. Nor may it be right to raise an historically-conditioned past situation or solution to the level of a norm to be applied to the churches of Asia today.

We know that in the New Testament, around Jesus' time, there was a plurality of forms in which Jesus communities developed. We must ask why only one of those forms among many should become the norm by divine right—*iuris divini.*[30] Connecting divine right with the present shape of the church has become a very delicate and difficult problem, especially in areas like sacraments, the place of women in the church, and so forth. The question turns out to be all the more difficult and complex when we are faced with the possibilities of different forms and grades of ecclesial community in a continent of cultural and religious pluralisms such as Asia. Deeper study and reflection in this whole area may be required in the years to come.

CONCLUSION

It appears that none of the current ecclesiologies responds to the situation of the church in Asia, which projects the image of an alien body. The root cause of this situation is the way the church exists as a theological and religious reality with no cultural foundation in the Asian soil. It is crucial to develop an understanding and praxis of ecclesial community that will have the anthropological and the cultural as its base, rather than as its consequence.

Being a community is first and foremost a cultural and symbolic reality, and not a matter of structures and institutions. Seen from the Asian cultural perspective, community exists primarily in the people. There is much flexibility and openness. This inclusiveness allows for various grades and levels of belonging to the Jesus community. Inclusiveness, which has the support of the New Testament, leads us to see a much larger number of Asians belonging to the Jesus community than those who are within its boundaries. Similarly, there could be various forms of ecclesial communities in Asia such as Ashrams and action groups. These communities with people of different faiths reflect the love, fellowship, justice, and freedom of Jesus' vision of the Reign of God, which is the ultimate unity of the human family. All this has implications for interpreting Christian tradition, its structures and institutions.

Finally, the churches in Asia should not simply try to sink their roots in Asia, but rather should have Asian cultures as their roots inasmuch as these roots are God's own grace and gifts to them. These are gifts through which they fashion themselves into unique and distinct communities. These are not expressions of much-feared nationalism or cultural chauvinism. To call for an Asian/Indian anthropological and cultural foundation for the local church could be just the opposite of what is being feared: it is not a church of power, ethnocentricity and exclusion, but a community of poverty and powerlessness, of interiority and selfless love for one's neighbor, and open to all castes, cultures, and faiths.

NOTES

1. Cf. Felix Wilfred, *Popular Religiosity and Asian Contextual Theologizing*, presented at a symposium held at the University of Nijmegen, Holland, January 3–7, 1990 (to be published).

2. Bede Griffiths has repeatedly drawn attention to this point. For example, see his article: "Nature, Technology and the New Society," in *Jeevadhara* 18 (1988): 23–31.

3. The January 1987 and January 1988 issues of *Jeevadhara* on human problems were dedicated to these two.

4. Cf. James Davison Hunter and Stephen C. Ainlay (eds.), *Making Sense of Modern Times. Peter L. Berger and the Vision of Interpretative Sociology* (London and New York: Routledge and Kegan Paul, 1986), 57–75.

5. Cf. M. N. Srinivas, *Social Change in Modern India* (Bombay: Orient Longman, 1972), 46ff.

6. Cf. Anthony Giddens, *Sociology. A Brief but Critical Introduction* (London: Macmillan Education Ltd., 1988), 136ff.

7. Cf. S. N. Eisenstadt, "Modernization and Dynamics of Civilization," in *Solidarity* 102/103 (1985): 3–11.

8. Ibid.

9. Cf. M. N. Srinivas, *Social Change in Modern India*. Cf. also Yogendra Singh,

Social Stratification and Change in India (Delhi: Manohar, 1989), pp. 91ff.

10. Cf. Brendan Lovett, *Life Before Death. Inculturating Hope* (Quezon City: Claretian Publications, 1986).

11. Cf. Masao Takenaka, *God Is Rice. Asian Culture and Christian Faith* (Geneva: WCC, 1986), 22.

12. Reported in *Indian Express*, Madurai edition, January 18, 1990.

13. Cf. Yves Congar, *L'Eglise, une, sainte, catholique et apostolique. Mysterium Salutis, Dogmatique de l'histoire du salut* (Paris, 1970); E. Lanne, "L'Eglise locale: sa catholicité et son apostolicité," in *Istina* 14 (1969): 46–66; H. Legrand, "L'Eglise se réalise en un lieu," in *Initiation à la pratique de la théologie*, vol. III (Paris, 1983), 146ff; J. M. R. Tillard, *Eglise d'églises* (Paris, 1987); Avery Dulles, *Models of the Church* (New York: Image Books, 1978); idem, *The Catholicity of the Church* (Oxford: Clarendon Press, 1987); Joseph A. Komonchak, "Towards a Theology of the Local Church," FABC Papers 42 (Hong Kong: 1986).

14. Cf. Hans Küng, *The Church* (London: Burns and Oates, 1967); idem, *Infallible? An Enquiry* (London: Collins, 1971); Leonard Swidler, "Demokratia. The Rule of the People of God, or Consensus Fidelium," in *Journal of Ecumenical Studies* 19 (1982): 226–43; J. L. McKenzie, *Authority in the Church* (New York: Sheed and Ward, 1966).

15. Cf. G. Alberigo (ed.), *L'Ecclesiologia del Vaticano II, dinamismi e prospective* (Bologna: Edizioni Dehoniane, 1981); G. Alberigo et al. (eds.), *The Reception of Vatican II* (Washington: 1987); Antonio Acerbi, *Due ecclesiologie. Ecclesiologia giuridica ed ecclesiologia di communione nella lumen gentium* (Bologna, 1975).

16. Cf. G. Gutiérrez, "I grandi mutamenti all interno della società e delle chiese di nuovo crisitianita dopo il Vaticano II," in G. Alberigo, *L'Ecclesiologia del Vaticano II*, 23–36; idem, "The Church and the Poor: A Latin American Perspective," in *The Reception of Vatican II*, 171ff.

17. Cf. Jon Sobrino, *The True Church and the Poor* (Maryknoll: Orbis Books, 1985); Leonardo Boff, *Church: Charism and Power. Liberation Theology and the Institutional Church*, (New York: Crossroad, 1985); Juan Luis Segundo, *The Community Called Church* (Maryknoll: Orbis Books, 1973).

18. Cf. Karl Rahner, "Basic Theological Interpretation of the Second Vatican Council," in Karl Rahner, *Theological Investigations*, vol. 20 (London: Darton, Longman & Todd, 1981), 77–89; Walbert Bühlmann, *The Coming of the Third Church* (Maryknoll: Orbis Books, 1976).

19. Cf. Johann Baptist Metz, "Im Aufbruch zu einer kulturell polyzentrischen Weltkirche," in Franz-Xavier Kaufmann and Johann Baptist Metz, *Zukunftsfähigkeit. Suchbewegungen im Christentum* (Freiburg: Herder, 1987), 94.

20. Cf. Anthony P. Cohen, *The Symbolic Construction of Community* (Chichester: Ellis Horwoord, 1985).

21. C. Geertz, "Thick Description: Toward an Interpretive Theory of Culture," in idem, *The Interpretation of Cultures* (London: Hutchinson, 1975), 5.

22. Cf. Jung Young Lee, "The Yin-Yang Way of Thinking: A Possible Method for Ecumenical Theology," in *International Review of Mission* 60 (1971): 362–70.

23. Rajni Kothari, "From Religions to Religiosity," in *Jeevadhara* 20 (1990): 74.

24. Cf. M. M. Thomas, *The Acknowledged Christ of the Indian Renaissance* (Madras: CLS, 1970); S. J. Samartha, *The Hindu Response to the Unbound Christ* (Madras: CLS, 1974); Hans Staffner, *The Significance of Jesus Christ in Asia* (Anand:

Gujarat Sahitya Prakash, 1985); P. J. Thomas, *100 Indian Witnesses to Jesus Christ* (Bombay: The Bombay Tract and Book Society, 1974).

25. Gerhard Lohfink, *Jesus and Community* (London: SPCK, 1985).

26. Cf. A. Grillmeier, "The People of God," in H. Vorgrimler (ed.), *Commentary on the Documents of Vatican II* (New York: Herder, 1967), 153ff; K. Morsdorf and Karl Rahner, "Kirchengliedschaft," in *LThK,* vol. 6, cols. 221–25; U. Valeske, *Votum Ecclesiae* (Munich, 1962).

27. Cf. Vandana, *Gurus, Ashrams and Christians* (London: Darton, Longman & Todd, 1978); idem, *Social Justice and Ashrams* (Bangalore: ATC Publications, 1982); Bede Griffiths, *Christian Ashram* (London: Darton, Longman & Todd, 1966); M. Rogers, "Hindu Ashram Heritage: God's Gift to the Church," in *Concilium* 9 (1965): 73–78; R. W. Taylor, "From Khadi to Kavi: Towards a Typology of Christian Ashrams," in *Religion and Society* 24, no. 4 (1977): 19–37.

28. Cf. Felix Wilfred, "Action Groups and Struggle for Justice: Ecclesiological Implications," in *Asia Journal of Theology* 3, no. 1 (1989): 237–59.

29. Cf. Yves Congar, "Christianisme comme foi et comme culture," in *Evangelizazione e culture*, vol. I (Rome: Pontificà Università Urbaniana, 1976), 99.

30. Cf. Karl Rahner, "Reflection on the Concept of Ius Divinum in Catholic Thought," in *Theological Investigations*, vol. 5 (London: 1966), 219–43; cf. also Carl J. Peter, "Dimensions of Jus Divinum in Roman Catholic Theology," in *Theological Studies* 34 (1973): 227–50.

2

CONFLICTING MODELS OF CHURCH AND SOCIETY IN BRAZIL

Ivone Gebara, CSA

INTRODUCTION

I wish to give a general outline of the different practices and theologies which exist in Brazil today and in particular in the northeast region of Brazil where I have lived and worked for sixteen years.

The point of view I offer you and the interpretation of what I call the practices and theology of the church is only one among many. Even if I try to be "objective" in my description of the various trends, my interpretation inevitably reveals my involvement, my political "color," as well as the fact that I am a woman. You will be aware of this throughout this paper which aims, on the one hand, to reveal the richness and complexity of the Christian phenomenon in Brazil, and on the other to highlight what is at stake in the actual ecclesial situation, especially in the most recent events in the northeast region of the country.

My reflection is divided into three parts. In the first, I shall describe the present situation in the northeastern part of the country; in the second, some of the practices and theologies in use in the church there, and in the third, the significance of the conflicts which are being experienced by the church. A short conclusion will bring me back to my hopes and to the vision I entertain for the years ahead.

THE ECONOMICAL, POLITICAL, SOCIAL, AND CULTURAL CONTEXT OF THE CHURCH IN NORTHEAST BRAZIL

Wherever the church is present as a community of believers, heirs to the faith and gospel values of Jesus, it is marked by its economical, political, social, and cultural context. It is this context and the practical options made by the faithful which determine the model of church in each era of history.

THE POOR

Even though there are some isolated areas which are rich and modern, northeast Brazil is still one of the poorest areas in the world. It has one of the world's highest infant mortality rates mainly attributable to hunger; 80 percent of the population is poor; 15 percent belong to the middle class; 5 percent are rich landowners who control over 70 percent of the land and wealth of the area. During the last two years, the country has experienced enormous rates of inflation. Last year alone it reached almost 2,000 percent over twelve months.

The majority of the population survives thanks to a "hidden" economy which does not figure in government estimates or official calculations. It consists in the exchange of petty services, in small businesses and artisan trades—in short, of an extraordinary inventiveness which seems to increase each year. This economy is actuated by the poor themselves; their humble "assets," their industry, and their will to live constitute the dynamics of this subterranean economy which ensures them their daily bread.

This population of the poor is often considered to be Roman Catholic, but in fact the majority belong to Pentecostal churches, the Assembly of God, Candomble (an Afro-Brazilian religion). What these people seek in religion is immediate help to survive, to live. Among them one often meets people who are going on a pilgrimage with Catholics and who then call on the *pai de santo*, a sort of priest of the Afro-Brazilian cult. At the same time, they have small sanctuaries in their homes with representatives of the "celestial" forces of the different cults. If one asks these people to which religion they belong it is not surprising to hear them say they are Catholics.

This reflects some of the complexity of Catholicism in Brazil and the diversity of the questions which arise regarding the practice and theology of the local church.

THE RICH

Although I am referring more specifically to the poor, the rich are no different; the ambiguity regarding a choice of religion is always present. One often finds that the rich favor tradition and negate everything that seems to be prophetic in the Christian life. They believe in an almost immutable religion, a religion which sanctions the established order without asking whether the established order is not in fact ethical disorder.

THE HIERARCHY

Political power in Brazil has always been in the hands of those who held economical power. Until about seventy years ago the hierarchical church, apart from some exceptions, blessed and legitimated to a certain degree the government in power. This attitude began to change during the period of military dictatorship (1964–85), when the hierarchy, pressured by the suffering of thousands of people, took a definite stand against the arbitrary exercise of power by the military government. Over the last five years, however, we have witnessed a certain withdrawal of the episcopate and of the hierarchy from this stand. Some church groups have taken up clear positions opposing the irresponsibility of the government in different sectors, and openly and effectively support people's movements, syndicates, and political parties which are trying to build an alternative plan for society.

There is thus a lack of homogeneity within the local church in its attitude toward the different political options. This is apparent not only at the pastoral level but at the level of its attitude toward civil society.

SOME PRACTICES AND THEOLOGIES

I shall give an overall explanation of five types of practices and theologies. No one of them alone corresponds completely to the reality. What I propose is diagrammatic and somewhat static; actual experience is larger than any confining interpretation. The typology I am presenting here is a yardstick to help understand what is happening in the church of Brazil.

POPULAR RELIGIOUS PRACTICE AND ORAL THEOLOGY OF LIFE

The religious practice of the poor is conditioned by the effort required to survive, or to protect life itself which is threatened by many mortal enemies. Chief among these is hunger. This struggle seems to grow more urgent every day. The life of the poor is continually exposed to death, much more so than the lives of those who live in stable economic conditions. Food is "for the day"; the house which shelters a large family is "for the day"; a storm or even the decision of a big landowner or of the government can destroy this roof which is just as fragile as life itself.

Religious practice is rooted in this basic historical precariousness. There are very few people to whom the poor can look for help or support, and it is in this fragile existence that "allies" from above (the saints) come to their assistance. When real and concrete expectations become more and more ephemeral, celestial intervention opens up the way to possible salvation in the short-term humdrum of daily life. Pilgrimages to "holy places," saints' days, candles and offerings and promises are so many expressions of their deep need to be made welcome, to be heard, and to have their sufferings eased.

Religious practices of the poor go beyond the limits of Catholicism, and it is often outside those limits that remedies are sought for their many trials. Different doors are knocked at in the hope that at least a window will be opened somewhere! Thus their religious "syncretism" is an expression of the struggle to live yet another day.

This way of life which often makes appeal both to God and to the "celestial allies" is what I call the oral theology of life. At one and the same time God is involved in human distress and yet is above all distress since everyone, men, women, and children can make God hear their suffering pleas, their desires for love, and their concrete expectations. This is no written theology. To write about God is a luxury the poor cannot afford. Quite simply, one lives on God, one speaks of God, one hopes in God. This is the theology of the majority of Brazil's population, but rarely is it considered to be such.

TRADITIONAL "CONSERVATIVE" PRACTICE AND THEOLOGY

What I term traditional "conservative" practice and theology is to understand the Christian faith as a compendium of religious practices that come from God and that lead directly to God.

Obedience is a primordial concept in this manner of living Christianity. Obedience to God is equated with obedience to authority, whether religious, civil, family, and so forth. It is by obedience that order is maintained and tradition preserved, and that a certain morality, rooted in principles believed to be eternal, is protected. To disobey is to transgress an established order, it is to sow doubt, and in the end it is to act contrary to God's will.

In this perspective, one acts with charity towards others, but because to do so is one's duty. Thus various charitable organizations have been founded here in Brazil, particularly since the last century up to the present time. The causes of the poverty of the poor are not questioned; the poor are helped to bear their poverty and God will reward us for our good deeds.

Sacramental practice, defending the catechism, and guarding the traditional formulation of the Catholic faith are the bastions on which this practice of charity and help rests. Liturgies, traditional songs of a somewhat nostalgic timbre, and at times an exaggerated stress on ecclesiastical laws and rubrics are also part of the fabric of life of this Catholic group. It is present mainly in the middle classes, in those bordering on poverty, or in the rich minority who are convinced of the value of a traditional religion which they see under threat of disappearing. In general, these groups are favored by the majority of those bishops and priests of the most traditionalist tendency. They have increased over the past decade. They advocate political neutrality, at least in public, but this "neutrality" often hides their real options regarding the structure of society. In fact, their "practice," what they do, reveals a rather limited social horizon, an analysis which does not go very deep, and an attitude of fear when faced by any proposed change, whether regarding society or the church.

TRADITIONAL "MODERNIZING" PRACTICE AND THEOLOGY

In Latin America in general and in Brazil in particular, religious movements began to emerge, especially following the Second Vatican Council. They were organized on a national level and had programs for action. These national groups have not only adopted modern ways of speaking and writing, but also make use of modern technical methods and trendy expressions which, however, retain a traditional content. These movements seek to gain access to the more affluent sectors of society as well as to youth, and to some extent to simple people who are involved in small trades and who struggle valiantly to keep the increasing threat of financial impoverishment at bay.

Their accepted model of Catholicism shows a uniformity achieved by adhering to the same theological thought and ideological position, both of which are strongly bound to the capitalist system prevalent in our societies. The reflections of these Christians show, at times, some of the causes at the root of the people's misery. However, the causes often identified have a functional origin—these Christians believe that with a little effort these problems can be solved. Their sociopolitical option is thus to maintain and improve the status quo. They do not preach radical change and often they advocate a conservative policy disguised as modernity.

Their religious practice is traditional. They attend Mass, prayers, organizational meetings, youth meetings, send their children to catechesis, and go to discussions on topical problems. They are always loyal to the teaching of the Roman magisterium. Usually, these movements have sufficient funds to construct well-built centers with very well-appointed modern offices. They want to be recognized as church institutions approved by the Pope. More and more they are introducing modern communication techniques. They favor a somewhat "sugary" tone when speaking of the wonders of the Christian life. Their reflection does not coincide either with reality or lived history, but echoes an ideal which can easily lead either to alienation or to fanaticism.

PRACTICE OF LIBERATION THEOLOGY

The theology of liberation in Latin America has been a burning question in the international press for the last twenty years. It has found firm supporters and violent adversaries who have not spared the representatives of this theology from ecclesiastical tribunals and public chastisement.

Liberation theology is, so to speak, the theoretical expression of practical faith. Its point of departure is that the call of God comes to us from our neighbor—the poor, the marginalized, the ones who, by their suffering down through history, demand that we take a stand in restoring whole life to them. The exponents of the theology of liberation do not see this as a question of choosing or not choosing to defend the cause of the oppressed. It is not a choice but an ethical necessity if one is to be faithful to the Christian faith, to the life-giving Spirit. It is this radical way of understanding the faith which requires actions of justice and caring. It demands a change in those world structures which are the causes of misery in different countries of the world. With this objective in view, a large number of Christians have joined popular organizations—trade unions, political parties, and popular movements of all sorts which seek to give everyone a more humane life. Christian life is primarily an "orthopraxis" for them, acting or doing right, and only later an "orthodoxy," that is, well-regulated, correct, logical thought.

These groups of active Christians of different social origins—poor, middle class, and ecclesiastical (Catholic Action, for example)—are not very numerous, even though propaganda often leads one to think that they are multitudinous. They expound both a practice and an alternative theology which maintain that faith in the values of the Kingdom must be able to bring about personal conversion, community and social change, as well as more justice in the world and in the church. Some of these groups meet in basic ecclesial communities, small church centers where they try to share responsibilities and services and, as far as possible, wealth. The different communities often have a rather original liturgical life which is not necessarily helped by the presence of a priest.

This practice and theology provoke fear among traditionalists who see the church being overrun by questions which are outside the religious sphere. They also provoke fear in the political authorities lest faith really become a yeast that raises the dough of practice. Following Jesus Christ and being fired by the values of the Kingdom have serious historical consequences that must lead to definite changes in our behavior. This practice and theology also raise the fears of religious authorities who see their power questioned by the sharing and division of power within the community.

PRACTICE OF THE FEMINIST THEOLOGY OF LIBERATION

Participation of women in the different popular liberation movements, as well as the daily struggle of thousands of women who bear almost total responsibility for the home, has begun to stimulate theological reflection among some women. They take the reality of their own situation as their starting point. Some of their number—I am one—began to suspect a theology, even that of liberation, which presented them with an ideal way to be human which took the male as model. They realized, and the majority still realize only vaguely, the potential contained in androcentric anthropology which is the basis of all the theologies that we have learned.

This anthropology leads us to consider "man" as the first of creation not only in theory, but also to draw practical conclusions. Women are outside the great decisions of history. They are either accessories or called upon to care for the wounded from the "wars" created by male reasoning. In the ambit of the church the woman's place is mainly that of a servant.

Significant changes are beginning to take place, especially at the level of awareness and at the level of some claims for action, even within the institutions of the Catholic church. Women are realizing that the task of educating children and young people in the church is in their hands, even if they have little say about the actual content of what they teach. Now, over the last three years, these women have begun to feel a certain disquietude concerning certain theological formulae. Questioning these, they are beginning to demand a revision and a re-elaboration of theology based on a more equal anthropology, with greater deference for the difference between the sexes.

Liberation theology is only now beginning to propose a theological argument which is inclusive of the sexual differences. The liberation of everyone must respect not only the diversity of cultures but the difference between the sexes as well. This is what is lived. It is what some women in Brazil, aware of the historical responsibility which devolves on them, are trying to say and to write about, whether they are religious or lay.

CONFLICTS BETWEEN THE VARIOUS PRACTICES AND MODELS OF CHURCH

The word "conflict," does not necessarily mean open, conscious, clear conflict, but it does imply conflict about interests to be defended, and about models of society and church which are being built.

In a very schematic way we may say that the stakes in all ecclesiastical conflicts center on the construction of two models of society and church. The first, more democratic model, seeks consensus and is founded on a perspective of social justice with a socialist stamp. The second, more centralized and hierarchical, is founded on the perspective of social justice according to the capitalist model, that is to say, a reformist justice, which does not try to plumb the actual causes of the problems. Nor does it question the prevailing model of society.

I do not wish to enter here into the debate about the crisis of historical "socialism," but only to touch upon the orientation of a vision of society or of church which is based on a certain set of values.

During the last ten years the centralizing model of the Catholic church has gained ground. This trend has been sanctioned from high up in the church and is molding the type of church unity which appeared to have been shaken by the openness set in motion after the Second Vatican Council.

Doubtless one finds therein a return to certain types of uniformity prevalent before the Council. At that time the role of authority was understood to mean obedience almost without dialogue. This manner of behavior is characteristic of different Vatican structures, especially as they relate to local churches which see their autonomy being gradually restricted. Opening up to the great social, political, and scientific questions was considered a threat to this unifying vision of the gospel which claimed the approval of authority.

In my view one must keep this vision in mind when trying to understand the Vatican's recent intervention in the Latin-American Confederation of Religious (CLAR) and in the closing of the Institute of Theology at Recife and the Regional Seminary of the Northeast. These are very disturbing events since these places which witnessed to the "alternative" vision of the church permitted the poor and people professionally qualified in different sciences, as well as women and men of different religious creeds, to meet as partners and discuss together the building of a more human world.

The work of these organizations questions the position of those who wield "religious" power. It calls for a serious revision of the manner of exercising that power and a revision of the institutions which depend on it. But such a revision is seen as insupportable by those in power who dismiss an alternative vision of the church and who declare publicly that this different way which follows a new path does not lead to truth and so must be eliminated. Behavior like this, without "dialogue," is the prerogative of all authoritarian regimes, and the hierarchy of the Catholic church is not exempt from this sin.

In all church conflicts there is something very deep which should be stressed. Both our traditional theology and the concept of power in the church are based on an anthropology which does not take into account the present reality of the human being in our pluralist, secularist situation today and our search for autonomy. It is an anthropology based on a bipolar, dualistic, and idealistic system which retains a rather pessimistic concept of the human person.

This is not the place to elaborate on this anthropology. We know its general characteristics. We know how jealously it guards a logic which in the long run always favors one extreme to the detriment of the other, even excluding one to the benefit of the other. We know the extent to which it has sacrificed the body, bodies, history, life itself, in favor of the soul, the ideal, principles, all in the belief that truth was to be found in the "higher world" and that the "lower world" was too mixed, transitory, impure to be recognized and esteemed. In reality it did not take seriously the wonder of creation since its reasoning and its practice often consisted in seeing opposition between the human and the natural world. Eventually, it actually came to oppose the human to God and in its desire for domination recognizes only the values of gain and profit. Today different movements throughout the world as well as in northeast Brazil are proclaiming a new understanding of the human being: a human being deeply related to all existence. We are still only beginning to understand the relationship between everything which exists. As this crystallizes and deepens, theology and church institutions will be increasingly obliged to revise their concepts, their manner of understanding the human person and his or her relationship to the Transcendent One. No doubt some Good News is being announced quietly as the dawn of the third millennium approaches, but it is still far from being heard everywhere. This hope is like a beckoning star which will not set as long as men and women have not yet celebrated their happy relationship with the whole of creation.

WHAT MAY ONE HOPE FOR?

While each of the five practices and corresponding theologies which I have described lays claim to Christian hope, each one formulates hope after its own fashion. Must we then speak of a conflict of hopes within the church? I am convinced we must. The conflict between the various groups, each building a different vision of the church, leads necessarily to a conflict of hopes.

Let me return to today's experience in the history of the church in northeast Brazil. It would seem that in the years to come there will certainly be an increase in the practices of both traditional and modern theology. This seems clear from the interplay of the forces actually present in the country, above all at the ecclesiastical level. But this does not mean that the hopes of the poor for liberation, their attainment of autonomy and self-determination, and the need to democratize ecclesiastical structures will not make progress. The way may perhaps be more difficult and may be lived differently, but the hope which characterizes it will always be present. Christians have made strides which cannot be made to disappear simply by decree. These strides are historical signs. I single out four to illustrate my point of view:

1. the presence of a grass-roots church made up of people who seek to understand and live by "Jesus' example" through their engagement with the poor. These people are either poor themselves or have taken the cause of the poor to heart;
2. the large numbers of lay people who have undertaken to proclaim the Kingdom and to confirm the faith of their brothers and sisters. Some of them

have committed themselves to the ministry of the theological magisterium at different levels of ecclesiastical life;

3. the feminist movement which is beginning to form within the Christian community itself, despite encountering some reserve and misunderstanding. Some women are rediscovering the importance of their role in passing on the faith and are seeking a place as equals in the church;
4. the movement of small communities of religious women inserted among the poor, trying to live the daily life of the poor and working for their liberation.

These four examples demonstrate the strength of the current of hope which wants to see a church born out of the poor by the will of the Spirit. This church which is growing slowly, despite the difficulties inherent in the historical process, is an invitation to believe that the God of Life, he who is in our midst, who is our flesh, is urging us each day to "restore justice," to "set the prisoners free," to "proclaim a year of grace," to be open to the unpredictable which can change the course of our lives.

COMMUNION

If all this is true on the level of our faith lived in the limits of history, it is also true that this invitation to restructure life is situated in the midst of conflicts and difficulties. I would like to highlight a few such difficulties in this conclusion.

— In the context of different practices of church, can one speak of communion within the local church? Should one not speak rather of communion between different church groups who have a similar practice and, in this sense, of communion that goes beyond the local level?
— The expression "local church" is sometimes too limited to express the complex reality of Christian communities living in the same geographical area. Today, to limit local church only to a geographical aspect is to forget the complexity lived by the different groups.
— A great number of Christians live a kind of communion which goes beyond diocesan boundaries and sometimes even beyond country boundaries. This communion is built upon the same interpretation of the faith and upon common action in building a more just and human society. Thus, one often sees that Christians (Catholics) have lived a fraternal, ecclesial communion with groups of churches coming out of the Reform and even with groups who do not identify themselves with religious creeds.

In my opinion, we are in the process of building a new communion, one which will give a different face to Christianity in the third millennium.

RELIGIOUS CONGREGATIONS

Religious congregations, through their members, are identified with the different models of church. There is not one congregation in Latin America that is homogeneous in its option, even if officially it commits itself to one plan of action or type of church. In reality, the options and actions are fairly mixed.

In the "movement" of small fraternities inserted in popular areas (inserted religious communities) there is often a communion that is created beyond the specificity of each religious congregation. It is a communion built on the same way of living religious life—near to the poor, sharing with the poor. It is an attempt at communion with their life and at helping them to rediscover their dignity. In this sense these small communities, although different in their congregational origins, come together in a "common charism" to put themselves at the service of and to listen to the poor—in theological terms, to be at the service of and attentive to the God of Life.

This new way of living consecrated life demands, more and more, a new reflection on the structures of religious life and on the theology and anthropology which support it. Religious who are very committed to the liberation of the poor often have the feeling of being "strangers" in their own Congregation, speaking another language because they are living another reality.

Can our old structures, modernized often from a "technical" point of view, welcome the "new wine" that is in the process of fermentation, or does one really have to discover new casks so that the new wine will not be lost?

3

BELIEVING COMMUNITIES
IN THE UNITED STATES

Teresita Weind, SND

On a very, very cold and wet Sunday afternoon into a May evening in 1983 I was with a group of adults and children who marched in front of Palmer House in downtown Chicago. We were there to focus attention on and pray for the adoption of the Peace Pastoral, *The Challenge of Peace: God's Promise and Our Response.* As you know, the Peace Pastoral was accepted. Since that Sunday afternoon there have been and continue to be many people walking for peace, disseminating information about peace and encouraging others to turn their lives toward the gift of God's promise of peace.

On a still colder day in late November in 1984 I was with another group of people who marched around the main building of the U.S. Post Office in downtown Chicago. We were protesting U.S. involvement in South America.

On yet another occasion, on a frigid Good Friday, and then again in the following year on a beautiful, sunny Good Friday, I was with a very large number of Christians who were walking the living Way of the Cross throughout the northeast side of Chicago. The pilgrimage took us to fourteen different places where we demonstrated against the way our local civic and state departments participate in the injustice, oppression and terrorism that destroy innocent people in our own and third-world countries.

I knew very few of the people with whom I marched, demonstrated, and protested in the name of Jesus. As we moved together, we were a prophetic sign of the justice and freedom of the Reign of God. As we moved together, we were an identifiable dimension of local church applying what we believed about the coming of peace and justice. I will probably never see many of these people again, but the identity I discovered and shared with them on those days helped to shape me into the Christian I am aspiring to be. These people called me to witness to my communion with the People of God.

Closer to home, I can recall that it was again a very cold evening in November of last year when a couple from one of our base communities came to take me with them to a scheduled meeting in the home of one of the members. I had been invited to be with them to listen to their concerns about our parish community. This same group invited me to return in January of this year so I could respond to what I had heard.

I was with a different base community for Mardi Gras—supper, socializing, and Evening Prayer. They had invited me to share the meal and then to preside at the communal prayer with their group.

GATHERED AROUND THE EUCHARIST

More frequently and more regularly than these spotted events just mentioned, I gather with our Christian community every weekend to "do eucharist." This phrase, "do eucharist," describes the shift from the practice of going to hear Mass to a growing conscious and active participation in the rites (Liturgy of the Word and Liturgy of Eucharist), and the determination to carry the meaning of eucharist into the work and play of every day. The People of God, gathered around the eucharist in a particular place, is the local church. I know many of these people with whom I "do eucharist." I know all of the members of the base community units. Those whom I know and those whom I do not know share in that common bond in the mystery we name "church." In this ecclesial reality no one is a total stranger. In this mystery of church I know I am intimately bound to many beautiful, justice-minded, peace-oriented people. These are people who made and keep making the commitment to live from the place of the Spirit and the energy of sacrificial love. Since that is more than any one person can ever do alone, these people keep coming together in many different ways to open each other to the gift of God.

One of the solid and stable realities of local church is that we are drawn into and gifted with a community of people whose conscious identity is rebirth in the risen Christ. We probably would not know these people, would not be privileged to serve and worship with these people, were it not for local church.

BEARING WITNESS TO THE REIGN OF GOD

A primary function of the local church is the gathering of a diverse group of people in a community of faith for the sake of bearing witness to the presence and coming of the Reign of God. Church actually structures that togetherness in mutual trust from a common origin. Church affords us the opportunity to work together on common interests toward a common direction arising from a purpose rooted in the redeeming Christ.

THE RELOCATION OF THE HOLY

Since the end of the Second Vatican Council in 1965, local churches have begun to bear witness in worship, in example, and in service to the relocation of the holy in the midst of community.[1] We are slowly moving away from attaching the holy to the ordained or the special commissioned ministers. We are growing into an awareness of ourselves as "the chosen race, the royal priesthood, the holy nation, God's own people who declare the wonderful deeds of God who called us out of darkness into that marvelous light of merciful love and peace" (1 Pet. 2:9). Living into and out of this mystery is sometimes awkward, frustrating, and even painful. It is not easy to share the responsibility of leadership after we have been led for such a long time. Experience bears out the other side: it is not easy to share the authority and power after having held it for such a long time. The passage into the new church is indeed a difficult one.

CALL FOR REFORM

The Pastoral Letter from Catholics concerned about fundamental renewal of our church takes this reality seriously. The letter is a call for reform in the Catholic church. The text of this letter, issued twenty-five years after *Gaudium et Spes*, was published in the *New York Times* as a full page advertisement on Ash Wednesday, February 28, 1990. The ad included the full text and 4,500 signatures. Those who wrote and those who signed the Call for Reform know very well that the relocation of the holy is alive and vibrant in the local ecclesial communities. We testify with the author of Revelation 21:3, "And I heard a loud voice from the throne saying, 'Behold the dwelling of God is with people. God will dwell with them, and they shall be God's people, and God will be with them.' " The Call for Reform is one response to this voice, spelling out some practical applications for realizing the relocation of God, the holy, in the midst of the people, the laity, the local church.

Heaven and earth are full of the glory of God. But sometimes this glory becomes crusted over and concealed by institutional structures that stand as a stumbling block to church members and society. To really experience the holy in the community, the Call for Reform reminds the church that:

—we need to have women incorporated at all levels of ministry and decision-making;
—we need to discard the medieval discipline of mandatory priestly celibacy, and open the priesthood to women and married men, including resigned priests, so that the eucharist may continue to be the center of the spiritual life of all Catholics;
—we need extensive consultation with the Catholic people in developing church teaching on human sexuality;
—we need to speed up the inculturation of diverse peoples through new forms of liturgy, language, and leadership drawn from the native culture of the people;
—we need a process that allows all those affected to be heard from, and to take part in decision-making.

These and several more needs are included in the Call for the Reform of our church. The letter concludes with this statement:

To be a clearer sign and a better servant to God's global family, our church must reform its own structures. We call on all people within our church, in the spirit of co-discipleship, to use their imagination and creativity. For the world's sake, let us make the church more faithful to its mission.[2]

EXPLOSION OF MINISTRIES

The Call for Reform comes within this twenty-fifth anniversary year of the Council that renamed us the People of God, the laity. Renamed and renewed, we are called to "full, active and conscious participation" in our local settings. There is no longer that certain someone who is going to come with hierarchical authority and do church for us. This is the reality that is slowly sinking in and reshaping American Catholics. This is the reality that challenges us to be continuously formed and transformed for interaction for justice and world peace, for global community and ecological harmony.

Peter Neuner, theology professor at the University of Munich, writes:

In all theologically significant places in the Bible, the term LAOS does not refer to the common people in contrast to the spiritual and temporal leaders. LAOS circumscribes the believers and baptized in contrast to those who are not baptized and who do not believe.

LAOS designates people of God, church as a whole. If we have a correct theology of people of God, we do not need a special theology of the laity.[3]

Local church is in praxis wherever the laity minister in the name of Jesus. With a global concern and local involvement we see ourselves as active participants in the great explosion of ministries.[4] In the arena of the local church, people reach out to people. Edward Sellner promotes mentoring as the authentic exercise of power that serves the needs of all involved in ministry. Mentoring is a form of peer ministry. Mentoring leads people to new perspectives, facilitates personal and institutional growth, helps others name their talents, clarify their dreams, and fulfill their potential. Mentoring moves people from disorientation and despair to new life-giving experiences of creativity and hope. This degree and intensity of active involvement frees the lonely and alienated from the sphere of isolation, self-doubt, self-hatred, and meaninglessness. It is a way of getting the church involved in the world. The real issue today is about getting the church involved in the world. Gregory Pierce of the National Center of the Laity maintains:

It's important to determine the rightness or wrongness of one's actions in the real world of work and family. We are not constantly called to take heroic stands. Church is not always heroic protest. Daily work inside our jobs is as important as the prophet in the desert.[5]

PEER MINISTRY

Peer ministry, self-help groups, and conscious witness to Christian values are a few of the ways that the local church practices the gift of faith in the risen Christ. The challenge facing every form of Christian ministry is to be prophetic for the growth of the Reign of God here on earth. It is not enough for Christians to be fulfilled and self-satisfied. As local church, the people are to bear witness to the gospel values of freedom, equality, forgiveness, and community. In North America this is a call to be countercultural and stand over and apart from the oppression, inequality, individualism, consumerism, materialism, violence, and dehumanism that pervade this society. Strong ties, frequent prayer, and commitment to the way of Christ keep the local church alive and active in present-day social trends. As more and more Christians grow in this conviction, more and more individuals form the connections that bring them in support of and with each other.

MINISTRY OF LISTENING

In 1981 Reverend J. Daryl Furlong and Sister Eileen, in the diocese of Madison, Wisconsin, began the Ministry of Listening. This is another form of peer ministry with a focused family perspective. It is an example of the explosion of ministries in North America. The Ministry of Listening draws the participants into a process of establishing support and healing for families at the parish level. The term that came out in Fr. Furlong's work is "like-to-like ministry." More and more of us keep learning that the ones who are compassionate and sensitive are those who have experienced or presently share in a similar or "like" hurt or pain. There are now many active groups for the separated and divorced, for those who are mourning the loss of a loved one, and for those who are care-givers for the terminally ill.

Fr. Furlong and Sr. Eileen developed a structure for listening to families. They expressed it in a cyclic ongoing process which begins with an awareness which helps to understand the situation; moves on to a caring which is enabling; then on to a like-to-like ministry which serves; and finally supports the families through structures that facilitate and free. The cyclical pattern of awareness, caring, ministry, and structures continues to make clear at the level of local church that the parish is here to serve the needs of others.[6]

With the relocation of the holy in the believing community and its actions, more and more of the laity come to see that Christian life is a way of achieving human fulfillment and implementing the work of the healing, redeeming Christ. Every Christian is called to share this mission and responsibility. Every Christian learns to serve as disciple and suffering servant. Every Christian discovers how to serve and share by listening.

Isaiah prophesied about this in one of the songs of the Suffering Servant:

The Lord God has given me the tongue of those who are taught, that I may know how to sustain with a word those who are weary. Morning by morning God wakens, God wakens my ear to hear as those who are taught. (Isa. 50:4)

NOTES

1. David Powers, "Evolution in the Priesthood," in *Church* (Fall 1988): 18.
2. Call to Action, 3900 North Lawndale, Chicago, IL 60618, U.S.A.

3. "The Laity," in *Overview*, The Thomas More Association, 205 West Monroe Street, Chicago, IL 60606-5097, U.S.A.

4. Edward Sellner, *America* (September 16, 1989): 133.

5. Gregory A. Pierce, *Overview* (March 1990).

6. Rev. J. Daryl Furlong, *The Ministry of Listening* (Chicago: Buckley Publications, Inc., 1987).

4

THE CHURCHES OF AFRICA: THEIR IDENTITY? THEIR MISSION?

Efoé-Julien Penoukou

The coming of Christianity to black Africa had, and continues to have, a deep impact on the life and mentality of numerous peoples in their happy or unhappy opening up to the Western world. This is true even if they have already been strongly influenced by Islam. The Christian phenomenon appears as an incontestable event in society in parts of Africa even if it generates nationalist messianisms, independent churches or so-called syncretist tendencies.

Even an empirical look at the statistics on Catholics shows clearly that although they represent only 13 percent of the inhabitants of the continent their annual growth rate of 3.5 million is greater than that of Catholics in Asia, Europe, and Oceania together. The rate of increase in the number of priests places Africa in second place after Asia and before Europe, America, and Oceania. It is also well-known that two-thirds of the world's 200,000 catechists are Africans. We could continue, but we must not lose sight of the fact that although these statistics are encouraging, the motives for conversion are sometimes ambiguous. So also are some "Christian" practices and even the content of faith. Nevertheless, one can observe a vitality and an undeniable aliveness in many ecclesial communities and their social environment. Many dioceses have made worthwhile efforts in the fields of liturgy, catechetics, theology, socioeconomic matters, and politics. Under the inspiration of Vatican II, prayer groups, gospel sharing, and fraternal meetings are all developing; new ministries for the laity, both men and women, are making their appearance; indigenous religious institutes are being born and faculties of theology established; many regional, national, and even continental associations of African theologians, biblical scholars, and moralists are appearing. Almost all local churches are developing their social involvement to link evangelization and human development.

These ecclesial practices obviously differ, often widely, from one church to another for various reasons such as the length and level of first evangelization, the personality of the bishop, the presence or absence of Islam, and so forth. They represent faith experiences which are most certainly sincere. They give birth to and nourish those men and women who are today building tomorrow's church on African soil.

THE DILEMMA OF THE AFRICAN CHURCHES

At the same time, the good faith of the African churches places them in a kind of dramatic dilemma with regard to their inauthentic or nonprophetic relationship with a continent ill at ease with itself. It is a continent subjected to international aid as well as international exploitation. It is involved in conflicts between tradition and modernization; between authoritarian one-party systems and a desire for liberty; and between a broken-down economy and the struggle to survive. It is said that the African churches constitute a kind of sounding box of the different disunities and contradictions existing in their societies. More precisely, the churches seem to be just as unable as the African states themselves to break out of these contradictions in spite of the newness and radical nature of the evangelical message. Without denying the faith which the Spirit upholds in the different ecclesial communities, the African churches present a dilemma with three characteristics. They are:
1. dependent churches
2. "wait-and-see" churches
3. outmoded churches

DEPENDENT CHURCHES

Implanted from outside and founded on models of "church" which were developed by and for other societies, the African churches are structured with a total dependence on alien plans—theological, pastoral, liturgical, financial, and so forth. This is after more than one hundred years of evangelization! The efforts at inculturation which can be seen here and there are mostly superficial without any real relationship to cultural symbolism. Ecclesial institutions are often imitations of those in Western churches and are a heavy burden. As a result, the African churches are permanently beholden to others for financial support. Projects are undertaken according to the possibility of obtaining outside help. Even Mass offerings come from churches elsewhere, their purchasing power and their "intentions" penetrating even the eucharistic celebrations of Africans. Numerous aid organizations are established and then compete with each other. Without them there is no survival for our dioceses, our institutions, our pastoral works, our seminaries, our theology faculties and our formation centers.

Along similar lines, the relationship between missionary institutes and some African churches remains ambiguous in spite of the excellent work of missionaries in first evangelization.

Such a situation gives rise to an ecclesiology of implantation which African Christians themselves have not been able to accept. This structural dependency is antiecclesial in the long run. It strikes at the very identity of the church as sign and sacrament of salvation. It brings into question the credibility of the church in Africa.

"WAIT-AND-SEE" CHURCHES

Churches accustomed to receiving everything from outside tend to wait for everything. In this sense, many of the local churches in Africa could be called "wait-and-see" churches, since they often lack imagination and prophetic creativity. They wait for and apply certain exhortations from Rome as if they were divine decrees. The forthcoming special Bishops' Synod for Africa is an astonishing illustration of this.

The "wait-and-see" church is one that is insufficiently helped by the gospel to enlighten, take responsibility for, or even create events. It rather waits for and submits to events instead of filling them with the leaven of the gospel, anticipating them or determining their shape. This is to be seen in both ecclesial and social situations. The most striking example of this for me is the attitude of total indifference shown by the sub-Sahara churches in the face of the racist system of apartheid.

OUTMODED CHURCHES

A "wait-and-see" church naturally courts the risk of becoming outmoded — overtaken by events and by the evolution of mentalities and behavioral patterns. This is why in certain areas — doctrinal, moral and pastoral — a specific type of ecclesial language no longer has any effect. In fact, this language shows itself to be outmoded in relation to cultural traditions as well as to present-day changes. As a result, many groups do not feel that the gospel really touches their ancestral religious convictions, their actual life situation, or their deepest aspirations. The phenomenon of syncretism is developing. Intellectuals and young people who seek companionship in centers of reflection and human solidarity are turning to the Rosicrucians or the Freemasons. Meanwhile, poor Christians faced with the aftermath of belief in witchcraft and the attendant need for healing are joining the new religious movements of charismatic healing.

THREE THEOLOGICAL CURRENTS

In the face of these characteristics of the African churches, three theological currents have developed which attempt to react to the dilemma in which the churches find themselves. They are complementary to each other. All want to establish an adequate relationship between the Good News of salvation and African reality.

AFRICAN THEOLOGY

This saw the light of day in the 1950s on the eve of the independence of the African states. It is characterized by a demand for the overt recognition of African values. It is the theology of adaptation, of finding stepping stones in cultural traditions in order to pass over them to a Christianity seen as a finished product. But this ongoing theology will become increasingly critical of the

ecclesial practices of the magisterium and will promote a growing awareness of
the need to incarnate the gospel in African reality.

THEOLOGY OF INCULTURATION

This follows the same lines as African theology but with three particular
traits:
a. a concern to specify the precise places for evangelical incarnation;
b. affirmation of the relative, partial, and circumscribed character of the teaching of the magisterium with regard to the unfathomable riches of the word
   of God;
c. development of a dialectical relationship between gospel and culture. If the
   culture has to accept the word of God as a factor of conversion and anthropological and cosmic fulfillment, it can only do so by deepening, by itself and
   under the action of the Spirit, the dimensions of meaning and hope which
   are inherent in this word.

Especially in Burkina Faso, the theology of inculturation focuses on a church/
family praxis and on a theology of brotherhood and sisterhood.

THEOLOGY OF LIBERATION

This theology first appeared during the 1970s as a result of the dehumanizing
situation in black Africa, the new awareness of the gospel as a promise for the
whole person and for all persons, and the Latin-American Colloquium of Third
World Theologians at Accra in December 1977.

> All theology of liberation is born out of the attempt to understand the
> suffering of those who are victims of oppression and institutionalized
> exploitation, of those who are rejected and treated like objects while they
> are human beings created in the image of God, redeemed by Christ and
> sanctified by the Spirit.[1]

All the practices and theologies in the African churches today represent not
only different faith experiences but also the limitations and demands of fidelity.
In this second part of my testimony, I would like to put forward a few theological
reflections on inculturation.

THE PARTICULAR CHURCH: COMMUNION IN DIVERSITY

The particular church has its foundations at one and the same time in the
gift of the triune God in Jesus Christ, and in the cultural gifts which also find
their origin in this divine gift. The inculturation approach is a search for maturity in faith. Because of its relevance and credibility in African societies it allows
us to rediscover the triune God, not as an abstract metaphysical concept, but
as an interpersonal relationship which is a perfect communion of differences.
The triune God is at the same time difference and communion in relationship.
The difference is not an obstacle to communion but a condition of communion.
God is only God as Father, Son, and Holy Spirit. All creation was made in the
image of this triune God before it was broken by the sin of division. Neverthe-

less, all cultures aspire to communion in the differences of their identity.

The mystery of the church which St. Paul expresses in Ephesians as the plenitude of Christ has no other identity than this trinitarian structure of unity and diversity (Eph. 1:22–23). The church actualizes in a sacramental way the communion which has been revealed and assumed by the person of Christ at the heart of history. The principle of the diversity and unity of churches thus originates in the communion-in-diversity relationship proper to the Trinity.

These few reflections indicate how being a particular church is firstly a requirement of faith. The local church draws its particular identity from the inexhaustible riches of the unique mystery of the Holy Trinity, principle and model of the church.[2] It is the Spirit which enlightens the peoples and makes them fruitful, thus enabling them to build a church through discerning and living certain specific aspects of their culture.

The local church is neither a ghetto nor an anonymous society. It is one specific expression of the unique church of Christ. In other words, the local church fulfills itself in communion with the totality of ecclesial communities as the one unique church of Christ. There is then a sort of interiorization, of mutual inclusion, which shows that it is only in agreement and in communion with other churches that a local church identifies itself with the church of God. The particular church is both church and particular insofar as it is a response to the gospel heard in a human situation, in communion with other local churches. No one local church can pretend to exhaust all the diverse meanings or the many historical forms assumed by the church of Christ.

In Africa the church can actualize its specific identity and show itself as sign and sacrament of salvation only by facing the major challenges with which it is presented.

THE CHALLENGES TO THE MISSION OF THE CHURCH IN AFRICA

CHALLENGE OF IDENTITY

The first challenge is that of the very identity of the local church. This challenge is applicable not only to actual ecclesial experiences but above all to its environment and to its sociocultural evolution. Many doctrinal and sacramental statements and practices still pose very basic problems and keep consciences in a state of perpetual turmoil. I am thinking here of the thorny question of marriage which prevents many Christians from receiving the other sacraments. In fact, the Christian family itself is threatened. The accommodation between Roman law and Germanic custom brought about in the ninth century by Archbishop Hinemas of Rheims still continues to weigh heavily on Catholic doctrine concerning marriage in Africa.

There remains also the delicate and complex problem of the eternal financing of projects and institutions pertaining to the African church. Certainly, the disastrous economic environment prevailing on the continent makes it difficult to see other choices in the immediate future, but this remains something paradoxical to a responsible acceptance of the gospel. If the church in Africa remains so very dependent on outside help, can we truly believe that the God of Jesus Christ has given what is needed to all peoples so that they might accept responsibly God's message of salvation? How can it faithfully proclaim itself as church, as sign and sacrament of salvation for all? In Africa we urgently need an ecclesiology of responsible participation. However difficult it may be, it is time that we ourselves increasingly undertake responsibility, area by area, for those projects which arise out of our essential needs and which are within our capabilities. Taking things in hand autonomously and responsibly, through a regional or even continental solidarity among the churches, portrays a prophetic witness of liberation for the future. This would be a testimony to carry to the heart of an Africa eternally assisted from outside.

CHALLENGE OF THE POLITICAL ORDER

It has been said in more than one African country that the African states are not legal states. The majority of them are shackled by one-party authoritarian regimes. These systems which attack both liberty and human dignity are being implemented, if not actually created, by Christians. Acknowledging well-known principles, we must undertake a political commitment by both individual Christians and ecclesial communities. It is where the destiny of human beings is being played out that the mission of salvation proper to the church is to be found. This salvation is neither an abstract principle nor a theoretical debate but an event which involves Christ and his church in the history of the human race.

CHALLENGE OF THE ECONOMIC ORDER

The permanent economic drama of Africa and its causes are well known. First there is the international economic system which contributes to Africa's underdevelopment in spite of whatever is signed by way of loans or aid agreements. The international speculators who deal in our primary resources, the bottleneck of debts and the accumulated interest on them, and the present plans for structural adjustments, all spell ruin for Africa. The figures, the facts, and the misdeeds are there. But the serious responsibility of Africans themselves for this stagnation is undeniable. Areas of real effort exist but they are isolated and sterile in the long run. The World Bank observed recently that the standard of living on the black continent is about the same as it was thirty years ago. The responsibility of Africans for this situation is enormous: lack of thought, laziness, a mendicant mentality, corruption, irrational interference by arbitrary political powers in the economic sphere, ill-conceived development plans—so many evils which crush people like a sordid and sinister fate. It is time to call all Africans to make a collective effort to change the situation in the name of their dignity and intelligence as human beings.

Faced with such a situation, many local churches have rightly undertaken micro and macro development projects. However, the often social and therefore nonproductive nature of these projects, their excessive dependence on external financial backing, and the partial nature of church involvement are all factors which make for self-questioning on the educative role of the church in economic practice. In what ways and for what reasons does the church's strategy of development differ from that of the state, and above all, how does it form the African for self-reliance? In a word, are the practices of social development undertaken by the local churches on the right road for the liberation of the poor, and thus for the coming of justice—a sign of the Reign of God?

CHALLENGE OF THE CULTURAL ORDER

For us in Africa the question of culture is an all-embracing one. I am not entering into the false debate between those who wish that we would no longer be African in Africa and those who wish to reduce our cultures to fossilized traditions. Culture is not a static thing. It represents, both in tradition and evolution, a way of being together. As transmitted and unceasingly interpreted it is both a vehicle for and a creator of values capable of helping a human being to become fully human.

For us the cultural question belongs to the theological order. Appreciating this leads to an understanding of how much the redeemer of humanity, who came to save the Jewish people in their particular culture, can only be truly accepted in the heart of a specific culture.

The liberation or human promotion of Africans as Africans does not exclude the urgent need for a judicious openness to the evolving realities of our present world. This is necessary in order to discover and develop the true values of their cultural patrimony.

CONCLUSION

In Africa it is not the people who reject the church but rather the church which does not recognize itself in the people, a people in solidarity with history. We do not have religious crises but religions in crisis.

I end on a note of hope with regard to all the sufferings of the local churches by quoting a celebrated sixteenth-century theologian, Erasmus of Rotterdam, who was a contemporary of Luther, and who was threatened and isolated in his struggle for the liberation and fidelity of the church of his day. He wrote these words full of emotion, humility and faith: "I therefore support this Church until I see in it a better one, and it is certainly obliged to support me until I become better." The church is not yet perfect and neither are we! We are called to become so in the perfection of the communion of the triune God, our very reason for existence.

NOTES

1. "Libération ou adaptation? La théologie africaine s'interroge," in *L'Har-mattan*, 1979:195.
2. Vatican II, *Decree on Ecumenism*, 2.

5

QUESTIONS FROM THE LOCAL CHURCHES IN ASIA

Michael Amaladoss, SJ

INTRODUCTION

Asia is a vast continent with a variety of cultures and contexts. Any attempt to speak of an Asian theology is bound to be general. It will also be conditioned by the particular background of the speaking, which in my case is Indians. My aim in this paper is to point to significant, sometimes problematic, new thrusts. I shall group my remarks around three challenges that the churches in Asia are facing. After presenting the new situation that gives rise to a new theological perspective I shall point to questions that theologians — at least some of them — are asking.

THE CHALLENGE OF THE GREAT RELIGIONS

CONTEXT

Asia is the cradle of all the great religions, including Christianity. All of them are experiencing a revival in a search for identity in a post-colonial context. This revival has given rise in some areas to fundamentalist movements. On the other hand, growing industrialization and urbanization is leading to a certain secularization. In this situation the religions are called to collaborate in the defense and promotion of common human and spiritual values. This was the theme, in fact, of the addresses of John Paul II to religious leaders of other faiths during his recent visit to India.

Since the Second Vatican Council this call finds a resonance in the hearts of Christians because of a growing positive approach to other religions that urges us on to respectful dialogue with them. A meaningful, experiential, and open encounter with the other great religions is really a new "sign of the time" in the life of the church. Such encounters are often occasions for humility when,

46

for example, the "mystic" religions think of Christianity as an inferior religion, still tied to rituals, laws, and structures, or when the church is admired for the wrong reasons, such as its efficient organization, its international network, or its schools that are bearers of modernity, and not for its spirituality or for the Good News it brings.

THEOLOGICAL PERSPECTIVE

In this situation a new theological perspective is emerging. One may call it a paradigm shift from a church-centered view of the plan of God for the world to a Reign-centered view. Without ignoring human sin and sinful social structures, all history is seen as salvation history. God, the word and the Spirit are active in the world from the beginning, leading it to the fullness of God's Reign. The religions too are elements of this cosmic covenant. The church is called and sent into the world to be at the service of this "mystery" as its first fruits. It does not exhaust or monopolize this mystery. Other religions too are playing a role in the history of salvation, because the salvific dialogue between God and the human person not only takes place in the secret of the human heart, but takes account of our social nature. The primary focus of evangelization, then, is the Reign of God and it comprises various activities like liberation, dialogue, inculturation, and proclamation according to the situation. The building up of the church is only at the service of the coming of God's Reign.

QUESTIONS

This new perspective raises various questions that need to be pursued:

Regarding the Church. 1) If the church is no longer seen as the center of the world and of salvation history, what is its self-awareness as the herald of the Reign? 2) What are the sociopolitical implications of the broadened process of evangelization, especially when the church is called to collaborate with other religions in the defense and promotion of common human and religious values?

Regarding Christ. How do we understand the unique and universal mediatorship of Jesus Christ in the context of the cosmic activity of Christ and his historical manifestation and continuing presence in the church? Some theologians speak of the cosmic, unknown Christ; others speak of Jesus proclaimed by those committed to him in faith. Still others seek to discover the dialectical links between the cosmic Christ and the historical Jesus in the overall context of the "mystery" of salvation. Some would distinguish between the spheres of Christ and of the Spirit. This is a question that is very much debated. While we may not be able to unravel the mystery, we could try to locate it more precisely and accurately.

Regarding Christian Life. For Asians dialogue is something intrapersonal, an attempt to come to terms with their own roots as Hindus, Buddhists, and so forth. We hear claims of people being Hindu Christians or Christian Buddhists. From this point of view which is a more positive and integral approach to other religions, prevalent ideas regarding syncretism will have to be revised. One will have to learn to live with pluralism. In this context how would we assess the claims of those who speak of the possibility of going beyond "name and form," of transcending structures and symbols?

THE CHALLENGE OF THE POOR

CONTEXT

The poverty in most countries of Asia needs no demonstration. But in recent years popular religiosity has also come to be recognized as an integral element of the Asian situation. Both poverty and popular religiosity have negative and positive aspects. Poverty is oppressive; but one can choose to be poor for the sake of the Reign. Popular religiosity can be superstitious and alienating. It can also be the source of prophecy and inspiration.

Another important element of the Asian situation is that the struggle against oppression is more and more engaged in by multireligious action groups. If we wish to avoid the privatization or marginalization of religion in such multireligious societies we have to see that the religions, while rooting each believer in his or her faith, also provide a common inspiration for the task of liberation. This is the collaboration we have already spoken of in the first section.

THEOLOGICAL PERSPECTIVE

There is a quest for integral liberation. One seeks freedom not only from economic injustice and political oppression but also from social bonds like the caste system. One sees the need for cultural change: a transformation of world views and value systems. One looks to the liberating motivation and inner strength of authentic religion. One sees the usefulness of tools for sociopolitico-economic analysis. But one also looks for new models of socialism. One seeks to integrate the insights and methods of leaders like Gandhi. One seeks roots in one's own tradition as a way of avoiding alienation, even if this tradition has to undergo transformation.

QUESTIONS

The Asians are searching for an integral humanism. Asian traditions have in the past perhaps promoted the ideals of personal growth and fulfillment through detachment and contemplation and have sought social harmony as a context and support for this personal sadhana. Today the communal dimensions of human existence, experience, and fulfillment and the commitment to historical action are more stressed. We need to hold both these dimensions in a dynamic equilibrium. As an Indian theologian, George Soares-Prabhu, has expressed it: "Asian thinking is always holistic. Experience in its totality (personal and communitarian, mystical and societal) will replace praxis as the hermeneutical key to an Asian theology of liberation." But this holistic perspective is still being sought.

Another area for research is how to make religions relevant and a force for unification rather than division in the experience of multireligious action groups. Otherwise these groups will become marginalized as far as religion is concerned and the church itself will lose the cutting edge of its presence to the world.

As a result of recent history the relationship between the church and state in Europe and America has taken a variety of forms. There is, however, no reason why these should be models for the countries in Asia with multireligious populations. These countries will have to evolve towards a situation in which we have states that are neither confessional (Islamic, Buddhist, Hindu, and so forth) nor purely secular-technocratic (with no respect for religious values). This is the only way in which minority religious groups can contribute to nation-building without feeling marginalized and defensive. But this is hardly possible as long as the church itself preserves its "foreign image" in its liturgy, its theology, and its organizational structures. This leads us to the next point.

THE CHALLENGE OF SELF-DISCOVERY AND GROWTH

CONTEXT

As early as 1974 the Federation of Asian Bishops' Conference, at its first meeting in Taiwan, spelled out the task of evangelization as the building up of the local church through a threefold dialogue: dialogue with culture, with other religions, and with the poor. At the International Mission Congress in Manila in 1979 evangelization was declared to be the task, primarily, of the local church. The three-self movements in China and the role of the church in the Philippines during the recent struggle for liberation have refocused the attention of Asians on the need to become local churches. There seems to be a gap, however, between desire and reality. Assessing the Pope's visit to India in February 1986, Parmananda Divarkar writes:

> As far as India is concerned, we are still suffering from the connection of a large part of the Church with the colonial expansion of western Europe. It is not just a question of a surface appearance of being foreign. The problem lies deeper and cries for a radical solution; we have not grown from a seed but are transplanted. At first sight it might seem an advantage to skip the slow stages of growth that lead from conception to maturity and to find oneself catapulted into adult-hood, with all the trappings of a fully developed Church. But the laws of life can be bypassed only at the expense of vitality and eventual fertility. . . .
>
> A journalist who followed the papal tour concludes his otherwise positive reports with the comment: "It is clear that John Paul II is a strong Pope, a fighter for what he believes in, while the Catholic Church in India is quite the opposite." Whatever be the measure of truth in this statement, would it be impertinent to suppose that John Paul is effective because he is free to be himself, whilst the Church in India is not . . . We are not a young Church, except in the sense that we have never really grown up.

THEOLOGICAL PERSPECTIVE

Over the last twenty years the focus in Asia has moved from adaptation, through inculturation, to the building up of the local church. The latter, while supposing a dialogue between gospel and culture, includes the creation of indigenous forms of Christian life and ministerial organization as well as contextual theological reflection in a community that is built up from below as a response to God's word. The dialogue between gospel and culture or inculturation is itself seen as an encounter between the church, which is a particular historical and cultural expression of the gospel, and a culture which is animated by other religions, popular or developed. Such inculturation is seen not merely as an incarnational process by which the word takes flesh again in a new culture, but also as a paschal process in which not only the new culture but also the church as the bearer of the gospel is called to die and rise again. Aloysius Pieris has called it a "baptism." This call to the church to die seems to be threatening to many. Obviously, the church as a people, as a movement and as a mystery does not die. But as an organization with structures that are historically and culturally conditioned, it must be ready to die and to take on new forms.

QUESTIONS

It is one thing to speak of a participative church from below as a response to God's word, and another to create conditions of freedom and responsibility that facilitate such a growth. Autonomy in communion, collegiality, and subsidiarity is an ideal often spoken of. But what seem real are structures of financial and cultural dependence that are internalized through formation and history. How can we create a participative church?

The church as people, the church as movement, the church as mystery will certainly endure. But are our models of church with their time-and-culture-conditioned structures called to die and to rise transformed into a new people? What is the role of tradition? How much of it is really normative and how much of it is relative? What are the criteria to be used to distinguish the essential? Does one historical development necessarily contradict, dominate or condition another historical development?

CONCLUSION

Let me conclude with three general observations on the characteristics of Asian theologies. They are, first of all, holistic. Tolerance is a characteristic of Asian peoples. Pluralism is a part of experience for them. Their world view is inclusive, integrating the "yin" and the "yang," the active and the passive in one total perspective. Sharp dichotomies are avoided. There is an attempt at consensus even in and through conflict.

Secondly, their approach is experiential. Realization (sadhana) rather than knowledge is the goal of life. Truth is experienced as a being rather than as a creed. A certain pragmatism accepts plurality of levels and methods in experience allowing for process and diversity.

Finally, Asian theologies are dialogical. If dialogue with other religions is a dimension of our life, a reflection on that life can hardly be exclusively Christian.

CHALLENGES TO MISSION CONGREGATIONS AND LEADERSHIP IN ASIA

I have basically three areas of reflection regarding Asian theologies:

Local Church. There is a growing sentiment that the primary evangelizer is the local church and that mission itself be understood as a concrete means of

communion among local churches. Some key elements of this reflection include:
— the invitation of the local church to participate in their missionary enterprise
— the theology of local church
— what the local churches are asking today
— the need for inculturation.

These four elements raise a number of questions:
— How do these affect our policies of inculturation, our commitment to a specific country?
— How can we be helpers, not leaders, sometimes even against the wishes of the local leaders whom we have first formed in our own image?
— How can we let the church be built up from below without imposing what we know of our church and its various structures, within, of course, the permissible limits?
— What are the implications of this for our policies regarding finances, aid for projects, and so forth? In India, for instance, we have discussed the possibility of making a distinction between development aid which is given through autonomous agencies, and the funds available to the missionary who should instead try to work with local resources. I think there is here a whole area of reflection regarding policies and action that concerns both leaders and members of mission-sending congregations.

Theology of Evangelization. The SEDOS Seminar of 1981 widened the focus of evangelization to include inculturation, liberation, dialogue, and proclamation. This obviously focuses evangelization on the Reign of God. I think that there is a growing awareness that liberation is an integral dimension of evangelization. But I do not think that the same awareness exists with regard to inculturation and dialogue. Dialogue should be seen not only in connection with the great religions so that it is confined to Asia, but also in connection with the popular religions in Asia, the Pacific, Africa, and Latin America. Dialogue is also relevant to Europe and North America because of the presence of sects and the large numbers of Muslims. There are proportionately more Muslims or followers of Asian religions in Europe than there are Christians in Asian countries.

Formation. The third area of reflection concerns the broad topic of formation. If we are thinking seriously of working in the local churches according to the broadened understanding of evangelization which includes the promotion of justice, inculturation, and dialogue, then we must ask ourselves some probing questions:
— Can relevant formation take place except through an experiential insertion in a place where these realities can be experienced and reflected upon?
— Can we form people for this kind of a situation in a hot-house, in so-called international formation centers?
— What is formation? And where do missioners get this experience during their formation period?

So, ultimately, the question is: where do we form missionaries and how? Where do we form the leaders of the local churches, the priests, religious, and lay leaders in Africa, Asia/Pacific, and Latin America? This is the basic question. I can see that in concrete terms, setting up formation programs that are inculturated locally may take time. In the meantime, what kind of initiation is being given to missionaries going out to Africa, Asia, and Latin America? Are they being formed in a hot-house and then thrown into a work situation? Is there any place in Africa, for example, where someone who will be working there could spend a semester being exposed to a particular culture and learning more about it experientially before he or she is thrown into a particular mission situation? This is over and above language school. I do not know of any place in Asia. I suppose each religious congregation places its people in a community where they might learn some of this, but today, with all our modern means of teaching and learning could we not begin forming all of the missionaries locally at all stages? I suggest that different Congregations working in the same area could collaborate and set up institutes of initiation for missionaries in a particular country and in particular cultural contexts within a country.

6

A THEOLOGY FOR AFRICAN CHURCHES

Boka di Mpasi Londi, SJ

If, when we speak of theology, we mean a body of ready-made formulae or abstract concepts, then we can say that Africa has no theology, and there is no reason to believe that Africa needs one.

In Africa, theology appears as life, as intellectual vitality emerging from a faith that is lived by all the People of God. It has three elements:

1) Expression. To be alive and viable, to live and to survive, faith needs to be expressed. The person responsible for this expression is the believer himself or herself.

2) Personality or identity. In Africa there is no such thing as an isolated individual. The person is an open world, a related center, a "being with," a miniature community. The person takes priority over things and over any system of ideas. We are all aware that the African personality has been disturbed by historical circumstances. Thus we can speak of an anthropological identity crisis of the African personality, a crisis that needs to be "resolved." The solution to the crisis is in the culture.

3) Culture. Culture simply means the specific vital expression of the human personality.

In Africa today it is difficult to separate the work of theological thought from these three constant factors: expression, personality, culture. There is one word that contains all three: inculturation.

INCULTURATION

This is the bedrock of African theology. If we must find a word to characterize African theology, it is inculturation. Its purpose is harmony within diversity. For this reason we should not wonder if, for now, socioeconomic and political imperatives of development and the challenges that they present come after the search for identity. Some would indeed focus primarily on the demands of development and social justice to build a Christianity concerned with African

53

society today, but my own focus here will be on inculturation. There is a very good reason for this. The imperatives of development are surely there challenging the people of Africa. However, to respond to the challenge, to act, and to promote their own development, Africans must first of all exist as Africans. So long as the anthropological identity crisis continues, all other undertakings are likely to fail, built as they are on quicksand.

John Paul II noted this and welcomed it on the occasion of his first trip to Africa. He said:

> [In Africa] there is certainly maturity, a youthful maturity, a joyful maturity, a strong maturity, the maturity of being themselves, of finding themselves in this Church as in their own Church, not in the Church imported from elsewhere. This is their Church, the Church lived in an authentic, African way.

And when he returned to Africa a second time, he pointed to the fundamental condition for this: "Africa needs space, freedom and creativity."

Already in 1969, Paul VI, speaking in Kampala, had proclaimed Africa's right to create her own Christianity. He said, "In the expression of a single faith, pluralism is legitimate, even desirable; in this sense you may and you must have an African Christianity." And in 1980, in Nairobi, John Paul II went even further when he said, "Not only is Christianity important to Africa, but Christ himself, in his body, is African."

There is no lack of encouragement from the popes and the same can be said for the leaders of missionary institutes and societies. Indeed, at a recent meeting of formators on the subject of inculturation, one superior general expressed surprise that one of his members, a missionary priest novice master, was somewhat reticent to embark upon this adventure that we call inculturation. The superior general said to him, "It is really so simple! The main agents of inculturation in Africa are the Africans themselves. You, as a guest who comes from abroad and who has been welcomed among them, can at best be of some assistance; at worst, you can be an obstacle. But you shall never achieve inculturation in their stead, neither for them, nor without them nor against their will."

All of these statements inspire confidence. They tend toward some sort of response to the aspirations of the African personality, some sort of decisive thrust to channel creative initiatives. After John Paul II's first trip to Africa, a book was published entitled *Voice le temps des héritiers (Time of the Heirs Has Come)*. The authors, Jean-Marc Ela and René Luneau, defined the main concerns of African churches and denounced the gap between statements of principle and their realization in concrete acts. A bishop presented a copy of this book to the Holy Father during an ad limina visit.

INITIATIVES IN INCULTURATION

Let us note some initiatives in theological expression where an African theology is actually in the making. A system for theological expression is spreading throughout the entire continent in institutes for formation, study and research centers, and theological reviews.

FORMATION INSTITUTES

Some institutes, such as the larger seminaries, used to be somewhat like landing fields onto which ready-made consumer goods were parachuted—from "above"! Today they are becoming centers for research and workshops for reflection. Their purpose is to rediscover traditional values and reclaim the cultural heritage in which we must incarnate our faith if it is to continue growing.

An example of this is the Major Seminary of Koumi, in Burkina-Faso. Their newsletter, "Voix des Séminaires," often includes reports of field studies done by the seminarians themselves. Some of them did not have the time to experience fully their authentic culture during their childhood and early youth. They began to do so now in order to discover the roots into which they will have to introduce the message of salvation. This is a new awareness of what it is to be a seminarian, to prepare oneself for the work of evangelization as a priest. The same kind of study can be found in the newsletter put out by the Seminary of Ouidah in Benin, "Voix de St. Gall."

To give one more example, a quick glance at the titles of ICAO documents shows a striking number of theses and reports that deal with traditional local values in an effort at authentic understanding.

RESEARCH CENTERS

Some centers are changing their methods. They now organize seminars to provide an opportunity for those who know the local culture to express and interpret it personally. In the past, the most common approach was to go and question people and bring back whatever they had said; they are given a chance to speak for themselves and to be heard. One center in particular is remarkable in its use of this method: the Ethnological Study Center in Bandundu, directed by the Society of the Divine Word in Zaire. In twenty years they have organized twenty seminars, one each year, and for each seminar they have published a report.

TWO SIGNIFICANT AREAS OF THEOLOGICAL EXPRESSION

At the risk of shocking you or at least surprising you, since we are so used to equating theological activity with the activity of professional theologians sitting in libraries and confined to academic circles, I must tell you that, in Africa, close observation will reveal that the center of theological reflection is moving toward the center of life, the faith community. The principal agent on a day-to-day basis is no longer the priest, whether foreign or native, but rather the lay person. It is through the laity that faith can take root in the culture since values in Africa are transmitted through the family.

LITURGY

The first place of creativity is the liturgy as it brings together the greatest number of ways of expressing faith. In the first place there is exploration of bodily expression, especially in terms of gestures and rhythms, and rhythmic movement that can even become dance. Artistic creations bring out lines, shapes, symbols, and colors that have special meaning for the particular community. Chants, punctuated by the throbbing of tam-tams and the festive beat of drums, find those particular rhythms and tonalities that are in tune with the soul. The composers of these chants are not always priests or religious—they are often lay people. Homilies are bringing back a climate of dialogue as a means of community participation in the thought of the preacher. At the same time, the thoughts of the preacher are thus tested and verified by the community. Members of the congregation express their reactions spontaneously and truly in these dialogues. The preacher can have direct feedback on his thoughts through these reactions, and know whether he has been understood, and whether there is agreement or not. When, at the end of such a homily, the congregation sings the Credo, this Credo truly reflects a consensus, an expression of shared faith: together they stand in the light of the word of God.

DIRECT REREADING OF THE GOSPEL

Finally, there is one last key concept: a direct rereading of the gospel message. Our younger generations are practically allergic to the unfolding of whole systems of abstract ideas about faith, the Trinity, the church, and so forth. A direct contact with the word of God is what they ask for, right there where the Spirit breathes. This requires an effort of interpretation. As if he intuitively understood this need, Pope Paul VI said in Kampala:

> You can remain sincerely African even in your interpretation of Christian life; you will be able to formulate Catholicism in terms that are absolutely appropriate to your culture, and you will be able to bring to the Catholic Church the precious and original contributions of "negritude" of which it is particularly in need at this hour of its history.

Two liturgical initiatives deserve special mention:

1) the liturgy of Ndzon-Melen in Cameroon—an initiative that came from below and was approved at the top, by the bishops; and

2) "The Mass According to the Zairois Rite," to use the official title—the idea came from above, from the bishops, and was approved at the local level. There are already the beginnings of African eucharistic prayers in both French-speaking and English-speaking countries. Throughout Africa there are initiatives and efforts at theological creativity seeking new ways to express faith in the liturgy.

CONTROVERSIAL POINTS

With respect to the changes in the Zairois rite, the invocation of the ancestors is one and the change in the order of the penitential rite and the rite of peace are others. The penitential rite comes after the liturgy of the word, and even after the homily, rather than at the beginning of Mass. The sign of peace is exchanged right after the penitential rite, and not after the Lord's Prayer. The Mass according to the Zairois rite has not been authorized officially "from above" to this date. The Pope has been in Zaire twice; despite the solemnity of the occasions, he could not celebrate Mass according to the Zairois rite. (In 1988 the Zairois Mass was approved. Eds.)

Two other controversial points concerning liturgy should be mentioned:

1) Since there are too few eucharistic celebrations due to the small number of available priests, should not the number of ministers be increased by ordaining lay persons who are already responsible for communities? No agreement has been reached as yet on this point, either theologically or politically.

2) Considering the economic implications, and because of the imperatives deriving from the incarnation of faith, do the substances of the eucharist (the bread and the wine) reflect an authentic fidelity to Christ's intention today? On this point as well, reflection continues and no agreement has been reached as yet.

SMALL ECCLESIAL COMMUNITIES

Whereas liturgy is lived in passing moments, small ecclesial communities are privileged places, permanent and essential, for witnessing to faith. Two vital elements can develop: the first is creativity in ministries where theological reflection is developing very fast. The second is an awareness of joint responsibility and solidarity. Solidarity founded on the extended family is the cornerstone of African sociology. This new awareness in our churches is already beginning to acquire a significant theological expression and will lead to development. It is not enough to theorize about development; it is essential to have a foundation. The emergence of small Christian communities is a reliable base from which to promote a holistic approach to development that will endure.

Christian communities provide:

— a setting in which the organic functions of traditional solidarity can expand. A sense of responsibility can be awakened, especially among the laity; a spirit of relationship and sharing — typical of traditional culture — can be fostered and deepened.

— a place where the spirit of evangelization can be assimilated. This spirit is becoming the new inspiration for a new culture, not only for Christians, but for non-Christians as well. The gospel increasingly inspires and animates social life and spiritual life for both Christians and non-Christians.

— a setting for self-criticism. It is easy to criticize others, but self-criticism is another matter! In a small community it is practically inescapable, as it is in a family. Here again, modern trends are picking up on traditional values and rediscovering self-criticism in a group setting.

— finally, a setting from which a truly responsible and committed laity can emerge. Herein lies the true guarantee of vitality and survival of our churches. What is new in this acceptance of responsibility by lay people is the fact that they are thinking and reflecting instead of expecting the priest to provide ready-made answers. Today lay people know that they are responsible for their church even to the point of expressing appropriate opinions, and this gives them a desire for information and formation.

CONTROVERSIAL POINTS

1) The introduction of a priest or a religious into these communities—is it artificial or natural or problematic?

2) The presence of the guest—the missionary!—is he or she a real member, a collaborator, a catalyst, a judge, a security officer, or a guardian of loaned goods?

3) Openness to other Christian faiths brings up the problem of intercommunion.

CENTRAL IDEAS

Let us now consider some central ideas and trends emerging from the activity of professional theologians.

ANCESTORS

Ancestors are the mediators of life, of blessings and of virtues, all of which have their source in God. Thus they are also the models for taking responsibility for life. This sensitivity, this acceptance of responsibility with respect to the life we have received and are to transmit, is not an abstract concept but rather a commitment that involves duties and moral obligations. In other words, it is a deep awareness of being an example or model, and this is why the ancestor is the saint of the family, the saint of the clan.

It is precisely this sensitivity and understanding that prepare us to receive Christ with hardly any reservations. How understandable that John Paul II should have been overjoyed in Nairobi to receive a book entitled *Christ as Our Ancestor*, written by an African priest, Charles Nyamiti, professor of theology at the recently established Catholic Higher Institute of Eastern Africa.

This is indeed a new movement that expresses concretely our desire to turn away from ready-made systems, formulae, and abstract concepts, toward a person, Jesus Christ, whom we recognize as our Ancestor. This is tremendously important when we know that the Ancestor is a vital global link, translatable into but not reducible to biological terms. Indeed, human life can never be reduced to biology alone. For an African who has been normally educated and not deformed, to be told that "Jesus is our Ancestor" is enough to make him feel vibrant, entirely cared for, and secure. Yes, Jesus is our Ancestor. He is no stranger since he is admitted and understood as Ancestor. He belongs to us and we to him; he is our own.

A few months after Professor Charles Nyamiti gave his book to the Pope, a group of nine young African theologians, some of whom were still students, grouped around their elder, Msgr. A. T. Sanon, and in collaboration with their

French friends R. Luneau and J. Doré published a first christological study which clearly states their position. Entitled *Toward an African Christology*, this work offers a way of thinking that is no longer oriented toward concepts of essence or nature, but rather toward a living person, through realities that are directly available to the African consciousness on a spiritual level. What is involved is a personal relationship with the living Christ—Ancestor, older brother, liberator. A vital relationship is established, one that challenges.

THE FAMILY

Thanks to patient and careful sociological research, an impressive documentation has been assembled. This has finally re-established the cultural truth concerning the traditional African practice of marriage in its various forms: progressive, polygamous, and monogamous.

The progressive form belongs to the realm of ceremony and ritual. Its stages are punctuated by dowries and births, depending on the region and the population concerned. It is not as widely practiced as had been originally thought.

The polygamous form is the result of social tolerance. It attempts to resolve certain problems raised by the experience of the first complete marital contract which is, in fact, monogamous.

The monogamous is the original, fundamental form of traditional marriage. The structure itself witnesses to this. It is a contract between two individuals, a man and a woman, and an alliance between their two families. A dowry is usually paid in the initial phase, not by the betrothed alone, but by his family with or without his contribution. It is true that on this point there has been in practice a certain evolution, but the structure has not changed. It is therefore incorrect to continue imagining that polygamy is the original and most common form of marriage in Africa. That form is monogamy, beyond all possible doubt.

A consensus has developed on this point, on the basis of studies published by the magazine *Telema* through the years 1976 to 1984. This was confirmed at the SECAM meeting in Yaoundé in 1981 and by the Plenaria held in Rome the following year.

One can state today as a definite fact that sociological proof has confirmed the cultural truth about these forms of marriage. A theological reflection can now lead us with some certainty to valid pastoral guidelines.

THE GUEST—THE MISSIONARY

The third key concept concerns the presence of the guest, the missionaries, and their role: Are they to stay? In what capacity? To do what? Or to leave?

Two Italian missionaries, Renato Kizito Sesana, former director of the magazine *Nigrizia* and now missionary in Tanzania, and Valentino Salvoldi, a professor of philosophy, have published a book, *Africa—The Gospel Belongs to Us*. They did not write "Christianity," they wrote "The Gospel." They attempt to translate what Africa feels today about the message it received, and what Africans consider to be the essence of the message before any baggage was added onto it. Finally, the authors propose a moratorium. In 1974, the African Association of Non-Catholic Churches (CETA) held a meeting in Lusaka at which a moratorium was suggested as a strategy. No more personnel, equipment or funds would be sent, in order to test the real capacity for survival of those churches that had been implanted in Africa. This was intended as a tactical measure and not as a sign of hostility. Now, twelve years later, two Italian missionaries, at the end of their experience, believe that such a moratorium would be appropriate, and that an African Council is becoming necessary.

A complementary book by Fr. B. Joinet, *Africans Gave Me My Freedom*, underlines both consistent and original aspects of the African personality, but it does not support the idea of a moratorium. On the same subject, Fr. Efoé-Julien Penoukou, Dean of the Faculty of Theology at ICAO in Abidjan, in his *Eglises d'Afrique*, provides an overview of the tasks facing the African churches. His reflections lead him to support the idea of an African Council but not a moratorium.

LIFE

A fourth key concept is life with its corollary, health, and its counterpoint—disease. Research is only beginning to shed light on the cultural, spiritual, moral, social, and scientific complexity of our African traditions. All expressions of evil, the counterpoint of life, have been lumped together and labeled "witch-craft." This is a pejorative label and one that is inappropriate. It has led to a marginalization of essential values which have been consistently ignored, mis-understood, and despised. Anthropological research has advanced considerably in this area, allowing theological reflection to engage in an organic thought process capable of justifying the use of terms such as savior and liberator as they are applied to Jesus Christ. If he is truly the savior, Jesus must free the people from evils that they know to be evils afflicting them. Jesus does not save them from evils that are listed in a catalogue of sins and presented as evils. A catalogue may appear to them suspect, or perhaps artificial, or even one that distracts them from the pressing preoccupations of their lives.

Jesus Christ, once he has entered our lives, has to free us from a real evil, an evil that we ourselves perceive as such, if he is to deserve the title of savior, or liberator. This is a challenge to theology. This challenge leads us toward a new consciousness and new demands for a theology of Christ. And we must boldly set to work.

METHODOLOGY FOR AN AFRICAN THEOLOGY

THE PEDAGOGY OF INITIATION

A book by Msgr. Anselme T. Sanon in collaboration with Fr. René Luneau, *Enraciner l'Evangile*, emphasizes that the pedagogy of faith should be based on the traditional experience of initiation. Today many formation institutes are beginning to realize that the African educational system known as initiation is quite similar to the early catechesis of the Fathers of the church. Many inspiring analogies with that catechesis are being discovered. For example, there is a desire to provide a global and participatory formation which is done better by story-telling than by reasoning, through experience rather than by teaching. As regards methods, it is certainly a sign of progress that we should be able to find inspiration in our own traditional experience, until recently considered useless and suspect and sometimes even harmful and reprehensible.

KENOSIS

This is a method inspired by the incarnation (Phil. 2:7). As we meditate on Jesus, we become aware on the one hand of a personal kenosis expressed in his incarnation, life, death, and resurrection. On the other hand, we see a cultural kenosis in the fact that having chosen to be born a Semite, he speaks with authority: "You have heard it said, but I say to you. . . ." He introduces a principle that is precious to us: an emptying that makes way for something new. This is the equivalent of the experience of conversion which involves the loss of something old to make room for something new.

For the sake of brevity, I simply note that cultural kenosis occurred clearly and visibly at Pentecost when different peoples were amazed and perplexed to hear their own languages spoken, rather than Hebrew (Acts 2:11). This was the first confirmation of cultural kenosis. A second occurred when the apostles discerned regarding the necessity of circumcision. Was it necessary to circumcise and therefore to judaicize those who were not Jews and who requested baptism? The answer was definitely no. Is the West ready to accept a similar cultural kenosis today in communicating the message to Africa?

CONSEQUENCES FOR AN AFRICAN THEOLOGY

— The universal can only be lived in the particular. The Son of God is universal; however, in his incarnation he became part of one particular culture—the Jewish culture. He did not wish to absolutize this particular culture. We see the necessity of a cultural kenosis in order to separate the universal from what is not universal, in order to avoid giving absolute value to that which does not have it.
— Initiation and creativity underlie kenosis. The central issue from the standpoint of methodology is kenosis, and its model is the incarnation of the Word itself.
— The missionary and pastoral aspects of inculturation are found in cultural kenosis. The missionary aspect of inculturation signifies the process of insertion of the evangelical message into an already existing culture to awaken faith. The pastoral aspect signifies the necessity for faith to express itself within an adequate culture, which inevitably needs to be created.
— Cultural kenosis is essential to the missionary aspect of inculturation as creativity is to the pastoral aspect.

AN AFRICAN COUNCIL

The above thoughts and reflections all lead to the conclusion that an African Council would be appropriate. Every attempt at theological reflection, whatever the path chosen, leads to an impasse, a blockage that is not normal. We feel that an African Council could result in a decisive discernment, analogous to that of the apostles in Jerusalem, analogous also to that of Vatican II, much closer to us in time. (On January 1, 1989, the Pope convoked a Special Assembly of the Synod of Bishops for Africa. Eds.)

The light of the Holy Spirit leads us to discover the problems; the strength of the Spirit will lead us to find the solutions!

7

The Church in Latin America: Basic Ecclesial Communities

Jose Marins, Carolee Chanona and Theolide Trevisan

We will share with you our understanding of the church in Latin America today and what that church is saying about the problems and challenges it faces. We speak to you from the vantage point of a pastoral theological reflection on basic ecclesial communities. We are in contact with grass-roots communities in many churches of Latin America and also in the Caribbean. Once a year we visit the Hispanic community in the United States of America.

The language of our peoples at the grass-roots level who are classified as illiterate is largely a language of symbols. And so we introduce them to you through their symbols, the cloth banners and pennants which they have made during workshops which we conducted with them. We present some of them to you now.

SYMBOLS

PANAMA

This symbolic greeting is a simple red pennant handcrafted by Panamanian Indians. It is dominated by the outline of a fish and was given to us at a meeting with basic grass-roots communities on the periphery of Panama City. Archbishop McGrath was present for the meeting. In their native language they told us:

> Panama means the place of the fish, so we drew this fish on our cloth. In our Christian tradition the fish is a symbol of Jesus but we selected it also because many of us earn our living by fishing and we want to tell you how we experience church. People who work on the land make paths and sometimes try to cement them. It is easier to walk on them that way. But when we work on the sea we cannot walk on a path. We cannot just follow

the paths of yesterday because they may not lead us to the fish today. Finding the fish each day means that we must read the signs—the tides, the sun, the shadows, the winds. We have to judge, and so we learned also to judge and discern in our basic grass-roots communities. It is not always important to repeat yesterday's ways. They do not lead to today's fish.

When we work on the small boats with nets we must work as a team, otherwise we get nothing. We do not all do the same thing on the boats; one directs, another handles the sails, others the nets. Doing different things we accomplish a common work. In the church, too, we accomplish a common work. It is not so different.

BOLIVIA

This Bolivian banner was given to us by several hundred people who were representing the miners and the communities involved with them—Indian campesinos, camp dwellers, and some people from the city. It was the first time they had come together to share their common experiences and in so doing they came up with the message on this banner. There are lights and shadows symbolizing the situation of constant debt in which they live. Then there is the figure which looks like an octopus or some kind of monster which is sucking out all the natural resources and wealth from the country.

Bolivia is the world's largest producer of pewter and has the richest subsoil of all Latin American countries, but these resources are being taken away and fed into foreign commercial companies. Thus there is alienation and also extreme hunger. At this moment Bolivia suffers from 14,000 percent inflation. It is practically at the stage of total collapse. The poor in Bolivia, as elsewhere, even crush each other as they ally themselves with the foreign interests so as to improve their lot.

Symbolized on the banner are the three groups—the miners, the Indians and the campesinos. They are simple people. As they come together they talk about the difficulty of surviving today. At the same time they share the faith that guides them to discover the resources they have in their own hands to improve the situation. One is holding a scissors to cut at the tentacles of the monster that entraps them. It seems a puny instrument, out of all proportion, but it is precisely the disproportion of a David and Goliath that is the strength of these poor people. The writing on this very colorful banner says that the basic grass-roots communities are the People of God helping to transform their society.

HAITI

Haiti's symbol was given to us before the departure of the Duvaliers and before the visit there of Pope John Paul II. It portrays the church as both a sign of hope and a stumbling block.

A drum dominates the whole banner. It is symbolic of the culture of the people. These symbols are all the more important in situations of misery and poverty, for many can only express their desire for life through music and dance.

The banner expresses joyful hope at discovering a church that helps them to be aware that Christ is also Haitian, that he is identifying himself with the Haitian people, calling them, helping them to go beyond and transform their situation. However, the little church building at the center of the cloth is half in and half out of the drum.

Even in Haiti, prior to recent events, the church had not drawn close to the people to hear them. It was seen as allied with the Duvaliers, a church where the appointment of bishops was largely controlled by the regime, a church that had not really made an option to be with the people, but maintained its position in close alliance with the powers supporting the status quo. It is not a unique situation. In Salvador, for example, not all the bishops are sensitive to the people; some of them continue as military chaplains in a situation where the role of the army is seriously questioned by others. Some are suspected of denouncing to the government Christians involved in supporting the people.

BRAZIL

The banner from Brazil represents the renewed faith of the Catholic church. Different situations are pictured on the cloth. Their human suffering is portrayed by their having to leave their homes. New technology destroys the natural resources. The primitive situation of the people gets worse. Jesus is crucified in the human person, men and women, black and white. But there is hope in the situation, for they are committed to change it, and the symbol of this commitment is the signatures of the participants around the border of the banner. Many could not sign it because they were illiterate, but these kissed the banner as a sign of their commitment and solidarity.

DOMINICAN REPUBLIC

Their cloth banner represents a similar situation. The same anger and pain is shared by two different peoples on the island—one French, the other Spanish-speaking. The Haitian people, as portrayed, have the worse part of the island. The dominant ideology of the stronger Spanish-speaking side means in fact the oppression of the weaker part. There is an incomplete figure of Jesus depicted on the cross, a sign that as long as they are divided they have to acknowledge that Jesus is incomplete. His face cannot be seen. They cannot grasp his full significance. To overcome this situation of injustice and lack of communion they have to "complete Jesus," that is, transform the reality.

THE PEOPLE WANT PEACE

Throughout the continent there are different levels of conflict:
— areas of constant war in Salvador and Nicaragua
— extermination of peoples in Guatemala
— organized guerrilla activity in Colombia and Peru
— permanent repression and violence in Chile and in Paraguay which has the distinction of enduring the longest period of repressive dictatorship in Latin America.

At the same time there are emerging alternatives in Brazil, Argentina, and Uruguay. Everywhere there is the basic desire for a change in the situation.

Our peoples want peace. There are signs of hope when the common people come together and through concerted efforts do something to improve their situation at the local level. In the next section we will try to show how the people became aware of their situation and how the signs of hope emerged.

VATICAN II TO MEDELLÍN

The Council was a moment of deep crisis for the church, the people, and the bishops, especially in Brazil but also in many other Latin American countries. The bishops during the Vatican Council at first felt that they understood little of what was going on, and with a deep spirit of humility they started to study in afternoon sessions with theologians such as Congar, Schillebeeckx, Danielou, and so forth. In the second and third sessions of the Council they heard experiences of other churches in Europe and Asia, and in the fourth session they began to plan a continental session to incarnate the Council in Latin America. This came about at Medellín where two and a half years after the Council the bishops, priests, laity, religious, and other Christians met to make options as they tried to interpret what was happening in their own situations.

We were all involved in this. Before Vatican II we had been very concerned about the lack of priests. We asked sisters and lay people to substitute for them and they were given responsibility to catechize, to baptize, to give the eucharist, and so on. This brought us closer to our people and was a turning point for many of our churches. At first we had been trying to do something for the people, but we soon learned it was they who were teaching us how to believe in God, how to be less complicated. Many discussions and meetings took place on how to learn from the real problems of life, how to survive.

The next step was to start working from the people's situation, the new *locus theologicus*. We as church discovered a new situation. In the past we had often supported government decisions and we discovered now that we were considered the enemies of the people. We began to examine why the people could not survive, not just during hard times, but in an ongoing way. We were not so naive as to think we could change the world in a few years!

We tried to do a theological discernment rather than a sociological study of the situation and we saw that it was simply not in accordance with God's will. We saw that it was sin. And so the church spoke with a very prophetic voice in Medellín, denouncing that situation and committing itself to change it. We understood well the Pope's statement later on when he visited Puebla: "It is not that there are poor and rich but that rich people become richer at the expense of the poor who become poorer."

"Evangelization" was understood as announcing good news to those who need good news. That meant liberation for people from the structures which maintained those situations contrary to God's plan. Not just liberation *from* but liberation *for*:
— to create space for a possible changing of those situations
— a liberation that would go from the personal, to the social, to the ecclesial

- a liberation at the personal level from a way of living according to values contrary to the gospel
- a liberation for the person to enter into relationships with others, not exploitative but collaborative, recognizing and respecting the dignity of the other
- a liberation for working together as a people conscious of a "collective identity," of a collective history and destiny. They are conscious that they are persons, social beings, not lone individuals, and that this defines their relations with other persons.

OPTION FOR THE POOR

The point of departure for this evangelization is this preferential option for the poor — not an option for poverty, condoning poverty, but for the poor who suffer the consequences of a subhuman situation. Option for the poor is the point of departure, not the goal. The goal is to create a situation of nonexploitation, of justice, and of recognition of the rights of others.

In this sense the option for the poor is not exclusive. But it is from the vantage point of the poor that the rich are evangelized. Poverty and riches are correlated, and if one's goal is to acquire material goods at the expense of others who do not have even the minimum of those goods, then something has to give. The option for the poor is not reduced to obtaining material goods only. Just having clothes and food is not the end of human living. The reflection of God's image and nature in us requires that we be able to develop social, religious, and cultural values to participate fully in society.

CONVERSION

Many times we seem to be opting for the poor but instead we are opting for ourselves, using the poor to bolster our feeling of being authentic, using the poor as our measurement of how self-sacrificing we are. We need the experience of the poor to help us to be completely empty-handed so that we may be evangelized by them and learn from them those values that are still so present among them. This can lead to a new experience of who God is, God's mercy, and compassion, and graciousness. The option for the poor by those of us who are not materially poor is an option that leads us to solidarity with them in order to change their situation.

At the same time it is an option to become evangelically poor ourselves. As Jesus divested himself of his Godhead and became one with us in order to redeem us, so we divest ourselves of riches to be with the poor. We can then begin to relate to other values, to mobilize, to organize, to create, to undertake activities that would change the situation. Puebla and Medellín foresaw the effects of this conversion, this "letting go." They call for a change in the way of being church, for a prophetic presence in society.

We are paying a very large price for this prophetic presence. Because of their option for the poor more than seventy priests, two bishops, nine sisters, and over six hundred lay leaders and church workers have been killed since Medellín and Puebla.

BASIC ECCLESIAL COMMUNITIES

The basic ecclesial community is the space, the forum, where the simple people, the poor who have been marginalized from both society and the church, have a place where they can speak, be heard, and discuss. The initial step is not, therefore, to gather people together for religious practices but to bring them together to experience relationships and to discover their human values. To do this you must pitch your tent in the land of the poor. This involves a whole process of conversion.

The basic ecclesial communities accomplish conversions in both church and society, because in both the poor are marginalized. As a result, the way of being bishop or priest or religious changes. Bishop Romero's conversion was such a change. He had not been prophetic or one to take risks. The people changed him. The ground from which a theological understanding on liberation emerges is reflection on the faith of the people and the consequences of this for society.

A NEW PASTORAL APPROACH

The situation, the place where we are present with the people is the theological locus. Where we are has not only a geographical but also a ministerial and even theological connotation. Often we spend time talking about external problems, or about the church as institution, but these are not the people's problems. Their problems are concerned with the Kingdom, the Reign of God.

Praxis. We analyze the situation. Then we evaluate the practice of our faith in this situation. We try to apply the Bible to our communities not in a fundamentalist way as the sects do, but taking into consideration the whole ancient tradition of the church. The scriptures are very important here. In them we meet the person of Jesus, his criteria, how he judged situations, his way of life, how he communicated his mission. We meet him not only in his historical situation, but Jesus present here and now in this community, in this church. This leads us to action.

The goal is the Reign of God. We emphasize the personal, social, ecclesial, and eschatological dimensions. Often we stress one dimension but we try to complement this one with the others for the sake of the Reign. The goal is not the church. Nor is it the search for vocations, religious institutes or parish organizations.

THE COMMUNITY

The community is the agent and the clergy is the servant of the community. We believe in resurrection even in very difficult situations, and we do not give in even when we are opposed by some members of the hierarchy.

Celebration is very important for us. The fiesta is often the people's first experience of God's Reign. It has an eschatological meaning for us. We celebrate because we have hope.

Evaluation. We try to evaluate constantly what we are doing. We try to learn from our mistakes, to complement our opinions with those of others, to face new challenges.

CHALLENGES

Some urgent challenges, both pastoral and political, have emerged. We single out the following:

BEC GROWTH

BECs (base ecclesial communities) are the basic church groups. If they are basic, they must have all the elements necessary to be church at that level. Because they are still in the process of becoming, it is vital that there be space and opportunity for them to grow as ecclesial communities. This is not always clear to those responsible for authenticating or recognizing the BECs officially. How to allow the communities to mature fully is a challenge.

THE ROLE OF THE PRIEST

The BECs challenge the role of the priest in mission. Priests often go through a crisis in this new situation. They feel useless. The ministry for which they have been trained and to which they are accustomed is no longer what is being asked of them. They may have suffered all the woes and pains of the people, but this sharing in pain is not unique to them. As the other dimensions of ministry are fleshed out and the laity's participation is acknowledged, the priests need to reconsider their place in a community where there is now a complementarity of roles. Given our recent experience of a very clerical, pyramidal church in Latin America, it is imperative that the priest today knows how and when to intervene and not to interfere in the growth of the community. He must be sensitive to a process that is emerging and to allow a seed just sown to grow. His role is one of helping the communities to form, accompanying them and not being the central authority deciding what the community does.

THE ROLE OF RELIGIOUS

Religious were asked at first to substitute for the priests. Now after ten to fifteen years' experience of Sisters working pastorally, they in turn are being challenged to examine what their role is in relation to the process. Are they merely substitutes, or does the Religious life have a unique and particular dimension to bring to this new situation which can be discovered in dialogue with the community?

THE ROLE OF WOMEN

They are among the most active and creative members in the basic communities. The liberation of women is seen in a special way in Latin America. Because a people that was oppressed and marginalized is discovered to be one people — men, women, youth, the elderly — the liberation of women is seen in the global context of the liberation of the whole people. This is not to say that the specific marginalization is overlooked, but it is seen in complementarity with the liberation of the whole people. In this process the man is also liberated from those structures and conditions which condition him to see woman only in a certain way.

COORDINATION OF MINISTRY

This is a challenge in each community. We are not looking especially for increased ordinations, but trying to inaugurate another style in which the community will indicate how to coordinate ministries. These are not necessarily life ministries; they are temporary; they include men and women. They do not include ordination to priesthood. We avoid this discussion and try to act in the real situation in which we find ourselves today.

POLITICAL MINISTRY

The vocation to a political ministry is another challenge. We know there is a lot of support for ongoing formation in these ministries. Communities, at times, cannot keep up with those in this ministry and this gives rise to a certain separation, but the persons in this ministry still feel the need for ongoing support. Related to this is the problem of how to ensure that the ecclesial dimension is not diluted as Christians and BECs become more committed to justice. This can create permanent tension in the effort to avoid reductionism and opposition while seeking to maintain integration and continuing reciprocity.

THE MISSION *AD GENTES*

In order to be a full church, the Latin American church must respond to the mission *Ad Gentes*. Over the last ten years different congregations have undertaken mission *ad gentes*. But for centuries the local church has not done this. Some people may have had an experience of mission, but not the local church as a whole. Now that we have had a good experience of other churches in Latin America—first from inside the same country and later from other countries of the continent—we are now to mission openly *ad gentes*—to all nations.

We would like to make the point that we are not interested in establishing national mission-sending institutes or congregations. This is the position of Brazil and in some other Latin American countries. On the other hand, Mexico, Colombia, and Chile have national institutes. But the choice of a number of countries is not to found such institutes but rather to implement the commitment of the local church to mission. They will try to do mission through teams of priests, sisters, brothers, and lay persons. Bishops who have finished their term can also serve another church as part of these teams.

We are inviting all members of our church to offer at least five years of their lives to mission. We recognize and are gladdened by long-term commitment to mission, but we are implementing another style. We do not deny a lifelong commitment but are complementing it. Serving another church for five years as a member of a team means a kind of itinerancy. We understand that this is impossible for countries like Japan and China in which three years are needed to learn even a little of the language.

But these itinerant teams insist on the need for a commitment between churches, both to give and to receive. Mission is not a personal affair but a church affair entailing a kind of dialogue, a receiving and giving.

We distinguish three points in this missionary commitment *ad gentes*:

1. With the local church let us go to non-Christians.
2. *Ad ecclesiam*—to the churches. Let us be with the native church in the process of inculturation. When we dialogue with another missionary church our concern is not only about local issues but also about the problems of the universal church. Let us not leave decisions regarding the universal church only to those in Rome but offer our views and our perspectives in a spirit of deep communion with the Pope.
3. *Ad invicem*—to one another. Let us have a more and more universal view of the church. We are Catholic. We are not concerned only about the few square miles of our local church but as Catholics we look at what the church is doing here and now in this world, and we are willing to contribute from our own poverty.

PROBLEMS

Inevitably there are problems which challenge us even further.

PROTESTANT FUNDAMENTALIST SECTS

These have lavish financial help and are committed to the ideology of a capitalist society. They are invariably supported by governments of countries where a policy of national security ideology is in force. In practice this means most of Latin America.

NEW RELIGIOUS MOVEMENTS

These movements which come from outside Latin America proliferate here. They come with preconceived ideas, "facts," answers to problems. They seek followers, vocations, not integration with the culture of the people or dialogue with the church. They do not listen to or collaborate with us.

NEW CONSERVATIVE TRENDS

The upsurge of the tendency to retreat, to go back to more conservative attitudes, is another problem. This tendency is seen in some Latin American seminaries today. Many aspirants entering the seminaries are content to follow a model of church which pre-dates the Second Vatican Council.

Consultation prior to the appointment of a new bishop does not seem to take place now. It happens frequently that men who are not in any way involved with the vital pastoral aspect of BECs are the very ones appointed bishops, and usually to key places. We cannot yet speak of a division among the bishops but there is definitely a sector that is gaining ground and that has a lot of support.

REFUGEES

More than one million Latin American refugees are in different parts of the world. How do we accompany them? How can we help them pastorally?

THE CHURCH IN AREAS OF CONFLICT

This challenge is particularly associated with the situation in Central America where there are areas designated "liberated." The church as church has been absent from these areas, yet there are large numbers of people who are Christian belonging to these communities. They are abandoned pastorally.

CONCLUSION

We began by presenting some symbols. We conclude now with two final ones. The first is from Chile, the second from Argentina. From Chile comes this small piece of bone which a political prisoner received in his soup. He has carved it into the image of a tiny dove, a sign of hope in the presence of the Spirit of God. From the suffering church comes hope, strength, peace.

And from Argentina comes this small piece of wood on which there is a drop of the blood of Bishop Angelelli from La Riota. We know that he and a lay church worker were killed because of their commitment. With them were two priests who were wounded. They got this drop of his blood on this fragment of wood from a local tree called *bel arbor*. I show it to you as a symbol of the bishop's death and of the deaths of so many others.

We end with a quote from this same bishop: "We are given two ears, one to be attuned to the needs of the people, the other to be attuned to the will of God for these people. Only with the two can we announce the gospel."

CHALLENGES FOR MISSION INSTITUTES

We wish to underline now how the missionary congregations can help us in Latin America.

LOCAL CHURCH BECOMING MISSIONARY

We think that missionary congregations can help the local church become a missionary church. They sensitize our church and make us more aware of mission *ad gentes* — to all nations. Missionary congregations can help by giving us the preparation we need, by investing in the preparation and formation of local people instead of bringing in more people from outside and by helping us to evaluate our missionary commitment, especially our methods, our priorities, and the commitment of the local people.

A HOLISTIC APPROACH

Missionary congregations are challenged to reread their charism from the perspective of the church or area where they are inserted, and to live their charisms in the situation where they are located. They are called to integrate and collaborate in what we call the *pastoral de conjunto*, that is, a holistic approach to pastoral work in a given situation, seeing the whole situation of the people to whom they are responsible and therefore not fragmenting their pastoral work.

In many of our countries and churches there is not a holistic approach so that the challenge for missionary congregations is to contribute an overview greater than that of the local church. In doing this, they must be aware of other groups with charisms in the local church and help to integrate these into the common plan. The local church has to avoid duplication and make use of the little it has to serve the larger and more common project.

LOCAL VOCATIONS

The very best members of our congregations, as well as those who have been in leadership positions, should be sent to the mission areas and not kept back at congregational headquarters for formation work or to produce the congregation's bulletin, for example. Local vocations to the missions must not be placed in parishes or traditional pastoral work just to keep up the congregation's commitments. We must believe that if we give our best personnel to the missions God will bless the congregation. We need to revise our ecclesiology and the image of the church from which we are operating. If missionaries come to the local church to get local vocations for their congregation they are helping themselves, but this is not the commitment we await from them.

GOVERNANCE OF CONGREGATIONS

A challenge confronting mission institutes today is to revise our model of internal governance. Many mission institutes have their general headquarters in Rome. To what degree do we in our congregations present to local churches of Latin America the same model of governance which Rome presents to them? Can we convey alternative models by decentralizing our own congregational central administrations?

Can we ensure that the renewal programs and opportunities available to Superiors General are made available to all members of the congregation? Sometimes there is a real gap in the thinking of leadership and that of the members of a congregation. Decentralization and collegiality are important in a congregation and benefit both the congregation and the local church.

8

THE THEOLOGY OF LIBERATION

John Fuellenbach, SVD

INTRODUCTION

Liberation theology originated and developed out of a particular situation in Latin America, a situation marked by "utter dependence and oppression" for millions of people. The church asks a very simple question: does theology or the gospel have anything to say to our situation that could help to overcome this hopeless and desperate state of affairs? If not, the church and the gospel will become utterly irrelevant to our situation.

It is a theology that asks for a radical commitment of Christians to the plight of the poor in order to help them to change the situation through an active engagement for social justice and human rights. It uses the tools of "social analysis" in order to understand adequately the causes of oppression and dependence. The theology of liberation sees itself as the correct interpretation of Vatican II and the papal documents *Populorum Progressio* and *Evangelii Nuntiandi* for the situation in Latin America. Theology cannot be done independently of the concretely analyzed situation.

Liberation theology is critical of all traditional theology because the social sciences have helped to uncover the unconscious presuppositions out of which all theology is done. All of our most lofty ideas and ideals, including theology, are conditioned by social, political, and economic factors. There is, therefore, no objective theology that could claim to be the *norma normata* for all theology, a claim often made or presumed by European theologians. In this connection the accusation of liberation theologians against their colleagues is twofold:

1. European theologians do not dare to subject their theological presuppositions to a critical analysis which would reveal that their theology is to a great extent the product of their social, political, and economic situation, out of which they unconsciously construct their theology. European theology operates from the basis of affluence and progress. The theologian in Europe does his or her theologizing from and for such a society.

2. The second accusation is that of arrogance: European theologians behave

as if they know what theology is and that everyone else has to submit to their judgment when theologizing.

My concern here is to show the biblical foundation of this theology. Its basic insights are the Reign of God and a correct image of God.

THE BIBLICAL BASIS OF LIBERATION THEOLOGY

THE REIGN OF GOD

God's ultimate plan and intentions for the whole of creation can be adequately expressed by the biblical term *Reign of God*. Bringing about the Reign of God is the ultimate goal of history, the fulfillment of the age-old dream of humankind and of nature—the new heaven and the new earth (1 Cor. 15:22–28). This ultimate goal of all creation is for Christians the vantage point from which we understand ourselves and the whole of reality. It is our Christian vision, the horizon within which we locate and arrange everything.

Jesus saw God's Reign not as a utopian vision that might come about one day, but as a reality breaking into this world, challenging all present structures and powers. The Reign is in our midst, it is now the all-determining reality in a world which is still under the mighty sway of evil powers and principalities.

The church enters precisely here. It is related to the whole of humankind and must see itself in the service of God's plan, the Reign of God.

The mission of the church today can be described in a threefold way:

1. to proclaim in word and sacrament that the Reign of God has come in the power of Jesus of Nazareth;

2. to offer its own life as a "test case" to show that the Reign is present and operative in the world today. This is realized initially in a particular phenomenon of history, namely, the Christian community.

3. to challenge society as a whole to restructure itself along the basic principles of the "inbreaking" Reign which are justice, peace, fellowship and human rights. This is a constitutive element of proclaiming the gospel since the ultimate goal of the Reign is the transformation of the whole of creation.

Salvation is something that affects all creation and all inter-human relations, autonomous, interpersonal, and social. Since the Reign enters a sin-permeated world, a world of oppression and exploitation, "salvation" is to be understood as an all-embracing liberation, that is, in a "holistic sense": spiritual, psychological, and sociopolitical. This "holistic view" of the human person and the world is decisive.

St. Paul has given us an almost classic definition of what the Reign of God is all about:

> The Reign of God is not a matter of eating and drinking but a matter of justice, peace and joy in the Holy Spirit (Rom. 14:17). Not in talk consists the Reign of God but in power. (1 Cor. 4:20)

Albert Schweitzer once called this text of Romans "a Christian creed for all times." To be a Christian means, then, to transform society, human reality, and human structures in the direction of justice, peace, and joy in the Holy Spirit; to commit oneself to change situations where the opposite is most evident and where tangible situations inimical to the Reign are present.

THE CORRECT IMAGE OF GOD

Liberation theology tries to answer the constantly asked question: why make a commitment first and foremost to the marginalized of our society? Commitment to a "liberating praxis," that is, an activity which transforms society on behalf of the oppressed and exploited, is regarded as the most important exercise of Christian charity. One could say similarly that the "option for the poor" becomes the central point of a true Christian commitment. The term "liberating praxis," however, is ultimately the key concept of liberation theology.

The word *praxis* refers to the primacy of human involvement in the process of living a commitment which embodies both doing and thinking together. Thinking or "theory" does not precede and guide involvement as happens in an abstract philosophy of life. Thinking, rather, operates from within involvement. In the involvement, theory can reflect both on itself and the involvement, and in doing so it sets involvement on the right path. This is called *orthopraxis*. Orthodoxy is useless without orthopraxis. In fact it becomes a cover for false praxis if it is considered "right" in itself.

The primacy of human involvement over theory as such is also found in other philosophies. The theology of liberation assigns primacy to the "praxis of faith," that is, the biblical doing of truth. It sees praxis as necessarily having a sociopolitical dimension. Christian orthopraxis must accordingly include a right sociopolitical involvement; it cannot be limited to private virtues.

Liberation theologians present the following biblical basis for their view that a "liberating praxis" is the core of any Christian commitment:

The Exodus Story. This is the model of revelation. "I have seen the miserable state of my people in Egypt. I have heard their cry to be free of their slave drivers. Yes I am well aware of their suffering. I mean to deliver them out of the hand of their oppressors" (Exod. 3:7–8; see also Deut. 6:20–23).

This is the primary theme of revelation within the Old Testament and the faith of Israel. God's first deed on behalf of the people was an act of setting a group of oppressed people free, a political act. Since God remains always faithful, all further revelation has to be seen in the light of this first act.

God's Demand for Justice. The great prophets like Jeremiah, Isaiah, Hosea, Amos, and Micah all had one decisive theme and priority in their preaching: justice and doing right towards one's neighbor.

In particular they contrasted liturgy and worship with their demand for doing justice (Isa. 1:11–17; 58:1–11; Amos 5:21–26; Micah 6:6–8). Jeremiah's phrase might be the best summary of their protest: "To know me, Yahweh, means to do justice" (Jer. 22:16).

Jesus' Mission. Jesus understood his mission as being in continuity with the great prophet of the Old Testament. Luke (4:16–21) and Matthew (11:1–6), quoting Isaiah, clearly indicate this.

Jesus and Politics. Libraries have been written about Jesus' stand regarding politics. Jesus did not present any political agenda or program, nor did he challenge the aristocratic and hierarchical world view of his time, but he did relativize all authority and put it under the judgment of the "in-breaking" Reign. He did propose a "metapolitics," that is, a system of values and a view of reality by which any context may be judged. The question which we have to answer is: what does Jesus want of us today, in the time after Pentecost?

Compassionate God. The Bible gives us many images and descriptions of who God is, but the most adequate description seems to be that our God is a compassionate God, a God who is with us, who does not redeem us by pulling us out of our misery while remaining in distant glory. God is a God who saves by coming down directly into our misery, our oppression and exploitation, and who suffers all our misery "with us" (Emmanuel). God redeems us by identifying with our true state. The amazing fact is that God can be found where people suffer, where the suffering and misery in this world are most obvious. This is the real mystery of our God in Jesus Christ, a mystery we will never understand.

The mystery of the poor is that God wants to redeem the world through them. Jesus demonstrated this in his own life and in his preferential love for the poor. His life's mission was that of accepting powerlessness, and by doing so he revealed the limitlessness of God's compassion.

From this biblical point of view liberation theology refers constantly to the "emotional aspect" of one's commitment to the poor. One who has never experienced oppression and exploitation will never understand what this way of talking about God (theology) is all about. Only the one who makes this commitment to a "liberating praxis" on behalf of the poor and against the existing social order will come to see and understand. It will lead him or her to the discovery of God's liberating power and to a new understanding of his or her faith.

THE APPROPRIATION AND REJECTION OF MARXISM IN LIBERATION THEOLOGY

The Vatican document on the theology of liberation accuses liberation theologians of borrowing Marxist concepts uncritically, concepts which are in its judgment "perhaps impossible to purify."

But liberation theologians have been critical of Marx and Marxism. They accept the validity of many of the standard criticisms leveled by Western intellectuals, both Christian and non-Christian. They also reject, quite contrary to the Vatican document's accusation, Marx's tendency to reduce all forms of alienation to an economic source. And they agree with the document that "sin" is the "most radical form of slavery," "the source of all evils," from which derive other forms of slavery. They also recognize that salvation is not simply reducible to historical liberation. As Gutiérrez puts it, the process of liberation will not have conquered the roots of oppression without the coming of the Reign, which is above all a gift. Liberation theology does require transhistorical faith for its justification.

Following are some main areas in which liberation theology seems to touch on Marxist themes.

SOCIAL ANALYSIS

It was Karl Marx who, through a rigorous analysis of the social and economic structures of society, discovered that these factors condition all our thinking, judging, and acting to a considerable degree. We as Christians hold firmly to the belief that free will determines the flow of history, but we recognize also the influence of the organic process of history as a factor that conditions all human actions. If we can admit a "Reign-process" and concede that it is in some sense incarnated in human history, then the use of sociological analysis as an interpretative tool for understanding this incarnation seems to be justified.

Theology cannot be done independently of society and history. We have to analyze society and understand history as the place of God's self-revelation if we want to discover and to talk about God in a meaningful way today. From the perspective of history, truth is conceived as historically mediated and dependent on both the situation in society and the interests of human beings in a particular epoch. Marx, the great master of suspicion, stressed the second part of this understanding of truth and viewed all human interests through the eyes of class distinctions. Liberation theologians have insisted that this holds true for theology as well. Before we can start theologizing at all, we must first critically reflect on our presuppositions and critically examine how far our own theological concepts are conditioned by socioeconomic factors. We have to uncover our "selective inattentions."

STRUCTURAL SIN

Human beings are first of all social beings. They are not lone individuals. They form a communal unity, a concrete social entity with its structures, relationships, and self-understanding. This need not deny that persons have a transcendent dignity or that they are the subjects of their own thought. It does mean that such dignity is necessarily bound up with concrete social structures which may promote or oppress it, and that the thoughts which are indeed our own are also conditioned, positively or negatively, by social environment.

Theologically we speak today of "structural sin," meaning the social objectification of sin. The Medellín and Puebla conferences especially put the stress on this aspect of sin. They described the dreadful situation in their countries as a "situation of sin," the product of the economic, social, and political structures that gave rise to this state of misery. These structures of relationship between economic and social classes, sexes, ages, and races favor the freedom of some persons to an astonishing degree while they deprive others.

The question constantly raised is: what lies at the root of the "situation of sin"? Is it individual egoism or is it the autonomous structures that foster egoism? If our focus is egoism, we will emphasize the forming of conscience; if we stress sinful structures, social change will have priority.

Of course, the answer will not be either/or but dialectical. There is a "sin" which individuals and groups imbibe from their environment that precedes and conditions every conscious choice; and there is the ratification of this sinful situation when individuals and groups become aware of such sin, yet opt to maintain the situation or to do nothing about it.

THE NEED FOR POLITICAL ACTION

While liberation theology pays special attention to eradicating the structural sources of injustice and oppression, it does not deny the existence of personal sin or the need for personal conversion. It only highlights the impact of structural sin, both the contextual origin and the consequences of personal sins. It thus recognizes the basic limitation and finitude of personal freedom which is subject to the pressures, challenges, and temptations of existing structures. Structural sin and personal sin are not two coequal realities; rather, structural sin functions as a totalizing context or condition within which personal sin occurs, far outweighing the latter in its scope, duration, and penetration. This also means that individuals as individuals cannot eradicate structural evil. What is required is political action in its classic sense, that is, action undertaken by individuals in their organized solidarity which is aimed at creating liberating social structures.

The question has to be asked not only in the traditional way: what impact does personal sin have on social sin? but instead: what impact does social structural sin have on personal sin? Puebla puts it this way: "To preach the gospel without its economic, social, cultural, and political implications may well mean that the church has been reduced to an instrument that functions as part of the established order." The failure to recognize structural sin can lead to acceptance of the grossest violations of human dignity, making those who deny its existence unconscious, uncritical defenders of ideologies.

CLASS AND SOCIETY AND CLASS STRUGGLE

Liberation theology accepts the fact that society is divided into classes. This is an historical reality. Class struggle is seen as something that neither Marx nor liberation theology invented or advocated. It has been a fact of life throughout history. Those with privileges will not voluntarily share their privileges with those who do not have them. This is not necessarily because they lack "good will" as individuals but because the weight of reified structures which are based on a division of classes will overrule such good will.

Liberation theology does not advocate revolution in order to overthrow an existing social order. It insists that society must change, but this does not occur automatically. All papal social encyclicals as well as Medellín and Puebla insist on the need for a radical change in society if the lot of the oppressed is ever to be changed. If the ruling class will not voluntarily change, then the agent of change and social transformation can only be the oppressed majority. It is they who suffer from the basic social conflict in its most degrading form and who have the strongest motivation for organizing their own emancipation. In this perspective Marx defined the oppressed class and not the ruling one as the true agent of social change.

THE CONCEPT OF LIBERATION IN LIBERATION THEOLOGY

Liberation theologians hold that we have become aware today of something that was always there but of which we were not conscious. We are aware that human history is to be interpreted and understood as a gigantic process of liberation from dependence, and that an adequate reading and understanding of the whole process can only be done from this new awareness. There were historical epochs which presented other readings of history: the metaphysical or the mythical. In these epochs liberation did occur but it was not thematized nor was there an awareness of history as a process of liberation. A new insight, a new awareness has emerged in the history of humankind, namely that history has to be conceived in terms of conflict into which the process of liberation explodes. What we are experiencing today is that humankind is becoming aware of this dependence-liberation process and starting to read history for the first time from such a point of view.

Marx's theory of class conflict and of class-consciousness is thus affirmed, but in a more subtle way, since the liberation theologians do not restrict the dialectic of "conflict-rupture-progress" to classes only but apply it more generally.

Linked with this process of liberation is, of course, the process of becoming human. But no one claims that humanization automatically creates more freedom. It only creates the conditions for a greater freedom and creativity. It does not guarantee the possibility of exercising the newly-found freedoms. What we do with these greater freedoms is in no way determined beforehand. It is quite correct to say that people living in the jungle may have more freedom today in relation to their environment than do those who live in "developed" countries in relation to theirs.

If the twin words *dependence-liberation* are understood adequately a new historical awareness appears. If this historical awareness creates a lens or a focus through which we can see certain phenomena which were there before our eyes but not seen, then it is important to identify what that lens is. Why did it appear precisely in our time? Why did people not wake up sooner to the awareness that history is a process of liberation?

THE ROLE OF THE POOR IN HISTORY

Liberation theology originates from a simple question which thousands of sincere Christians have to ask themselves: what does it mean to be a Christian in a world that is marked by massive injustice? What is the biblical meaning of the immense movement of the poor who do not ask for anything except the right to live? What is the significance of organizations of the poor that fight for their lives? What theological meanings emerge when we enter into such movements of love?

Thus the question of the role of the poor in history has come to the forefront. Liberation theology, however, argues more from a biblical than from a Marxist

point of view concerning the role of the oppressed classes in society. It shows
how the God of the Bible chose the poor to become agents of salvation for
humankind. They are treated as favorites. The mystery of "the poor" in the
Bible consists precisely in their being the chosen instrument through which God
wants to redeem the world. There is a similarity but also a marked difference
between Marx's proletariat that will lead the great revolution and bring about
a classless society and the oppressed and exploited poor whom God chose to
accomplish salvation for all the exploited as well as the exploiters.

> God purposely chose what the world considers nonsense in order to put
> the wise to shame, and what the world considers weak in order to put
> the powerful to shame. God chose what the world looks down on and
> despises, and thinks as nothing, in order to destroy what the world thinks
> is important. (1 Cor. 1:27)

What the world considers "nonsense" and "weak" in this passage is identified
with concrete people in history—the powerless and exploited of the present
world. The whole of scripture is reread from such a perspective. The exodus
story in particular is seen in a new light.

Zaccheus had to come down from his perch in the tree and join the people
around Jesus in order to understand the Good News. This vantage point was
the only one that could enable him to see and to understand what Jesus was
all about.

Liberation theology is to be understood as the effort to think of and grasp
our faith from a commitment in solidarity with the poorest; walking with them
and affirming that on this road where the Lord is present (Alvarez: 15).

Liberation theology is considered dangerous not so much because it contains
marxist elements but because it creates a fundamental insecurity. A church that
has installed itself over centuries among the "established" will find it extremely
difficult to welcome a message that comes from the poor and oppressed who
question the church's support of the status quo. The reaction quite naturally
will be one of anxiety, fear, and insecurity because such a message is dangerous
for society and for a church that is part of such a society.

THE PHILOSOPHICAL PRESUPPOSITIONS OF LIBERATION THEOLOGY

Hegel's world view is the philosophical underpinning for the theology of
liberation. For Hegel, history is a history of liberation with a twofold meaning:
in its historical content, it is political; in its absolute finality it is also religious
and transcendent. The one cannot exist without the other.

THE RELATION BETWEEN SALVATION AND LIBERATION

Liberation makes salvation concrete and effective, but salvation itself as a
totality effects and inspires liberation.

Salvation embraces all human reality, transforming it and leading it to fullness in Christ. Nothing escapes this process; nothing is outside the pale of the action of Christ and the Spirit. Those who diminish the meaning of salvation are really those who limit it to the strictly "religious" sphere, unaware of the universality of the process.

As Segundo posits: If an absolute is unwilling to immerse itself in the relative, it ceases to be absolute; indeed it fails to attain even the value of that which is "relatively" alive and operative. The salvific process gives human history its profound unity, and sees this as a history in which Christ's liberation is at work.

LINK BETWEEN HISTORY AND THE REIGN OF GOD

The question remains of how history is linked with the process of the coming of the Reign of God. All will agree that a total discontinuity between Reign and general history cannot be maintained in view of the witness of scripture and our own experience of God's presence in the world. Yet the difficulty of the "how" remains. The official magisterium fears that the theology of liberation goes too far in its stress on the Reign as present here and now.

In *Gaudium et Spes*, 39, we read: "Earthly progress must be carefully distinguished from the growth of Christ's Reign. Nevertheless, to the extent that the former can contribute to the better ordering of human society, it is of vital concern to the Reign of God." And in the Profession of Faith of Paul VI (1968) we find similar statements. While the Pope is eager to make sure that the Reign "consists in an ever more profound knowledge of the unfathomable riches of Christ," he also urges all "to contribute . . . to the welfare of their earthly city, to promote justice, peace and fraternal concord among all," and to help especially "the poorest and most unfortunate."

Evangelii Nuntiandi speaks of people seeking the Reign, "building it up, and implementing it in their lives" (13), and again: "Men and women, created in God's image, received a mandate to subject to themselves the earth and all that it contains, and to govern the world with justice and holiness . . . " (34).

There remains a certain ambiguity, and yet how will one interpret terms like "sign" or "flowering" or "building up" if not to mean that a more just world is a sign of the growth of God's Reign? None of the major liberation theologians ever identified the inner earthly processes with the Reign of God. They all keep what is called the "eschatological proviso" of present history. None of them sees the fullness of the Reign in an affluent society. The third-world problem is not that the Reign has not yet come in its fullness, but that even the "proviso" of the Reign is formally denied.

THE RELATION OF THE CHURCH TO A GRACED WORLD

Liberation theology sees the church itself as servant—not at the center of the stage but at the service of a graced world. The church is then defined as the community which knows through revelation the full meaning of what is going on in the history of the world and which is committed to witnessing to what it is to be fully human.

Faith makes three specific contributions to the work of political liberation:
1. it provides an effective inner motivation in political involvement;

2. it makes us conscious of the sin of oppression and injustice and of the temptation to absolutize our own motives as strategies when engaging in social transformation;

3. it provides hope against despair through the conviction that a just society is something possible.

By stressing total liberation, liberation theology reacts against the traditional tendency of limiting the scope of salvation to the religious dimension. By emphasizing the political dimension of liberation as a means of making salvation historically and socially concrete it reacts to the traditional tendency to stress the importance of ultimate ends and to neglect the concrete means of making such ends effective and actual.

Salvation must become effective by liberating the totality of human existence from the reign of sin in all its dimensions. As the ultimate fundamental alienation, sin cannot be touched in itself, in the abstract. It can be attacked only in concrete historical situations, in particular instances of alienation. In subordinating the "totalistic" ambition of Marx's materialist dialectic to the equally "totalistic" imperative of Christian salvation, liberation theology has brought Marx into the inner chamber of Christianity; he no longer remains outside as an enemy.

THE EMERGING SPIRITUALITY OF LIBERATION THEOLOGY

We distinguish between monastic, medieval, and Eastern spirituality; therefore, it should be justifiable to talk about a spirituality of liberation theology. The common basis for these different spiritualities is that the gospel experience is lived in different cultures and different life situations which demand different responses.

The different authors of liberation theology stress different elements of this spirituality, but I think we can single out three basic emphases that emerge in all of them: the historical Jesus; lived experience with the poor; love expressed in terms of mercy and compassion.

THE HISTORICAL JESUS

Vatican II insisted that the essence of discipleship must be the following of Jesus as he presents himself in the gospel. This is regarded as the supreme norm for every Christian, religious congregation, and community. The historical Jesus and the central theme of his message are the determining factors of liberation spirituality. The reasoning for this is the following. The activity of Jesus during his historical and earthly ministry can be defined as a "sacrament" of the Reign in its fullness which makes itself visible in human history. "Sacrament of the Reign" means a sign pregnant with the reality of the future fullness of the Reign, as the dawn is the sign of a new day.

The Reign as a present reality makes itself visible to us on two levels: on the level of Jesus' activity and on the level of his behavior.

Jesus' Activity. Jesus' miracles demonstrate that God wants to heal the brokenness of human existence and to let us participate in God's own life. Healings as well as exorcisms demonstrate the presence of God's Reign now in the world as "integral, all-embracing salvation."

Jesus' Behavior. In relation to God (i.e., vertically) Jesus lives as Son with a total dedication to the Father who is everything to him. In relation to human beings (i.e., horizontally) he welcomes sinners; behaves like a servant; puts brother- and sisterhood over and above religious cult; subordinates the Law and sacred institutions like the Sabbath to the physical welfare of actual persons; disregards all qualifications that arise out of the social status of persons, including the past of those persons, and demonstrates that every human being has a future to look forward to.

The historical Jesus remains absolutely necessary for us in order to experience concretely what it means to live the Reign now by following him. Any spirituality must orient itself to Jesus and his central message. True conversion includes the same attitude of Jesus towards the poor, the outcast, the rich, the powerful—the attitude of compassion with which he offered integral liberation.

The Role of Mary. This relevancy of Jesus' humanity becomes possible in Latin America because of an increasing familiarity with the gospel. Again, because of this familiarity, the mother of Jesus, so highly esteemed in Latin America, takes on a new role. She is primarily seen now as *the* true disciple of Jesus and devotion to her could become a real incentive for a liberation spirituality.

In the Midst of the World's Turmoil. Commenting on the spiritual life Bernard of Clairvaux insisted that the place from which our spiritual nourishment must come is the place where we ourselves think, pray and work. Gutiérrez in his book *We Drink from Our Own Wells* refers to this quotation and points out that it is from "our own well" in Latin America that we must drink. This well is located within the liberation process to which we are committed. The spirituality of liberation theology is therefore located in the midst of the world's turmoil, rather than in a safe haven of retreat. It touches every aspect of life and it draws on the daily concrete experiences of its practitioners. That leads us already to the second basic element of spirituality.

THE LIVED EXPERIENCE WITH THE POOR AND NEEDY

The concrete experience of life among the poor is the source from which a real concern for justice and solidarity emerges. Our first reaction will most probably be compassion which will move us to action. The discovery of a compassionate God whom we want to follow is a great step in this spirituality. In the commitment to the poor we discover that compassion was the driving force in Jesus' concern for us, it was what moved him, what lay at the core of all his action. The Bible uses this word twelve times in connection with the suffering, distress, and sorrow which affected the people whom Jesus encountered. His reaction to these predicaments is compassion, meaning that he "suffers with" people before he heals them.

The poor become the place where we discover God's compassion and predilection for them. The experience of living with the poor leads to a deeper understanding of Jesus and of the central message of the Reign which is, first of all, a message meant for the poor. This is what Puebla meant by saying that "the Poor also evangelize the church." They make it easier to find God, to understand the gospel and to purify our prayer.

FOUR STAGES OF GROWTH IN COMMITMENT TO THE POOR

The South African theologian Albert Nolan, in a talk on "The Service of the Poor and Spiritual Growth," distinguishes four stages in our growth in commitment to the poor:

1. Compassion emerges out of exposure to suffering and misery which in turn moves us to action, be it to relief work or to the simplification of our own lifestyle.

2. We discover that poverty is a structural problem based on particular social and political situations that are manufactured by humans and which create oppression and injustice. Our reaction is anger and indignation, in particular toward the rich and toward politicians. We must master our anger and come to see that it is the system that must be changed. We are all victims, the rich included.

3. We come to discover that the poor themselves are perfectly able to save themselves and that they do not need us to save them. We learn from them rather than teach them.

4. We move from disillusionment and disappointment with the poor to true solidarity. The realization has to be made that the poor are not saints and the rich sinners. The problem is structural. Once we come to discover that the cause of the poor is God's own cause we will be able to overcome the feeling of disillusionment and disappointment which we will experience with particular poor people once we are involved with them.

LOVE EXPRESSED IN TERMS OF MERCY AND COMPASSION

The greatest value of any spirituality is, of course, love. But love must express itself in terms of compassion. Compassion in its original meaning means to suffer with people, to go where people suffer and to be with them in their suffering, before we do anything for them. Ultimately it means solidarity with them in the way Jesus showed solidarity with them. As we cannot understand the poor without Jesus, neither can we understand compassion independently of Jesus' own compassion. The demand of the gospel is most accurately expressed in the demand of Jesus: "You should be as compassionate as your Father in heaven is compassionate." In the measure that we come to discover God's own compassion for the poor, in that measure our way of prayer, contemplation, and meditation will grow because we will come to discover who God really is. Many have commented that there is a growing awareness and realization in Latin America of the need for true contemplation and prayer in order to discover the Lord in the poor and the poor in the Lord.

9

AN INTRODUCTION TO POPULAR RELIGIOSITY

Everyone knows the phenomena referred to when speaking of popular religiosity: pilgrimages, devotions, sacred times and places, ritual and ascetic practices, symbols, and so forth. Customarily one tends to view them in a condescending manner either as opposed to the "official" liturgy or as different from the religion of the cultural and religious elite. Recently one sees a more positive assessment of popular religiosity as the religion of the poor and the oppressed as opposed to the religion of the rich and the powerful. How can it be evaluated in itself as the religion of the people? Do not more developed forms of religion have their roots in it? Is there not a popular religious dimension in each one of us?

What is the place of popular religiosity in the life and culture of the people? The power of symbol and its roots in human-natural and sociocultural conditions of existence have to be explored. Popular religiosity can be alienating. It can also be prophetic and inspirational. It can be a means of exploitation. It can also be a force for liberation. What are the criteria for discernment?

Does popular religion disappear with the onset of secularization in the modern world? Or does it take new forms such as gnosis or spiritism? How do we understand the new religious movements? Is there no popular religion in Europe and America?

In the project of building up the Kingdom through evangelization how does one assess the role of popular religiosity? How tap its potential? How enter into an authentic dialogue with it, without marginalizing it? How inculturate the gospel in a popular religious milieu? How enable the people to live their religious life meaningfully in view of the coming of God's Reign? Are the people in the "secularized" part of the world being starved of popular symbolic expressions of religion? How can we mediate between and integrate the popular and the elite, the popular and the official, the popular and the powerful?

A suitable focus for a study of popular religiosity would deal with three areas: a right understanding of popular religiosity, a sociocultural and religious analysis of the same, and a reflection on its place in the project of evangelization as inculturation, dialogue, and liberation. A good starting point for this study may be *Evangelii Nuntiandi,* 48, and Puebla, 444–69.

The three following chapters attempt to deal with some of these questions. They are edited versions of papers presented at a SEDOS Conference on this theme.

10

POPULAR SPIRITUALITY IN INDIA

Jyoti Sahi

I came into contact at a deep personal level with what might be called popular spirituality or popular religiosity when my wife and I moved to the village where we are now living. Before that I had been familiar only with the more intellectual approach to religion. I had first experienced this within the reformed Hindu tradition of my father and then within the Catholic tradition after I had become a Christian.

I have been struggling for some time now with the term "popular religiosity." It is possible to make two broad distinctions in India: there is a popular faith which one could call a folk religion and a very philosophic Brahmanic religion which has its own traditions comparable to the Greek and Roman philosophic traditions of the West.

BRAHMANIC HINDUISM

One of the basic ideas of inculturation, going back to De Nobili and others, has been that, in Asia, Christianity need not be presented only in terms of Western philosophical thought processes. Early missionaries felt that they could build on the philosophic traditions of Brahmanic Hinduism, Buddhism, or other Indic religions such as Jainism because they approached the religions of the East from a philosophical perspective. There are still many people in the Indian church today studying the relationship of Shakaracharia to Thomas Aquinas or comparing a particular Hindu mystic to a Christian theologian. It is at this level that much inculturation has been done in India heretofore.

FOLK AND TRIBAL RELIGION

The irony of this approach has been the neglect of what we might call folk, tribal, or popular religions. They have been looked upon as superstitious or pagan and thus not much effort or study has gone into understanding them. In fact, official Christianity in India has tended to relate to what we might call the great traditions and not to the folk or "little traditions." Yet the fact remains that the people who have become Christians in India have come largely from simple village and tribal backgrounds and not from the great philosophic traditions. One could say that 90 percent of our Christians in India do not come from what might be called the "high caste" or "elite" group. Ironically, inculturation and dialogue have been directed toward this group and little has been done with regard to folk religion and popular spirituality. Michael Amaladoss, SJ, and other theologians have pointed out this irony. The question is much debated in India today because there is an increasing realization that folk and tribal religions are very different from the great philosophical traditions of Hinduism and Buddhism.

CHARACTERISTICS OF FOLK RELIGION

Folk religion is based on symbols, images, myths, folk stories, and parables. These do not follow a systematic theological structure, nor do they manifest a systematic theological approach. This symbolic approach to life is not open to propositional statements, but rather functions through the processes of the imagination. This very basic aspect of what we call popular spirituality affords me personally as an artist an entry to folk religiosity. The functioning of symbols and the way in which the more imaginative and intuitive mind approaches reality are what interest me. This imaginative approach to religious belief has been criticized as superstitious, pantheistic, or animistic. These are categories which people like to use when speaking about popular spirituality but I would prefer to say that this spirituality constitutes a cosmic religion—a creational religion. It is concerned with images which have their origin in nature and a sense of the sacred in creation.

I am uncomfortable with the way in which popular spirituality is spoken of as something merely childish. The people are often spoken of, from an elitist point of view, as children or simple, ignorant people who need to be schooled by those who have a "higher" religion. And so evangelization is often seen as a process whereby people who have this simple, almost childish religion are gradually brought to a higher form of spirituality. One of our important insights today is that there is nothing especially childish about folk religion. It follows a different process, a different way of experiencing reality, and has an integrity and an importance all its own.

WHO ARE "THE PEOPLE"?

Rather than accept an elitist definition of the people who practice popular religion, we may ask ourselves: who are these people? They are rooted in the experience of nature, the earth, the universe, the cycle of the seasons, the movement of sun and moon, the journey of the stars. Some may define the people as "the poor." That may indeed be true. The majority of the human race, the whole mass of human beings who constitute "the people" in any nation, are those who live close to the land, who are subsistence farmers or food gatherers, who rely for their daily bread on the fruits of the earth, and are therefore poor. They are poor in the proper biblical sense—they are dependent on the bounty of creation, and that means ultimately the bounty of God. They have no "tomorrow" because they always live in the "now" of divine providence.

COSMIC AND META-COSMIC RELIGIONS

In order to help us understand popular religiosity I will use the categories which have been developed by Aloysius Pieris, SJ, who distinguishes between cosmic and meta-cosmic religions. Cosmic religion which forms the basis for a popular spirituality is a faith expression that relies on symbols and on the wholeness of human experience. It is not just intellectual. It gives meaning to the wholeness of life which includes feeling, the imagination, the psychic and physical experience of the human being, as much as the intellectual power of understanding and knowing. What characterizes this folk religiosity is its appeal to all that comprises the human experience of life.

What he calls the meta-cosmic are those religions or faith systems capable of raising spirituality to a philosophic level which is more speculative and abstract. So, for Aloysius Pieris, Buddhism, Hinduism, Christianity, Islam, and Judaism are all meta-cosmic faiths.

All religions, including Hinduism, Buddhism, and Christianity, have within themselves cosmic and meta-cosmic dimensions. These exist together, but how they do so is one of the questions which perhaps we should reflect upon at some length. I suggest that these two dimensions of any belief system are complementary in many ways, but I would insist that though they are complementary, we should question placing one above the other or whether we could say that the meta-cosmic is higher than the cosmic. I will return to this question again.

CONVERSION FROM A COSMIC FAITH

In India, where we are beginning to reflect on tribal theology, not many people are conscious of the fact that twenty percent of the population comes from a tribal or non-caste Hindu background. This represents a large number of people coming from a background which is either purely tribal, or "tribal" in the sense that they have been absorbed somehow into the outskirts of the Hindu system. We call this latter group Dalits, meaning "the oppressed"—but they are people who originally came from a tribal background. It is largely from this twenty percent of the Indian population, the Dalits and the tribals, that the two percent Christian population comes. Aloysius Pieris argues that "conversion" takes place from the cosmic to the meta-cosmic, but in general there is no possibility of conversion from one meta-cosmic faith to another. Only dialogue is possible there. A tribal group, for example, having a cosmic faith can all become Christians, or Buddhists, or Muslims, but this kind of conversion will not take place from one meta-cosmic faith group to another. Very few

Brahmins would ever become Christian because they feel that their religious system is as great as the Christian religious system.

"Missions" from any one of the meta-cosmic religious systems are therefore oriented to those who profess a cosmic or creational faith. Christianity is not the only meta-cosmic faith concerned with evangelization and mission. Islam is involved in this missionary process, as is Hinduism and the Rama Krishna mission.

CHALLENGES TO EVANGELIZATION

One of the great challenges to evangelization and mission in the Indian context is that after two thousand years of mission activity only two percent of the Indian population has become Christian. During that time many great missionaries, some of them central to the whole idea of mission, came to India, where they labored indefatigably. That conversions have been so meager is a great shock to people in the church. What happened? What went wrong? Deep down it challenges and hurts some Christians who tend to think they have a much greater religion than anyone else. They see that in the large nation of India there are many people who are not ignorant of Christianity, who have seen many missionaries and are aware of their work, and who still do not feel that the Christian religion is a superior religion. This is the context in which we are working.

META-COSMIC WORLD VIEW

Cosmic religion has a rootedness in the land or in the locality through experience of the cycle of seasons and festivals. This the meta-cosmic does not have. Meta-cosmic religions are universalistic and are not rooted in the lived reality of ordinary people. In a way, one could argue that the meta-cosmic religions have emerged out of an alienation from the land and many problems have come along with that alienation. An example would be the growth of modern urbanization, which is in a sense very closely linked with meta-cosmic religion. Hinduism also led to this phenomenon of urbanization. Brahmins believe they must not do manual labor, they must not dig, they must not dirty their hands. They are now no longer linked with the land. Farmers, food gatherers, people of the forest, people of popular faith are, but not people of the city.

Christianity as a meta-cosmic religion tends also to the same alienation from the land. Throughout India Christianity is rooted in the cities and Christian tribals or farmers seem to follow the same pattern. They move to the cities because their newly-found faith is perceived as closely related to the attitude of the meta-cosmic religions, for which land is not so important. Relationship to the land and nature is often seen as something low. It is in this context that we are now becoming increasingly aware of certain negative aspects of the meta-cosmic world view.

EXPLOITING LAND AND PEOPLE

The philosophic assumptions underlying the meta-cosmic religions are often negative to nature. In India, as elsewhere, the basic assumptions which have led to the ecological crisis in our country often come from meta-cosmic religions. The blame cannot be laid only at the door of the Christian and Judaic attitudes towards nature in which human beings are supposed to rule over nature – the idea of domination over nature is also to be found in Islam and in Brahmanic religions. Alienation from the land has led to exploitation of the land and the people connected with the land. Ecological issues in the Third World, and especially in India, are not just vital issues concerning forestation or desertification – they also concern the people. The people who are very close to the earth and who now do not have firewood or drinking water are precisely the ones who suffer the most. So attitudes towards nature are also attitudes toward whole groups of people who are close to the land. There is a relationship between issues of social justice and the whole ecological crisis.

IS THE META-COSMIC BETTER?

Is the meta-cosmic better than the cosmic faith of popular religion? Communal tension and conflicts between religious groups all over the world are legitimized by dogmatic religious pronouncements. We are very conscious of this in a multireligious nation like India, where we see how religious fundamentalism leads to communal violence between, for example, Muslims and Hindus or Hindus and Christians. It could be suggested that much of the world's violence is related to meta-cosmic propositional statements. There is much truth in Hans Küng's belief that peace will only be possible in our world if there is peace and dialogue between religions. I have found that in folk religion there is a kind of dialogue going on at both the human and spiritual level, and it is much easier there because folk spirituality is not based on dogmatic statements. One aspect of folk religion is that it is basically human and therefore links all people together. When I went with my family to live as Christians in the small Catholic village where we now are – a small village in an ocean of folk, Hindu, and Muslim villages – we observed that at this popular level there is much less religious tension than in the cities.

DIALOGUE OF LIFE

In folk spirituality there is a lived dialogue and sharing in one another's religious practices. In Bangalore there is a basilica dedicated to Mary. Every year on the feast of Our Lady, special buses cater for the crowds that come from all over the countryside to the basilica to celebrate the feast. Large numbers of Muslims and Hindus will be among those celebrating! In the same way, Christians in the villages will visit certain Hindu shrines occasionally if they feel that they would get some healing or some blessing from so doing. Christian villagers go to a shrine to have their child's hair cut off and dedicated to the shrine in the same way that Hindu families dedicate their child's hair to the temple. This is all part of folk religious practice. In our village there are also many folk practices connected with the cycle of human life. For example, when a baby is born there will be rituals to receive the baby into the community; likewise, marriages or funerals will have their peculiar rituals. At each stage in a person's life there are popular folk practices to sanctify the rites of passage.

BORROWING OF TRADITIONS

At the folk level a constant inculturation of Christianity takes place. The way in which people bury their dead, the way festivals relate to the seasons, the blessing of the harvest, and so many other seasonal events all have links with local village faith. At Christmas time in our village the people will plant different seeds to sprout in a pot. These are then put near the Christmas crib and used later during the year for planting. This is actually a folk tradition which is also found in Hindu folk practice. They sprout the grain in pots for the new year and these are the same grains which will later be sown in the fields at planting time. This new year ritual is seen as a blessing on the harvest and assures a healthier crop. At this level you find a borrowing of traditions which are common to all agricultural people.

Meanwhile, at the level of a more intellectual, elitist dialogue it is becoming more and more difficult for Hindu, Muslim, and Christian intellectuals to discuss and share with one another because of growing suspicion between the meta-cosmic faith systems. These present a great challenge to the whole understanding of what mission and evangelization are about.

INCULTURATION

In India, a country with both cosmic and meta-cosmic religions, inculturation presents a yet deeper challenge to our understanding of evangelization. Inculturation can be seen in different ways. Firstly, according to De Nobili and other famous missionaries, inculturation has been seen as a means towards evangelization; secondly, it has been seen as a means towards dialogue. The two views and objectives do not always work well together. In India Hindus are upset by the whole inculturation process and especially by the Ashram movement. "You tell us it is dialogue," they say, "but in fact you are really concerned with converting Indians from their faith to yours! You are just pretending to dialogue by wearing orange clothing—the clothes of the Hindu Sanyassi, but the whole purpose of this is to dress yourselves up like wolves in sheep's clothing. You are really getting into the Indian community as fifth columnists."

Integrity within Oneself. Inculturation presupposes an appreciation of a plurality of cultures and a relationship between culture and faith. Leaving aside the question as to whether a Christian is going to convert or announce the gospel to someone else, the Christian is faced with his or her own conversion. Deep down within each Christian there are many levels of belief, and these derive not only from the Christian faith which an individual embraces but also from the whole history of belief going back to one's ancestors. Since I became a Christian while in my teens I hold very strong Hindu values and beliefs. The challenge is to relate these different dimensions of faith in my own individual personality. Inculturation is not primarily about converting others, but about creating an integrity and wholeness within oneself. Inculturation is a process of creative self-expression which enables Christians to be true to their history and particular culture within the local church. I, as an Indian, have a right to express myself authentically and creatively in my local context, and I should be able to use my culture in that effort. Inculturation is therefore a process of radical humanization. We all need to be inculturated in order to discover what it means to be truly human.

Liberation from Colonization. Inculturation is a process of liberation from colonization or enslavement to the culture of another nation. Many people in India believe that what we are really dealing with when we talk about inculturation is de-colonization. We have been colonized by the British, by the Portuguese, and before that by the Syrian peoples of West Asia. Conquerors have used culture and religion not only to spread religion but also to oppress our indigenous peoples and to drain the Indian economy. Therefore, when we speak of popular spirituality we are also dealing with what we may call countercultural movements.

Inculturation can be called countercultural in the sense that popular spirituality represents resistance to those meta-cosmic forms of religion which have often supported, directly or indirectly, the colonizing efforts of the dominating group. The countercultural element of popular spirituality is one which insists on the localness and on the authenticity of the incarnated reality as opposed to something that comes from outside. The meta-cosmic tends to stress the "universal," whatever that is, and marginalize what is specific and local.

Inculturation and the Feminine. Inculturation as counterculture is linked up with movements which we would now call women's movements. In India, for example, there has been a realization that women's movements are the ones closest to what we are terming popular religion. Women all over the world have a closeness to popular religion, and this is in large part due to the elements in popular religion which stress the feminine aspect of faith and deity. These aspects have been marginalized by the meta-cosmic religious systems which tend on the whole to be male dominated. All meta-cosmic religions are culturally male dominated.

Countercultural. Ecological movements or movements concerning peace and justice are linked to popular spirituality and are countercultural. There is a relationship between popular spirituality and all these countercultural movements. We can now no longer be complacent about the "superiority" of the meta-cosmic. In the world around us, meta-cosmic organized religions are contributing much toward global tension in the form of growing fundamentalism and religious intolerance. There are evils in the meta-cosmic understanding of reality as dangerous to the future of this planet earth, as anything to be found in the "superstitious" or "pantheistic" beliefs among tribals or village people. In fact, there is now a growing belief that the cosmic faith systems have much to teach us about how society should live in harmony with nature.

A **New Tribal Theology** is emerging which does not think it is necessarily a step forward to adopt a meta-cosmic world view. The list of "core values" of the tribals as suggested by Bishop Nirmal Minz and Ram Dayal Munda gives a rather comprehensive picture of what we might call "gospel values." This may even bring us to question how far the biblical faith is itself "cosmic" rather than meta-cosmic. It is certain that a very important central core of the Old Testament's teaching concerning creation and the relation of the people to the land is firmly based on what we might call a cosmic world view, as we find it in tribal or folk religious values all over the world.

POPULAR RELIGIOSITY AND TRADITION

In addition to being countercultural, popular religion is also very tradition-bound and lacks a prophetic vision. Folk tradition is not self-critical in the way that the meta-cosmic is. This is clearly manifested in folk art. This art is in many ways wonderful and has an integrity of its own to which many creative artists have returned to find the sources of their own imaginative life. But folk art is also rigidly traditional, resisting creative innovation and evolution at every stage. Popular spirituality functions as the real conserver of traditional symbols, and this is one of its important values. Without this conservative world of meaning, symbols themselves easily become alienated — hijacked, so to speak — by individual interpretations which lack the real authority to communicate. Symbols, if they are to be channels of communication, must be rooted in a tradition. This was clear to thinkers like Ananda K. Coomaraswamy. What he speaks of as constituting a "Christian and oriental philosophy of art" is precisely a culture rooted in tradition, and that means a cosmic world view. But is art only to be traditional? Is not the function of art also to be a counterculture, a tradition of dissent? Does not the individual conscience, and by extension the consciousness of a whole society, only grow through a dynamic questioning of the tradition? What we are calling the cosmic world view does not have a power of self-criticism, given the parameters of its own cosmic symbols. For that we need the intervention of the meta-cosmic.

The cosmic world view which we find in popular spirituality has been exploited by those who seek to control the masses, precisely where it is most tradition bound. Nothing serves the interests of rulers better than popular spirituality. And so, those who seek to lay special stress on "mass movements" and the importance of the "common people" as against the governing "elite" can easily destroy their own argument in favor of liberation, when they fail to notice the liberative dimension of the "meta-cosmic." They may simply categorize this as the belief system of a powerful elite and therefore irrelevant to the struggling, marginalized masses. By an irony which is itself at the very heart of what we might term the dynamics of culture, the cosmic culture of the people is itself in constant need of revitalization and reinterpretation by that elitist critical culture which also carries in itself the potential to empower the people. A tradition cannot grow, or live, unless it is questioned.

WHO IS "THE PERSON"?

If we are turning today toward popular religion to understand better in what way spirituality can empower ordinary people, we must do so by looking also at the personal responsibilities of the individual to the whole of creation.

Earlier the question was asked: who are the people? We must ask rather: who is the person? There can be no liberated people without liberated persons. This is the challenge to a cosmic faith needed for our time. Such a faith must address not only the future of the planet but also the evolving person. Processes of democratization, which have profoundly influenced people's political consciousness all over the world, have also given a new meaning to the importance of the individual person as a responsible being. There must be a vital dialogue between traditional popular religiosity and modernity. Liberation movements must take into account the cosmic, earth-affirming spirituality of those who live in intimate solidarity with the earth. On the other hand, folk spiritualities must develop a prophetic voice which is critical of the tradition in a positive way.

All the major religions of the world need to re-evaluate their popular spiritual sources, not simply as a "lower" element to be tolerated for the sake of the ignorant and simple, but as preserving a real insight into what it is to be truly human. We need what some call a "democratization of mysticism."

The insights of the great mystics must be given back to the poor of the land in a way that both empowers the ordinary people and also links the professionally religious to the living traditions of the whole community.

11

POPULAR CHRISTIANITY IN AFRICA

Sidbe Semporé, OP

It has been said that Africa is a *terra religiosa*; indeed, throughout the whole continent, religion continues to be a lived reality that has a profound impact on attitudes, behavior, plans, and destinies. On all levels, collective and individual, religion inspires reactions and dictates options. Traditions and customs have for centuries been imbued with a religious spirit that appears in persistent and typical forms. This is seen in the manner in which new religions, such as Islam or Christianity, are understood and assimilated. I will attempt to show that the Christianity of most Christians is nourished both at the source of the received message and at that of lived traditions.

A GLANCE AT THE PAST

When the first missionaries arrived in the Congo at the end of the fifteenth century they had little difficulty in baptizing the king and his subjects. However, three years after he was baptized, King Joao I reverted to the religion of his ancestors. His son Alfonso I, the "very Christian" king, did not succeed in keeping his people faithful to the religion of the missionaries. An old historian tells us that the king undertook a campaign with the missionaries against the paganism of Christians in the kingdom. "In less than one month," he writes, "all the idols, deviltries, masks, the objects that were adored and looked upon as gods, were brought to the court . . . They were set on fire and burnt. Then, King Alfonso gathered all his people and distributed, in place of the idols, crosses and images of the Saints that had been brought by the Portuguese."

The epilogue of this first evangelization of the black world took place in the seventeenth century with Kassola, and in the eighteenth century with Dona Beatrice, both members of the Bakongo tribe of the kingdom of Congo and Angola. In 1632 the neophyte Francisco Kassola broke away from the Jesuit Father Pedro Tavares and founded the first independent native movement in black Africa. He carried along with him crowds of people captured by the passion of a new kind of preaching in the language of the Bakongo people. The crowds were also attracted by his reputation as a new sort of medicine man. Healer and seer, he attempted to deliver people from illness, from fear of witchcraft and spells, from anxiety about the future. People were also reassured by his tolerance for ancestral customs that they considered sacred: ancestral worship, sacrifices to the spirits, observance of taboos and interdictions.

Less than a century later, in 1704, a young Mukongo woman of twenty-one, Kimpa Vita, also known as Dona Beatrice, caused a serious rift in the missionary work of the Capuchins in the Congo and in Angola when she founded a movement known as the Antonians. This young prophetess, who was later burned alive in 1706, succeeded in revitalizing the kingdom that had fallen into decadence and bringing about a consciousness of national identity. More importantly, she was able to introduce into Christian territory traditional concepts and practices that were hardly compatible with the missionaries' view of Christianity. While rejecting certain aspects of the beliefs and the doctrine of Christianity she had received (Father Colomban of Bologna, a contemporary of Beatrice, tells us that the "false saint" had forbidden fasting during Lent, refused the practice of individual confession and the celebration of the eucharist, broke to pieces imported crosses and icons, authorized polygamy, and so forth), the prophetess preserved some elements that she cleverly integrated into the Mukongo religious landscape. Just as Kassola had done, she saw that Christianity can only take root in a lasting way if it is grafted onto the roots of the religious and cultural world of the African people.

THE PERMANENT FOUNDATION OF THE AFRICAN RELIGIOUS UNIVERSE

It is dangerous to embark on a schematic presentation of the African religious world. Differences in concepts and practices from one group to another are often not a mere matter of superficial variations. Furthermore, confrontation with imported religions and with modernity has resulted here and there in a breakdown of beliefs and practices. Finally, despite the African tone of religious expressions and feelings, we must avoid claiming for Africa a monopoly or a specificity in an area which constitutes the common heritage of all humanity.

THE LIVING GOD

Keeping in mind these limitations of any approach to the African religious world, we can say that African religions are based essentially on an existential relationship to the Living One, to God whose real presence to the world and to people is perceived and lived in discretion. In general, all that the African knows about God and expects of God is expressed through stories, proverbs, God-bearing names, daily greetings, invocations, and prayers. Only occasionally does the worship of the Supreme God involve ritual sacrifices. It is important to stress the pivotal importance of the African vision of God as ultimate source and guarantor of life. African religions are religions of the Living God.

INVISIBLE POWERS

The path of African religious practice leads to a relationship with the world of invisible powers. The African vision of the world assumes the existence of a hierarchy of invisible beings ruling over the world and influencing the destinies of people. This ambivalent world of invisible powers includes a whole range of benevolent and malevolent forces and spirits, as well as the unbreakable lineage of the living dead, that is, the ancestors. These amphibious beings, participating in both worlds, are invoked as intermediaries. Their cult is accompanied, depending on the need, by conciliatory, conjuring, or reparatory sacrifices. Here we are dealing with one of the key dimensions of African religions, the one that not only resists the assimilating power of Islam and of Christianity, but will actually constitute the very heart of the religion of blacks for four centuries in the form of the candomblé in Brazil and of voodoo in Haiti.

PEOPLE AND THEIR ASPIRATIONS

Finally, African religions assume responsibility for men and women and their aspirations here on earth by offering solutions and suggesting behaviors. Morality, based as it is on taboos and prohibitions, is essentially hedonistic and inseparable from a religious vision of destiny. The agonizing problem of evil finds outlets in tragic faith in witchdoctors and in the obstinate recourse to sorcerers and healers. An affirmation of the transcendental dimension of people can be found in the importance that is given to dreams, to episodes of trance and of possession, and to belief in reincarnation.

SYNTHESIS

The religious vision and practice of Africans can be synthesized as follows:
God. He is the source and river of life, Lord of all and Father, *fons vitae*, the source of life. Relationship to God is characterized by extreme sobriety both in words and in worship. The latter includes few sacrificial acts and hardly any temples. People do not exteriorize their relationship to God except through a basic attitude of gratitude and submission.

Invisible Powers. They are seen as ambivalent and versatile — sometimes protective and benevolent, at other times querulous and vindictive. They are the object of a cult of honor on the part of the humans whom they haunt. Relationships of communion or consecration can bind people to some of these powers. The *vodunsi* in Benin and the men and women devoted to *orishas* and to *loas* in Brazil and in Haiti are examples. Such relationships are sometimes expressed in phenomena of possession or trance. Worship of the ancestors turns people constantly toward their own end and gives an eschatological dimension to their lives.

Men and Women. Their lives are a search for fullness, for happiness here on earth and in the hereafter. This search is dependent on:
— the observance of social customs in their entirety
— the performance of religious obligations. These involve sacrificial acts accom-

plished by themselves or by others in favor of spirits or ancestors. Such acts of worship owe as much to veneration as they do to fear. They also involve the duty to protect life, threatened by the intervention of jealous invisible powers and by the evil spells cast by certain humans. This duty to protect life is accomplished in a threefold way:

1. by seeking the advice of a seer at various stages in life all the way from conception until death and including all moments of crisis such as sickness, poverty, adversity, and also times of plenty
2. by observing a code of purity and a ritual of fertility
3. by the continued use of means and objects of protection vested with powers from above.

THE CHRISTIANITY OF THE MISSIONARIES

In order to understand the religion of African Christians today we must, of course, study the soil which received the seed; but we must also see what kind of Christianity was offered at the beginning. Without going as far back as the contents of the first evangelization of the Congo, to which we alluded earlier, it is useful to glance at the end of the nineteenth century. Christianity as it was introduced by the missionaries at that time was essentially a rural form of Christianity, deeply marked by the spiritual and doctrinal legacy of the Middle Ages and of the Renaissance years, as well as by the peasant mentality of the European countryside of the time. Religion was taught to the people in an abridged form.

Catechism. It was a condensed form of the Catechism of Trent expressed in simple and brief phrases.

The Bible. Ordinary people were not allowed to read the Bible. A brief digest of the combined four gospels was provided in which emphasis was placed primarily on moral conduct and practical matters of cult and devotion.

Religious Mentality. The mentality underlying the missionaries' Christianity stressed the mysterious and transcendental aspects of religion and accepted a spontaneous and unquestioning belief in the existence of angels (kindly and protective spirits) and of demons (living incarnations of evil). There was an emphasis on the effectiveness of sacraments and sacramentals, the influence of prayer and ritual acts on the course of events and the wills of men and women, and the important role of invisible mediators in the drama of salvation. This was a popular Christianity that invested time and space with its seasonal rituals, its daily worship of saints, the veneration and use of icons (images, statues, medallions, and so forth) for spiritual and temporal purposes, its temples, its objects of worship, its hierarchy of celebrants and the magic of its language. Such a Christianity was easily received and remodeled by the African mentality which was fascinated by the effectiveness of a religion whose rites, language, and protagonists seemed, by their very strangeness, to have fallen from the sky!

It is possible to say, without straying too far from the truth, that, despite differences of inspiration and form, popular pre-Conciliar Christianity and African religions have many of the same sources and express similar tendencies in their understanding of God and of the universe.

POPULAR CHRISTIANITY IN AFRICA TODAY

Popular Christianity in Africa is the response of the people as a whole to evangelization, and the manner in which the people understand and incarnate the message. This response grows out of the religious mentality of the people and the specific inputs of the new religion. The process thus involves the encounter with, acquisition of and acclimatization into African religious soil of elements originating from various sources. The faith of simple people — and most Christians are simple people — deserves consideration and respect and must be taken seriously, even when it surprises and disturbs by its excesses, its oversimplifications, and its deviations.

A PRAYING PEOPLE

Christianity has always been popular in Africa in the sense that it has always attracted crowds for worship and prayer. Before baptism Africans tend to be reserved in exteriorizing their relationship with God. Yet once they become Christian they are uncommonly assiduous in prayer. For about twenty years prayer has been experiencing a revival with respect to both practice and fervor. Many prayer groups have sprung up all over Africa. Some came about spontaneously, others were initiated by pastors or Christian associations. The large mass of Christians keeps prayer alive in its own ways.

Most of the time prayers are prayers of petition, of appeal for help, of imploration, and supplication. As it was long ago in Palestine, so today, the same needs find expression in the same ways: Lord, help me to see, to hear, to walk; my daughter is sick; my child is dying; my only son is possessed by demons; be a judge between myself and my creditor; make my brother share his inheritance with me. And there are the prayers of the many who have spent their last pennies paying for medicines and witchdoctors and who turn for healing to God, to his saints, or to miraculous fountains. Most Christians turn to prayer, to devotional practices and objects in order to obtain, and to guarantee their possessing, what they need in life and in love — health, fertility, wealth, security.

God. The Christian is convinced through African tradition and through the gospel, that God, source and Lord of all life, holds the key to the happiness of men and women. And so they turn to God in prayer and ask for the essentials of life. But this is only a last resort. The underlying mentality is flawed by fatalism, just as it was in the Israelites of biblical times. God does what he wants, he distributes good luck or bad luck to people according to his own decision. However, he can be moved or persuaded. To do this, the prayer must go through mediators and intermediaries of all sorts, spirits and saints who are closer to men and women and therefore more easily accessible and effective.

Mary. She occupies a privileged place in the hearts of Christian people. She is the universal mother and has great power to obtain graces from God. Many people have images or medallions of the Virgin; some have statuettes from Lourdes in their homes; all have rosary beads, even though those who actually recite the rosary regularly are few. People care little for the scruples of theologians and pastors. For many the choice between the mother and the Son, between the statue of the Virgin and the tabernacle in the church is easily made. It may be that with Mary they spontaneously relive the African relationship to the mother with whom deep and unbreakable bonds of complicity are established.

Much like an African mother, Mary—quiet, discreet, yet ever present and active—appears as the mother of perpetual recourse, ever ready to move the heart of God in favor of the one whom she protects and adopts—*Advocata nostra*. All that is related to Mary—sanctuaries, objects, images, devotions—is supposed to provide efficient protection against ill fortune. Furthermore, Mary is considered to be one of the most real and certain elements of the Christian religion since she so frequently appears to humans in various parts of the world and delivers precise messages for the good of human beings. This explains the huge success of apparitions and of Marian sanctuaries like Lourdes, Fatima, Medjugorje, and Kibeho, and of Marian associations and devotions.

Jesus. Yet for all that, Jesus is certainly not forgotten! But here again African piety has spontaneously made certain choices. Jesus, Son of God, incarnate Word, second Person of the Trinity, is known from the catechism. But, after all, what he is concerns him alone, whereas what he does concerns the destiny of each Christian. And Christians will linger on those aspects of his person that make him truly the servant, attentive and respectful of the needs of all. The mysterious host of the tabernacle is a reassuring presence in the jungle of hostile powers surrounding people. The eucharist is venerated and received as a mysterious and awesome force capable of neutralizing the evil forces at work in men and women and in the world. It is true that many of those who can no longer receive the eucharist because they are not "at rights with the church" do not suffer greatly from this. Most people, however, continue to see in the eucharist a mysterious force of a unique kind.

Popular Piety. In Africa popular piety is attracted to those devotions in which Jesus appears in a state of weakness or of solidarity with the human condition— the infant Jesus, the nativity, the via crucis, the face of Christ, the Sacred Heart, and, of course, Jesus on the cross. The humiliation of Christ, his sufferings, and the unjust fate that befell him elicit a very special response in the hearts of African Christians who can empathize easily with a destiny so close to their own. This piety, that seems to emphasize suffering, that vibrates when evoking the leper-servant in Isaiah 53 or the suffering Christ of Calvary, is an instinctive attempt to find a way out for human suffering and to escape the dilemma of helpless revolt and of annihilating fatalism.

The sensitivity and the reaction of African Christians faced by the dramatic event of salvation are in some ways reminiscent of the reactions of Western Christians in the early Middle Ages. Their spirituality, devotions, literary and artistic works were centered on Christ's passion and on the anguish of the mother of all sorrows. The aspect of the paschal mystery, on which the faith of the African Christian focuses in a special manner, is "the kenosis of Good Friday," the deliberate humbling of the Son of Man, folly for the disciples of the past, scandal to the African Christian of today. The way of the cross of Good Friday is re-experienced by the crowds as a unique sacramental liturgy. In Benin, in Burkina Faso, and no doubt elsewhere, the passion of Christ is commemorated and acted out, and climaxes in a poignant burial according to ancestral customs.

Resurrection. Despite the vividness of the paschal liturgy, resurrection is perceived as a rehabilitation and a reparation, a vindication of the innocent. Good Friday is still, for many, the most important date of the religious year. On that day, lifted up from the earth, Christ attracts to himself the weeping and compassionate African crowds. Seraphim of Sarov taught that "every day is Easter"; but for the African Christian, the statement by Pope St. Gregory has particular relevance: "The life of every Christian on earth is a continuous Good Friday." Finally, this shift of emphasis in popular piety signifies perhaps an unconscious identification of the poor and the small with the suffering Christ and a silent protest of those who fulfill in their flesh the continually actualized passion of Christ.

A PEOPLE STRUGGLING FOR HAPPINESS

For those who have received baptism, the search for earthly happiness is part and parcel of the religious quest. In their struggle for a full and happy life, African Christians feel dispossessed and unprotected. From the start, they feel at a disadvantage. They therefore use all the advantages of religion and all the weapons made available by Christianity to acquire strength and protection.

Saints venerated in the Catholic church are invoked as providential allies. In Africa we have inherited the saints of the Roman calendar along with devotional particularities attached to their cult. Most often, Christians know little or nothing about them. It is enough to hear that a particular saint is powerful and helpful and right away every problem is brought to him or her. Saints are venerated above all as mediators and protectors. Most of the time people will be quite happy to use the prayers and the objects brought from abroad to address the heavenly benefactors. And those who can read are delighted if one day they come upon a prayer said to be infallible, foolproof, and miraculous, one of those that circulate now and then and guarantee—so they claim—health, success in all undertakings, happiness in the home, protection against accidents, witchdoctors, evil spells, lightning, and even hell!

For protection and success in all things, there are a number of practices to choose from: novenas to St. Bridget and meditations on her revelations; invocation of St. Anthony or St. Christopher; recitation of St. Michael's rosary, of the prayers of St. Martha or the prayer of St. Charlemagne; the cult of St. Jude; the use for multiple purposes of the "key to the Psalms" or of the writings of Father Julio.

Devotional Objects. In addition to prayer and invocation many use symbols and devotional objects exclusively for purposes of protection and welfare: a rosary carried in a pocket or handbag; a miraculous medal around the neck; holy water or water from Lourdes always within reach; pious images and relics worn, or perhaps hidden between the pages of a book or under a pillow; statuettes protecting households; blessed palm leaves or twigs to keep away lightning; pendants to exorcise and weaken the attacks of the enemy. In other words, all the concrete supports to faith that the Western Christian ritual or the peddlers of piety can offer are requisitioned to become part and parcel of an elaborate system of protection.

Religious objects and symbols brought in from abroad are very naturally adopted. The traditional religious mentality is itself very ingenious in imagining and creating amulets and *gris-gris* richly endowed with powers from above, and predisposes to this easy adoption. Because Africans feel constantly threatened they try to build an armor around themselves seeking security and invulnerability from the powers above. The same mentality endures in the veneration of saints and the use of devotional objects.

Sacrifices. These were frequently offered to the dead, to ancestors and spirits in order to obtain peace, wellbeing, and security on earth. In the same way, people try to obtain the same favors from heavenly benefactors by offering Masses, going on pilgrimages, surrounding themselves with devotional objects, reciting specific prayers, and participating in certain rituals, burning candles and incense. Masses are greatly valued; some even prefer them to novenas. At times, Masses and novenas can satisfy customary obligations or family duties with respect to dead persons.

Souls in Purgatory. This cult originates in a sense of piety, affection, and compassion for the dead, and also, perhaps, in a fear of those who have died and might feel neglected. Characteristically, prayers are said for the most neglected souls in purgatory. In the past, if ancestors were neglected, the living could expect trouble. Because of this, there is a widespread feeling of guilt associated with this cult of the ancestors which in some areas has an obligatory and exaggerated aspect. In some churches, both in East and West Africa, popular piety prefers requiem Masses chanted in Latin for the dead. This adds something to the mystery of the hereafter.

In their daily struggle for bread, for a fertile life, for personal wholeness, and harmony in relationships, believers reach indiscriminately and nonexclusively into the ancient testament of African religions and the New Testament of imported Christianity, thereby achieving a spontaneous inculturation of the Nazarene's message in their own way.

AN INCULTURATED CHRISTIANITY

As we have seen, the meeting of missionary Christianity with African religions has brought about among simple people a popular religion that is expressed in a variety of ways. It is characterized by a particular exuberance and originality in the Afro-Christian churches founded and directed by Africans. These countless independent churches provide space for popular African faith to express itself and to evolve in a climate of total freedom and spontaneity. If we can see beyond the slightly folklorical and even at times aberrant aspects of certain elements and practices, we can find in many of these churches the essential characteristics of what can only be described as a typically African Christianity.

Prayer is understood and lived as an activity that situates people anew within the universe and within society and has a profound impact on spiritual forces. Those who pray are not only in relationship with God, they are in contact with a network of forces. Prayer becomes a manifestation of power capable of setting off a state of trance in a troubled people. This can be a phenomenon of liberation (by the expulsion of maleficent powers) or of possession (being inhabited by protective powers—"guardian angels"). Prayer is always a renewed experience of the vulnerability and the nothingness of people (an awareness of being undeserving and impure) as well as of the salvific and liberating power of spiritual forces. Such a conception of prayer engages people fully in every dimension and mobilizes them, body, heart, and spirit, in space and in time.

Visions and Dreams. Special importance is given to visions and dreams as channels through which God and spiritual forces communicate with men and women and symbolically reveal to them the path that leads to happiness. African cultures teach that dreams and nightmares always contain messages, and "seers" in certain independent churches attempt to decode them. These "seers" actually practice an authentic ministry of counseling by responding as well as they can to the needs and anxieties of a never-ending flow of clients.

Salvation and Health. Traditionally there is a close link between salvation and health, and it is strongly reaffirmed in these African Christian churches. Much as in biblical days, sickness in the African perspective is seen as an aggression and healing as a victory. Disease is a challenge put to God by the powers of the occult, or a trial sent by God to teach endurance or to punish. Prayer, fasting, and confession of sins prepare the way for God's salvific intervention. A cure, even if it is obtained in association with local medicines or Western drugs, is frequently attributed to the far-reaching hand of the God of the exodus or to the strong and powerful hand of the Nazarene. Healing is accepted as an act from above, a miracle, a sign that God is with men and women. Is it not significant that the Catholic church still requires miracles and healings as an assurance that God is with those Christians whom it wishes to raise to the altar?

Solidarity. Finally, solidarity lived in a spirit of brother- and sisterhood and especially of compassion for the weak is a constant element assumed in the faith and in the structures of Afro-Christian churches. African tradition in its pure state exalts sharing and tolerance and gives Christianity a tone that is less rigid.

THE FUTURE OF POPULAR CHRISTIANITY IN AFRICA

In the independent churches a spontaneous and deliberate inculturation of the Christian message is underway. In the Catholic church this inculturation is much more timid and awkward. As a result a fair number of faithful are forced into clandestine and questionable practices. It has sometimes been said in

Africa that we make Christians and then life takes them away from us. Recently a bishop of Rwanda commented, "Many citizens of Rwanda remain good baptized pagans, happy to be doubly religious." The attraction of "sects" and independent churches leads some people to practice in several different places. The recent Roman document on sects, cults, and new religious movements is correct in pointing out that sects go out to meet people where they are, in a warm, friendly, personal, and discreet way. They bring the individual out of anonymity, promote participation, spontaneity, responsibility, and involvement. They provide an intense follow-up through frequent communications and contacts, visits, continued support, and guidance. They help people interpret their own experiences, reaffirm their own values, and face up to essential questions. Frequently they make convincing use of words—preaching, literature, and mass media. A strong emphasis on the Bible is frequently accompanied by healing ministry.

Renewal. Popular Christianity, indeed, Christianity itself in Africa, is called to an *aggiornamento*, a permanent renewal. Its weaknesses can be summarized in two points, two insufficiencies:
1. the absence of a solid biblical foundation. Christianity, the religion of the Book, must become once again the religion of the word for the masses of the illiterate
2. the absence of a "rootedness" in African reality because of a doctrinal and canonical superstructure that is far too Western. Inculturation must go beyond the simple phase of adaptation and folklore.

Permanent Conversion. This conversion to which the gospel calls Christianity in Africa implies a break and a change on the one hand, solidarity and rootedness on the other:
—a break from the structures of sin and alienation of societies in search of salvation
—a change of mentality and a change of perspective in the definition of happiness and human relationships
—solidarity with the aspirations and struggles of individuals and peoples
—rootedness in the culture and essence of contemporary peoples.

A THREEFOLD QUESTION

The future of Christianity in Africa, and more specifically of Catholicism, raises a threefold question: will the church have the will and the freedom
—to "speak God" in Africa's way and to read the gospels in Africa's way? — to pray to God and celebrate him in Africa's way with African rites rather than africanized Latin rites? — to promote African art, African calenders?
—to incarnate and practice the gospel in Africa's way with a moral discipline and sacramental pastoral in an African context, especially in matters pertaining to baptism, the eucharist, and marriage?
—to adopt a structure and a form of self-government that is African with reorganization and adaptation of ecclesial structures, ministries, and law?

Ultimately the goal of inculturation is to make Christianity more popular and more evangelical, and this in a spirit of unconditional fidelity to the message of Christ and of sympathy of heart and spirit toward men and women and their own milieu. This is a task that belongs to the church as a whole. Such an authentic approach will allow the church to avoid the risk of closing in on itself, and will be a forceful invitation to openness to mission and involvement in the world such as it is, with its gigantic planetary challenges and its immense hope.

12

POPULAR RELIGIOSITY AND EVANGELIZATION IN LATIN AMERICA

Bishop Samuel Ruiz

Popular religiosity was not considered a significant issue by those involved in theological reflection or pastoral planning until recently. Even Vatican II documents which inspired widespread renewal throughout the church did not explicitly mention such now familiar terms as popular religion, popular catholicism, and people's religion. Yet it has always existed in the church. From earliest times the Christian faith has been concretely expressed both in the essential message of the gospel and in a synthesis of the religious practices and beliefs of the people—be they Romans, Greeks, or slaves.

HISTORICAL BACKGROUND

History shows that as long as popular religiosity remains passive and develops without questioning "the established order," it is tolerated. When it protests and challenges a worldly and rich church, then popular religiosity and its "prophets" are silenced or persecuted. Both Protestantism and the Enlightenment—with their heirs, liberal capitalism and dialectical Marxism—have looked on popular religiosity with contempt. It was accused of ignorance, idolatry, obscurantism, sentimentalism, and alienation.

In attempting to ameliorate the negative effects of the Reformation and the Enlightenment, the official church created and promoted devotions which we now would consider traditional, such as particular prayers, Marian devotions, and devotion to the Sacred Heart. One of the purposes of these devotions from the perspective of the official church was to improve the popular expression of religion which was seen to be dominated by feeling and emotion. The emphasis was thus put on the objective and the rational. The liturgical movement and biblically-based renewal programs were also directed toward this goal. Between the world wars, the Catholic Action movement aimed at deepening the popular understanding and expression of faith by encouraging the social involvement of Christians in their society.

POSITIVE ATTITUDES EMERGE

From 1950 to 1970 popular religiosity was the stepchild of Catholic pastoral workers. Though it was relentlessly opposed it simply would not die. On the contrary, it continued to blossom. Gradually, new and more positive attitudes began to replace the former negative ones. Pope Paul's encyclical *Evangelii Nuntiandi* was the first papal document to dedicate special attention to the topic of popular religiosity. In Latin America the parameters of the new attitude are history and culture. Using these two parameters rather than a strict criterion of orthodoxy, popular religiosity in Latin America today is seen as a hope for the future. The Third General Assembly of the Latin American Bishops in Puebla in 1979 declared:

> By the religion of the people or popular religiosity or popular piety, we mean the whole complex of underlying beliefs rooted in God, the basic attitudes that flow from these beliefs, and the expressions that manifest them. It is the form of cultural life that religion takes on among a given people. In its most characteristic cultural form, the religion of the Latin American people is an expression of the Catholic faith. It is a people's catholicism. (Puebla, 444)

After Puebla popular religiosity had its "identity card." Previous to this it was a suspect movement, a devalued evangelization, a hodgepodge of superstitions, something which needed to be transformed and purified.

PUEBLA'S ASSESSMENT OF POPULAR RELIGIOSITY

The characteristics of this popular religiosity are described in various numbers of the Puebla document from 444 on. Puebla speaks of the essential historical identity of the Latin American continent; it says that this popular religiosity, even if it is lived out in a preferential way by the poor and simple, takes in all social sectors, uniting them in spite of their multiple diversities. It says that popular religiosity is a wisdom which responds to the great questions of life; that popular religiosity is a Christian wisdom which enables the people to discern and sense when they are being given the authentic gospel or when there are other hidden interests which are called gospel but which are something else.

Popular religiosity is capable of bringing together multitudes, in this way giving the church, especially at the shrines where the people gather, both a vision of universality and an opportunity for a deeper evangelization of the masses.

Popular religiosity is an active way in which the people evangelize themselves. It is a movement of implicit and sometimes explicit protest against the fact that social justice has not been fully lived out, and that the demands of being children of God are not reflected in the structures of society.

The lack of concern for popular religiosity and its abandonment by pastoral agents explain the weakening, deformation, and deterioration that took place in popular religiosity because there was no real pastoral effort to accompany this religiosity. A new evangelization is called for. Before examining the elements of this new evangelization, let us look at the effects of the earlier evangelization which was partnered with colonization.

EVANGELIZATION AND COLONIZATION

A meeting was held recently in Ecuador by indigenous people in connection with the projected celebration of the fifth centenary of the evangelization of Latin America. There it was said:

> We, the indigenous representatives of thirty nationalities and fifteen countries in the 2nd Ecumenical Consultation of the Latin American Indigenous Pastoral Apostolate in Quito, Ecuador, on July 6, 1986, declare our total repudiation of these triumphalistic celebrations of the five centuries of evangelization for the following reasons: genocide, the war of occupation, the violent usurpation of our territorial dominions, the disintegration of our organizations, etc. . . .

They asked for an authentic evangelization of accompaniment, dialogue, and unity among the churches which professed themselves to be Christian so that they may work together in a united way.

CHAPLAINS OF THE CONQUISTADORS

The first priests who arrived were chaplains of the conquistadors. Only afterwards did missionaries arrive. Not having independent means of transport, they used the means provided by the state, the ships of the empire. Not only did they arrive on the same ships as the conquistadors, but they also depended on imperial power to evangelize. The consequences were sad. Refusing to be evangelized meant refusing submission to the emperor. Bartolomeo de las Casas wrote to the emperor, telling him what was happening. The emperor issued an edict to protect the people. However, in order to circumvent this, the emperor's edict was proclaimed outside the towns in which the people were living, at two or three o'clock in the morning, and in a language the people did not understand. If the people were reluctant to submit they were forced to do so. The alternative was to emigrate from where they were and to form new groups in new towns. Thus did the people lose their land and property, sometimes including even gold mines.

AMBIGUITY OF TERMINOLOGY

Ambiguity begins with the very terminology. Spain, in its conquest of our continent, sought economic gain. It sought a new merchant route to bring from the East Indies the materials the Spaniards needed for their markets. Christopher Columbus reached land which he supposedly believed to be on the way to India. He therefore called it "The Indies." The subsequent invasion brought us life, but it also brought us death. "Indian" is the terminology of the dominator. There were no Indians on our continent before Columbus came. There were ethnic groups—Quechuas, Guaymies, Guaranecs, Mexicas, Olmecs, Toltecas—many different ethnic groups. The word "Indian" is a term of domination, a term used by the people who crushed others. Being indigenous or "Indian" in the sense of having a determined culture is not a biological phenomenon. A similar situation is true for the numerous Japanese in Brazil today: biologically they are Japanese but culturally Brazilian because many of them were born there.

"SANDWICH RELIGION"

Quite simply, political domination and religious domination went together. There was no dialogue between the religions, natural and revealed. Religion was imposed by force. Monuments, codes, and writings of the indigenous people were destroyed in order to wipe out every trace of their religion. The result was a "sandwich religion." On top there was a light covering of Christianity, and at the bottom there was a hidden natural religion which emerged to "accept" and to "reinterpret" the religion which had been imposed officially. This "sandwich religion" is illustrated by many of the myths which are still part of the culture and are given a Christian meaning. These myths tell of the creation of animal life from the earth by a celestial Father and Mother figure who rewards and punishes, of the origin of sickness and wellbeing, of saints and protectors who are mediators, and so forth.

A SOPHISTICATED CULTURE

The Spanish were amazed at the cultural development of the "primitive" peoples whom they met. Their descriptions of the social organization and development they found expressed their wonder. I lived in a place where the culture of the Guaymies is still alive. These people used the zero in numbers before Europeans did, enabling them to make sophisticated calculations, including calculations of stellar distances. Twice a year at sunset some ancient buildings in the middle of Yucatan cast a shadow which is the image of a snake. For the indigenous people this is a vivid reminder of the mythic story of a divine snake which descends from heaven to earth. The precise calculations used in these buildings presupposes a very advanced knowledge of heavenly bodies. There is not any doubt today that these people had quite a profound technical development and knowledge of nature.

POPULAR RELIGIOSITY IN INDIGENOUS COMMUNITIES

Popular religiosity in Latin America manifests itself most clearly in the religious practices of indigenous communities. This is a point of fundamental importance. Their religiosity sometimes runs parallel to official religion, sometimes it is outside it or even beneath it.

At this moment we in Latin America are in the presence of a completely new development. It can be called the emergence or the rise or the irruption of the poor on the continent, but it is also the emergence of the indigenous people on a continental scale. Some indigenous groups have recently called on linguistic anthropologists to investigate their language. They were forgetting it and realized it was important to preserve it. They are becoming aware of the fact that they have something unique to give to society. Their community consciousness and their personal disposition to serve in the community are elements which are constitutive of being indigenous. This essentially communitarian dimension of indigenous populations is characteristic, not only of Latin America, but also of the whole of the Americas from Canada in the north to Chile in the south.

I experienced an extraordinary example of this some time ago. An eight-year-old boy was given candy by his teacher one day. The following day he had to go on a long errand, but he kept the candy all day, and only on the following day when he met his school friends did he eat it — sharing it with them. Three days! But the strong community consciousness of the indigenous people is such that he could not allow himself to eat the candy alone. This is not a value that was transmitted by evangelization — it was there before the gospel arrived. The indigenous people are aware today that because of the values of their culture they can contribute a lot to answering the questions which arise in the search for a new society.

CULTURAL DIVERSITY

A simple example illustrates this diversity. Thirty years ago I arrived in Chiapas where I am now a bishop. It was my first contact with strong nuclei of indigenous communities. I came in contact very soon with the diversity of their cultures and customs. When I visited Chamula, one of the largest communities, during the carnival celebrations at the beginning of Lent, I wished to greet the indigenous Chamulas. About four thousand of them were gathered there but not one shook hands with me! The priest who was with me said, "My Lord Bishop, people do not greet one another like that. Here they bow their heads so that you can touch them with your hand." In recognition of the dignity of each person, they bowed in veneration of the pastor.

A few days later I went to a place where the people spoke a dialect of the same language but were a different tribe. I was ready to greet them by touching their heads but the situation was quite different there. People greeted first with the right hand and then with the left. So for two hundred people I had to give four hundred handshakes. Later I went to another region and was ready if necessary to greet the people with my nose, but in that particular place one did not begin with the greeting at all! First, one had to have a conversation and develop a human relationship in order to get to know one another, and only then was one able to greet the other formally.

CULTURAL UNIQUENESS

I should like to preface my further remarks by two short comments on culture in general and "civilization." Culture is a human phenomenon, specific to humanity. It is transmitted in different ways—through education and through accumulated experience passed on through human language. Animals too accumulate experience but they have no language to transmit it. We could define culture as the ensemble of responses which a community gives and transmits to others with regard to questions posed about transcendence (about the one we like to call God)—about human relationships with other groups and with one's own group, and about questions which arise from contact with nature.

The questions which arise from these three areas—transcendence, human relationships, and relationships with nature—and the responses to them transmitted from generation to generation are what we call culture. Stated simply, culture represents diverse ways of being a human person.

Each human group which is aware of being a human group has a culture. No matter what degree of development a particular group has, the culture which they have been taught from childhood is a culture validated by that particular group. It may not be valid for another human group. Each culture has its own personality and internal unity. The culture which is best for a human group is the one which is its own, which is the fruit of its historical journey, and not a culture which comes from the outside, even though that one might seem to be better.

CIVILIZATION

What we call civilization is something different from culture. It is characterized by the subjection or control of natural forces and by technical development. The values of a culture do not have their origin in technical development, although they may be involved in some way in technical civilization. So a human group, both theoretically and practically speaking, could have a very developed technical civilization and a rather precarious ensemble of cultural values. The opposite could also be true. A human group could have very great cultural wealth and a poverty of civilization which is necessary for the survival of that human group.

EVANGELIZATION AND INDIGENOUS CULTURES

How is evangelization done in the context of cultures that differ so much? Gospel and culture are not identical. Evangelization does not mean changing the "Indian's" natural religion into a Christian religion if this destroys the natural religion which is the basic nucleus encompassing all the cultural factors of the people. Surely destroying a culture is not evangelizing. Nor does it mean just joining in prayer and contemplating the culture of the people without doing anything else about it. Nor does it mean rebuilding the culture again to its pre-colonial splendor. That could be archaeology, not evangelization. Because people have a destiny which goes beyond this world and time, should one destroy the various cultures and build up a universal monoculture? But then why did Jesus become a Jew in a Galilean subculture, fulfill the Jewish law, speak Aramaic, and act according to the customs of his people? Why did God permit the existence of so many rich cultures if they were all destined to be destroyed in the process of evangelization? What is evangelization, really?

THE "SEEDS OF THE WORD"

Great credit must go to the African bishops who did so much to produce the document *Ad Gentes* on the missions during the Second Vatican Council. They protested strongly against cultural domination. The document was rewritten many times and finally passed with the highest vote in the whole Council, but the process was painful and slow (see *Ad Gentes* 2–15).

Throughout history God had a universal plan of salvation. But this plan did not just remain in God's heart—God acted in history. In the incarnation Christ became one of us through the action of the Spirit. The church continues his mission. It is the Spirit who inspires, accompanies, and anticipates the presence of missionaries. In the salvific plan of God for human groups we find what the Greek Fathers called the "seeds of the Word" which exist in the cultures of all peoples in their search for the transcendent. These "seeds of the Word" are not just a pedagogical tool for Christianity; they are already part of the content of the proclamation, even though this content will become more explicit through a gospel proclamation based on years of faith experience.

Thus, before proclaiming the word to a culture where the gospel has not yet arrived, the church and the missionary have the task of sitting down and listening, observing and understanding the culture in order to be able to say, "The Lord be with you," or "The Lord *is* with you." To know how the Lord is there, the missionary must know how God's presence is being lived out in that people and how they approach the divinity. The church, discovering all this through its missionaries, should insert itself in the human group in order to incarnate itself just as Christ inserted himself in humanity. A gradual liberation of the people will be brought about in this process of incarnation which is accompanied by growing intensification of the values and a purification of the countervalues which exist in every human culture.

MISSIONARIES

Missionaries arriving in indigenous communities were unfortunately ethnocentric. They judged the culture by the criteria of their own culture which they considered to be the only valid one. Some examples:

Clothing. Given their ethnocentricity, they experienced cultural shock at finding people naked. They made moral judgments on the lack of clothing and did not see this as a natural response to the climate. They insisted that indigenous people should wear clothes. This had unfortunate consequences. Firstly, the clothes caused infections which resulted in the death of many from diseases they had never before known. Secondly, communication in the community suffered because men and women communicated with a language tattooed on their bodies.

Food also caused cultural shock. In Bolivia, the food called *masato* is prepared by using a leaven which is produced by being chewed by the oldest woman of the community. After the leaven is chewed it is put in the dough to make it rise. The cultural shock from this is in reality no greater than the shock caused to indigenous people seeing others drink cow's milk or eat horse flesh. Indigenous people eat tarantulas. Needless to say, some stomachs react differently from theirs to this food!

Time is perhaps the cause of the greatest cultural shock. "Coffee break" is a norm in modern life. In the Northern countries there must be coffee breaks — but indigenous people do not have time for coffee breaks! Time is at their service. If there is something they are not going to be able to complete then they do not begin it. When they do begin something they will finish it, even if they have to stay at it for two or three days consecutively. Time is thus quite important. There is the evident danger that evangelization based on ethnocentrism results in the Europeanization or Westernization of indigenous peoples.

Missionaries must be humble as well as patient and not try to modify the culture of the people to whom they are sent. They must try to discover the "seeds of the Word" in the culture of the people. They must try to understand the totality, the inner cohesion, and the integrity of the culture. It is the converted people themselves who will transform and evangelize the culture.

The serious way in which the people hear the gospel message and interpret it in their own culture is shown by the way a group reacted to the catechesis of a Dominican priest in our diocese on the theme of reconciliation. This incident occurred during the year that our diocese was preparing for the Synod on Reconciliation. The Dominican had reached the penitential service at Mass but the indigenous people were deeply divided within their tribal group. They stopped the Mass and took three days to work through a reconciliation process before they could say they were ready to continue. The depth of the penitential act was based on their cultural understanding of the word of God perceived in its fullness.

A SENSE OF HISTORY

Cultures are not islands separated from history. Some cultures have been dominated and destroyed in history; others, because of their geographical situation, have been protected, but will eventually be dominated and oppressed by the West. In Latin America, as far as the indigenous people are concerned, there really is no history because history, as it has been taught in schools, dates only from the conquistadors. The people do not know their past as Europeans do. They have been obliged through the school system to look for their points of reference in Europe. So they run the risk of forgetting the myths, the life experiences, and the richness of the ancient peoples. There are changes now and history is beginning to be written from the perspective of the conquered people rather than the conquerors. The church too is beginning to appreciate how indigenous people viewed evangelization and the conquest.

When a people has no history there is a problem for evangelization. Christianity itself is a history of salvation rather than a religion of rules and regulations. How can we build the church when the people have no history, when they have no autochthonous heroes, celebrations, or feasts? They celebrate the feasts of saints imported from Europe! Now pre-confirmation catechesis tries to give a historical view of events in the community in order to awaken the people's awareness of history. People have also begun to celebrate anniversaries such as ordination to the diaconate and other events.

I once knew a lay sister, the cook in a convent. She did nothing but cook year after year for twenty years or more. I suggested to her that she should write out her recipes and make them available to the people. She began to do this, and when a year later I met her she was a changed woman. She had become pastorally involved with the indigenous people through her recipes, which were a great help to them. She was now entering into debate and dialogue with the missionaries about indigenous customs and culture. She had enough confidence to dialogue with a Jesuit theologian at a meeting. They were able to speak on equal terms about pastoral involvement.

If we dialogue and debate with the people on the basis of their history, and not on the basis of orthodoxy and formulated religious ideas, there is a potential richness. The debate is no longer between élites and a poorly instructed people. It is rather a commitment to a historical manifestation of the religious experience of people whose lives are given in the service of others. The indigenous people with their popular religiosity could give themselves in service to a transformation of history, and the élite could understand them and even change their point of view in a dialogue of love, commitment, and service.

AUTOCHTHONOUS CHURCHES

This brings us to the birth of autochthonous churches, churches that will be established with their own ministers and ministries emerging from within the culture. These churches will reflect on the faith, not from the perspective of Greek and Thomist philosophy but from the mythology with which the particular groups reflect on their own life. They evolve their own expressions of faith. They are not expressing the faith of others but the faith of their own community. Therefore they use their own symbols and cultural signs in a liturgy which is their own and not just an adaptation of an imposed liturgy. The liturgy expresses the faith of that community with rites and signs which are intelligible to the people. Finally, in this context, evangelization will be an enrichment of all that is held to be the final goal and objective of their culture. These principles are nothing new. They are a repetition of what we already know.

While preparing for the Medellín meeting in 1968 the bishops were impressed by the talks of two anthropologists who spoke on the importance of anthropology for evangelization. As a result, our diocese sent thirteen missionaries to study anthropology for one year, to appreciate our people's understanding of the values of their own cultures and to begin an incarnated evangelization.

There are now seven thousand indigenous catechists whose formation is arranged from within the community. It is they who now bear the weight of evangelizing.

CATECHISTS

There was a time when the catechists in our diocese had diplomas from catechetical academies. They had followed a lot of courses, but their catechesis proved to be in their own image and likeness. That stage is now past. At a meeting of two hundred catechists recently we asked the question: what does it mean to be a catechist? There were various replies: "to give good example"; "to preach the word of God"; "to seek the good of the communities." But we said, "Does not every Christian have to do all this? So what is a catechist, really?" Having thought further about it they came up with this description: "Well, to be a catechist means gathering the harvest of the thoughts of the people on the word of God" – and that really changed their objective. They go now with the scriptures and with two or three prepared questions, not only to teach but to share their reflection with the reflections of the people. They receive the people's sharing. Catechesis becomes something which they not only give but something which they receive too.

The plan of their catechesis is very simple: what is God's plan? How do people respond to this plan? How can we live faith, hope, and charity in realizing the plan of God? This plan of God is understood in a triple dimension. They discuss what God's plan is in economic affairs, in politics, and in their culture. They discuss how people respond to God's plan in these three areas. The replies which emerge are really extraordinary. It is said about charity, "Charity cannot be defined, charity is lived." We could say the same about faith. Conversion happens first on a community level, then on a family level, and lastly on an individual level. Then the people become politically aware and become involved in politics. Cooperative movements emerge.

MINISTRIES AND THE HOLY SPIRIT

Catechesis is, of course, only a step. Ministers also must emerge from the community. There are traditional ministries which have to be revised on the basis of a people's life of faith. I would like to illustrate the people's attitude towards ministries by a simple anecdote. We were discussing the diaconate in a catechists' meeting one day. The facilitator asked them, "Brothers, suppose the bishop called away all the priests from the mission. Or suppose all the priests and religious were traveling in a bus which crashed and they were all killed. What would happen?" There was silence. Then the father of one of the permanent deacons got up slowly, and said:

Listen: What you are saying to us is very serious. You have been preaching the word of God to us for the last twenty years and you are afraid that the church will come to an end just because you leave. What have you done so badly that you are so afraid? I don't think that you have given us the Holy Spirit. Although Jesus Christ had only three years to preach he gave his Church the Holy Spirit and that is why it was able to continue. Your preaching is all about Christ. The Holy Spirit—the dove—has escaped!

I recalled that when I was at the Vatican Council, even though we were sometimes less than fully attentive to a speaker, we knew immediately if he was Eastern or Western by the emphasis he placed on Christ or on the Spirit. This community reflected for a year on the diaconate based on the Acts of the Apostles. As a result, the role of the Holy Spirit in the Christian life was seen as something vital and dynamic, even though the Spirit as such had never been part of the catechesis they had received.

PRIESTS EMERGE FROM THE COMMUNITY

I know a community which could not have Mass because they had no priest. They were simply too far away from a center and priests could not get there. They had no bread or wine either. Yet they managed to make bread and wine from what was available to them. They now had bread and wine and permanent deacons and wondered why they could not have the eucharist, why they could not have Mass. The difficulty of passing from the diaconate to the priesthood is almost incomprehensible for the indigenous people. There is great frustration here. There exists a fundamental cultural problem which they want to try to explain to those in power.

The Vatican Council says that ministers have to emerge from the autochthonous people. In our indigenous cultures no young man has authority. A man is considered young when he is not married and has no children. He may be thirty years of age, but if he is not married he is considered young. He cannot have authority. If we want priests to emerge from the autochthonous community we must have priests who are married and have children.

So the question arises: if we cannot have a church for the people, emerging from the people, how can the church be called truly catholic?

13

AN INTRODUCTION TO MODERNITY

The amount of knowledge in the world continues to increase because of constant research. It is rapidly diffused through very efficient communications systems. *Modernity* is what happens when this knowledge is transferred into technology which has increasing and unforeseeable effects on economic growth, on social systems and on political decisions. Inevitably, the individual too is affected in his or her values, attitudes, beliefs, and behavior.

It is with the human effects of modernity that we are concerned in this section. These are sometimes good, sometimes evil, and often ambiguous. Modernity can lead to human community and comfort or to pollution and poverty for millions; it can facilitate or disrupt human values; it can enrich a poor country or steal its unrenewable sources of energy; it can help in the diffusion of truth or of lies through the media, and it can pass on productive information or child pornography.

The word *secularization* is being used to describe the challenge of all this to the person of faith today. Secularization manifests itself when explanations of reality previously attributed to mythical or religious sources are shown to have rational ones. It is also manifest when the scientist takes over from the witch doctor, the psychologist assumes some previously priestly functions, or a technological discovery disintegrates a traditional explanation. A group of animists in Java lost their gods a few years ago when a new seismographic station began to foretell and explain volcanic eruptions more accurately than the local holy man. For some people, the study of a good theology of providence could have a similar effect. These people are experiencing secularization.

The church is challenged to evangelize this new and emerging person who seems to need an experience of God quite different from that of the past. Secularization is forcing us to find a new presence of God, a presence which permeates, integrates, energizes for action, and which brings human and divine values into secular realities.

In the following four chapters we explore the phenomena of modernity and secularization as they are manifest in various parts of the world.

14

Evangelization:
The Challenge of Modernity

Desmond O'Donnell, OMI

THE PROCESS CALLED MODERNITY

When Thai teenagers throng into a discotheque in Bangkok, when Kashi tribals in northern Bangladesh discover video via a car battery, when a Javanese student threatens suicide if his parents refuse to get him a motorcycle, when Muslim women in Jolo say they are too educated to wear the purdah, and when a scientist in Sydney experiments with DNA, modernity, and the significant change in human consciousness which accompanies it, is taking place. Let us note carefully that modernity is a process more than an event.

Because of constant research the amount, depth, and accuracy of information increase with ever greater rapidity today. This knowledge is then rapidly diffused through very efficient communication systems and is transferred into technology — cars and computers, hair dryers and dish washers, seat-belts and space travel, telephones and televisions, airplanes and air conditioners, electricity and amplifiers, weather prediction and nuclear weapons, radio and video, seismological stations and genetic engineering.

Each new piece of technology affects or will affect the human family:
— ecologically: controlling pests and damaging the ozone layer
— economically: encouraging trade and causing unemployment
— politically: centralizing power and diffusing information
— culturally: challenging traditions and undermining symbol systems
— religiously: answering questions scientifically and purifying faith
— humanly: developing genetic engineering.

Modernity Is Morally Neutral. A helicopter can drop food or bombs on a village; a car can bring one on an educational tour or for a weekend of adultery; a computer helps both dedicated demographers and tyrannical dictators; genetic engineering can prevent prenatal defects or kill human embryos. Modernity counts the immediate cost of most things but it assesses the deeper value of few. Values are not in its vocabulary.

As the process of modernity pushes forward, persons become more self-conscious, less willing to admit or accept limits, less able to make long commitments, easily caught up in control-and-consume syndromes, frequently distrustful of communal purpose, and uncomfortable with mediating authorities.

Religiously also, most people become restless because of the apparent withdrawal of God, the decrease of the sacral spheres in life, and the increase of the secular. Because the immediacy of God is not so obvious, they suffer "the sting of contingency." They are then challenged to find a new and deeper presence of God, but many sidestep this demanding process.

Some move towards fundamentalism by believing more and more in less and less; others slide into secularism by believing less and less in more and more.

Modernity Seems To Be a Monoculture reducing traditional cultures to its own image and likeness. At the same time it is a metaculture criticizing other cultures in a subversive way. Thus, the dominant dialogue might no longer be between traditional cultures but between modernity and all of them.

Self-propelling. Because of unlimited access to knowledge and research, technology is subject to "rapidation," giving modernity its own momentum. It seems to be self-propelling: it develops under its own momentum. It can be creative for good purposes, but productive, too, of evil.

Much Technology Is Addictive. Initially at least, it is not only painless but pain-reducing. It satisfies curiosity, power, prestige, and possessive instincts. It is addictive. It says—often accurately—that:

—faster is better than slower
—newer is better than older
—now is better than later.

It lures each of us subtly through five almost imperceptible stages of addiction or acquisitiveness exemplified in advertising:

—from the superfluous to the attractive
—from the attractive to the useful
—from the useful to the necessary
—and from the necessary to the indispensable.

Modernity Seems To Be Irreversible. Because of its addictive potential, modernity seems to be irreversible. People seem mostly to want more of it. If they hesitate at any of those five seductive steps, the advertisements tell them what they are missing—again, for good or for evil. Its addictiveness is facilitated by the illusion of apparent control which it offers at each step—always just a button away.

Mindless. Modernity opts for motion regardless of the direction in which one is going. Its criterion is mostly functionality. It is apparently mindless and calls for unquestioning participation. It promises "progress," a high quality of which it often delivers, but not always—and especially not in the long run.

Reductionist. Because of its stress on functionality and immediacy, modernity disregards or tends to reduce to irrelevance the higher manifestations of human life—religion, philosophy, art, and so forth. It measures, weighs, and instrumentalizes even the person, because anything beyond biological needs and instinctual urges is not manageable. This reductionistic tendency means that modernity deals with everything piecemeal or in terms of technical problems. Its approach is, "Get the job done."

Unpredictable. For all these reasons, modernity gives the impression of being unpredictable. It encourages many good ideas, such as openness to information and constant communication, which facilitate interdisciplinary mutual respect. But where it is all going in terms of the human is not clear. In fact, it is far from clear because both beneficial and harmful effects continue to emerge, as genetic engineering shows us.

Centricist. Urbanization appears to be an effect of modernity. It might thus be called centricist because it draws people functionally together for both productivity and pollution. It also gives the opportunity to centralize power and wealth. One result we observe is that the poor and the rich are growing farther apart everywhere.

Modernity Maximizes the Power To Choose. In the past the corner shop of our towns and the omni-shop of our villages certainly limited our choices by present standards. But the supermarket, while increasing choices for a while, can eventually limit them by monopoly trading and higher prices. The increase in the power to choose which modernity brings is not always, and certainly not automatically, a good thing over a long period.

In the fields of city planning, space travel, and genetic engineering, modernity maximizes human choice and increases the need for well-discerned decisions. Because human persons are now the subject of their own research, education for choice could well be the greatest human need today.

CHALLENGES OF MODERNITY TO EVANGELIZATION: SECULARIZATION

People in all religions experience discomfort at the point where their previous awareness of God becomes problematic. When the Australian government's CSIRO scientifically seeds the clouds to bring rain during a drought it becomes less easy to say that God sends the rain. And one cannot escape the challenge by replying, "Yes—but who brought the clouds?", for the CSIRO may eventually "create" clouds too.

What Is Secularization? Secularization is usually defined as the experienced, gradual disintegration of all mythical and religious legitimations of society. Notice that secularization is not atheism. Neither is it secularism, which is a sort of undeclared atheism. Nor is it materialism. It is not usually a chosen stance. Many sincere thinking Christians today are desperately trying to hold on to an image and experience of God which no longer fits their lives. It is as if God is withdrawing rather than being discarded or argued away by these people.

Secularization manifests itself when explanations of reality previously attributed to mythical or religious sources are shown to have rational ones. It is also manifest when the scientist takes over from the witch doctor, when the psychologist assumes some previously priestly functions, or a technological discovery disintegrates a traditional explanation. There is less need to look outside and above for a God to give meaning to life when explanations from within and answers from below are increasing.

The Second Vatican Council expressed the origins of the secularization process rather optimistically in *Gaudium et Spes*:

> Through their labors and natural endowments people have ceaselessly striven to better their lives. Today, however, especially with the help of science and technology they have extended their mastery over nearly the whole of nature and continue to do so. Thanks primarily to increased opportunities for many kinds of interchange among nations, the human family is gradually recognizing that it comprises a single world community and is making itself so. Hence many benefits once looked for, especially from heavenly powers, are now enterprisingly procured by people for themselves. (33)

As we saw earlier, many find this religious earthquake too much and they then move away into the temporary security of secularism—believing less and less in more and more—or into fundamentalism—believing more and more in less and less. Both of these groups can remain "in the church." The secularist keeps up external religious behavior without belief; the fundamentalist withdraws into a private, very limited parameter of orthodoxy. If religious leaders move towards either of these, they increase the fragmentation within their religious group. Secularization is a fact. Secularism is an ideology—an altogether different matter.

THE CONSEQUENCES OF SECULARIZATION

Some of the more obvious results of secularization are: the privatization of belief and practice; selectivity and pluralism about doctrines and moral behavior; the questioning of religious institutions; a decreased religious influence in the public sector. Churches lose their direct influence on civil legislation and lose control of social service institutions such as hospitals and schools.

There is even a desacralization within the church as it becomes more difficult to attach the word "holy" to people, roles, and organizations. "Sacred" congregations become an anomaly; the papal tiara loses it meaning; medals are no longer visible; public prayer in schools causes acrimonious debate; grace before meals in restaurants is a thing of the past. A hospital is a hospital—sacred images do not make it a better one. The use of sacramentals declines, new theologies and spiritualities emerge.

Perhaps I can illustrate the process by sharing with you an experience from my own family. My grandmother rode in an automobile with some trepidation. Before starting the journey she sprinkled holy water liberally and made the sign of the cross; my mother sprinkled holy water, made the sign of the cross, and used the seat belt; my sister uses the seat belt and makes the sign of the cross! What will my niece do? Have they four different conceptions of God or are they relating to the same God in four different ways?

Ecclesiastical authority becomes more healthily hesitant as it recognizes itself to be but one more interpreter of meaning for the modern person. The church is challenged to evangelize the new and emerging person who seems to need an experience of God quite different from that of the past. Secularization is forcing us to find a new presence of God, a presence which permeates, integrates, energizes for action, and which brings human and divine values into secular realities.

CHALLENGES AND QUESTIONS

1) Is the process of secularization evangelically valid? Is it beneficial toward a deeper experience of God?

2) In the midst of secularization how should the church cooperate with other sectors and institutions in society in its mission to announce Jesus Christ? What and how should it criticize?

3) In relating to secularized societies what are some of the changes which the church itself should make to be both true to itself and also credible to the society it evangelizes? What forms of inculturation should faith institutions adopt?

4) Evangelizers are challenged to become aware of the changes in a people's mind-set and capacity for belief resulting from technological advances.

5) When technology changes patterns of living in a culture, what can a missionary do to help people profit from the benefits of technology without totally disrupting their beliefs and the religious context provided by a more traditional culture?

6) What is the possibility of direct proclamation of Christ in a secularized society, and how might this be done? What symbols and what language should be used?

7) What ministries should missionaries and all pastoral ministers favor in a secularized society?

PLURALISM

Because of modernity, the individual has discovered himself or herself with a new degree of self-consciousness. At the same time this new person is being bombarded with an unprecedented flow of information and options. This is a very volatile combination—high self-awareness and an almost unlimited supply of information.

Freedom. Combined with these two elements of modernity is the reminder from *Gaudium et Spes* that "only in freedom can the human person direct him- or herself to goodness," possibly one of the most dangerous and challenging statements of Vatican II. Freedom adds a very creative aspect to the two elements of self-awareness and information. Pluralism is then inevitable. It becomes increasingly difficult for any reflective individual today to give him or herself totally and unquestioningly to any institution, system or conceptual framework.

Relativity. No wonder modernity creates an inquiring and inventive attitude of mind and relativizes previously accepted "certitudes." It disrupts cultural and religious unity and helps to produce a person who is fragmented, competitive, conflicted, and critical, a person who in addition may have a very significant underlying anxiety-laden insecurity. As in the political arena, where the neutral state gives rise to interest-group pluralism, so within the church too there is a growth of theological and spiritual pluralism. The sources of this are in the variety of christologies and ecclesiologies now present in most groups of believers.

The Consequences of Pluralism

On the outside, Christianity and the Catholic church have become one more item on the religious shelf. We have become a church of shoppers, infected by religious consumerism. Paul Johnson puts it well in his book *Enemies of Society*:

> The Roman republic and early empire was a market-place for a multitude of rival private religions and it was the triumph of Christianity that it scooped the poor. The process could occur again . . . and the sociologists have a good deal of evidence that we are in the market-place of the modern world now.

Centralism. Perhaps we need even more of a marketplace within the church at this time. The Roman centralism as we experience it now has not always been part of the church. The call of the popes for deeper inculturation of the Christian message is the rationale needed to counter this centralism.

Variety. The great faiths of Asia have considerable pluralism within them and a great ability to adapt to new cultures—to inculturate without any overall authority structure. Can we rediscover Christianity as an historical movement capable of being more at ease with variety both within and without?

Fear. Has our fear of pluralism inside and outside the church been motivated by defensiveness since the time of the Reformation? In psychology we recognize that fear is a dangerous motivation for human responses, especially coming from someone in authority. The church is now surely secure enough to hear and name its own fears and to develop great confidence in the message it carries. A healthy internal pluralism—despite the fear of the fundamentalists among us—seems inevitable today unless we are prepared to return to, or take up again, a "walled city" approach.

Heresy. Peter Berger says that modernity tends toward the "universalization of heresy." "Heresy," in this sense is here to stay as thinking people today will not be easily corseted into any one ideology or doctrinal system. And even if it is possible to corset them for a time, they will not stay in it. To evangelize the modern person we need to discover more deeply Christ's "Fear not," based on the power of his gospel, and then be prepared to live with a lot of looseness or "heresy" around the edges.

THE MOVE FROM "FATE" TO "CHOICE"

Another major challenge to evangelization is the move which the modern person has made from a mode of acting based on fate—a given which could not be controverted—to a mode of acting based on personal choice.

A common purpose and mediating authorities were generally accepted in nonmodern cultures, and so there was not a high level of personal self-awareness apart from the group. Most nonmodern persons did not feel or at least did not activate a desire to investigate, to compete, to control or consume. They were thus less anxious and felt less threatened than people today. Also in the past there was less education in the sense of learning to question. These factors combined to produce attitudes which were based on fate rather than on choice.

The "given" influenced decisions more often than the "chosen." The accepted past deeply influenced the present; the future was often enough left to fate and to faith!

Modernity is in the process of changing even the attitude which might favor such behavior and certainly the behavior itself. The supermarket has replaced the corner shop; a wide variety of routes and means of transport have taken over from the local bus; transnational companies have pushed the limited local factory aside. Sexual intercourse plus birth has been replaced first by intercourse minus birth and now by birth minus intercourse, and so on. Choice continues to overcome fate and the given.

MAXIMIZATION OF CHOICE AND ITS CONSEQUENCES FOR EVANGELIZATION

There are serious implications for evangelical reflection in this apparent maximization of choice for the modern person. Let us examine the nature of choice.

Apparent. Choice is "apparent" because everywhere, perhaps especially in the less developed world, this choice is being centralized. It is increasingly found in the hands of educated elites who manipulate the economy in poorer countries; in the hands of the already rich who own the land (sixteen families own most of Pakistan); in the hands of young technocrats or military dictators who direct the use of a nation's resources to their own whims and benefit. Even in highly developed "democratic" countries, lobbying groups have highly significant, if not the final, choice in government policies.

Temporary and Illusory. Choice can be very temporary and very illusory in many situations, as we saw in the case of the supermarket which gobbles up the corner store or in the case of the medical center which takes medical care away from the family doctor.

Final. The finality of some of the choices before us today, especially in the nuclear and medical fields, makes these choices rather frightening for the future — or no future — of the human race. This surely calls for evangelical concern and action.

For Progress? "Progress" is the motivation most frequently proposed by modernity. This seems innocent enough, but on scrutiny we now know that it is a mixed blessing and that it calls for frequently discerned choices. So often too it appeals to the immediate and instinctual, to its painlessness and pain-reducing gifts. Observation, however, shows us just how painful and pain-increasing some aspects of modernity can be. *Inside America*, just published by

Louis Harris of Harris polls, shows that ninety percent of Americans report experiencing high stress, even if 95 percent still believe in God; 28 million are alcoholics; 81 percent think that the rich are getting richer and the poor poorer each year; 60 percent feel they are alienated from the power structure.

Instant. Finally, choices need to be near-instant as technology talks its way across all borders and cultures. A teacher in Bangkok told me that by studying the good and bad effects of industrialization in other countries they had some chance to prepare themselves for it before they accepted it. But when it came to information technology there was no time to choose; it just seemed to arrive and take over. Any Western video is now available in Bangkok in its original language or dubbed in Thai.

This clear bias for choice over fate, be it on the personal, local, national, or international level, calls out for an informed evangelization like so many other aspects of modernity. Education for choice is probably the greatest challenge before all of us today.

THE DISCOVERY OF THE INDIVIDUAL

The individual has discovered herself or himself with a new degree of self-awareness in modern society. We have noted some of the consequences for society of secularization, pluralism, and the possibility of making choices. I will now briefly outline some of the effects of modernity on the individual who is both the object and the subject of evangelization today.

THE NORTHERN HEMISPHERE

Identity. It is a major "plus" of modernity in the "First World" that it has enabled the individual to gain an identity independently of the group. The existence of listed human rights and an acknowledged respect for personal conscience have made major advances. More highly-developed communication and openness, encouraged by technology, are largely responsible for this.

Alienation. Modernity does bring people together more, but mostly in a functional way, thereby instrumentalizing them in some way. Thus it might be said that alienation is the pathology of the so-called developed countries of our age. Big cities continue to grow alarmingly and people live in closer contact, but they are not more present to or for one another.

Anxiety. While modernity has greatly increased people's self-awareness as distinct from groups and institutions, it is an anxious self-awareness, an unhealthily tense and tired self-consciousness. This probably explains the rise in emotional and mental illnesses today in developed countries.

Consumerism. People in the more highly-developed countries today are subject to the continual battering of modernity's subliminal message—"Faster is better than slower, newer than older, now than later." Thus they approach their world with a "master-and-use" attitude rather than with a contemplative one. Consumerism is one of the results of this change in human consciousness today.

Mobility. The human organism can suffer from cyclical dysrhythmia or jet lag. As geographical mobility becomes excessive the whole person is affected. Modernity seems to be a cause of this dysrhythmia. Families in the USA which move every five years find it costly in more senses than the obvious one.

Bureaucracy. Many pressure groups today use polls, surveys, and questionnaires to organize effectively against increasing government interference. They believe that the instrumentalization, mechanization, rationalization, and bureaucratization of the human person is being overdone for the sake of control. This control is exercised in the name of "progress" or national security, both of which appear to be linked with modernity.

ASIA

It is difficult if not impossible to attribute characteristics to the peoples of Asia because of their extraordinary diversity. Nevertheless, it would seem that most Asians have lived and continue to live with five deep and permeating experiences. Each of these is now being questioned by modernity.

Belonging. Most Asians have a strong feeling of belonging without perhaps being consciously aware of it, because its opposite has never been present. Each person belongs to a wide family, a village, a language group, a caste, and a religion. The pressures of modernity, however, may change this. Higher material standards combined with easier mobility enable the barrio Filipino to find work in Manila or in the Middle East where village togetherness is not so obvious. Even in very modern Japan, belongingness is an economically motivated experience in which the company almost possesses the employee.

Sharing. Most Asians live with another gospel value—sharing. I have seen so many intelligent, highly-motivated young Filipinos quit college after their second year in order to finance a brother or sister through grade school by earning their school fees. Many young Asians put off marriage for the same reason. But this also is breaking down as young people choose a love-marriage and elope, rather than delay or accept an arranged one.

Transcendence. Most people in Asia, from the so-called "animist" to the temple-going Hindu or the mosque-going Muslim, seem to inherit some sense of the transcendent. In a way they breathe God. But modernity threatens this. The Kiaks of central Borneo have chosen to live in villages along Kapuas or smaller tributaries rather than to build their villages in the forest. They have seen the forests as the place of ghosts and gods. Australian bulldozers and French missionaries have combined to remove the gods and have disturbed the traditional religious experience to some degree.

Order. Every Asian village has order. There are clear hierarchies of caste, society, and religion. But the economics of modern society upset this as "lower" class no longer means a person who has less money. Education too has shaken the order as bottom-of-the-ladder people have more access to training. Technocrats too take the place of gurus as power people in big cities like Karachi and Kuala Lumpur.

Patience. Some call it passivity. It may be that patience is a cultural characteristic of Asian people in the face of much pain and oppression. They have an extraordinary capacity for exercising the virtue of long-suffering. Victor Frankl reminded us that the ability to overcome and to put meaning in meaninglessness characterizes the human person at her or his best. The Asian people have a remarkable patience and ability to feel at home with their environment in both pleasant and painful moments. But this patience and "passivity" is now being challenged as they see the possibility of greater comfort constantly portrayed in the cinema and on video. They see too how often this is portrayed as achievable through violence towards others.

The above observations are a brief and necessarily simplified outline describing the phenomenon of modernity and its apparently emerging "modern person." Jesus told us to proclaim the Good News to all people. The problem for evangelization today seems to be that modernity has made many people "religiously unmusical." And yet this may be true only of a certain "dated" kind of music.

The question now is: can we recognize a new kind of music, the kind of music which enables the modern person to resonate to God's unfailing, never-ending invitation? This is the challenge modernity presents to evangelization in today's world.

EVANGELIZATION AND THE MODERN PERSON

Our model of evangelization is based on how God evangelizes each one of us. I see the process of evangelization for the modern person evolving in seven never-ending steps.

Identification. Our first step in evangelizing the modern person is to identify with them, to laugh and cry with them, to feel their pleasures and their pains, their personal and cultural experience. I must do this firstly with myself to identify my personal and cultural bias, and then go through a continual kenosis as I try to enter into the experience of the modern person.

Acceptance. God does not love me more or less after long prayers or after adultery; God cannot. Here is the second step in my evangelization of myself and of others: to accept fully.

The modern person will have to be accepted in his or her fragmentedness and confusion, perhaps also in their constant questions and aggression against the church or even against God. The communication of my full acceptance of the other is a basic condition for their growth in integration and self-acceptance without which all evangelization is problematic.

Call to Life. In my own willingness to be evangelized and to evangelize today, I have the privilege of calling people to the fullness of life. I do this by manifesting this life in myself as far as I possess it within myself.

I too am part of modernity, sharing in its confusions and questions. Because of faith I can do this with serenity, the evidence of which attracts others to ask where it comes from and to seek its source in God. To the modern person who is pressured to sacralize so many things and so many ideologies, I must say clearly that there is no god but God; that God alone is holy. I must challenge myself and them to be convinced that the most perfect legislation, the most advanced technology, and the most excellent GNP will never answer the deepest human needs. Love, joy, peace—the gifts of the Spirit (Gal. 5:22)—will always be necessary.

Offered Help. I offer help—but only after having taken the first three more difficult steps. For if I help before I hear or fix it before I find it, I am not really helping at all. If done as God does it, this help will be given at the right time, in the right amount, and respond to the right need.

This need may be basic self-respect, deeper integration against modernity's disintegratedness, or it may be the service of God's word in the explicit gift of telling who Christ is if the person is ready to hear. Jesus responded to the Syrophoenician woman at the point of her need—physical healing—but he knew that he should not ask the then impossible: to join the Semitic people.

Forgiveness. None of us ever responds fully to God's call to be evangelized, and so we come to the next step—forgiveness, seventy times seven. God's forgiveness, unlike merely human forgiveness, is not given after my failing; it is given before, during, and after because it is an attitude. God's merciful love is God's clearest and most constant quality. Neither must I have any timetable or limits to my patience in my own being evangelized or in my evangelization of others. I must live in God's time, with endless patience. Even in practical terms it will prevent "burn-out."

Missionary. The Good News is a fire to be passed on. While evangelizing us, God is sending, missioning us to do the same. We are empowered by the Spirit to announce God's justice and peace.

The modern person hesitates about commitment. Receiving this sense of mission can help to overcome this hesitancy. I must send this modern person to be a missionary—to walk with others on this journey of evangelization. Today especially I must remind him or her that each individual is made to God's image and likeness—a creative lover—and that this is more than a privilege; it is an obligation to be creatively loving in calling others and in changing systems in line with God's own justice and truth.

Invitation To Celebrate. The deepest step in my evangelization is taken when God invites me to celebrate—to dance with God. I am called to the feast of God's word and sacrament, especially in the eucharist where I experience symbolized *shalom*. This is a step which I may never see many modern persons take, but I must be ready to invite them at the moment of their readiness. While waiting, I can continue their evangelization in and through many minor, richly human celebrations such as eating, drinking, laughing, and relaxing together.

True evangelization means going over these seven steps unendingly and more deeply each time. But I must recognize that it may not be my privilege to bring a person or a people beyond the first, second, or third step. Evangelization is God's work, God's gift.

A SPIRITUALITY FOR MODERNITY

"All day long I am taunted: where is your God?" (Ps. 42:4).

This question might have been addressed to any modern Christian. In the not so distant past Teilhard de Chardin posed the question this way:

All around us the physical sciences are ceaselessly discerning new relationships between elements of the universe. . . . Is the Christ of the

Gospels, imagined and loved within the dimensions of the Mediterranean world, capable of still embracing and still forming the center of our prodigiously expanding universe? Is not the world in the process of becoming more vast, more close, more dazzling than Jehovah? Will it not burst our religions asunder? Will it not eclipse our God?

An Anglican spiritual writer underlines the urgency of spirituality for the modern person when he writes, "This may be the emergence of a new sort of spiritual person ... there may be no option if meaning is to be sustained" (Happhold in *Faith and Modern Man*). This brings me to what I think is the first and central aspect of this spirituality for modernity—it is going to call for a new mysticism unlike that of the "mystics," and unlike the passing mystical moments most of us have had in our lives.

A NEW MYSTICISM

It is extraordinary that when St. Paul met a secular society for the first time in Athens, he may have given us the answer, or a direction, when he quoted, not the scriptures, but the words of the sixth century B.C. poet Epimenides:

From one single stock he not only erected the human race so that they could occupy the entire earth, but he decreed how long each nation should flourish and what the boundaries of its territory should be. And he did this so that all nations might seek the deity and, by feeling their way towards him, succeed in finding him. Yet, in fact, he is not far from any of us since it is in him that we live and move and exist as indeed some of your writers have said: "We are all his children." (Acts 17:26–28)

This is the presence of God which the modern believer must deepen or rediscover. Note the words "seek," "feel their way towards him," and "not far from any of us," because they are very modern indeed. This is the immanent God whom we "find" by "feeling" our way towards God. But God is not far from us because we live, move, and exist in God who must be the center and source of a modern spirituality. This is far from both secularism and naive fundamentalism. A long time ago the English historian Christopher Dawson wrote, "People today are divided between those who have kept their spiritual roots and lost their contact with the existing order of society, and those who have preserved their social contacts and lost their spiritual ones." Unless each of us finds what John Ruysbrek describes as "the God in the depths of us who receives the God who comes to us," we will be in either one of these un-Christian categories.

FINDING GOD IN THE WORLD OF TECHNOLOGY

The Danish philosopher Wittgenstein reminds us, "It is not *how* the world is that is the mystical, but *that* the world is." The modern believer has to discover this and to experience the world of modernity as "a diaphany of the divine" (Teilhard de Chardin).

Tillich spoke of "a God who is the personality of everything," and in the *Vedanta Mandukya Upanishad* we read, "There is nothing in the world that is not God." This is a mysticism that enables us to experience God in the world. "Christ," as Bonhoeffer reminds us, "is no longer the object of religion but Lord of the world."

The modern believer has to be deeply convinced that she or he has nothing to fear from the basic thrust of technological discoveries. "Called or not called, God will come," as Carl Jung inscribed over his doorway.

The poets have always seen this. Elizabeth Browning wrote, "Earth is crammed with heaven and every common bush afire with God, but only those who see take off their shoes. The rest sit around and pick blackberries."

The modern mystic will agree that every computer is afire with God ... but some sit around to pick out what has already been inserted in their program. Only those who see with deep faith will find God in technology.

FINDING GOD IN MYSTERY

Nonmodern persons met God deeply in sunsets, sunrises, starlit nights, in nature — and many of us still do. They met God also in gothic arches, papal cavalcades, and in crimson cassocks. God was also experienced in statuary and shrine more deeply in the past than now.

The Anglican writer John Macquarrie puts it this way:

Nowadays, the kind of natural theology that saw God in mountains, stars and clouds has declined. Nature has been made the subject of scientific research. ... If we believe in God now, it is not likely to be because we have seen attested God's wisdom and beneficence in nature. Rather, if we can still see God in nature, we do so because we already believe in God on other grounds.

This other ground may be the presence of mystery within and around each of us, mystery in the sense of something which is so deep that it is endlessly enriching. Today it might be parental courage with a crippled child, vows fulfilled, recovery from drug addiction, caring teachers, dedicated artists, being oneself.

St. John reminds us: "God is love and those who live in love, live in God and God in them." This love, seen with a contemplative heart, either in our own struggles or those of others, might be a rediscovered revelation of God in an age of technology.

CHARACTERISTICS OF THIS SPIRITUALITY

A Pilgrim Spirituality. Modernity means motion and it may just be that it is a grace continually calling us away from our fixed idols and immovable images of God. A spirituality for now will be one of searching, evolving, discovering, of uncertainty and transition, of parting and of letting go—a call from God to become what we ought to have been always: pilgrims on a journey "not knowing where we are going" (Heb. 11:8). It may be we are being called into a corporate dark night of the soul as old images and concepts crumble and as God, through God's creativity in current technology, beckons us forward in trusting love.

A Creatively Loving Interdependence. Modernity is centricist and so it gives the power-hungry and the money-seekers the possibility of making this a very uneven and unjust world. This demands that we become more and more like God, creative lovers, loving creators of a world in which real progress is the progress of peoples, *progressio populorum*. Latin American writers speak rightly of the need for "political saints," of people who will become conscientious about and willing to work at changing systems, so that we can "reconcile all things in Christ." A modern spirituality must learn from the Japanese economic motivators—"I'm OK because we're OK"—and live this in the marketplace of daily life.

A Spirituality That Gives Unity. Modernity is subversive and disintegrative, and so the modern Christian must live a spirituality that creates unity: between Christian and non-Christian religions; among Christian religions themselves; between prayer and action; between solitude and community; between the material and the spiritual; and surely between woman and man. Like so much of what I am saying, this too is very old but by no means old-fashioned; it may indeed be the price of the modern person's survival. This unity, of course, must be taking place first of all and more urgently within each of us.

An Interiorized Spirituality. Modernity brings the individual to the fore. Good! But it deprives him or her of cultural support in the transmission and development of faith. Thus the faith experience has to be very personal, very interiorized today. As this happens, each of us, having rejected the magic of many of our Catholic symbols, may rediscover them more deeply as his or her very own. Then too we need not fear "losing the faith" because it is part of us, like our lungs which continue to grow as we do. That is why "having the faith" might be better described as "faithing" today.

Community-Supported and Explicated. In spite of its increased potential for communication and bringing people together functionally, modernity is probably responsible for the pathology of our age—isolation and alienation. Thus a modern spirituality will have to be a community experience. Never before, except perhaps in the act of martyrdom, has it been so necessary to explicate, to exteriorize faith, and where best to do this than among "faithing" people— a Christian community? This is not the monastic model which, too, has its important symbolic presence in modern society. It is a question of structured, qualitative time willingly spent together to share our experience of God.

Apostolic, Earth-Based Prayer Life. To live faithfully today in a time of rapid change calls for frequent discernment, even about the locus of God's presence. We must recognize the need for what Macquarrie calls "prayer as thinking"— passionate, compassionate, responsible, and grateful thinking. All reality is opaque and when it is moving fast, it is still more so. And so we need to withdraw, not to escape nor to "refill" spiritually, but to sharpen our spiritual eyesight, to see what is really there in technology and the things it produces. We need to discern what each new discovery is doing to ourselves and to our brothers and sisters, and especially how it might be contributing to a system that could stimulate real growth or strangle the human within us.

A Spirituality of Hope. Finally, it has to be a spirituality of hope, of "joyful hope" and of a "sure hope" (1 Pet. 1:3) which keeps telling us that we live in an already christified world—that God created the creativity of the modern person and "saw that it was good." Concern merely for the secular city not only robs religion of its meaning, but denudes humanity of fundamental dignity. When the first Russian cosmonaut came back from space he said he had looked around up there without finding God. A newspaper reporter cabled Martin Buber with this piece of news and asked for a comment. Buber's reply: "Relax; read psalm 8."

> Yahweh, our Lord,
> how great your name throughout the earth!
> Above the heavens is your majesty chanted
> by the mouths of children, babes in arms.
> You set your stronghold firm against your foes
> to subdue enemies and rebels.
> I look up at your heavens, made by your fingers,
> at the moon and stars you set in place.
> Ah, what are we that you should keep us in mind,
> That you should care for us?
> Yet you have made us little less than gods,
> You have crowned us with glory and splendor,
> Made us supreme over the work of your hands,
> set all things under our feet . . .

15

CHALLENGES TO INCULTURATED EVANGELIZATION

Marcello Azevedo, SJ

Modernity presents a challenge to all of us involved in inculturated evangelization. We will briefly examine some of these challenges which can be clustered around three major relationships:
1. Evangelization, modernity, and technology/science
2. Evangelization, modernity, and social/political change
3. Evangelization, modernity, and secularization.

EVANGELIZATION, MODERNITY AND TECHNOLOGY/SCIENCE

A crucial task of religion in the contemporary world is producing and articulating a new vision of technology as well as creating the social pressure for the implementation of this vision. This convergence of vision and pressure seems to be effective in achieving technological changes for the sake of humankind. For example, the ecological approach to environment as perceived and urged by a community or population has sometimes been effective in bringing social pressure either against the use of a specific destructive technology or to improve pollution control. A growing appreciation of tranquility and silence coupled with social pressure to achieve these values publicly has brought about a remarkable reduction of the noise produced by airplanes and other means of public transportation. The church and other religious or secular institutions should be active in the implementation of values which can lead to a better quality of life.

ORIGINATORS OF VALUES AND MEANINGS

Pope John Paul II's encyclicals have valuable aspects and recommendations. Unlike his speech at UNESCO, however, the encyclicals are conceptualized and then phrased in a language that is less acceptable or not even understandable to contemporary persons. One of the main tasks in the modern world as well as in the church is to develop an ongoing cooperation between originators of values and meanings and effective communicators in order to produce new comprehensive and understandable visions powerful enough to trigger social pressures for change. The attempt at doing it in a consistent and concerted operation all over the world will entail changes in international political and economic relations. This active commitment to produce change goes beyond the static ethical evaluation of technologies according to standard Christian values.

PATTERNS OF ACCEPTANCE OR REJECTION OF TECHNOLOGY

Researching the patterns of cultural acceptance or rejection of technologies by various populations around the world would be helpful for the following reasons:

1) First, this could assist entire populations and national administrations in designing public policies to counteract negative technological effects. Japan, for example, increasingly stresses the artistic education and creativity of children on a national scale as a means to offset the impersonal, anonymous influence of its highly-developed technological society.

In developing countries much could be done in a preventative fashion before they reach technological levels which have already proved elsewhere to be destructive of cultural or human values or of the quality of life.

2) Second, this could enlarge and empower the protest against some forms of harmful technology, shifting the protest from the private to the social arena, from a decentralized, small-scale, local phenomenon to a large-scale international movement, for example, the ecological movement.

3) Third, this research could provoke a reorientation of some policies of transnational corporations regarding the transfer of technologies, or promote the production of commodities which are more responsive to cultural needs instead of being simply imposed on entire peoples.

SHARING OF TECHNOLOGICAL BREAKTHROUGHS

Up to now, most international relations have been exclusively conceived of in terms of East/West political and military confrontation. This dominant and determinant standpoint has catalyzed a whole network of international policies and organized them accordingly. What was gained by it? Practically nothing. Instead new meanings and values need to be promulgated throughout the world and strongly backed by national and international social pressure, pushing the superpowers and their allies as well as the transnational corporations towards an effective sharing with the developing countries of the technological break-throughs which improve food, health, and education.

THE CHURCH'S RESPONSE TO TECHNOLOGY

When the church decided to face up to modernity in Vatican II, its position on technology contemplated the older technological processes and the products and procedures of the agricultural and industrial revolutions. These processes led to the external modifications of the environment, they improved human efficiency, and they affected individual and social consciousness. *Gaudium et Spes* praised science and technology in a relatively uncritical way. With bio-technologies, however, the church faces a more complex and weighty challenge. If we are not to miss another crucial watershed, scientific discovery will have to be closely monitored and organically integrated into our theological research and reflection. It demands a far greater theological understanding of creation than we have now. It also demands of the church not its traditional defensive posture, but an attitude of both critical and positive openness to unfolding scientific processes. This has to be an interdisciplinary task that urges the theological community to work together with other members of the church, particularly with the scientific community, on the meaning and extent of these discoveries.

An attitude of coresponsibility and mutual trust would replace a sheerly negative position of condemnation; it would arouse concern about how to put such a high degree of knowledge and technology at the service of humankind; it would protect human populations from the consequences of misuse of the most brilliant scientific discoveries of our times. This is not a simple task. It certainly is a crucial challenge to evangelization of today's world as it touches the cultural structures of the modern world.

EVANGELIZATION, MODERNITY AND SOCIAL/POLITICAL CHANGE

The human ability to change the world according to God's design of love is the radical meaning of the Christian message and the very reason for its inculturation. However, one of the strongest arguments linking modernization and religious ineffectiveness refers to the impact of bureaucratization on all forms of morality. The moral prescriptions of Christianity were and still are relevant for interpersonal relations, for face-to-face contacts, for the privacy of individuals and families. But they have much less application to the mass society with its impersonal and anonymous interaction of role-performers. Many authors suggest heavy declines of religious influence with the growth of large, impersonal systems. We certainly are less prepared for and less sensitive to the ethical aspects of large-scale societies, especially at the international level. It is necessary to expand the ethical analysis which is now concentrated on results and consequences in order to understand the processes themselves that produce such results.

STRUCTURAL INJUSTICE

The modern world, which once emphasized the difference between center and periphery, now needs the periphery for the very survival of the center. The periphery is kept dependent but is allowed to reach a certain level of development to make the expansion of markets and ideologies possible. This explains the intricate international debate among developed countries over the fate and future of developing countries. It is the inspiring thread of foreign policies. This is also the main reason for accelerating by force, and at any cost, the stages of modernization which were denied to those same countries until very recently. Thus the link between political goals and large-scale economic imperatives built a world of structural injustice at individual and social levels.

The impressive technological mastery over nature and over human beings which we have recently attained is often used to exploit individuals, groups, and entire populations rather than to distribute the resources of the planet more equitably. It has led to division rather than to union, to alienation rather than to communication, to oppression or domination, rather than to a greater respect for the rights of individuals and groups. Modernity has been achieved at great cost—costs exacted at the time of its inception in Europe and still being exacted today. Huge material sacrifices, dislocations and migrations, expropriation and expatriation, mass hunger and virulent new epidemics are a recurrent page of modern history. Economic transformation and social dislocation have frequently generated repressive mechanisms in the political order. In the developing world there is a growing awareness of the impact of structural injustice and, consequently, an experience of failure as the paramount result of the whole process of modernization.

LIBERAL CAPITALISM

On the side of liberal capitalism there is very little understanding of the problem of structural injustice and a very low value placed on human cost when economic goals are at stake. This kind of economic determinism underlies the political choices of almost all nation-states. Moreover, it has become the very core of the decision-making process of transnational corporations and of some highly-developed countries which are so powerful in determining the fate of humanity. The interaction between technology and consciousness, strikingly fostered by the mass media as a vehicle of economic supremacy, has built up a consumer society both in industrialized societies of affluence and deplorable waste and in the developing societies, many of which aim at a one-sided and almost exclusively material and economic development.

The capitalist society which is deprived of ideas and values that go beyond the dominant economic perspective has no message and nothing to offer the real human growth of today's men and women. The material inertia of advanced technology will be able to support a purely immanent conception of life for a long time, a life which is empty of any inspiring world view.

SOCIALIST-COMMUNISM

On the socialist-communist side, the absolute power of an all-pervasive and imposing bureaucratic and totalitarian state radically reduces individual aspirations and limits social possibilities. The high human costs of modernization in the Soviet Union, especially from the 1920s through the 1960s, are repeated now in a more subtle and sophisticated way wherever a country starts modernizing under communist rule.

Modernity—its ideas, values, aspirations—continues to be a crucial theme of our times and it is fully integrated into all of the different versions of socialist-communism. Its program is based on all of the standard assumptions of modernity—history as progress, the perfectibility of humanity, scientific reason as the great liberator from religious illusion, and humanity's ability to overcome all or nearly all of its afflictions by taking rational control of its destiny. In these assumptions socialist-communism, like liberal-capitalism, is a child of the Enlightenment. This point has been totally overlooked by the sponsors of a polarized world, by strategies of East/West confrontation and by the advocates of radical capitalism or socialism as an exclusive alternative.

Socialism has successfully incorporated some countermodern themes such as the theme of renewed community in the midst of alienation. Both liberalism and socialism have upheld the threefold promise of the French Revolution— liberty, equality, fraternity—although they have very different definitions for these terms. Whereas liberalism has said little about fraternity, socialism by contrast has made this one of its most inspiring ambitions. Socialism is the secular prototype of projecting the redemptive community into the future. Its secularized eschatology embodies the central aspirations of modernity: a new rational order, abolition of material want and social inequality, and complete liberation of the individual. Socialism, in other words, promises all the blessings of modernity and the liquidation of its negative costs, including, and most important, the cost of alienation. To grasp this essentially simple fact about the socialist myth is to understand the appeal of socialism.

BEYOND CAPITALISM AND SOCIALISM

We should recognize the basic values of both the capitalist and the socialist system but at the same time be aware of their structural limitations, their functional shortcomings, and some of their unacceptable principles. There is no question, therefore, of an exclusive choice of one of them nor of a suitable synthesis of their positive aspects, since these aspects, as a matter of fact, are structurally and functionally articulated in and with the given system and ideology. The solution will be to go beyond capitalism and socialism and creatively try to open another path. This path should be based on different assumptions even if it has to reassume in a different perspective some permanent aspects of the pre-existent systems such as the dignity of the individual and the meaning of community.

THE CHURCH AND THE CONSTRUCTION OF A JUST SOCIETY

In today's church there is a growing awareness of the structural injustice of the modern world in all of its forms. Practically everywhere a commitment to the struggle for justice in the world has become a hallmark of the church. This commitment has entailed concrete decisions by individuals and communities for sharing the lot of the poor and of the oppressed, for being with them, for being the voice of those who have no voice. The more the church is able to realize the everyday consequences of injustice and oppression in itself, the more it will understand the real needs of the people. The hierarchies of some countries, especially in Latin America, have taken relevant risks when they assumed the defense of the poor and affirmed the overcoming of social injustice as a central concern of evangelization. Perhaps no continent more than Latin America experiences in the flesh of its people the consequences of capitalist domination through the policies of its own governments, the actions of the developed countries, and the transnational corporations.

LIVING AND CONSISTENT WITNESSES

All of us must be the living and consistent witnesses of the Lord in the concrete situations in which we are present. This is crucial for re-establishing lost or forgotten evangelical values which are also fundamental human values. This is the way to help men and women to be open to God as well as to their fellow human beings, thus building together a new world where it is possible to share the resources and benefits with individuals, societies, and nations in peace and justice.

EVANGELIZATION AND SECULARIZATION

Secularization is the most crucial challenge to inculturated evangelization because it touches the very heart of both the nature and the mission of the church. The main concern of the church is how to be faithful to the Good News of Jesus Christ and the sound development of tradition while making this content of faith present to the people who actually live in today's historical context.

CHURCH RESPONSES TO SECULARIZATION

DEFENSE AND ACCOMMODATION

Referring to the attitude of the churches in relationship to the whole problem of secularization, Berger distinguishes two basic positions: defense and accommodation. "In the defensive posture, vis-à-vis the dimensions of secularization and pluralization in the modern world, the institution continues to affirm the old objectivities and, as far as possible, goes on with its own life and thought despite the regrettable developments on the 'outside.' " The Catholic church before Vatican II and some sects today are examples of such a position.

Should the accommodation posture be an alternative? "In the accommodation posture, the old model of a pre-modern Church was still held as the determinant and normative standard. Concessions would be then made accordingly. The accommodation posture springs out of the need to maintain the basic institutional dimension and not primarily to foster the life and the inspiration which can faithfully shape a deeply renewed institution." Does this model resemble the present church after Vatican II?

THE CHURCH—TRANSPARENT MILIEU FOR THE ACTION OF GOD

However, the fundamental challenge cannot be how to rescue a specific sociological pattern of the institutional church. The fundamental challenge is how to shape the institution in such a way that it can be a transparent milieu for the constant action of God amidst humanity—amidst this very concrete humanity of men and women of which we as church are all a part. Putting it another way, how can we keep the institution consistently faithful to its only meaningful vocation of being a mediator and not an end in itself? Neither defense nor accommodation, but a critical and honest facing up to modernity is the only consistent attitude of a church which believes, hopes, and loves not for its own sake but for the sake of all women and men in the world.

ULTRA-ORTHODOX OUTLOOK

We must deeply believe that God speaks again and again through Jesus Christ and the Holy Spirit in the concrete language of a time and a culture, and not only in the patterns of one particular time and culture. Here is precisely the failure of an ultra-orthodox outlook within religious institutions which do not have a sound historical instinct of faith. What they try to preserve is the sociological face of the church of a specific time outside of this time. What they try to impose on all cultures is one concrete cultural version of the church. That is why an analysis of the church as a whole can hardly be done through the focus of one science only, and still less only through procedures of a historical analysis. Sociological research must be complemented by a historical viewpoint and interdisciplinary approaches.

MEANINGFUL THEOLOGY FOR THE HUMANITY OF OUR TIME

While being faithful to the original faith and tradition, theology must rethink and re-express the timeless truths in accordance with the mental categories and in the language of a concrete time. Theology therefore cannot be content with the successful formulation of a specific time as though it were valid for all times. Theology must be in a certain way a creation of each time for its own time. It has to make God's initiative for the humanity of any time meaningful for the humanity of our time. Thus, the goal is not to secularize theology but to enable it to introduce the transcendent God to the secular person of today. That is only possible if theological reflection refrains from the attempt to sacralize the whole of human life and recognizes that humanity can provide itself with many answers which were formerly sought from religion. Ironically, secularization may then become a way of purifying religion and faith.

The awareness of secularization is a means for shaping truly new and acceptably plausible structures for today's men and women. At the same time, theology may help modern women and men to discover and realize the limits of immanence and the unavoidable necessity of transcendence. In other words, an inculturated church may lead modern humanity to overcome the modern dogma that humanity is the master of its own destiny. This naive assumption of the industrial revolution has become meaningless for the frightened men and women of the technoelectronic revolution. Inculturation seems to be the only way for the church to engage in a dialogue with modernity throughout the world.

THEOLOGY STARTS WITH REALITY

Whatever the culture in which the Christian message has to be inculturated, reality must be the starting point of theological research and reflection. An interaction between professional theologians and people in their everyday life, as well as in their historical, social, cultural, political, and spiritual reality, could lead to a meaningful conceptualization of the Christian faith for today's world.

A theological process which centers its research and reflection exclusively around itself and its internal structure of sources, principles, and methods could hardly answer the existential religious problems and aspirations of men and women who live in an unstable, rapidly changing, and challenging world. If theology is not for the people, what is it for? Theology, therefore, can no longer be a distanced, noncommitted enterprise. It must be intimately tied to the people, to their history and their concrete, cultural reality. This kind of theological research and reflection is a necessary and effective means for a mature inculturation of the Christian message.

INCREASINGLY ACTIVE LAITY

The interrelationship between the Christian message and the complex modern secular world is bound to be quite ineffective if the church does not allow the laity, and especially women, to share genuine responsibility in the decision-making process at different levels of church life and organization.

THE CULTURAL ROOTS OF POPULAR RELIGION

An acute sensitivity to the cultural roots of popular religion should help in finding the symbolic level that makes religious language more immediately available to a particular people. Through this cultural awareness Christian beliefs and paradigms may be inculturated without losing their original meaning and inspiration but without falling into a noncritical cultural and religious syncretism.

INDIVIDUAL RESPONSES TO SECULARIZATION

Hopefully, for the modern person the answer to secularization will not be the sheer negation of religion or escape into a rather functional, dichotomous approach to religion which allows for the coexistence of the incompatible domains of the sacred and profane. The latter position tends to re-establish and foster old sacred patterns and symbols as a kind of stable and secure point of reference. Most of these old sacred patterns and symbols were shaped out of mysterious unknown dimensions of nature or person. These are no longer a mystery.

Modern human beings should be helped to become aware of their limits and the limits of science as the apex of current knowledge and power. Transcendence therefore should not be imposed on humans from above. Transcendence will become an urge, an internal demand felt by modern women and men when they realize and experience the inevitability and the evidence of human limits. Science will then no longer pretend to be in full control of nature. Science will lead to an openness to the unpredictable, to the new, to nonreachable fullness, to the need for God. Science will bring with it the truth of "limit" and, therefore, of existential humility which makes humans open to receive and to commit themselves. Acceptance and commitment are two important dimensions of religious paradigms.

CONCLUSION

We face modernity as a cultural reality with values and meanings—some positive and life-giving, others negative and destructive. Developing new meanings and values from within the dynamics of a given culture in general and of modernity in particular seems to be the way to improve it without denying it; the way to go beyond its cultural shortcomings and at the same time to redeem and restore it. The Christian message would then be part of modern culture and would not be experienced as outdated or irrelevant.

16

MODERNITY IN AFRICA

Ngindu Mushete

SIGNIFICANT ASPECTS OF MODERNITY IN AFRICA

This paper aims to explain at what levels of truth and religious depth the problem of modernity is located for people in Africa, people whose cultural roots do not go back to Athens and Rome. As we shall see, evangelization must reach the Africans where they are. We are not dealing here simply with geographical location but with cultural and epistemological location. The place where they stand is not an enclosure from which others are excluded; rather, it is a place that is fundamentally open in a dynamic, critical and discerning way. African anthropology calls for a philosophy of the finite, of the unfinished; contrary to modern and contemporary Western thought, people are not masters and owners of the world, they are not a complete reality, they always yearn for something more.

MODERNITY AND EUROPE

In Europe there is much talk of *aggiornamento*, inner renewal. There is need to rejuvenate a body, breathe fresh life into it, revitalize it—but it is still the same body since it remains in fact in the same universe of meaning. Despite a multitude of cultures and subcultures the Western universe today consists of a single sociocultural matrix through which the evangelical message has travelled for close to two millennia. Dialogue will thus be primarily intracultural, within the boundaries of a single cultural universe. In this dialogue Europeans today are using the language of their ancestors. There is communication along a chronological line: the past of one particular people enters into dialogue with the present of the same people and communicates its meaning to this present, which in turn assumes this meaning as its own and actualizes it in a more appropriate language. What is true of language is also true of institutions. We examine and criticize institutions, not to destroy them, but rather to revitalize and rejuvenate them, so that they may truly serve life rather than threaten to stifle it.

MODERNITY AND AFRICA

In Africa dialogue does not really take place between Africa's past and its tormented present with a view to its future. Rather, it takes place between Africa's present and the Western present as well as the Western past. Need we remind ourselves that it is the West that evangelized and still today evangelizes Africa? Christianity in Africa cannot claim the past of Western civilization as its own, since in no way did it participate in the ancient schisms or heresies that we only know through the evangelizers to whom we submit. Catholics, Orthodox, Anglicans, and Protestants all came to us with their fervent zeal for Jesus Christ, but divided among themselves, hurling anathemas at one another and inviting us to do the same and more.

Colonialism. In addition, the problem of modernity in Africa has to be viewed in the context of a reaction against the colonial situation. As a background we shall use here the elements of a definition of that situation provided by G. Balandier:

1. supremacy of a foreign minority, racially and culturally different, over a native majority that is materially inferior, in the name of racial and cultural superiority dogmatically affirmed;
2. encounter between two heterogeneous civilizations where a mechanically advanced civilization of Christian origin imposes itself from outside on a radically non-Christian civilization that has no complex technologies;
3. the antagonistic quality prevailing in the relationship between the two societies, a consequence of the role of instrument assigned to the subjected society;
4. the need to adopt pseudojustifications and stereotyped behavior in order to maintain domination.

SCOPE OF MODERNITY IN AFRICA

Viewed in the African context, the problem of modernity raises a number of issues. One in particular will have to be analyzed separately: the delicate question of the relationship between religion, tradition, and modernity, a complex issue, one that invites us to study the changes affecting African society and its present evolution. These changes can be grouped under three main headings.

FUNCTIONAL LEVEL

This includes various transformations pertaining to clothing, landscape (housing, new roads, and so forth), communications (vehicles, airplanes, ships, telephone, television), population (volume, composition, displacement or mobility, land use, and so forth), production techniques, work, and so forth. There is a new configuration, a new human and cosmic environment affirming itself and imposing itself all over the continent. African cities provide the best examples of this refashioning along Western lines. Change is most rapid and most radical at this level. New tools and new means of exchange (money economy) are easier to adopt than new meanings involving a radical change in the basic interpretation of human life and of the destiny of the universe. Commenting on this, P. Temple said:

We realize better and better each day that the European civilization handed over to the Bantu is only a superficial layer that has no profound hold on their souls. We see that those whom we call evolués are simply those who have reached the point where they no longer dare to profess their original wisdom in front of whites, thus in practice denying their ancestors.

STRUCTURAL LEVEL

Along with customs and behaviors, Europe introduced its systems to Africa, superimposing them upon traditional systems. Thus, European medicine coexisted alongside African healing methods: European-style families and their narrow structure alongside African families that are so elastic and flexible; law courts imported from abroad alongside customary courts; Western scientific educational methods superimposed upon traditional African education profoundly imbued with symbolism.

The point is not to deny or minimize the scope and the importance of the changes that took place within social structures and institutions. We must note, however, that this is a level where people already feel more involved, and the security of their position in the world considerably restrains their taste for untested innovations. The "rate of change" will clearly be slower here than it is on the functional level.

REPRESENTATIONAL LEVEL

The representational level is the level at which we define the most fundamental meaning of life, and it is the one where there is most resistance to change, although it is not necessarily static. This is where we find basic concepts, fundamental metaphors, powerful symbols, the great doctrines concerning God, humanity, the world, life, the afterlife. This is where we find the deeper meaning of important rituals with which we consecrate and celebrate the crucial moments of existence—birth, initiation, marriage, enthronement, death. This is where we must seek the meanings of the central values of African societies—solidarity, hospitality, respect for life, sense of the sacred, and so forth. It is at this fundamental level that we must attempt to understand the Africans as they understand themselves, their history and their relationship to the universe.

Fragility. The problem we face, stated in negative terms, is the pervasive fragility of the very foundations of existence:

— Social fragility, caused by destruction of the foundations of traditional society and by the instability of an elite educated abroad and frequently foreign to its own people;

— Structural fragility of the newly-established political and economic structures, which were copied from the West and have no meaning for the people;

— Cultural fragility due to cultural neocolonialism through the schools and the mass media on the one hand, and on the other hand, the absence of a committed and rooted elite of leaders and thinkers capable of developing original and autonomous views.

A Summary of the Significance of Modernity in Africa

The question of modernity is formulated differently in Europe and in Africa. The Africa of today is deeply marked by its colonial past. The continent has undergone a modernization and a social upheaval which go hand in hand with a certain secularization and the breaking up of traditional African societies. Industrialization and all that goes with it seriously menace our peoples with alienation, causing irreparable damage and the disintegration of a fabric of life woven over the centuries. These changes affect Africa on three different levels: functional, structural, and representational.

This is the present African world—a world in which the church is situated. It is a "monitored church," one which seeks the way to its integral development hesitantly through suffering; a church which lives in a state of more or less latent violence and permanent frustration. In short, it is a church which is fragile and at a disadvantage, whether at the level of personnel, material and institutional resources, or its own theological thought.

The birth of several independent churches and the springing up of sects in Africa are perfectly clear expressions of an effort on the part of the peoples to free themselves. They are expressions, too, of the search for salvation on the part of peoples who feel themselves to be in danger of perdition.

Having said this, we may go on to note and stress that the question of modernity in Africa includes at one and the same time the processes of integration, inculturation, the crisis arising from the imbalance provoked by these processes, and lastly the efforts being made to ensure the success of the processes and to avoid or surmount the crisis arising from the imbalance.

THE CHALLENGES OF MODERNITY TO THE CHURCH OF AFRICA

The Basic Difficulty

The evangelization of Africa today makes us ask some fundamental questions concerning the meaning of divine revelation under its various aspects; the meaning and significance of the faith which answers to it; the value and validity of the dogma which it proclaims; the role of the church which enshrines it, the nature of the theology which attempts to establish the changing contents of evangelization—in short, the problem of the originality of Christianity considered as an historically revealed religion. One way or another this problem constantly recurs in the writings of African clergy and theologians. We find it implied in the three main questions which sum up and synthesize African theological research:

1. the problem of inculturation or the religious problem of a revealed truth
2. the question of the local church or the pedagogical question of authority
3. the question of development or the moral question of Christian life.[1]

Certainly, the question of the originality of the revealed message is not a new one. Christianity has always had to, and will always have to, justify itself, reflect on its profound nature, on what is implied by its metaphysical and theological point of view, resist the compromises and accords which confuse Christianity with the thought trends which have sometimes been used to express it.

It is doubtless this difficult and pressing problem which confronts the churches of Africa. One can never repeat too often that today, for numerous Africans, the Christian West represents and designates a privileged civilization. This civilization, by having incarnated the Christian message historically with a degree of success, seems to be the only one capable of doing so adequately. It also designates as the universal church that one which, in practice, disposes of nearly all the central posts in the government of the church. And it is the criteria of that one particular culture which determine the formulation of doctrine, the conception of moral values, the expression of cult, the organization of ecclesial life.

CULTURAL IMPERIALISM

This is the dominant feature of the Christian West for many Africans. Essentially it consists in considering what has been termed the cultural imperialism of the West as profoundly unjust and unjustified. Whether voluntary or not, consciously or not it seems to reduce Christianity to the dimension of its historical realization in the West.

This problem is clearly identified by young African intellectuals. For example, V. Y. Mudimbe writes:

> Why must one believe in a foreign religion? Be it Catholic, universal, or what one wills, the problem remains that Catholicism is a religion marked by the West even to the understanding of its message. Upheld as it is by European structures, it is impossible to embrace it without entering into the history of the world.[2]

Here one grasps the entire question of religious acculturation in Africa. The delegates from Africa who attended the Ordinary Plenary Assembly of the Synod of Bishops on the evangelization of the world today noted with chagrin, "Insufficiently incarnated Christianity is often lived only exteriorly because it lacks any real link with the authentic values which convey the traditional religions."[3]

This both underpins and frames the problematical African question of "pluralism." In the last resort, this question concerns only the need for a theology which endorses as valid both the religious experience and the cultural values of Africa. And this conforms with the wish of the Second Vatican Council when it recommends that the young churches borrow any customs and traditions of their peoples that may contribute to the glorification of the creator, or heighten the light and grace of the savior, for the benefit of a good Christian life (*Ad Gentes*, 22).

WHAT MISSION FOR MODERNITY IN AFRICA?

To the question of what is the aim of mission and the best way to achieve it, one can give four rough answers, all of which may be culled from recent Catholic missiology: 1) to convert heathens, 2) to plant or to implant the church, 3) to adapt doctrines and practices to another sociocultural situation, 4) to give light to the church and to help it to grow so as truly to fulfill itself and share full responsibility, in Christ, with other churches.

Salvation of Souls. The theory of the salvation of souls or the conversion of the heathen rests firmly on the adage, *extra ecclesiam (Romanam) nulla salus.* This theory logically should disqualify the religious traditions of all evangelized peoples. As H. Maurier writes:

> The language of Church growth and of Christian charity was based on the pity which the deplorable moral, human and supernatural state of "savages" inspired. There was no question of recognizing the intrinsic values of other religions — about which little was known. Even their values, if they had been perceived, would have been an impediment to the uniformly saving romanization which prevailed.[4]

Carried away by excessive zeal to defend the unity of Christianity and to distinguish it from what in popular and poorly defined terminology is called paganism, the theorists of the salvation of heathens forgot that God is omnipresent and that there is not only a universal reality beyond the Jewish and Christian revelation, but a salvation which may be obtained by nonecclesiastical mediations as diverse as are the different ideas and humanisms among the human race.

Implantation. The theory of the implantation of the church developed from 1920 onwards. Whereas the conversion of unbelievers regarded the souls of the poor blacks as *sedentes in tenebris et in umbra mortis*, the theory of implantation reveals a different preoccupation, firmly ecclesiastical and even ecclesiocentric.

Here it is a question of consecrating or implanting the church just as it stands in its developed Western state and historical reality, with its personnel, its works, and its methods, on the culturally impoverished backdrop of people lacking in civilization. The missionaries, notes H. Maurier, worked effectively to implant the Roman Catholic Church in the countries where it had not been present before.

> Missionaries are not usually aware that they are the agents of Roman Christianity on non-Western soil. They say their wish is to save souls, spread the true faith, preach the Gospel, and this, without doubt, they do, but they work to implant the Roman Church, its doctrine, its liturgy, its discipline, and its organization. They do it without saying so. It is part of their common conscience since it is taken for granted that the Roman Catholic Church is the only true Church of Jesus Christ, the only sure way to salvation.[5]

The consequences are known. The theory of implantation has led to paralyzed communities deprived of creativity or originality, praying with borrowed words, thinking with borrowed thoughts which have traveled via Rome, Paris, London, Bonn, and other European capitals.

Adaptation. Those who support this theory consider that a meeting should be brought about between the church as it has evolved historically in the Western context and the African reality. To this end they undertake to adapt the practices of this church as best they can to the sociocultural life of African peoples.

In a word (a word which needs much clarification), one could say that the main defect of this method is "concordism" which consists in confusing the Christian revelation with the thought trends which have served to express it historically. At what depth of religious truth can one make the comparison between Christianity, considered in the absolute as an arrested system of religious truths, and certain African elements isolated from their global context?

Inculturation. Enlightened thinkers see the task of inculturation as a decisive test which calls for a thorough renewal of Christian thought—a decisive break with the political inspiration of the 1960s. The term "new culture" is used by almost all authors. St. Augustine's colossal effort to infuse antique culture with the lymph of the gospel—an effort which paved the way for the later Christian flowering of the Middle Ages—is cited as a model by theologians who hide neither the size of the undertaking nor the difficulty of the task. Msgr. Tshibangu describes this very well:

> Today, the hour has come for the profound incarnation of Christianity in Africa. The preliminary short historical stage although lasting only a few decades, which the present generation has experienced, is of fundamental and capital importance for the specific—and let us hope, definitive—implantation of the Christian Church in Africa. If we should fail in our endeavour, the very future of a deep, far flung and mature Christianity may be compromised for centuries . . . The task which falls to us African Christians—apostles, thinkers, theologians, Church directors—is irreplaceable and indispensable. We are but at the outset of the foundation of the African Church. As an African bishop rightly declared recently, by analogy with the historical situation at the beginning of the Church, we have a real role as founders and builders of the Church of Christ in Africa—a Church yet to be firmly established on both institutional and doctrinal planes.[6]

EVANGELIZATION IN AFRICA: DIRECTIONS FOR RESEARCH AND COMMITMENT

The churches of Africa are increasingly rooted in their cultural and social context. The precise nature of the post-colonial period has brought to light other priorities and employed other methods of evangelization than in the time of the Vatican Council. Three traits characterize African mission theology over the last ten years:

1. the link between the gospel and culture is firmly maintained
2. it is sensitive to the problems of the world and of development
3. it is open to ecumenism and dialogue.

THEOLOGY AND CULTURE

Taking the theandric structure and experience of faith as our cornerstone, we are elaborating in Africa a strongly inductive theology of culture and the "non-Christian religions." A deep conviction is both the cause and the justification for our initiative. Christian religious language appeared and took on meaning at the heart of an already existing religious language, which it assimilated, completed, and transformed. In concrete terms this means that the African religious experience constitutes a privileged link by which Christ may be met and recognized by Africans. In illustration of this principle we would say that the prayer of the African is and continues to be the place where he or she grows spiritually, the place where he or she meets Christ and eventually hears his messages. In it Christ is recognized, for he has already been met through the help of the Holy Spirit in the course of the prayer journey. African prayer is a privileged link, the first step in following Christ, giving a true response to basic human questioning, giving meaning to the fullness of human destiny. African prayer thus remains one of the areas where the development of the Christian faith finds expression as a new undertaking. It is like a theandric drama where God interacts with humankind.[7]

Given this perspective, the fundamental question is not simply, how can we make Christ African? but rather, how can we recognize, confess, and think Jesus Christ present in our history and destiny? This theology has a direct influence on the Christian mission in Africa today. It can no longer start, as formerly, from the abstract universality of Christianity, but from its peculiarity. The abstract concept of Christianity as a universal religion easily leads to imperialism. Christianity considered as one religion beside others obliges us to think of God not as a requisite inscribed in a single tradition, exclusive, intolerant, and conquering, but eschatologically as one discovers God in encounters, in the meeting of cultures in their insurmountable diversities. His face will not be fully unveiled until the last day. "I was a stranger and you welcomed me."

The ever greater awareness that the world itself is one of God's sacraments will certainly widen the perspectives opened by the Second Vatican Council. The world as has been noticed is becoming more and more secularized. Everything suggests that the church will have to act in the world as the leaven in the dough or the city on the mountain top.

Concluding these reflections on the theology of culture, let us recall John Mbiti's observation:

> Christianity has spoken for too long and too much; perhaps it has listened too little. For too long, it has sat in judgement on other cultures, religions and societies while it considered itself to be above criticism. Perhaps the time has now come for Western Christianity to adopt a humbler approach towards other religions and cultures if it wants to succeed here in Africa. In particular, I would ask our brothers and sisters in Europe and America to allow us to make what, in their opinion, may be considered to be errors; allow us to make a muddle of Christianity, just as you did in Europe and

America. . . . When we speak or write on specific subjects treating Christianity or other academic subjects, we must not be expected to employ the vocabulary and style adopted in Europe and in America. Allow us to say certain things our own way, wrong or not. Our main concern here is to hand on, as best we can, the Gospel message which does not change.[8]

THEOLOGY OF HUMAN PROMOTION AND SOLIDARITY

Closely linked to the task of mission, the theology of human promotion and solidarity is of capital importance in the Africa of today. We are firmly convinced that the faith in Africa is not menaced so much by dogmatic beliefs as by the imperatives of action. Will Christians in Africa figure among the most active and effective agents for social promotion in Africa? Will they know how to respond to the cry of the African? J. M. Ela asks himself:

How can one believe in Jesus Christ in a context where the well-off nations refuse to recognize Black peoples as subjects of history? . . . How can we express our "belongingness" to God in a continent which does not belong to itself? Must we allow ourselves to be confined in a religious universe of three dimensions,—sin, the sacraments and grace—at a time when, under the cover of cooperation, business groups openly dispute land, beaches, the bauxite and copper mines, the diamond mines, commerce and tourism, not forgetting the uranium and oil industry and, naturally, the very conscience of the African people? Since economic penetration is always coupled with cultural domination it will become more and more difficult to separate questions of faith in the African milieu from the questions posed by the process of recolonization taking place in African countries. They appear to be a sort of fiscal paradise for the multinationals which demand a degree of stability and security to facilitate the pillage of national resources.[9]

A whole series of burning questions challenges the church of Africa today. The foremost among these are racism, the increasing poverty of the peasant masses, materialism, military coups and the democratic challenge, political and economic instability, corruption, modern African ideologies such as "scientific socialism," "planned liberalism," and "African socialism." We could go on. It is in this context that the church must find an appropriate way to proclaim the gospel and the primacy of Christ the liberator (Col. 1:15–20).

JUSTICE, PEACE, SOLIDARITY

The stakes are clear. The contemporary African masses are very sensitive to the values of justice, peace, and solidarity. Failure to act in support of these will lose evangelization most of its credibility. And this is not all. Action for justice and participation in the transformation of the world are an integral part of evangelization. They are a meeting ground for Christians and non-Christians, a place reserved for dialogue and solidarity, a sign of authentic love for humanity which is at the center of the gospel message.[10]

Such is the task of the church in Africa today. It is not a lesser challenge than that of changing a way of life, of changing the world, and of giving purpose and value to the struggle for justice and peace, linking it to the whole revelation of God's plan of love, the revealed mystery of Jesus Christ. This brings an assurance based on faith in the liberation through the passion and resurrection. As J. M. Ela writes:

> The Church of Africa is called to be vigilant, to have courage. . . . It must leave behind the well used paths of a praxis which holds it in a sort of dogmatic inertia in face of the violence of man, the blind attacks, the mutilations, the structures of inequality and of domination found among the people where the neo-colonial system everywhere deploys its huge tentacles. This they do with the complicity of the bureaucrats in power, while the scandalous prosperity of a small stratum of privileged people leads to the unemployment of so many people, young and adult. . . .
>
> If the Church wants to be part of the present-day history of Africa, it must fully understand that its identity is at stake at all levels of African society. Thousands of young Africans cannot turn their backs on the peasant and working masses from whom they sprang only to be recruited by the well-off set which lives by exploiting the disinherited social strata. The Church must be present to this problem. It is with those deprived of their rights and reduced to silence by the terrorism of the state, with the menaced and the intimidated, that the Church must side. If it is really the crucified body on Golgotha, it must enter into our original situation, beginning with the circumstances and the struggle which led us to revolt against the perpetuation of our people's misery. The meaning of salvation through Jesus Christ is all that matters to us today, to us Africans subjected to sub-human conditions imposed on us by so many convergent factors.[11]

ECUMENICAL THEOLOGY OPEN TO DIALOGUE

Any reflection on the evangelization of Africa must include a conscientious examination of ecumenism and dialogue. We are very aware of the question of Christian unity and the unity of Africa. Is not the unity of the world somehow linked to visible unity among Christians joined in a single faith?

In fact, faith alone is our response to the unique word of God proclaimed in the unique person of Jesus Christ. It is dreadful to think that Africa is condemned by history to know only a divided Christ. Africans have in fact embraced the form of Christianity proposed to them without exact knowledge of the origin of schism in the church. Our ecumenism rejects useless sterile controversies in favor of the serene and humble meaning of Christ's message to our peoples (Rom. 6:16–22). As Catholics and Protestants we are invited to question ourselves and to share what we have understood and discovered in Christ according to our respective confessions. We must work together to proclaim Jesus Christ effectively in the Africa of today and tomorrow. Collaboration already exists in several areas: social progress, religious education, translation of the Bible, and theological research.

The dialogue of the church in Africa equally concerns non-Christians, and needs people qualified in traditional African religions and Islam. African religions, as we have noted, contain great spiritual riches: a unified outlook on life, the significance of family life, a belief in life after death, and so forth. The same goes for Islam in which many elements common to the two religions must be pointed out, principally belief in one God and the understanding of brother- and sisterhood.

CONCLUSION

The fundamental problem, which is facing clergy and theologians alike, would seem to be the building of African churches centered around salvation, rooted in local structures and cultures, fully responsible for the spiritual destiny of their peoples. In view of this problem the question of the formation of pastoral agents and more particularly the training of men and women formators is an urgent priority.

At the close of this survey on evangelization in Africa in the context of modernity, at least two areas seem more particularly to demand our attention as they reveal the difficulties and hopes which the gospel may encounter on the eve of the second millennium:

1) The local church. It is essential that the local church, which is not only part of the universal church but the true embodiment of the whole church of Christ in one place, assumes and fulfills the mission of Jesus Christ, under the direction of the bishops, in communion with the universal church. In order to evangelize, a true local church must first be created and established. We need to consider: what is being done on the spot to create a local church? What types of cooperation exist between the young churches and the other churches? Evangelization in Africa is characterized above all by the problem of religious inculturation. What efforts are being made to train pastoral agents and to set out pastoral methods that are fully inculturated?

2) An African council. The future of Christianity in Africa is of great importance. Many call for a particular council where the clergy and the faithful of the church of Christ in Africa would meet in order to take stock of the actual state of Christianity in Africa, to draw up conditions for its development and its deep implantation.

The challenges are important and delicate. Responding to them requires clearsightedness, discernment, historical commitment, and even heroism.

NOTES

1. Ngindu Mushete, "Les thèmes majeurs de la théologie africaine," in *Bulletin de théologie africaine* 13–14 (1985): 279–92.

2. V. Y. Mudimbe, *Entre les eaux. Dieu, un prêtre, la révolution* (Paris: 1973), 35.

3. "La Déclaration des évêques d'Afrique et de Madagascar: Promouvoir l'é-vangélisation dans la coresponsabilité," in *La documentation catholique* 1664 (1974): 995.

4. H. Maurier, "La mission demain à la lumière d'hier," in *Eglise et mission* 205 (1977): 41.

5. Ibid., 35.

6. Msgr. T. Tshibangu, "Les objectifs et le programme de l'action de l'AOTA," in *Parole de Dieu et langages des hommes. Actes de la rencontre de Yaoundé* (24-28 Sept. 1980), (Kinshasa: 1980): 20–21, 35.

7. Ngindu Mushete, "Rapport général," in *L'Afrique et ses formes de vie spirituelle, 2e colloque international du CERA* (Kinshasa: 1983): 372–73.

8. John Mbiti, "L'inculturation du christianisme comme problème théologique," in Ngindu Mushete (Dir.), *Combats pour un christianisme africain. Mélanges en l'honneur du Prof. V. Mulago* (Kinshasa: 1981): 18.

9. J. M. Ela, "De l'assistance à la libération: Les tâches actuelles de l'église en milieu africain," in *Foi et développement* 83/84 (January 1981), and *Le cri de l'homme africain: Questions aux chrétiens et aux églises d'Afrique* (Paris: 1980).

10. SECAM: "L'Eglise et la promotion humaine en Afrique aujourd'hui (Kinshasa: 1985).

11. J. M. Ela, "De l'assistance à la libération," 7–8.

17

THE IMPACT OF MODERNITY

Reflections of Participants
at the SEDOS Conference

Whether modernity is seen as good or bad, positive or negative, helpful or destructive, actualized or potential, mission takes place, in fact, in the midst of these challenges. The manifestations of modernity describe us to ourselves. We recognize the all-pervasiveness of the phenomenon. Reactions vary. We accept, question, or reject, are disturbed by or fearful of the process. Often we are surprised.

We try to measure the impact of secularization on evangelization, the challenges arising from technology, growth in self-awareness of the individual person, and his or her ability to make choices rather than accept the course of events fatalistically. And we are aware of the immense increase in the availability of information. All these lead to an irreversible growth in pluralism affecting human living.

Inevitably and forcefully this awareness of pluralism leads us to two major considerations:

1. Only in freedom can men and women direct themselves to God;

2. The fundamental root of pluralism is the diverse cultures which are the basic matrix of all human groups.

We question whether these two factors are given the significance they deserve, either in human institutions with their social, political, and economic potential, or in the institutions of our church, not only at the level of the central administration but also in the very institutes of which we ourselves are members.

Evangelization must take into consideration the great diversity of cultures and subcultures even within the same country. There is no faith or religion outside a culture. Even the models of evangelization presented in the context of modernity by the writers of these papers cannot be applied to all situations.

Missionaries called to cross over cultural boundaries are not called to become Indians or Brazilians or Germans or English or whatever. They must be authentic to themselves and in their own cultures but they must be challenged by the gospel and enter sincerely into dialogue with those among whom they live and work. In view of the immense diversity of peoples and the diversity of their cultures, outside which there is no faith or religion, one questions the value of a universal catechism.

If evangelization is to respond to the processes of modernity, new ways are called for of understanding authority and obedience in the church and in our own missionary institutes, new understandings of the processes of decision-making and sharing, of subsidiarity and collegial (team) leadership.

A centralizing, overly directive, largely monocultural, controlling form of leadership will be destructive of creativity and the development of true unity, in our institutes, and in the church.

Formation in general, and formation of formators in particular, emerges with renewed urgency. Evangelization today needs well-centered people, formators/ educators possessed of a spirituality that can cope with the rapidity of change, and who can empower people to be at ease with diversity of cultures and the pluralism of our times.

Formation programs today need to incorporate an experiential aspect. Inductive models of learning become more significant. International mission teams and international collaboration in mission means that more emphasis will have to be placed on experiences of internationality in formation.

Modernity implies the need for a profound examination of missionary vocations, the policies and criteria associated with recruiting, accepting, and training people for mission, and the need to clarify motivations.

Formation and international formation in particular must be affected by challenges of modernity to inculturated evangelization.

In spite of the lip service paid to inculturation, the Greco-Aristotelian-Roman-based model of formation remains the operative and consecrated model in practically all theological institutes, whether in Africa, Asia, the Americas, or Europe. New models do inevitably appear in spite of the lack of encouragement, if not opposition, but their acceptance and recognition will perhaps come about only through the influence of sincere holy people who sponsor them.

An inductive approach is all-important when considering the process called modernity. Will the process evolve in Asia and Africa in the same way that it has in Europe and the Americas? Will it in fact provoke a loss of religious values in Asia? Is it applicable to Asia's countless millions who have still scarcely been touched by it? And does the "Western" process of modernity really apply to the profoundly different African cultures and traditional religions?

Living amidst the challenges of modernity calls for a new spirituality. We need to resonate to the beauty and wonder of the modern world and to recognize that

> It is not how the world is that is mystical,
> but that the world is.

We need a new mysticism, to see that

Earth is crammed with heaven,
And every common bush afire with God.

We need deep faith to open our eyes to the wonder of the world of technology, to see that "every computer is afire with God."

18

MINISTRY IN NEIGHBORHOOD
COMMUNITIES IN LUSAKA

Andrew Edele, MAfr.

The experience of urban ministry in Lusaka which I am going to relate is spread over a little more than fourteen years. Lusaka has about six hundred thousand inhabitants of whom roughly one quarter are Catholics. One in three of the inhabitants live in shanty towns that surround the city. Being the capital city of Zambia it has people not only from all the seventy-two tribes of that country belonging to six main language groups, but also an important number of people from the surrounding countries, mainly Malawi and Zaire, and a small number of Europeans.

I was appointed to a parish in the center of the town where up to 90 percent of the people lived in city council houses of different sizes and qualities according to the income of the tenants. These ranged from unskilled laborers to upper civil servants and included a considerable number of soldiers. At that time the parish had a population of about forty-five to fifty thousand, with about twelve thousand Catholics.

URBAN APOSTOLATE

Urban apostolate was totally new to me at the time. Thus for three years I practiced what my predecessor had introduced me to: family visits whenever time allowed for it. Being the only priest in the parish, it took almost three years before I had visited all the Catholic families and the many others who had invited me into their homes. The work was tedious but not without consolation. A good number resumed their attendance at Sunday services after having been visited, hundreds of marriages were validated, and large numbers of children were brought for baptism. Still, the system proved very unsatisfactory. When I began my second round of visits, I realized that no progress was apparent. What surprised me most was the fact that within those three years about 25 percent of the population had changed, so that I was continually knocking on wrong doors. Many of those who were still in the same houses had to be reminded again of their Sunday duties. However, what really disturbed me was the fact that the majority of the people could not tell me whether their next-door neighbors were Christians. It was mainly this fact that made me look for alternatives.

Although I was the only priest in the parish there was a host of active Christians belonging mainly to two groups—the Legion of Mary and a group called "Aktio." They too were engaged in house visits, although far less systematically than I had been. With their help I hoped to enable the Christians to meet their neighbors so as to overcome the anonymity in which nearly all of them lived. Without going into details, the fact is that after one year of great effort I had to concede defeat. The problem remained but I would persevere in seeking a solution.

A PASTORAL PLAN

Nearly two years later a Sister who had been doing pastoral work in a rural area came to work in the parish. I told her about my experience and together we evolved a pastoral plan which I will try to explain. We began by dividing the parish into geographical areas containing about sixty houses each, on the assumption that about fifteen of them would be occupied by Catholic families. We chose one such area at a time and gave it all the attention it needed. First we visited each family. Knowing that it would take us about ten days to see them all, we chose a date beforehand and invited all of them to meet in one of the houses. In most cases we chose the house of a Legionary or an Aktio member. Generally speaking, 80 percent of those we visited attended the meeting. After a short time for introductions there was an opportunity to discuss what was good and what was bad about being a Christian in the city. Most of them had already experienced village life, so they easily came to the conclusion that it was lack of social pressure from their neighbors that was responsible for their not going to church on Sundays, for not having their marriage blessed, and even for their not avoiding moral misconduct.

It was quite evident during the first meeting that it had done them good to be able to talk about their life as Christians. We had no difficulty in getting them to agree to meet again the following week. During that week we put ourselves at their disposal to discuss personal matters or family problems, and to validate their marriage if that were necessary.

The meetings of the following weeks—we had planned a series of eight meetings—were used for adult catechesis on the central truths of our faith: redemption, conversion, the church, the sacraments, especially baptism and eucharist, and so forth. Although it would be beyond the scope of this report to give you details of this catechesis, I am convinced that it was the determining factor for the success of this pastoral venture. We were able to communicate to the Christians that belonging to the church meant sharing of the faith, community in prayer as well as brotherly and sisterly concern. Our concentrated efforts at renewal for the area culminated in the celebration of the Holy Eucharist in one of the houses as a visible sign that they were now a Christian community with Christ in their midst.

CHOOSING LEADERS

When the now emerging community felt ready to choose their "elder," we encouraged them to do so. In the beginning we helped the one chosen for this task through individual coaching, but as the number of communities increased we were able to call the leaders for monthly training sessions. After those eight weeks of intensive renewal the group was asked to meet on their own at a time and place most convenient to them.

Most communities agreed to meet every two weeks at each of their houses in turn. In order to avoid aimless discussions or being side-tracked by trivialities, we prepared handouts for the "elders" as guidelines for each meeting, leaving, however, enough scope for them to do things at their own pace.

It was not always easy to decide when to start off a new community, or where to start it. Sometimes we managed to start a new one while we were still meeting with the previous one; sometimes the routine parish work made it advisable to take a break. Choosing the right places was also important. We hoped that the areas around the community would hear of it and the whole parish would become more and more open to this new pastoral approach. Thus when after two years in this work I was asked to hand over the parish to a successor and to go elsewhere, about one-quarter of the parish already formed part of these Christian communities.

A NEW PASTORAL SITUATION

The experience of those two years was a great help in my new appointment, where, however, the conditions were quite different. I was assigned to a slum area which, although it had at least ten thousand Catholics at the time of my arrival, was still only an occasionally visited out-station of a town parish. During the year before my appointment the parish had seen a priest only very rarely. My first task was to reassemble the Christians because the most fervent ones had, in the meantime, looked for other parishes in which to worship. It is difficult to describe the pastoral situation of that parish. Those who had managed to receive First Communion before getting married were indeed fortunate. Some adults had been baptized by a busy priest, although they were in irregular marriage situations. I had, however, one big bonus to start work with: everybody was rejoicing at the fact that they finally had "their" priest.

Although the majority of the people lived in near destitution the population was generally more stable because they owned the huts in which they lived. As can be imagined, I did not inherit a *status animarum*, nor even a single sheet of paper, but I did find a kind of "church council." Christians who presided over the Sunday service maintained a couple of lay movements and had even acquired a voluntary catechist who instructed the catechumens. It was with them that I discussed the pastoral priorities, inevitably mentioning my experience in the previous parish.

About two months later a few of them surprised me with the news that they had started neighborhood communities in their areas. I did not want to discourage them, although, given my previous experience, I did not imagine that anything very useful would come of it. In the meantime I was fully engaged in clearing up, somehow, the mess I had inherited, preparing for First Communion, arranging marriages, and so forth.

FORMING THE LAITY

About eight months after my arrival the parish was fortunate to receive a community of three Sisters, each one qualified for pastoral work—catechesis, pastoral theology and social work. They agreed to visit those communities which had sprung up in the parish. After three months we were able to work out a pastoral program which we felt was geared to the priority needs of the parish.

The emphasis was clearly on forming the laity to share in the pastoral and social activities of the parish. For one year each of us had training sessions at two-week intervals in topics that seemed most important: leadership in the neighborhood communities, catechesis, marriage guidance and preparation, and, finally, conducting prayer services and community rites such as initiation ceremonies, burials, and so forth. The formation sessions were designed in such a way that those participating could very soon put into practice what they had learned. Thus, gradually, we hoped to hand over the greater part of our pastoral responsibilities to the hands of the laity and become more and more free to train more people. Every year new training courses were worked out as the needs within the community became more apparent. Even training in social skills was arranged for those who were ready to hand on their knowledge to others within their community.

Three years after the beginning of the work the whole parish area was organized into these neighborhood communities and they had even taken on, although still in varying degrees, care of the sick and care of the poor, newcomers, and visitors. They collected and partly administered the tithe and were consulted about receiving people into the ranks of catechumens, admitting people to baptism, and the marriage of people within their community.

About once every month those with special responsibility within their communities met together at parish level in order to exchange their experience, to ask for advice, and to look for help from other communities if certain skills were lacking within their own.

AN ASSESSMENT

I am aware that all this sounds too good to be true, and so it is necessary to point out that not all was "plain sailing." Especially in the first parish in which I worked, some of the communities died out after having survived for only a few months. Two main reasons were responsible for this.

LEADERSHIP

The work in the community demanded a kind of leadership that was very different from the authoritative models in the already existing lay apostolate groups and catechists. These people lost their influence within a community if they were not able to adapt to the new pastoral program, but they were often still influential enough to divide the community.

In other instances there were not enough people with leadership qualities, or when they did emerge they were transferred before being able to share their leadership with others.

We never forced the people to undertake these community meetings when they were not ready to accept the new concept. However, they usually became convinced of their advantage when they saw that the neighboring area was very active.

This pastoral concept can only be realized if the pastoral team is ready to hand over responsibilities even at a certain risk. It is obvious that people need long and continuous training before becoming competent in their tasks, but giving them responsibility only after they have reached that stage would discourage most of them.

COMMUNITY GROWTH

The second condition for success is to accept the fact that each community progresses at its own pace. Quite a few communities which took a long time getting off the ground were the most lively ones later on. It takes a certain subtleness to adapt oneself to the different circumstances that influence a community. I mention just one significant example. In a few communities it seemed impossible to find a time for the meeting suitable to both men and women. Grudgingly we agreed that men and women would meet at different times. This proved to be a blessing in disguise because usually women kept quiet when their husbands were there. When they were by themselves they spoke up freely and thus developed their own convictions which they were not afraid to verbalize later on even when men were present at certain meetings.

EXTENDED FAMILY

Concluding this account I want to point out a fact that may escape someone who has not lived in a country like Zambia for a long time. I am convinced that this pastoral concept of neighborhood communities, or "small ecclesial communities" as they are often called, succeeded well in a town. There they managed to satisfy a need of which we were not even aware in the beginning, namely, the need for an alternative community to their extended family which they had left behind in the villages. The small ecclesial community created a substitute for their extended family without which they felt insecure.

19

PASTORAL PROBLEMS AND OPPORTUNITIES IN SUPERCITIES

Pierre Delooz

When you arrive by plane in Mexico City on a Mexican airline, you hear a voice saying, "You are welcome to Mexico City, the largest city in the world." Mexico City has over 15 million inhabitants. There are twenty-six hundred more inhabitants each day; by the year A.D. 2000 it will have over 30 million.

In the nineteenth and at the beginning of the twentieth century Western missionaries went out to the four corners of the world to serve people, mainly in rural areas. Only one-tenth of the people in non-Western countries then lived in towns. Today, however, the situation has changed completely. Between now and the end of the century two-thirds of these people will live in cities.

How can the churches make manifest the divine initiative of the gospel in the concrete situation of urban growth? Pope Paul VI responded modestly in a message to a Congress on Urbanization and Pastoral Care: "The situation is so unprecedented that it calls for a new way of being Christian and of proclaiming the Gospel, consequently let us seek together . . ." I cannot be less modest than the Pope. I too have to say, "Let us seek together." But in what direction?

The supercities are a chaotic collection of vast and daily changing problems. All solutions are uncertain, complex, desperate. Can we do more than identify some of the principal problems from a pastoral point of view which presupposes a specifically Christian theological vision of the city? Is there a theology of the city?

THE CITY: PLACE OF LIBERATION?

Can we use a careful, positive, nonmarxist liberation theology to praise the city as the providential locus of a possible human liberation? Following a particular but well-founded reading of the Bible, must we condemn the monstrous supercity as a place of human arrogance? Peter and Paul in the Rome of their day chose to proclaim salvation, making no attempt to solve the overcrowding, the educational, housing, and public health problems. They did not concern themselves with urbanization; they spoke of Jesus and of Jesus dead and risen. Is it perhaps too late for choice? And the situations are so different! In developed countries the old supercities such as London or New York are declining. There the churches remain major institutions but are compartmentalized, each caring for its own declining membership in a context of general de-Christianization.

In the supercities of developing countries the role of the church varies considerably. Emerging supercities such as Mexico City, Manila, or São Paulo are, in principle, Christian cities where the Catholic church is present with bishops, priests, religious, lay people, basic communities, and parishes. The church plays a role of social integration there.

In other developing countries emerging supercities like Cairo, Bombay, and Jakarta are not at all Christian. The churches there are only tiny minorities, unable to play a role of social integration, unable to influence the urban problems.

What kind of pastoral care and pastoral theology could be common to such different situations? None at all! That could be our first modest conclusion: no general pastoral guide can be adapted to fit all these different situations. Each Christian community has to start from the beginning, interpreting the signs of its own time, being responsible for its own answers, knowing that it is not building the celestial Jerusalem on earth. God alone will build that one day.

This negative conclusion can be extremely useful if it provides us with peace, a spirit of initiative, a sense of humor, and if it leads to a variety of pastoral programs emerging from dialogue between the needs of the people in the urban area and the talents of pastoral team members.

RELIGIONS IN THE SUPERCITIES

It may be necessary to pursue our reflection in another direction. In most of the Christian centers affected by growing urbanization it seems that secularism, indifference, and indifferentism erode the Christian life and even the religious capacities of many migrants—Britons in Paris, Irish in London, Italians in New York. Christians in the supercities seem to follow this pattern. It is not so in the Hindu and Muslim centers. The urban lifestyle, it seems, is not on the fringe of their systems. For Islam it is the system.

MUSLIMS AND HINDUS

Cities often possess a special sanctity for Muslims and are regarded as the only places in which a full and truly Muslim life may be lived. It is as if Islam's religious goals and rituals were more easily achieved in an urban context. Why does the Muslim not suffer the same culture shock as the Christian in moving from town to city or from a rural to an urban area? The usual urban problems—overpopulation, housing, education, unemployment, family planning, health, transportation, and so forth—remain problems also in Muslim supercities such as Cairo, Baghdad, Damascus, Teheran, Karachi, or Dacca. Their growth is also parasitic and creates severe problems for the poor, but the problems seem more manageable in the framework of the Islamic faith.

What does this mean for us? Does Christianity really make people more vulnerable in the supercities? In India, the Harvard-Bhubaneswar Project carried out a study for twelve years, between 1961 and 1973, on the transformation of the capital of the state of Orissa, an old sacred town, into a modern city. The situation seems an ideal context for studying our question. The results are clear. "Religion is neither disintegrating nor secularizing . . . New expressions of religion have developed that creatively utilize traditional elements."[1]

Have we something to learn from the Islamic experience of the supercities? Is it perhaps possible, or at least not entirely utopic, in Islamic countries, to have experiential Christian communities unafraid to affirm the validity of their Muslim cultural roots and yet, at the same time, unafraid to affirm Jesus as the final prophet of God in the midst of the megalopolis?[2] Can the same be relatively true for Hinduism? It is extremely difficult to answer these questions.

THE CRITERION OF EFFICIENCY

Almost no Christian scholarship exists that has even begun to study the Muslim and the Hindu city as a field of experience for us. The explanation for this, if it is accepted as true, might be that "Western" Christianity is largely the prisoner of its own cultural and historical heritage and has not really been free to incarnate itself in alien soil. Efficiency is one of its main hallmarks everywhere and tends to be the touchstone for judging church organizations, expressions of faith, relation to politics, and so forth. How does the criterion of efficiency apply to the large urban sprawls, the Latin American *favellae*, the peripheries of a Calcutta or a São Paulo? How can people be contacted? How do they relate to one another within their Christian heritage or with their neighbors, Islamic, Hindu, Afro-Brazilian, or other?

RELIGION AND CULTURE

The relationship between religion and culture is fundamental in attempting any initiative. "Hinduism" was found where ten Hindus were together, while a similar group of Christians necessitated sacraments, a relationship with priesthood, observances, and structures. What is the essence of being a Christian in the supercity?

Islam exercises considerable social pressures while Christianity emphasizes individual values and rights. Perhaps this emphasis needs to be reassessed today as the communal values of other cultures are recognized, for example in various African societies. While avoiding generalizations it would still appear that Islamic social pressures, regarded critically or even negatively by Christians, seem to have preserved Islam against enormous political pressures in the Soviet Union or Turkey.

We need to avoid presuppositions about the definition of church in the context of the supercity. The aspects of organization and power seem to be overemphasized.

There are few if any precedents. Each Christian community in these new situations has to start from scratch. There appears to be no pastoral theology or pastoral care common to the different situations. Thus the importance and significance of grass-roots groups and basic Christian communities is one possible way in which to go.

PLAUSIBLE ANSWERS

I would express a personal conclusion after a careful study of the problems of pastoral programs for the supercities: the plausible answers given by the churches confronting the problems of the supercities are at one and the same time so general but so different, even contradictory. I cite some examples to show that many contradictory propositions are put forward. Are they equally true?

— the number of parishes should be increased
— the parishes are outdated and should be replaced by basic communities
— pastoral care has to be centralized
— pastoral care has to be decentralized
— schools and hospitals are desperately needed
— schools and hospitals are obstacles to true evangelical mission
— the churches should avoid political implications
— the poor are totally alienated by political oppression and the churches have to be politically involved
— the most needed services in supercities are family ones, including birth control assistance; churches have to be involved in population problems, family planning and so forth
— population growth is not a matter that concerns the church directly . . .

Perhaps the churches do not see the true questions because they are too deeply implicated in the Western way of thinking—in terms of efficiency. They value efficiency in the human vocation, believing that the Christian vocation duplicates the human vocation in the religious field.

The rapid growth of the cities is changing the world daily in such a way that we experience the limits of "Western" efficiency. Is it perhaps a providential invitation to us to become aware of the fact that a new measure of our vocation as human beings is necessary, and also a new understanding of our Christian vocation?

Exploding supercities call us to perspicacity and to magnanimity, but also to humanity and to readiness to listen to new designs of God. We are enabled to perceive these new designs only after much intelligent and courageous effort, and only when we come to see ourselves, without losing heart, as "unprofitable servants."

NOTES

1. See Seymour, ed., *The Transformation of a Sacred Town* (Westview Press, Bhubaneswar and Boulder: 1980).

2. See the Westminster Theological Seminary Urban Mission Programme (September 1984).

PART TWO

MODELS OF MISSION
AND MINISTRY

20

THE DEVELOPMENT OF MINISTRIES IN THEIR HISTORICAL CONTEXTS

Robert Schreiter, CPPS

INTRODUCTION

The new ministries now arising in many Christian communities, as well as the redefinition of the tasks of ministry in other situations, have led to our looking again at the history of Christian ministry. We do not do this out of some antiquarian interest; rather, this need arises out of our hope that some guidance might be found in shaping the practice and theology of ministry in local church settings today. Christians have always believed that ministry is shaped by more than pragmatic or sociological circumstances, although, to be sure, these play a significant role. Christians believe that ministry is a gift from God in the Spirit. To fail to grasp the interplay between the work of God in the Spirit and our historical circumstances is to end up with something less than Christian ministry.

The purpose of this presentation is not to sketch out a full history of ministry in the Christian church. That is too vast an undertaking for our purpose here. There have been a number of recent attempts to reconstruct significant parts of that history—that is, significant for the kinds of questions which are now before us.[1] Some of these reconstructions have been controversial, either because of how they organize the scarce data we have or because they challenge some of our received notions of what our history has been. Some recent historical research has also turned up things in our history of which we were previously unaware, things that can have an impact on how we respond to the challenges before us today.

History is never just a recounting of facts; it is always also an interpretation of the past from the present. Some of the debate about how we are reading our history has to do with what kinds of lenses we use to focus upon our past. As will be seen, the data we have often allow for a variety of interpretations. These need to be sorted out as much as the data themselves.

This presentation focuses upon recent research into the history of ministry. More particularly, it looks at recent interpretations of that history with three questions in mind:

1. Where is the consensus of scholarship around controverted or controversial points in the history of ministry which are of importance for us today?

2. Which historical developments shape our contemporary understanding of the theology and practice of ministry in a special way?

3. What other points do we need to be aware of as potential resources in our history for a theology of ministry today?

Much of what follows presents the results of that historical research, not the argumentation which has led to it. It is in the nature of a map through the maze of work now going on in the study of the history of ministry. It moves by fits and starts, but it is hoped that in doing so it will help highlight some important points for our discussion. The presentation looks at four parts of our history:

1. Jesus and the New Testament
2. the second to the fourth centuries
3. issues in the medieval period
4. other factors shaping our contemporary understanding.

Because the presentation is somewhat topical in shape, rather than entirely chronological, there will be some moving back and forth between these periods.

JESUS AND THE NEW TESTAMENT

A renewed reading of the New Testament, plus recent research into the social world of early Christianity, lead us to look at some of the New Testament history in a different way. Among the questions this recent research addresses are the following:

WHOM DID JESUS CHARGE WITH THE CARE OF THE CHURCH?

Catholics have traditionally answered this question by saying that the care of the church was entrusted to the twelve apostles, under the leadership of Peter. There is a body of Catholic exegesis which continues to reflect this answer.[2] This approach contains part of the historical truth that we have been able to reconstruct, but does not adequately reflect the entire picture. The gospel points to three groups closely associated with Jesus and the early Christian movement, all of whom were involved in ministry: the Twelve, the apostles, and the disciples. These groups overlap in the New Testament writings, and so sorting out the differences is difficult and perhaps ultimately impossible.

The Twelve. There is a fair consensus among the contemporary exegetes that the institution of the Twelve does go back to the lifetime of Jesus. The Twelve were probably instituted as a prophetic act of Jesus; that is, as a symbol of the restored Israel with its twelve tribes. After the resurrection of Jesus, the ancient account in 1 Corinthians 15 says that the Lord appeared to them. They seem initially to have been leaders of the main community in Jerusalem. The extent of their authority in this community and other communities is uncertain. When Paul finally visits Jerusalem in A.D. 35–37, he does not mention the Twelve, only Peter and James (Gal. 1:18–19). Their significance for the Jerusalem community seems to have faded by the 40s, with James taking on the leadership. The notion of the Twelve is then revived especially by Luke, in that period in the latter part of the first century, when concern for maintaining pure teaching became a principal concern of the Christian movement.

"**Apostles**" is a larger category, and its precise meaning is uncertain. On the one hand, it was used to refer to those who had walked with Jesus of Nazareth and experienced him after his resurrection with a commission to continue his work. On the other, it referred to those who never knew the earthly Jesus (such as Paul), but who had come under the influence of the Spirit, and went out to preach and found communities. The Gospel of Luke uses "apostle" in a restricted sense, referring only to the Twelve. For Luke, a criterion of apostleship is having been with Jesus since the beginning (Acts 1:21–22). However, other parts of the New Testament clearly have a broader use in mind. It would seem that both men and women were designated as apostles. The clearest example in the New Testament is Romans 16, where Julia is referred to as an apostle by Paul and as one who had been an apostle already before him (Rom. 16:7). The commissioning of the apostles, as Paul points out in his own defense, seems to have come directly from the risen Lord, not via the Twelve. Apostles would exercise authority within the churches where they lived, or in churches they founded. That authority was sometimes shared with "prophets" – that is, those who would speak on behalf of God under the influence of the Spirit.

"**Disciples**" constitute an even more vague category. The Gospel of John uses it as a comprehensive category, and avoids the term "apostle" altogether. His writings are also more suggestive of leadership of early communities: the role of the Samaritan woman in founding the Jesus community there, the role of the Bethany community, the distinctive place of Magdalene in the Jerusalem community (or perhaps in a community separate from the one led by the Twelve). Women play a distinctive and decisive role among the disciples.[3]

Which of these three groups did Jesus commission with the charge of his church? There are various commissionings recorded in the gospels: of the disciples to go out and preach, at the Last Supper, and in post-resurrection appearances. To take here only the Last Supper stories: Mark and Matthew recount that the Twelve were present; Luke says the apostles (by whom he probably means the Twelve); but John says the disciples. Does John mean the Twelve only when he speaks of the disciples in the supper stories? We cannot say with any certainty. This and other situations in the New Testament texts have led contemporary exegetes to say that Jesus does not seem to have left any single individual, or group of individuals, in charge of the movement which became the church. There is clearly too much diversity in first century Christianity which speaks against such a possibility. By the end of the century, more uniform order is starting to emerge or to be imposed, particularly against gnostic teachers.

The Pastoral Letters reflect that. But that has to be seen as a later insight or development, some fifty years after the death of Jesus.

HOW WAS MINISTRY ORDERED IN THE FIRST CENTURY?

While there was great diversity in the ordering of ministry in the first-century church, that does not mean that there was utter confusion. The safest thing to say is that there was indeed some form of order in each community, even though there was not any clear pattern of organizing the ministry between churches (at least in the first decades of the Christian movement). Many of the first-century communities patterned their leadership on that of the synagogue. This leadership was often a collective one, of those who "presided" or served as "elders." The mode of the Seven in the Hellenistic community at Jerusalem recounted in Acts would be an example of this model.

In other instances, particularly outside Palestine but also within it, whoever's house served as the meeting place for Christians became the leader of the local community. This person, as host or hostess, presided at gatherings of the Christians. The case of Phoebe at Cenchrae, or Prisca and Aquila in Romans 16, would be an example of this, or the case of the "noble lady" called the elder (presbyter) of the church in 2 John 1:1. Often these first two models were combined. There is evidence that some Hellenistic synagogues were ruled by a body of elders, among whom someone might be called "father" or "mother" as the first among the elders.[4] Often those so designated provided either the space or the financial foundations that made the gathering possible.

Another pattern followed one that was found among social groups in general in the Eastern Mediterranean, especially in Asia Minor. Groups gathered into associations or clubs often called, for that reason, *ekklesiai*. These associations would gather for companionship, recreation, and especially festive meals.[5] In view of the central Christian ritual of the eucharist, this model of organization seems to have been used in Antioch and Asia Minor. The one in charge of the association was sometimes called the *episkopos*, often a wealthy patron who provided for the meal.

Romans, 1 Corinthians, and Ephesians give us lists of ministries.[6] Two are from Paul, and the third from disciples of Paul. None mentions *episkopos*. The lists are no doubt illustrative rather than exhaustive. *Diakonos* is used either of specific ministry, or of ministerial service or leadership in general. It seems that a *diakonos* could be either male or female. Thus Phoebe is called the *diakonos* of the church at Cenchrae by Paul in Romans 16:1, indicating, it would seem, the role of leadership of the community.

To answer the question, then: there was no single pattern for ordering the ministry in the first-century church, although, by the end of the century (when the Pastorals were written), more standard forms or uniformity were beginning to appear. Organization was borrowed from other models available in the environment, especially that of the synagogue, the larger household, and the club or association. Nor did the same vocabulary (*diakonos, episkopos*) mean the same thing everywhere. Our concerns for uniformity were not those of first-century Christians.

HOW WERE MINISTERIAL RESPONSIBILITIES PASSED ON TO THE NEXT GENERATION?

An egalitarian spirit marked many of the first-century communities, witnessed in Galatians 3:28, which may have been a baptismal acclamation. Indeed, it was this egalitarian spirit, evoking the memory of Jesus' invitation of all into the Reign of God, and now experienced in the seemingly indiscriminate outpouring of the gifts of the Spirit on believers, that attracted many Hellenistic Jews and Gentiles into the Christian movement. Thus the early Christian movement was made up of people from all classes, and seems to have had a disproportionate number of people whose upward social mobility was halted because of societal circumstances (for example, aliens not eligible for Roman citizenship, women, wealthy slaves).

The problem with any movement strong in egalitarianism is the discernment of leadership. The spontaneous bestowal of gifts of the Spirit, and the resources of a large house or financial backing for the festive gatherings, seemed to be prominent factors in determining leadership, along with the direct commissionings from the Lord. More often than not, the problem was probably too many people in leadership rather than not enough.

The problem of discerning true from false leadership, that is, of discerning between those endowed with the Spirit of God and those endowed with other spirits, was clearly a problem. The silencing of women in 1 Timothy 2:11f. was probably directed at certain women teaching what was considered heterodox doctrine, probably of some gnostic sort.

But how was leadership passed on to the next generation, especially when the gifts of the Spirit were less in evidence? The most obvious way was a direct commissioning from the leadership of the local community of the previous generation. A second way was the emergence of someone or some persons endowed with the gifts of the Spirit similar to those in the first generation. The practice of the laying on of hands was borrowed from rabbinic tradition, where the laying on of hands symbolized the transmittal of wisdom from teacher to disciple. This ritual came to be used widely in first-century Christianity, certainly for the transmitting of the responsibility to teach or preach. Exegetes and historians of early Christianity see it used in either of two ways: either as the passing on of a commission, or as a way of a community affirming its recognition of the power of the Spirit in that individual.

THE SECOND TO THE FOURTH CENTURIES

The second to the fourth centuries were times of the consolidation of forms of ministry. It was not until the end of that period that uniformity throughout Christianity was evident. A number of things from this period are important for our consideration here.

The Emergence of the Monoepiscopate. Ignatius of Antioch is a strong witness to the emergence of one person leading the community in the early second century. It was still not uniform throughout Christianity at this time, however;

when Ignatius addresses the church at Rome, he singles out no individual. It would seem that Rome at this time was still under the leadership of a group of elders (*presbyteroi*). One of the sociological factors which led to the monoepiscopate (that is, only one *episkopos* in each city or community) was probably the more widespread acceptance of Christianity. The one *episkopos* in a church paralleled the role of the *episkopos* as overseer or inspector in civil government. This was firmly established when Christianity took over the Roman civil forms for its organization a little later on.

Apostolic Succession. The idea of an unbroken succession has its roots in philosophical schools of the period. If one could establish the succession of one's teachers, one had a guarantee of the quality of what one taught. The later writings of the New Testament, and other writings of the turn of the century (1 Clement, the Shepherd of Hermas), point to the problem of teaching in the early Christian communities. The genealogy of teachers became a way of assuring sound doctrine. Lists would be drawn up similar to those found in the philosophical schools, showing how the teaching in a given community went back to the *apostoloi*, those who had been commissioned to preach by the Lord himself.

The Reduction of the Number and Kinds of Ministries. As the church became more established after several generations, and its social acceptance led to increase in membership, leadership became more of an issue. From the second century onward there was a concern for safeguarding the kerygma which led to attempts to establish a canon of writings and a clearer regulation of who would do the teaching. In this period we see attempts, as in Irenaeus, to establish a norm or rule of faith for these purposes.

Ministry became more focused in a limited number of offices. *Diakonos* became more restricted in meaning, referring especially to the administrative assistants of the *episkopos*. We see church orders of a body of *presbyteroi-diakonoi* or *episkopoi-diakonoi* or a combination of the three in larger cities. The other ministerial functions mentioned in the New Testament writings get absorbed into these three. Subsequent history in the Western church shows a continued focusing of ministry until the time of the Second Vatican Council when the distinctiveness of separate ministries is again recognized.[7]

WHO MAY LEAD THE EUCHARIST?

The first-century church does not give a clear answer on this. It seems that whoever was the acknowledged leader of a community, or whoever's house was the locus of the celebration, presided on behalf of the community. Leading the eucharist was not seen as a separate ministry; it fell to whoever led the community in other things. This says two things to us: the eucharist was seen as an act of the entire community; not just anyone could take it upon him- or herself to lead the eucharist. Because it was not a specialized ministry, the thought of a community not being able to celebrate the eucharist would have been unthinkable.

As ministries became more focused in the second and ensuing centuries, so did the celebration of the eucharist. The prophet no longer led the celebration; it fell rather to the *episkopos* or the *presbyteroi*, or these together. However, it seems that in emergency situations, other possibilities were still present at least as late as the fourth century. The Council of Arles in A.D. 314 (canon 5) forbids the celebration of the eucharist by deacons, which had been going on in many places. It is speculated that this practice had been tolerated or permitted by bishops, especially during the Diocletian persecutions, when many presbyters had been arrested or executed, leaving the communities to be cared for by deacons. The purpose of the canon at Arles was probably to stop this practice now that the emergency situation had passed.[8]

The Emergence of the Priest. The New Testament writings scrupulously avoid designating ministers in the communities as *hiereis* or priests. It has been suggested that this was to distinguish Christian from Jewish cult, but after A.D. 72 this would not have been an issue. More likely it was a way of distinguishing Christian cult from mystery cults. However, in the period under discussion it comes to be a common appellation for the one who leads the community. The full reason for this change is hard to discern. Seeing Christianity as the fulfillment of the Hebrew Scriptures in every detail led to comparisons between Jewish and Christian leadership patterns. And the growing custom of paying the church leaders for their services evoked memories of the Levitic priesthood.

It has even been suggested that the title *hiereus* was taken over precisely to show that Christianity was the equal, and not the inferior, of other cults. To call one's leader "priest" sounded better than to call such a leader "inspector" (*episkopos*). Whatever the reason, the introduction of the title brought with it connotations from its other usages. It started to weaken the bond between the leader and the community which provided legitimation for the leader's tasks, and it also started to separate the leader's competence or license to lead from a clear sense of a gift of the Spirit. Both of these bonds, with the community and with the Spirit, were never broken. Canon 6 of the Council of Chalcedon in A.D. 451 condemned absolute ordination, that is, ordination without reference to a community. And Cyprian of Carthage's affirmation of the dignity of the priest even when signs of behavior did not indicate the presence of the Spirit became an important grounding for a theology of the priesthood in the Donatist controversy. But the scene was set for talking about ministers and ministry in isolation from a concrete community.[9]

THE MEDIEVAL PERIOD

A number of things developed in the eighth to the sixteenth centuries which affect our contemporary discussion of ministry. Among them:

A SHIFT IN THE UNDERSTANDING OF THE EUCHARIST

Three factors have intertwined to shape an understanding of the eucharist in the West, factors still strong today:

The first of these had to do with the priest. Connotations of priesthood easily led to seeing priestly ritual activity as sacrifice. In the Christian community, this meant that the eucharist came to be seen as a renewal of that great priestly sacrifice spoken of in Hebrews. Thus the action of the eucharist came to be understood more and more as the action of the priest and less and less as the action of thanksgiving of the community under the leadership of the priest.

A second factor was the shift away from the emphasis on the action of the eucharist to a focus almost entirely on the eucharistic elements of bread and wine. This was prompted partially by the role of relics in Christianity from the sixth century onward, the eucharist becoming the relic par excellence. Controversies about the eucharist led to an ever greater focus on the elements as the physical presence of Jesus Christ. The consecration of these elements becomes more and more the focus of the eucharistic celebration, enhancing the role of the priest.

A third factor was the role of the people. As Latin became less the common language, the language of the eucharistic ritual took on more a sense of mystery. The action of the priest took on a correspondingly greater sense of awe, creating an ever greater distance between priest and people.

While all three of these factors have been recognized and to some extent corrected by the liturgical reform since the Second Vatican Council, they continue to inform understanding of the eucharist, the priest, and of ministry in general.[10]

THE PRIVATE AND THE DAILY MASS

The factors mentioned in the previous section led to a more individualistic sense of the eucharist, and a focusing upon the priest as the consecrator of the eucharistic elements. Increasingly, this meant less emphasis on the leadership of the community in eucharistic thanksgiving and prayer, and more emphasis on the power of the priest as renewing Christ's sacrifice in the eucharist. It became possible to consider celebrating the eucharist with no congregation at all. The power of the priest and the efficacy of the renewal of Christ's sacrifice meant that the eucharist could be offered for specific "intentions," for the dead or for some other boon. This led to a proliferation of the number of Masses. This same emphasis on efficacy also led to the practice of daily Mass in monasteries and then in other churches throughout the West, a practice which has never been followed in the East.

What this has meant for ministry is that not only has ministry been focused more and more in a single person, but that this person's prime ministry is the celebration of the eucharist. This makes it hard to establish any other ministries alongside this one, or to consider other ministries of equal status.

A SHIFT IN SACRAMENTAL THEOLOGY

All of these factors had their impact on how the priest as minister came to be understood in the Middle Ages. The gift of God which makes leadership of the community possible is seen less as a gift of the Spirit or the Spirit of the Lord, and more as participation in the activity of Christ. In other words, ministry comes to lose its pneumatological character (a gift of the Spirit on behalf or for the sake of the community), and becomes more a replication of the person of Christ himself. The priest sacrifices by participating in the one sacrifice of Christ. This christological understanding of the priest comes to be mirrored in medieval sacramental theology[11] and makes the priestly character one of an *alter Christus*, with all the sacrality which that implies. The priest then becomes the mediator between the people and God, rather than the leader of a community before God. Any dimunition of priesthood becomes a dimunition of Christ's presence in the church. A highly sacral image of the priest results, and a spirituality is developed which centers upon the person of the priest rather than the gifts of leadership of a community. This spirituality also means that it becomes harder to share out those focused functions of ministry to others or to reshape them into separate ministries.

THE REFORMATION

The sixteenth-century Reformation, in the persons of Luther and Calvin, tried to bring about a restructuring of ministry which would both reflect the New Testament reality more faithfully and meet the needs of the world then emerging. Luther re-emphasized the priesthood of all believers, grounding ministry in baptism rather than in the sacrament of holy orders. The threat of the radical Reformation, however, led Luther back to an emphasis on the ordering of this baptismal charism by the community. Calvin also tried to "desacerdotalize" the ministry by returning to some of the New Testament ministries. But despite three- or fourfold orderings still found in Reformed churches today, the role of pastor still predominates in the minds of most people.[12]

The sixteenth-century Reformation experience speaks to the twentieth-century experience in a number of ways:
- a de-emphasis on some order for leadership can leave a community open to manipulation by powerful, charismatic individuals
- a genuinely shared ministry between a number of equals, each exercising different ministries, is difficult to establish and to maintain
- to see Christian action in the various walks of life as ministry (as Calvin suggested) may so dilute the sense of ministry that the community becomes actually impoverished rather than enriched.

OUR CONTEMPORARY UNDERSTANDING

A number of historical factors have been mentioned in the course of this presentation which have contributed to our contemporary understanding of ministry. We have seen that the beginnings of the Christian movement are now most often read through the lenses of the end of the first century, when a greater ordering of the church was needed. We saw models of priesthood from the Jewish tradition and a Hellenistic environment help shape our notion of community leadership. We saw how eucharistic piety played a major role in defining the relationship of the leader to the community. Not only the past shapes our current sense of ministry; factors in our own environment play a role too. I would like to note three such factors which are operative in some of the cultures where the church is present.

TO WHAT EXTENT DOES THE EXPERIENCE OF RELIGIOUS COMMUNITY LIFE SHAPE OUR UNDERSTANDING OF MINISTRY?

Through long periods of history, religious orders and institutes have been special repositories of Christianity's egalitarian ethos. They have structured their leadership according to their perceived needs, from powerful Celtic abbots to highly egalitarian models in contemporary religious life. If we look at the contemporary situation—the fact that we elect our leaders from our own midst for a term of appointment; that it is the Chapter or some similar body which constitutes the highest authority; that we have tried to reduce internal differences of status (say, between priests and brothers in male communities)—how do we experience ministry within such a context? Does not ministerial leadership become something growing out of the community, for the period that it is needed, and more accountable to the community and its needs? When this model is placed alongside models of a more hierarchical ordering, can we see how our own situation is influencing our understanding of what ministry ought to be?

WHAT EFFECT DO THINGS LIKE PROFESSIONALISM OR PROFESSION HAVE ON OUR SENSE OF MINISTRY AND THE MINISTER?

Does part of our sense of a need for a plurality of ministries grow out of the sense of professionalism common among communities primarily situated in the North Atlantic community? In other words, a sense of division of labor, of competence, and of accountability. The idea of professionalism in its nineteenth- and twentieth-century forms derives from medicine and law particularly, when attempts were made to standardize the licensing procedures. That such professionalism is most successful only in certain kinds of societies (technologized and urbanized ones, mainly) has been clear in many parts of the Third World. Part of it, too, grows from the experience of many women in ministry being far more capable than their ordained male counterparts to perform effectively in certain areas of ministry. How does professionalism interact with our sense of the charism of ministry?

WHAT IS THE RELATIONSHIP BETWEEN FORMS OF MINISTERIAL ACTIVITY AND MODELS OF LEADERSHIP IN A CULTURE?

There are two aspects to this question. On one hand, to be prescriptive of what forms ministry ought to take, based upon the models of leadership in the dominant cultures of our institutes, may simply be a shifting of hegemonies. In cultures where leadership, and especially spiritual leadership, is based upon age, our democratic models may be so countercultural as not to be understood at all. While pleading for a greater sensitivity to modern Western patterns, one cannot forget other cultures as well.

Secondly, we come back to a question implicit in this whole presentation. What is the dogmatic value of those points in our history to which I have pointed here? How is one to discern revelation within these historical situations? Is it simply a matter of choosing what is most convenient?

My intention here is certainly not to denigrate the history of ministry as it has developed. One cannot simply sweep this history aside as though two thousand years of history have no significance for us today. That history has to be taken as seriously, if not more seriously, than those elements I have mentioned here. But the situation in which we now find ourselves is one where the models given us in our most recent tradition are not working, and so we have a responsibility to reflect on the entirety of our tradition.

One cannot jump back to the first century and canonize that as the only way to go, or as the pure revelation prior to contamination. To engage in such positivistic approaches to revelation and tradition is a little simpleminded; it is like saying that the acorn is in every instance superior to the oak tree. Calvin and the Reformed tradition have tried to do this with their concepts of "the New Testament church." But there is a plurality of churches in the New Testament, and our choice of a model will probably say more about our own times than the first century. So what are we to do?

REAPPROACHING HISTORICAL MATERIALS

To go into all the hermeneutics of reapproaching historical materials is too complicated for our purposes here. But let me suggest at least one key which might be of use: some of the hermeneutics of the Second Vatican Council, especially *Sacrosanctum Concilium* and subsequent documents on the reform of the liturgy. Both that Constitution and subsequent documents, building upon historical research, saw fit to find their models for reform of the liturgy in patristic models of worship. That is, they reached back beyond the medieval patterns which shaped our liturgical experience up to the middle of this century. There were many reasons for this—historical, dogmatic, ecumenical, and cultural. But it seems to me that the historical reasons (growing out of a vision of the history of liturgy), the dogmatic reasons (the authority of the patristic period's theology for subsequent theology), and the ecumenical reasons (the liturgy of the undivided church) had to come together with the cultural. In other words, those factors had to come together in a model which more adequately represented patterns of experience and leadership within Western, secularized culture.

Could not a similar interpretive key be used in ministry, bringing together historical, dogmatic, and ecumenical concerns within a meaningful cultural pattern? That might provide a way of respecting the present, the immediate past, and the origins of the Christian movement.

TOWARDS THE FUTURE

QUESTIONS BEING RAISED

A major question already upon us is: how are experiences of new ministries changing our definition of ministry? And how does what we are calling ministry relate to a more general sense of service or Christian witness? How does service come to be acknowledged as a special work of the Spirit for the community and come to be affirmed and supported by communities as a ministry of the church? We see a need for careful theological reflection on this question, guided by experience of these ministries and by a faithful listening to previous experience given us in scripture and the traditions of our church.

A second major question is how these new ministries will relate to other ministries already in the universal church. In light of this, some ministries are now seen to be renewed ministries rather than totally new ones.

Nonetheless, this major question brings with it a series of other questions for which we seek answers in light of this new vision of the church, yet one faithful to the best of our tradition. Among those questions are:

1) What impact are new ministries having on our understanding of the role of ordained ministry in the church? Historically, an earlier diversity of ministry has come to be consolidated in the ministry of the ordained priest. Now some of those ministries are coming to others. What will this mean?

2) What does this new diversity of ministries mean for what has been the sacramental commissioning for ministry—ordination? How do we arrive at discerning what the Spirit is doing in communities, and how do we come to affirm and commission or ordain persons in these new ministries?

3) The diversity of new ministries affects not only the sacrament of orders. It is already having an impact on other parts of the traditional sevenfold division of the sacraments. In ministries of healing and spiritual direction, the results of those ministries lead naturally into rites of reconciliation. Can we rethink who might be the appropriate minister of the sacrament of reconciliation in those circumstances? The renewed awareness of the relatedness of ministry to community reminds us of the close connection between leadership of the community and leadership of the eucharist in earlier periods in the church. Might the ministry of this sacrament also be rethought?

4) Ministry in sacrament recalls to us the Second Vatican Council's reaffirmation of the priesthood of the People of God, the priesthood of all the baptized. These new situations are making us think more about what might be the true and full meaning of this priesthood, and how it will affect the priesthood of those now ordained.

5) We also need to clarify more for ourselves what we mean by "the community" when we say that ministry is connected so closely with a community. Does this mean the basic Christian community, the parish, the diocese, or even the missionary society in some cases? And what is the relation of the community's affirmation of new ministries to their acceptance and affirmation between local churches and the universal church?

6) How are we to understand the charisms or gifts of the Spirit that give rise to ministry, and their ordering and institutionalization in the church? What kind of process guides this ordering, and who are to be the ones guiding the process?

7) This new vision of church and ministry is not one universally shared. It operates alongside another vision of the church which emphasizes the ministry of the central leadership of the universal church as directly and clearly guiding local churches. This other vision of the church wants to enhance the role of the ordained priest and to maintain a clear distinction between this ministry and other, subordinate ministries. Even when encouraging a diversity of ministries in the church, its chief concern is their hierarchical ordering, even in the local community. It also excludes certain persons, especially women, on the basis of status in life rather than call of the Spirit. Both of these visions are found in *Lumen Gentium*. How shall these two visions of the church relate to one another, and what shall be the future of new ministries as a result of that relation?

8) The visions of ministry in these two models of church are distinguished further by different understandings of the work of Christ in his church. The newer vision emphasizes Christ's work in the Spirit, guiding the church, and calling forth the ministries needed for the building up of the church and for the mission of the church in the world. This vision is reminiscent of one found in the earliest part of the church's history, and never completely lost. The other, more hierarchical vision sees Christ's work especially through the bishop and priest, who stand in the place of Christ in the leading of the community. Thus to diminish in any way the role of priest or bishop is to diminish the role of Christ. How shall these visions be seen in a balance that supports and protects what is happening in ministry in the church?

UNRESOLVED TENSIONS REGARDING NEW MINISTRIES

These last questions point to profound tensions, not only between those who hold to differing models of the church, but also among all concerned for the wellbeing and authentic witness of the church to its Lord. These tensions have not been resolved, and at this time show no ways of easy resolution. Among the most troubling of these tensions we see:

1) How shall we maintain the unity so important to Catholic Christianity, and yet acknowledge and even affirm the pluralism of the current situation? The resolution of the tensions caused by the interplay between unity and plurality will require great patience on the part of all involved in this discernment. This is especially important, given the fluidity of the current situation in ministry.

2) How will effective coordination between local churches be brought about in the midst of a diversity of ministries? Can a process be developed for recognition of ministries from local church to local church where this is needed, and for situations where ministries can span more than one local church (such as justice ministries)?

3) What happens when new ministries are discerned and accepted in a community, but are not accepted by the bishop or the central government of the church, either because of the restriction of universal law or because of the preferences of a bishop or the central government of the church? How can such situations be adjudicated?

4) The major portion of authority for leadership of the church continues to reside at the level of the bishop and of the central government of the church. How are we to deal with the ways of exercising that authority and the use of power in those situations which, to our best judgment, seem to be harmful to new ministries?

5) In the midst of these tensions and the conflicts which sometimes then arise, how do we maintain the unity within our missionary or religious societies which we are required to preserve, and how do we maintain credibility when what we say is contradicted by what we become obliged to do? Our concern is not so much for our personal fate in such situations, as it is for a faithful rendering of leadership for our societies.

6) The current situation has to a great extent become one of an impasse for women called to ministry. Both in recent legislation and in pronouncements from the central government of the church, the way for women into many of the ministries to which they now feel called is blocked. This seems to us to be impeding both the development of a genuine mutuality in ministry between men and women, and a renewal of traditional ministries of which we have received glimpses in many places. How can a dialogue be initiated and carried through that can resolve this impasse?

7) The tensions now felt and the conflicts we see already emerging could well lead to the departure from our societies of some of our most prophetic and creative members. Within communities, it could lead to persons breaking bonds of communion with parts of the larger church. These prospects create fear and sadness within us, feelings that still seek adequate expression. How can we deal with these prospects for ourselves and within our societies, and in the communities we serve?

TASKS AHEAD FOR MISSIONARY SOCIETIES

The questions and tensions we see and have experienced in these new situations remind us of our roles within our missionary societies. These societies live out a charism, recognized by members and approved by the central authority of the church. The experience of living from a charism means that societies are often able to feel at home more quickly with new and prophetic models of the church and ministry than are members of the hierarchy. That same charism often prompts societies to prophetic action which causes tensions in the church, tensions which we hope are signs of new life rather than of sin and death.

Within the context of these considerations we see a number of tasks ahead for societies and their leadership. Among them:

1) We ought to aid in the discernment of new ministries, and in the process of raising up and affirming them in Christian communities.

2) We need to support those members of our societies and other Christians who are working in new ministries.

3) We need to educate and help form our members to the reality of new ministries, both those members who are called into these ministries and those who are not. Likewise, we should lend our support to the education and formation of persons called to new ministries in the communities we serve.

4) The fact that our societies span many countries and many local churches gives us channels of communication which can be put to the service of helping coordinate ministries between local churches. We need to explore ways in which this might be done.

5) Because of the experiences of our members with new ministerial realities, we need to continue to work toward representing those realities to church authorities at all levels. We also need to continue to work toward reconciliation where differing views of these realities in the church come into conflict.

6) We must prepare our members to see the role of our societies decrease in situations where local people come to assume greater leadership in the ministry of the church.

7) We must find ways to prepare our members to face the painful situations where conflicts find no resolution, and church authorities at some level ask our societies to leave a particular area. We must be prepared also to see some of our members leave our societies in those situations, but we must also try to promote and sustain dialogue to the greatest extent possible.

8) The experience of new ministries may lead us to abandon some ministries long thought to be central to expressing our charism, causing us to rethink our role in the church in order to reflect more faithfully our charism in changed situations. This can be a very painful process, but one to which we may be called. Such change in our own ministries may bring us into conflict with those communities whom we have served through those ministries in the past. Again, we must promote dialogue and reconciliation as much as possible in those situations.

Our dominant mood about the new directions which the mission of the church is taking is one of joy and even of excitement. We rejoice in sharing in the experience of people finding a new identity in the church, leading them into the furthering of God's Reign. And it is because of that great hope that we are willing to face the challenges which new ministries pose to us as missionary and religious societies. And it is within that hope that we pray for the continued guidance of the Spirit in meeting the difficult situations ahead.

NOTES

1. Bernard Cooke's *Ministry to Word and Sacrament* (Philadelphia: Fortress, 1976) is the most extensive. Perhaps the best known at the moment is that of Edward Schillebeeckx, *Kerkelijk Ambt* (Bloemendaal: Nelissen, 1980), translated as *Ministry* (London: SCM Press, 1981). This book has evoked a good deal of discussion and critique. Most of the disagreement centers around his interpretation of data rather than the data themselves. Schillebeeckx has refined his argument on developments from the second to the thirteenth century in "De sociale context van de verschui-

vigen in het kerkelijk ambt," in *Tijdschrift voor Theologie* 22 (1982): 24–59. This article is being incorporated into a revised version of his book.

2. One strain of Catholic exegesis is anxious to restrict the origins of Christian ministry to the Twelve, and is much taken with questions of authority and its transmission. Albert Vanhoye's review of Schillebeeckx's use of the New Testament material in ministry is an example of this. First published in *Nouvelle revue théologique 114* (1982): 722–38, it has been reprinted in *Clergy Review* and *Vidjayoti*. Despite its widespread dissemination, it should not be taken as representative of contemporary exegesis in these matters. A more refined version, sensitive to both contemporary exegesis and the concerns of conservative Catholics, is Pierre Grelot's book-length response to Schillebeeckx, *Eglise et ministères* (Paris: Cerf, 1983).

3. The Twelve are certainly essential to any discussion of ministry, but hardly constitute the entirety thereof. For a comprehensive survey of the current consensus of exegesis on ministry and the New Testament, see Jurgen Roloff, "Apostel/Apostolat/ Apostolizitat: I. Neues Testament," in *Theologische Realenzyklopadie (TRE)* III, 430–45; idem, "Amt/Amtsverstandnis: IV. Im Neuen Testament," in *TRE* II, 509–33, with extensive literature. Elisabeth Schüssler Fiorenza, *In Memory of Her* (New York: Crossroad, 1983), presents extensive literature on the leadership roles of women in the first century. The disciple category is complex and has not yet been studied comprehensively, particularly in its relation to other categories of following Jesus and leading the community. My colleague Robert Karris at CTU in Chicago has been helpful to me in seeing the complexities involved. For one such example of the complexities, see Elizabeth Struthers Malvon, "Fallible Followers: Women and Men in the Gospel of Mark," in *Semeia* 28 (1983): 29–48.

4. On the issue of women serving as leaders of a synagogue, see Bernadette Brooten, *Women Leaders in the Ancient Synagogues* (Chico, CA: Scholar's Press, 1982).

5. Much of this history has been explored in the study of the social world of early Christianity. See the treatment of this question especially in Wayne Meeks, *The First Urban Christians* (New Haven: Yale University Press, 1983).

6. Thomas O'Meara, *Theology of Ministry* (New York: Paulist Press, 1983), 79–87, gives a good but succinct treatment to the question of nomenclature.

7. Knut Schaferdiek, "Amt/Amter/Amtsverständnis. V. Alte Kirche," in *TRE* II,533–52 gives a comprehensive overview of this period.

8. Schillebeeckx, "De sociale context," 58, note 129, both corrects his statement from *Kerkelijk Ambt*, 94, on this and develops the hypothesis presented here.

9. Schaferdiek, "Amt/Amter/Amtsverständnis," 541–45.

10. Schillebeeckx, "De sociale context," 43–47.

11. Ibid., 56–58.

12. O'Meara, *Theology of Ministry*, 114–16, is a good discussion of this. The issue of Reformation ministry is important for Roman Catholics since attempts to rethink ministry within the Roman Catholic Church are often branded as Reformation or "Protestantization" of Catholic ministry. For example, Walter Kaspar accuses Schillebeeckx of doing this in his book *Ministry* in a review published in *Theologische Quartalschrift* 163 (1983): 185–95, which has also appeared in English in *Communio* 10 (1983): 185–95. Kaspar characterizes Schillebeeckx's approach as a "free-church" approach.

21

A THEOLOGICAL ASSESSMENT OF MINISTRIES TODAY

David Power, OMI

There are those who consider that the new Code of Canon Law is the juridical instrument which will allow the Roman Catholic Church to realize, both efficaciously and harmoniously, the directions assumed by the Second Vatican Council. Others, however, while fingering through its pages have been heard to mutter "Vatican One and a Half!", and in a more detailed analysis to show how it fails to meet the aspirations engendered by the Council on such points as the relation of other churches with the See of Rome, or the position of the laity in the life and mission of the church.

Mention of these two examples reminds us that we seem to have arrived at a point where the road forks, some taking one direction and some another on matters of church polity. Together, however, because of the Second Vatican Council, we have attained a common consciousness of local churches, of the active role of the laity, of greater communication within communities and between churches, of the appearance of new churches independent of Europe and North America, and of greater cultural pluralism. Now, however, this new consciousness is being assimilated in two quite different ways. It is not a matter of division between those who accept the Council and those who do not. Those who do not accept it seem to be a minority and not to have a significant impact. The division is more within the ranks of those who appeal to the authority of the Council to justify their choices by a reading of its documents. Two evident differences concern the relation between local churches and Rome; and the position of the laity in the church.

CONTRASTING MODELS OF CHURCH

LOCAL CHURCHES AND ROME

We are familiar with the experience of the Synod of Bishops which offers its views to the Pope on a given topic and then awaits the promulgation of a pontifical document. A very different ecclesiology would be operative and a very different ecclesial experience emerge if, for example, the African bishops were to call a church council, with participation from other continents, at which the bishop of Rome would agree to preside. The council would address matters which the bishops consider binding or vital to the church in Africa. Such matters might include liturgical pluriformity, matrimonial law, ordination to office in the church and its conditions, and the role of the gospel in the North-South tension affecting global human relations.[1] The ecumenical significance of such a council would lie in the form of its convocation and in the way in which its agenda would be proposed. There would be a recognition that these matters concern one region of the church, but because of their nature, they need to be resolved in communion with other churches and under the presidency in charity of the bishop of Rome.

As things now stand, synods and councils are centered on the initiative and decisions of the Pope. In restructuring the Curia and in structuring the Synod, it was the aim of Paul VI to allow the Pope to have direct personal contact with other churches, to receive information and advice from bishops around the world, while retaining considerable personal independence in making decisions and in giving orientations to the life of the church.[2] This is not a return to preconciliar days, for it provides structures for communication and coresponsibility, or collegiality, not previously known. It does, however, interpret collegiality in a way that assures a maximum responsibility and autonomy for the bishop of Rome as universal head of the church.

DIFFERING MODELS OF CHURCH LIFE

In local churches we see a similar contrast between images of church life. One way of being church is realized in a parish. Although the priests are often in dialogue with lay members of the parish, the power of decision and direction rests with the priest. Education committees, parish councils, study groups, youth teams, special ministries, and the like have considerable impact on the life of the parish. The role of the laity, however, could only be called auxiliary and consultative, rather than constitutive and life-determinative.

A very different way of being church is realized in an ecclesiastical division which encompasses a number of basic Christian communities, enjoying directional autonomy, aided by and knit together through the ministry of priest and bishop. The action and will of the laity is life-determinative; orientations emerge from a consensus in faith of the members, attained in a variety of ways, related to hearing the word and discernment of the Spirit.

These are but rough examples calling attention to the point that we are living out two distinct ecclesiologies, differing not simply in theory but in ecclesial practice, both justified as an implementation of the Council. One is an example of ecclesiastical practice where the center is more in touch with the periphery, not merely transmitting more signals to it, but receiving signals from it. The other is an example of an ecclesial practice of converging circles. In this second example the starting point is the activity within each circle, but the vitality of the circles requires communion between them, and some convergence in regard to the meaning and power of the gospel. The presence of these contrasting models of the church[3] is verified both within local communities and in the relation between particular or local churches and Rome.

DILEMMAS FROM VATICAN II

Both of the above examples have their roots in the Second Vatican Council. We seem to be facing the practical dilemmas of a theoretical disjunction that was pointed out to us by the observers from other Christian churches and communions during the Council. They commented that it would be impossible to live simultaneously with the first two chapters of *Lumen Gentium* on the People of God and the third chapter on a hierarchical church. The observers from Eastern churches in particular pointed to the inevitable clash between a pneumatological ecclesiology and a christonomy.[4] On the one hand, there is the image of the People of God, an image of coresponsibility and collegiality involving all the faithful, a church coming to be, under the power of the Spirit in its local realizations, and then in the communion of communities. On the other hand, there is the image of a hierarchical church, founded on and empowered by Jesus Christ, brought into being in its episcopal succession and in concrete uniformity within diversity, assured by a collegiality of bishops, *una cum et sub Romano Pontifice*, Vicar of Christ on earth. At the Council also, we were asked not only what recognition we could give to other Christian churches, but how much of the Reformation and Protestant or evangelical experience we could incorporate into the life and ministry of Roman Catholic communities. Rather awkwardly, the Council put the call and priesthood of all the faithful into relief, while at the same time repeating the statement of yore that the difference between the ordained and the faithful is of essence and not only of kind. This, in effect, is not merely to complement one statement with another, but to put two diverging points of view alongside one another.

CRITICAL TURNING POINT OR IMPASSE

It is typical of a critical period in history that two divergent models of society and communion exist simultaneously. An older model is challenged by a new one, each one having its own rhetoric. The two conflict with one another in ritual and juridical structure. The new model appeals particularly to new experiences and claims to make sense of them in ways that the old does not. The old model promises continuity and allows for change by internal modifications that can be encompassed within an unchanging framework. Not being in possession, the new model has difficulties in forging its ritual and juridical structures.

A model, to be effective, needs these three dimensions:

1. appropriate rhetoric that appeals to the affective as much as to the cognitive (for example, contrast the images of perfect society with People of God)

2. ritual that transforms experience in relating it to a vision of life (for example, contrast the sacrifice of the Mass offered by a priest with the eucharistic memorial celebrated by a community)

3. juridical structures (for example, contrast a pastoral council having a con-

sultative voice or commissioning to ministry by a parish priest, with discernment of ministry by a community).

Given these divergent models a historical impasse is reached when there is no resolution to the conflict so that fragmentation and schism ensue. Instead of an impasse, there is a historical turning point if the new model is received and finds its appropriate ritual and juridical implementation.

Another resolution of conflict is, of course, possible. The old model can adapt its workings so as to contain new experiences while giving primacy to the need for continuity. It contains them by, in some measure, satisfying what is felt to be important in the new experiences, but more importantly by limiting them and their impact. This is what people mean when they use the tag "neo-conservatism." One current typical example of this is the present ritual of eucharistic concelebration in the vernacular. The desire for an understandable language and the desire for a common celebration are met, but the model of church which is ritualized remains strictly priestly and hierarchical.

Another example is that of the movement Comunione e Liberazione in the Italian church: it accepts the reality of the secularization of society and the diminished place of the church in public life, but continues to expect a centrally determined social teaching, a ritual practice that will enable the church to function as a social entity of some vigor in public life, one that transcends the realities of local communities even at their expense.

THE RECEPTION OF COUNCILS

We can grasp the meaning of what is happening among Roman Catholics only if we realize that as a historical event, the way in which a council is received is as important as what it actually decides or teaches. Looking back to the Second Vatican Council actually means looking back from considerably changed historical circumstances while at the same time making the effort to be true to the conciliar experience.

Ecumenical councils do not affect the life of the church simply by happening and promulgating decrees. They and their decisions have to be received into the life of the church. Historically, a Council becomes an event and not a mere happening by the way in which it is received. The fifth Lateran Council as a council of reform had little impact, not only because of its own internal weaknesses, but also because few people had any desire to respond to its impulse toward reform. The Council of Trent, on the other hand, occurred within a historical context where reform had become necessary to survival. Even then, it has been reasonably well shown that the historical reality of Trent results as much from the precise plan of implementation adopted by Pius V and subsequent popes as it does from the council's decisions. This does not simply mean that to be implemented the council needed the papal arm, but that the papal arm gave a particular coloring to the council's movement.

One area alone may illustrate the importance of reception, namely, the liturgical. The Council of Trent expressed its view that using the vernacular and giving the chalice to the laity were not fitting but it left open the possibility of some regionalism on these points and of a later more favorable decision. Subsequent papal action, however, made the bishops' statement irreversible for four centuries.

HISTORICAL SETTING AFTER VATICAN II

In this process of reception, changing historical circumstances make a difference. The political regimes in Europe affected the reception of both Trent and Vatican I. This is significant for us who live in an age of such rapid and global historical change. It is apparent that what we call the vision of the Second Vatican Council, and its specific teachings, have to be received into today's historical setting which is different from that of 1960 or 1965. Since historical consciousness and a definition of the church as sacrament of Christ and God's Reign in the world were integral to the conciliar vision, it is obviously very important for those who wish to be faithful to the council to keep this in mind. In particular, it is an important factor in our consideration of the future of ministries in a dynamic local church. We will now consider some of the changes in the world and in the church that have occurred since 1965, the year the Council closed.

THE RECEPTION OF VATICAN II

CHANGES IN THE WORLD

There are six changes in the world situation that, I believe, deeply affect our understanding of the church's mission and its ministries. Others, I am sure, emphasize other changes.[5]

1. Within the enormous economic and scientific expansion of these decades there has been a shift from an East-West tension to a North-South tension, the East-West conflict being translated into a conflict over the influence of the superpowers and their alliances in the South. Within this tension, the world has to record considerable failure in meeting the challenge of human poverty and suffering. There is also large-scale economic failure giving birth to a new poor, the landless, the unemployed and the marginalized.
2. There is a threat to human survival from nuclear perils, various kinds of genocide, and the impossibility of controlling natural disasters, an impossibility not unrelated to the North-South tension.
3. The human rights issue has taken on new dimensions because of both a new awareness of these rights and continuing violations of them. This issue itself has been expanded to include new categories of persons, for example women, children, and prisoners, and also new categories of rights, some pertaining to the right to work and conditions of work.
4. New peoples and new countries emerge, claiming cultural and political independence but bedeviled by their own internal conflicts and by global politics and economics.
5. There is the re-emergence of religion, of Islam especially, as a social and political force in world history.

6. Few countries have not been affected by the changing condition of women and of the family in society.

It was the intention of the Second Vatican Council that the church might consider the world as its partner, seeing it as a locus of both divine presence and absence (what was meant by reading the signs of the times). How can we be true today to what was said, more than twenty years ago, about partnership with the world? Certainly there was much more historical optimism then than there is now.

CHANGES IN THE CHURCH

Correspondingly, in the church itself we note the following changes as significant for our theme:

1. a loss of optimism in the vision of partnership with the world and a sense that a different reading of human history may be needed
2. a changing religious consciousness resulting particularly from the recognition of and dialogue with other religions
3. curiously enough, this is accompanied by what has proved to be a slow and somewhat flawed ecumenism among the Christian churches, where good will of a vague sort seems to exceed the possibilities of real achievement, and wherein the Catholic partnership, always marginal, is affected by decisions of other churches on ministerial matters (for example, the ordination of women) and moral matters (for example, attitudes toward the divorced)
4. a new cultural pluralism within the church, and a sense of the cultural particularity of local churches
5. the loss of institutions which formed the basis of the church's place in society and its influence on it, and hence the quest for a new basis
6. the emergence of the laity, and in a very particular way of women, as a tremendous force for change in the church
7. a growing number of unchurched believers as well as a continuing decline in traditional religious practices
8. the continuing appeal, on the other hand, of what is variously called popular religion or mass religion
9. a growing sense, among many, that the church is the church of the poor, not only a church for the poor, but churches emerge, constituted through the power and force of poor people.

FAITHFUL TO THE EXPERIENCE OF VATICAN II

If the inspiration and teaching of the Second Vatican Council is to be received into this rather variant historical situation of both world and church, how are we to be faithful to it in the local churches? It has been suggested that one is not faithful in the face of new experiences, and that one cannot simply quote texts to confirm a position already taken. And has it already been asked whether it is legitimate to make a distinction between the texts in themselves and the Conciliar experience out of which they sprang? Can we find the way of being faithful to our own experience by being faithful to the fundamental experience of the Council?

The fundamental experience of the Council, has been described as:

1. consciousness of experience itself as historical and cultural and as the place of God's presence
2. a new openness to the challenges of word and Spirit by people ready to give up some of their security in old positions. As Professor Antonio Acerbi puts it:

> The experience of the church, reforming itself in light of the Gospel, is the framework within which the Council documents belong and within which, transcending all cultural variations, the unchangeable elements are determined.[6]

He described this experience further as follows:

> The Church that was questioning itself about its mission and the conditions in which it carried it out, intended to set aside the human securities that were a result of its past in order to place itself in an attitude of listening and obedience before the Word of God, and to acquire once again the freedom and strength that come from fidelity to the Gospel.[7]

3. the ecumenical experience. For the first time since the Reformation, the Roman Catholic church felt itself impelled to consider the history and way of being of the Orthodox and Protestant churches as evidence of God's salvific presence and design. It could no longer ignore these experiences or consider them second-rate.

THE COMMUNITY MODEL OF CHURCH

Historical contingency, cultural pluralism, ecumenical interaction, evangelical witness, as elements of our new ecclesial experience, seem to call for a model of converging. The root of this ecclesial understanding and polity lies in the life of a local church as a communion of subjects, itself a subject in its relation with other churches. It is a communion of the one Lord and Spirit diversely manifested and witnessing according to historical and cultural conditions. In fidelity to word and Spirit, and in a reading of history, each church evolves its own life in a corporate way which involves the responsibility of all the members. To say that a church is a subject is to say that it has the status of an "autonomously dependent" person in relation to other churches, and that it itself functions as a corporate personality which is constituted by the interaction of its members.

To understand this model better we need to do two things: first, to see how it has been affected by critiques of Roman Catholic ecclesial polity and organization, and secondly, to look to current ecclesial experiences to see how the model is being developed.

CRITIQUES

Constructive Critique. Roman Catholic ecclesiology and practice have nothing to fear from the constructive critique that others make of it. Indeed, it is largely in virtue of an ability to listen to that critique that advance has been possible in recent years.

The Orthodox Critique. The Orthodox critique questions the way in which, over centuries, the Roman Catholic church organized its ministry and chose its ministers. It came gradually to place too much reliance on hierarchical structure and transmission so that not enough attention was given to the special charisms of the Spirit and to the way in which the Spirit guides a community in the appointment or reception of ministers. The need to base the understanding and practice of ministry on a discernment of spirits is one of the major consequences of the Orthodox critique of Catholic polity.

The Protestant Critique. This is both explicit and implicit. It is explicit in as much as it raises questions about the responsibility and role of the faithful in the church, about the relation of the minister to the community, as well as about the nature of her or his role in relation to word and sacrament. The critique is implicit inasmuch as ecclesial practice in the Protestant churches shows an alternative experience of ministry whose real efficacy presents a valuable contrasting experience from which the Catholic church may gain fresh insight into ministry.

These contrasting experiences, with their implicit questions to Catholic practice, are perhaps most vivid today in Evangelical and Pentecostal churches. These churches or communities give witness to the ways in which community may be lived in mutual support and care. Their ministry reveals the power of the word and the witness of a life lived according to the gospel. When some of these churches make their criticism of Roman Catholic polity on ministry explicit they ask two questions:

1) Have we not come to rely too heavily on institutions and on institutional training, so that little room is left to the freedom of the Spirit?

2) In the emphasis on the apostolic succession of bishops have we not neglected the importance of the apostolic succession in evangelical witness? Is this last not as important a criterion for the legitimacy of ministry as the regular practice of ordination within the prescribed canons? These churches also give evidence of the variety of ministries in a church and of the reception into church life of ministries that have their seed in cultural experience. Perhaps the most striking evidence of this lies in the place that their communities give to healing and divining ministries where these have a link with a people's cultural religious experience.

Social Sciences Critique. This notes that one must distinguish between unchanging elements and social or cultural particularities. Specifically, the question is raised about the role given to women in the church and about the stress on the celibacy of the clergy. Ritual enactment itself can reinforce a power structure and prevent the collegiality of community. Some theological theories about the power of the priest in the celebration of the sacraments have as much to do with a sacralization of the priest that maintains his authority as they have to do with genuine theological insight.

The Catholic church's openness to learn from the experiences of other churches, as well as an openness to an internal critique of its own power structures, are then some of the important factors which contribute to its ministerial renewal. Besides these, there is the important experience of poor churches for the most part within the historical continuity of the Roman Catholic communion itself. These recent experiences help us to see how an alternative model of church and ministry is being developed.

CURRENT ECCLESIAL EXPERIENCES OF THE COMMUNITY MODEL: BASIC ECCLESIAL COMMUNITIES

One would first say of a local church, viewed within the Catholic tradition, that it is a eucharistic community. This does not mean that wherever people regularly gather together for the celebration of Mass there is a local church. It means that, given certain types of communion and relationship in faith and hope, a community celebrates its *koinonia*, and roots its *koinonia*, in a celebration of the memorial of the Lord's death. This is what constitutes its vision of itself, its basic vision of history and of the Lord's presence in history. However, what makes up these relations in faith and hope is not immediately evident, just as geographical vicinity or rubbing shoulders does not of itself constitute community.

Some practical evidence of such relations is available to us, particularly in the experience of basic Christian communities. The term basic Christian community is not univocal because the experience is not identical from one country to another and because even within the same country it is used to designate different components of the overall reality. In Brazil, the term has at least two distinctive meanings. Clodovis Boff explains: "Basic Communities are made up of small groups of an average of ten people; it is most usually a number of these groups — generally ten — grouped in one area, usually a parish, that is known as a basic community. A large parish may encompass more than one basic community. ... But the small groups themselves are also sometimes referred to as basic communities."[8] The permanent Council of the Conference of Brazilian Bishops in a statement issued in 1982 stated: "Basic Communities as communities are formed by families, adults and youth, in a tight interpersonal relationship of faith ... they celebrate the word of God and are nourished by the eucharist ... they enjoy solidarity and a common commitment ... they are cells of a greater community."[9]

Positive Experiences

The Brazilian bishops are helpful in listing the factors that led to a positive experience within basic Christian communities, factors that we can extend to any renewal of community life in the church. They mention in particular four factors[10] to which we can add a fifth and sixth which emerge from the document and are pertinent to a model of Christian community.

1. The church is considered as the People of God, in which "to each is given the manifestation of the Spirit for the common good" (1 Cor. 12:7).
2. The church is considered as sacrament, sign and instrument of a profound union with God and of the unity of the human race (*Lumen Gentium* 1).
3. The role of the laity is considered in itself, not as participation in the ministry of the priest, and is deemed constitutive of the life and mission of the church.
4. The communities possess an integral vision of history where the story of humanity and the story of salvation are interconnected, an interconnection which, in Latin America, means the quest for justice and for the liberation of the poor.
5. These communities are the churches of the poor, not for the poor but of the poor, where ministry and leadership and social force come from the poor, are exercised by the poor, and constitute a new form of being a force for social change.
6. The prayer and ministries of these communities receive much from the forms in which the general religious experience of the people in their culture is expressed and nurtured.

If we abstract these factors from any particular experience of basic Christian community and see them as open to a cultural and historical diversity in the way in which they are embodied, we can take them as the key to an understanding of how church life may develop in this present age. It is the kind of development which allows a local church, as subject, to develop a new relation to self, a new relation to the world, and a new relation to the universal church. The new experience of being church carries within itself a model for new juridical structures, pertinent to the government and leadership of a church. Structures exist that emerge from church life, but as yet they are not canonically affirmed in full since they are called extraordinary. However, what Rome is prepared to recognize as extraordinary and episodic can readily one day be confirmed as normal and normative.[11]

The relation to self of these communities is that they are communities of the baptized which exist in virtue of the individual and corporate responsibility of all. There is need for an ordained ministry but no room for a clergy/laity distinction. Indeed, at present many communities have a great capacity to realize communion with only marginal help from ordained ministers.

CHARACTERISTICS OF THIS MODEL OF COMMUNITY

PRAYER

The center and source of a community's life is its prayer. This prayer is marked by six qualities.[12]
1. Fundamentally, it is a listening to the Word of God.
2. It shows a growing consciousness of the grace and power of the Spirit in daily life, especially in the midst of human vulnerability and weakness when hope is shared with others.
3. It is a common prayer, in which the active and heard voice of all is welcome and is not hindered by class distinctions, whether social or ecclesiastical.

4. Its symbolic expression finds its "stuff" in the things that belong to the community and its people—their bread, their water, their hands, the tents and awnings that they themselves have erected.
5. It is a prayer in which the poor are present and active, with their popular religiosity and native religious expression.
6. It is joyous and festive, with a joy that springs from the knowledge of Christ and the freedom of the Spirit.

The community has participatory structures that are grounded in the experience of prayer and eucharist. Affiliation to the community means initiation into the communion of prayer and reflection, of listening to the word and discerning the Spirit. Any decisions affecting the life of the community follow this model, for they too are rooted in a life of shared faith.

CHARISM AND MINISTRY

The call of the Spirit is born in the community; ministries are exercised by members of the community and for the community. Whatever training in faith and professional competence is needed is undertaken as a responsibility of the community. The relation of any minister to the community is that of birth within its life, of discernment and recognition within its womb. When such ministers are ordained, communion with other churches is thus signaled and effected.

Leadership, as now practiced in many communities, is guaranteed, not by office or delegation or title, but by charism, including its discernment and public affirmation within the community. Delegation by ecclesiastical authorities is used to effect relations with the wider community, but this is not the source of the minister's authority among the people. If a leader appeals to the authority of office or delegation, she or he has to be able to base the claim on witness and acceptance. According to the ancient tradition of the church this is what is expected of ordained ministers. Reception of their witness by the community is an essential component of their authority.[13]

RELATION TO THE WORLD

It is within the community of prayer and reflection that a church, in faith, sees its relation to the world. In Brazil the option for the poor and the vision of liberation constitute the shared vision of God's presence in the world. Granted the historical and cultural particularities of each continent and country, the understanding of itself as the church of the poor would appear to be a constitutive element of every eucharistic community, even in the more affluent countries of the North.

Firstly, this means a community in which the poor of society feel at home and free to express themselves, able to contribute to the life of others. Secondly, it also means that the community is a place in which there is a living critique of class divisions, including those affecting access to ordination. Thirdly, it means that mission to the world is the responsibility of the community as such, not of the laity as distinct from the clergy. Fourthly, it means a relation to the earth and awareness of the gratuity of life and of all living things. Fifthly, it means that this mission to the world is undertaken with modesty and in an openness to those not of the community, since there is no pretension that the church possesses a comprehensive social ethic. In the place of such a pretension there is the hope of receiving the sign and signals of the presence of the Spirit in the human and in the cosmos, given one's readiness to listen and to discern.

FREEDOM AND GRACE

In their vision of the world, Christians share a utopian vision of the future, born not of power but in the experience of freedom and grace, unassured by institutional presence or even by a uniform teaching on issues. The hope of freedom arises from spiritual liberation, constituted by: the absence of fear; the gift of the Spirit that assures us of God's love; the knowledge that the cry of Jesus is one with that of suffering humanity; our own compassion for suffering humanity and a suffering earth; freedom from the desire for power over others; the hope that survives in the midst of darkness.[14]

MINISTRIES

Ministries arise in these communities that are not simply to the community, but that represent the action of the community in society. The struggle for justice and freedom is carried out in small ways as much as in big organizations. Barefoot doctors and centers for herbal medicines put health care under peoples' own management. Small-scale credit unions and cooperatives empower people trying to live out their own autonomy. These are not in themselves church organizations, but are often served by those who find their vision within the eucharistic community and who are supported by that community.

In more affluent and educated societies, that is, where education is measured by length of years and institutional internship, it is gradually being discovered that a problem like drug addiction can be faced only when responsibility is accepted on the local level in communities that involve the families and friends of the addicts.

It is necessary that these communities give not only support and care on an interpersonal level, but also give an analysis and vision of reality that will enable its members to challenge the social effects of depersonalization, family breakdown, unemployment, and so forth. Adequate use of the aids provided by society cannot be made without the support of a community of vision and Christian faith. Here, too, the aim is not simply to help the handicapped or the unemployed, but to enable them to find their own power and their ability to contribute.

LOCAL CHURCH AND COMMUNION OF CHURCHES

There remains the question of the relation of local churches to the communion of churches. There is a need for new juridical structures that go beyond what is timidly approached in the revised Code of Canon Law. Three remarks in particular seem appropriate:

1. Juridical structures do not of themselves constitute the church but they facilitate its life which derives from sacrament and prayer. This life is given shape in sacrament and prayer more than in law.
2. The laity belong *pleno iure* to the church; this is not recognized unless they

are given discretionary and participatory roles in decision-making. Some provision of a deliberative voice for the laity has to be made in local communities, in parishes, in dioceses and in every form of church council, including the ecumenical.

3. The canonical experience of other Christian churches, in keeping with what has been said earlier, deserves examination and consideration in arriving at proper norms in this regard.

PROBLEM AREAS

Before ending the analysis of the community model of the church it is only proper to mention some of the problems encountered in its implementation:

1. The process of discernment is difficult, whether it is a reading of the signs of the times, a discernment of God's presence in life, or a discernment of charisms and ministries.
2. There is therefore the risk of substituting democratization for discernment, especially in choosing leaders.
3. Some communities, especially when they undertake the work of social liberation, can find themselves victims of ideologies of power.
4. Rather than unity in pluralism, the independence of local churches could give rise to fragmentation if bonds between churches are not fostered.
5. Given the persistence of mass religion and the genuine piety and need of those who adhere to it, the Christian community has to work out its responsibility toward those not interested in accepting the invitation to membership, but anxious to have sacraments and other forms of religious expression.

NEOCONSERVATIVE, HIERARCHICAL MODEL OF CHURCH

It has already been said that we are living in a time when some continue to live out of a hierarchical model of the church, feeling that the best way to face new experiences is to adjust rather than to change this model. The image used was that of a center in touch with the periphery. There seems to be a rather powerful resurgence of this model in recent years and some appointments of bishops who are expected to adhere to it. Its qualities are:

— it is hierarchical in structure while attentive to people and what they say; centralized, though ready to listen
— it is interested in the concern of its members to present the face of an institution that can have influence on public life.

Following are some of the reasons for the present attraction of this model:

1. It responds to a concern for the ordinary faithful who are felt to be unable to work out their own personal stand on matters of faith and morals and who need strong direction in order to deepen their faith life. Structural and ritual means of religious practice, clear and unequivocal ethical teaching backed by institutions, are felt to fall within the divine mission given to the hierarchy.
2. There is pessimism about taking the world as a partner in dialogue or as a locus of divine revelation. Though other cultures and religions are appreci-

ated, the primary task in this model is that of bringing the faith to peoples. The appreciation and understanding of cultures is important, but in the end it is only in the light of Christ that understanding comes in full. There is, therefore, an effort to build up a Christian culture, that is, an expression of faith socially attainable as a directive to personal and public life. This will provide symbols, ritual, office, custom, and teaching that offer guidelines and directives as well as a clear and distinct Christian identity. The appeal to witness is part of this view, but it is not the foundation of Christian identity but rather a public affirmation of its truth.

3. There is the effectiveness of working together as a clearly identifiable social body with social power rather than working through the medium of small communities whose members insert themselves into the fabric of social life.

APPLICATIONS OF THIS MODEL

Following are some of the reasons which appear to make a neoconservative model of the church persuasive:

1. Importance is given to the social relevance of sacraments, for example, infant baptism, church marriage and such visible practices as Sunday Mass. These practices connect people with public life as Christians so that the church and its impact on life are made visible.

2. The hierarchy remains the radiating center of communication, not only through the exercise of sacramental ministry, but also through juridical structures that are careful to distinguish between consultative and deliberative voice.

3. The old institutional base of schools and public institutions is being replaced by strong movements coordinated from the center, preferably Rome. Good examples of this are Opus Dei and Comunione e Liberazione. These foster a strong and uniform position on public issues transcending the action and interchange of local Christian and eucharistic communities.

4. In church-state relations the concordat is replaced by:
   — the politicization of forms of church presence such as Christian parties, trade unions, even large credit unions and banks
   — the social teaching of the universal church is preferred to the power of communities to analyze their own situation, and in the light of the gospel to discover their own social project and presence. The encyclical *Laborem Exercens*, for example, combines an analysis of work (the "new" in neoconservative) with a conservative reading of the book of Genesis and of the doctrine of creation. It thus brings a "concept of humanity" into the situation which is globally analyzed, rather than discovering the human in the situation.

5. The role of the laity, especially that of women, is contained by enhancement of the sacred character of the priesthood, as well as through an approach to lay ministries which accentuates the force of delegation and commissioning. We are told that in the priest the sacred character of the gospel and of the church are founded. From this it follows that the primary "holy" of the gospel is not the community of believers, but the priest, whose role it is to sanctify the baptized, and to celebrate the sacraments in which the holy of

holies, Jesus Christ, is present to the church. The letter of John Paul II on the eucharist, *Dominicae Coenae*, developing the notion that the priest acts *in persona Christi*, comes to the conclusion that the priest participates sacramentally in the sacrifice and holiness of Christ, while the faithful, through the instrumentality of the priest, participate spiritually.[15] Within such a vision there is little room to change the requisites for ordination to ministry or to change the process whereby candidates are chosen. Ordained ministry seems to come before community rather than being based in community, and apostolic succession of bishops comes before the churches in the succession of faith.

MINISTRY TODAY: THE DILEMMA

In this paper I have presented the practical dilemma in which we seem to be presently caught on ministry in the church. I believe that we have to face this dilemma squarely, though I do not know how we can move out of it. Let me conclude by listing some points on which there may be common agreement and then those areas in which tension seems greatest. First of all, I will list seven points on which there may be common agreement.

POINTS OF AGREEMENT

1. In ministry it is important to attend to the human dimension of life and its openness to the transcendent. Discovery of what generates a sense of human love and a sense of the holy among any people is important to the teaching of the gospel and the work of Christian ministers.
2. In all forms of ministry it is important for the minister to be close to the people and to be conscious of their modes of expression and of their approach to the sacred.
3. Ministries have to be fostered within communities, their seed-bed being the life of faith of the community.
4. The emergence of new ministries is rooted in the hearing of the gospel and in faith in the presence of the Spirit.
5. Care for the suffering and the marginalized, and the defense of justice, have to mark the ministry of the church in today's world, in all quarters of the globe.
6. Christians bring to the efforts and problems of humanity, as well as to its hopes, the unique experience of the cross of Christ, their understanding of the presence of Christ among the poor and their suffering.
7. Some elements of culture and popular religious expression can and should be incorporated into local ministries.

TENSIONS

I list now seven questions, the answers to which provoke tension:

1. What is the extent of coresponsibility and collegiality among the baptized in local communities, and in the communion of communities?

2. What forms and approaches to ministry does the Catholic church take from other Christian churches?

3. Who is to invite a person to ministry, or who is to approve ministry of whatever form? What are the respective roles of the community and of the community's leader in the promotion, recognition, and affirmation of ministry?

4. What is the relation of the ordained minister to a community; what changes in the conditions of such ministry are possible, and perhaps imperative to the future of the church?

5. What is the extent of the influence of a particular culture on the kinds and forms of ministry undertaken? What services, that are found in other forms of religious experience, can be integrated in the life of a Christian community?

6. How does a community address social problems? Is it through the implementation of a social ethic, or through a discernment by those in the situation, and a hope in the presence of Christ among the suffering? Which is more modest in the vision it presents and the claims that it makes?

7. How is the relation between local churches and the bishop of Rome to be shaped? What initiatives in the policy of ministry are appropriate to the local churches in a region?

This is a brief analysis of the current situation of ministry in the church. It is an analysis which highlights problems and tensions. Some might have preferred solutions. The solutions may well come from the dynamic local churches themselves.

NOTES

1. Tshishiku Tshibangu, "Full Christian Maturity of a Young Church," in *Concilium* 144, English ed. (April 1981): 63: "What is clear is that at this moment African Christians are so conscious of representing a different sort of ecclesiastical world that there has been considerable talk over several years of a general meditation and reflection on the Church in Africa and its specific problems, a reflection in depth to be conducted in the course of an African Council or at least an African Synod to be presided over by the Pope of Rome." The author refers to an address of the Bishops of Zaire to Pope John Paul II, Kinshasa, May 3, 1980.

2. Cf. Antonio Acerbi, "L'ecclesiologia sottesa alle instituzioni ecclesiali postconciliari," in *L'Ecclesiologia del Vaticano II: dinamismi e prospettive, a cura di Giuseppe Alberigo* (Bologna: EDB, 1981), 203–34.

3. "Model of" is an attempt to explain what already is; "model for" is a projection of what might become.

4. See Yves Congar, "Implicazioni cristologiche e pneumatologiche dell'ecclesiologia del Vaticano II," in *L'Ecclesiologia del Vaticano II*, 97–110.

5. See J. Kerkhofs, "Principali mutamenti nelle societa cristiana istituite enelle chiese dopo il Vaticano II," in *L'Ecclesiologia del Vaticano II*, 5–22; V. Cosmao, "Spostamenti dei centri di attrazione," ibid., 37–43; François Houtart, "The Global Aspects of Dependence and Oppression," *Concilium* 144, English ed. (April 1981): 3–10.

6. A. Acerbi, "Receiving Vatican II in a Changed Historical Context," *Concilium* 146, English ed. (June 1981): 81f.

7. Acerbi, "L'ecclesiologia sottesa alle instituzioni ecclesiali postconciliari," 80.

8. Clodovis Boff, "The Nature of Basic Christian Communities," *Concilium* 144, English ed. (April 1981): 53.

9. Conselho Permanente da CNNBB, "Comunidades Eclesiais de Base," *Comunicado Mensal: Conferencia Vacional dos Bispos de Brasil* 362 (November 1982): 1180–95. Cf 30: 1184. An Italian translation is given in Il Regno/Documenti XXVIII (1983) 451–57.

10. Ibid., 12: 1191f. Cf. sect. III A CEB e los pobres.

11. This is one of the major points made by Edward Schillebeeckx, *Ministry: Leadership in the Church* (New York: Crossroad, 1980).

12. See Inacio Neutzling, "Célébrations dans les Communautés de Base," *Spiritus* 24 (1983): 115–25.

13. See David Power, "The Basis for Official Ministry," *The Jurist* 49 (1981).

14. See Romans 8, which could read as a model for prayer in these communities.

15. *Notitiae* XVI (1980): 138; *Osservatore Romano* March 19, 1980.

22

MINISTRY IN A RURAL PARISH IN GUATEMALA

Graciella Estrada, MB

Our pastoral team began with a parish priest and four Sisters. We started to examine the local needs and then the priorities of the diocesan pastoral team.

THE NATIONAL SITUATION

Guatemala is a small Central American country which suffers from ever-increasing violence and death. The roots of this lie in socioeconomic and political structures which marginalize and exploit the majority of the people who live in poverty in the rural areas. They are dependent on external structures and a system that relies on force to continue in power. The population may be called one-hundred–percent religious and even Christian.

THE LOCAL SITUATION

Our parish consists of some thirty thousand inhabitants. It is located along the coast in a zone of vast private landholdings exploited for the production and export of cash crops such as coffee and sugarcane. These estates, called *fincas*, spawned small villages of permanent agricultural workers–tenant farmers. As a rule these settlements are made up of two hundred or more families whose living conditions are simply below human standards. The average daily wage today is about US $3.50. Until four years ago it was only US $1.50. Public transportation is in poor condition and functions, as a rule, only when it is needed to transport the produce of the *fincas* at certain periods. During the rest of the year the roads are virtually impassable. Distances within the parish are considerable.

THE THEOLOGICAL FRAMEWORK

As the parish pastoral team became more aware of the local situation, they worked out a theological framework to help us understand the situation in the light of the gospel. It appeared to us that what was needed was not just a program of action geared to outside aid or assistance, but a comprehensive evangelization in line with the orientations of the Medellín and Puebla meetings and Paul VI's *Evangelii Nuntiandi*. We asked ourselves how we could accompany these people so that they would become the authors of their own history. They would need to be committed to a process of transformation based on gospel values. We asked ourselves how would we announce a God who is Father of all, a God of life, of salvation for all, and especially for these poor people living in an environment that violated the basic truths of our faith.

PRIORITIES EMERGING FROM THIS ANALYSIS

We established priorities for our work, relating all our activities to one unifying goal. We formulated the goal thus: we want to arrive at an evangelized and evangelizing parish community which has as its starting point a consciousness of the dignity of the human person. Following from this was the right to live a worthwhile life, a life which presupposes that each person has been created in the likeness of God. We felt responsible for constructing a community of people who were brothers and sisters within the People of God. We were convinced that this program rested on a firm biblical foundation.

Our priorities were as follows:

1. The formation of men and women catechists who would be Christian community leaders. We recognized that they should be catalysts, animators of the faith in their communities and at the same time bridges of communication with the parish.
2. We used any means of social communication at our disposal for programs of religious and cultural formation, health–care education, the advancement of women, and other programs.
3. Regular visits were organized to the different communities to keep in contact with them and participate in their faith celebrations, such as the eucharist when a priest was present, or the liturgy of the word and other celebrations. An additional purpose was to motivate the people so that more catechists and ministers would emerge, persons disposed to carry out the different tasks needed to serve the community better.
4. We developed teaching materials and coordinated programs of pre-sacramental catechesis.

A PLANNED PROGRAM FOR CATECHISTS

The discovery of these catechists or animators came about through a direct invitation which we extended to all those who felt called by God to offer Christian service to their community. We started with a group of about fifty people which gradually grew until it reached two hundred fifty. All of these had the recommendations of their respective communities. Five formation centers were established within the different zones of the parish.

The program was built mainly on a four-year biblical formation cycle. Meetings took place every two weeks. Each meeting lasted from four to five hours. In addition we arranged intensive short courses of three full days twice a year.

These included topics such as: learning to analyze one's own situation; the importance of the prophetic sense of the gospel; and knowledge of labor legislation. Finally, diocesan and national meetings were held once or twice a year.

COMMUNITY RESPONSIBILITY

During a special eucharist in the parish, attended by people from all the small communities, each catechist received a diploma. Receiving this diploma meant that the catechist assumed a public commitment before the parish and community. Each catechist was called individually to receive it, the gesture making explicit the kind of service she or he was now disposed to render. Naturally this required a prior dialogue with the community so as to clarify needs. There was a dialogue also with the parochial team which had to give its opinion on matters referring to the biblical, theological, and human formation of a candidate.

As time passed the opinions of the communities and catechists received ever more weight in the decision to accept or not to accept candidates for the ministries they wished to perform. A pivotal point was the witness of their Christian life and their individual as well as their family life. The community showed itself to be very demanding in this regard.

ACHIEVEMENTS

The catechists became real evangelizers of their communities.
— They use the Bible as their basic tool in evaluating their own situation in the context of the history of salvation. They direct the liturgy of the word and prepare the people for baptism, first communion, and marriage along the lines of this biblical orientation.
— They have achieved a critical sense and a capacity for judgment which enable them to play a prophetic role. They discover signs of life and light as well as of death and sin within society.
— They develop their human talents in a way which makes it possible for them to express themselves with ease in public.
— They also know how to organize themselves. All this is developed for the purpose of better service, not to gain power or to dominate.
— They have also developed their creative capacities so that they can present topics within the particular manifestations of their own popular religiosity. This was shown for example in pilgrimages, the celebration of Holy Week, and other paraliturgical occasions.

After four years they suggested starting a catechists' organization. They wanted to become the agents of their own coordination, formation and mutual protection. They intended to form commissions in which they could take up very concrete tasks.

POLITICAL REPRESSION

As we moved ahead with this project, we were aware that repression was increasing in the country as a whole. We felt this in our area too.
— The catechists were now looked upon as dangerous people in the *finca*

because quite often it was they who spoke out to the administrators about the needs and the claims of the communities.

— Protestant sects were constantly increasing their membership. Their converts often became spies and denounced the catechists to the landowners.

— Relations between the *finca* owners and administrators and the personnel of the parish (priest and Sisters), which in the beginning had been very cordial, became strained until there was a complete breakdown. The work of evangelization interfered more and more with the interests of the landowners.

— It became increasingly difficult to use the chapel in the *finca* for community celebrations.

— There were threats against the life of the parish priest. Attempts to kill him failed.

— Persecution of catechists began. Some of them were killed.

— Spying on the house of the Sisters began.

MARTYRDOM

Persecution has now grown to such proportions that the work has to be pursued through the "Pastoral Bureau of. . . ."* We Sisters remain present with the catechists, running risks, still working with them, organizing materials in order to keep hope alive despite the situation of martyrdom of the church. We want to celebrate the faith with them to the extent still possible.

The time is over for pursuing projects and measuring accomplishments. Now we are convinced, even in the silence forced upon us, and through the blood of so many martyrs, that this project of the poor will one day turn into a triumph. After all this suffering we know that God is our help. He came to us with the Good News for the poor. And God is faithful.

---

* (The name was not supplied for fear of reprisals. Eds.)

23

FORMING CHRISTIAN
COMMUNITIES IN ECUADOR

Sara Casanova Lozada, MMI

The Latin American Congregation of which I am a member has as its charism, evangelization and human development among the poorest of the poor, especially among the indigenous people. So it was that I, a Colombian, have worked for nineteen years among the indigenous Native American people of Ecuador. I share with you briefly my mission experience working with these native peoples in a parish. I do this with special reference to the place of lay ministries.

San Cristobal is a parish of thirty-five hundred inhabitants spread out over some 205 kilometers. There are no public facilities or services; there is neither light nor telephone. Water is very scarce and, at best, obtainable only in some centers. There are only three public schools. The sole means of traveling to the parish center is over a poorly maintained country road. In 1980, the parish was entrusted by the archbishop to me and two other Sisters. We were responsible for the organization of pastoral work as well as the administration of the sacraments not reserved to the priest. We worked in coordination with the diocesan pastoral commission.

The indigenous people of our area own small plots of land of half a hectare or less. The soil is poor, dry, eroded, and stony, and so there is only one harvest during the year. Men group together to work, but they cannot avoid migrating to the big cities in search of casual labor as builders or workers in a sugar factory. In the absence of their husbands women have to assume all the responsibility for the family, for work in the fields, the care of the animals, and so on. They also work in cottage industries, using their weaving skills.

BASIC CHRISTIAN COMMUNITIES

Our parish did not have a parish priest for eighteen years. From time to time a priest would come for the administration of the sacraments, especially on the occasion of the feast of the patron saint. In order to build basic Christian

206

communities we started with the already existing geographical and social units — the neighborhoods. There are now twelve such base communities.

While we were engaged in this work we stayed in the homes of the indigenous people, participating in their daily family chores and eating the food which they ate. We had daily meetings with them and reflected together about their way of life, their poverty-stricken situation, their marginalization, their values, and their abilities. We tried to do this reflection in the light of the word of God. Eventually, after one year, the first ministers of the word emerged. After that, in response to the existing needs, other ministries developed: health care, literacy training, community organization, ministers responsible for social and religious affairs.

Frequent short courses were held within the parish to train these ministers. These were organized with the help of the Episcopal Conference's Department for Indigenous People. The courses of between three and eight days gave the ministers the opportunity to practice what they were learning and also to reflect on what they were already doing. While ministers were away taking a course, the rest of the community "pitched in" for them at home. After all, the ministers worked without pay. This kind of education is basically development of the human person and a formation of conscience based on the scriptures. The goal was that the indigenous peoples would become the authors and agents of their own development and Christian way of life.

I myself have learned much from the indigenous people. Above all, they taught me to share with others in great simplicity and in an unassuming manner. They give what they have without worrying about their own future security. They have awakened and strengthened in me the great sense of community which is so typical of them. They do not make a distinction between their life of faith and their daily struggle to survive. They feel themselves to be God's children at all times—when they work in the field, when they are united with their families to share their bread, or when they dance during a fiesta.

24

MINISTRY IN A UNIVERSITY IN HOLLAND

Catharina Halkes

GROWING FEMINIST CONSCIOUSNESS

Growing up, I was struck by two aspects of my church—male domination and clericalism. When I finished my studies I decided to take part in the struggle to declericalize our church and to make room for participation and the exercise of responsibility by lay people. I was convinced that the church needed to listen attentively to the reflections of the faithful on human sexuality as experienced by men and women in their relationships.

I gradually discovered that there was a special problem regarding women in our church. Not only had they been disregarded as lay persons, but also as women. And this in two ways: they were always expected to follow special roles and exclusions were always prescribed for them.

I became involved in the traditional Catholic women's movement and also in the lay movement. Eventually I was appointed by the bishop of my diocese as codirector of a training center for women and men who were being trained in pastoral care and counseling to serve afterwards in parishes or other ministries.

During that period I saw the potential and the commitment of lay persons, especially women, who discovered that they themselves could grow as mature, whole, and responsible persons. This experience led me to study pastoral theology. I was later appointed to the theological faculty of the Roman Catholic University at Nijmegen. Part of my work was to help seminarians and pastors attending renewal courses to become more sensitive to interpersonal communication. I also facilitated processes of growth within themselves for an optimal functioning in their priestly ministry, a ministry from which I myself was excluded because I was a woman.

All aspects of my work were interconnected and concerned declericalization, promoting laity participation, women's consciousness-raising, male domination in society, an exclusively male hierarchy in our church, and other aspects.

Through this process I became more and more free of alienating roles and expectations and more and more connected with my own roots. Feminism has meant for me personally a journey inwards and a deepening in terms of living from my own roots. I received the inner strength to leave all stereotypes behind me and to go on a social and spiritual quest to live on my own terms and not on the terms of others. In biblical symbolism, this was for me a quest for an exodus to a new promised land.

It is the quest of many women. In the Christian feminist movement our primary God-experience is one of God's immanence. This quest is a cry for liberation from onesidedness for both men and women so that they both may become more whole. Today women are building new communities to do feminist theology either in small groups or in institutes of adult education. They are studying feminist theology at theological faculties. The new Chair of Feminism and Christianity which I occupy in Nijmegen University is a first victory in this search.

LAY MINISTRIES

I do not like the term "lay ministries." I prefer to speak about the variety of ministries that build up the People of God. One might make a distinction between volunteers and professionals, between non-ordained and ordained, but I prefer to speak about the commitment of all and about the charisms of each one. The number of priests is seriously diminishing in the Dutch Roman Catholic church. There is a strong movement toward secularization. Many people have left the churches, both Roman Catholic and Reformed. Many look for new forms of religiosity or spirituality. On the other hand there is still a great number of faithful women and men committed to all kinds of church work. There are many base communities, experimental groups, ecumenical parishes, student and university parishes. Many of them came together to form one movement—the Dutch "Base Movement." In this movement one can distinguish four basic elements:

1. the so-called *leerhuis*—a coming together for careful, critical, political reading of the Bible in the context of Israel and of our own modern structures of injustice
2. political action
3. pastoral care for each other
4. liturgical celebrations.

The feminist critique has played an important role in this development. In 1983 the first European Congress of base communities was held in Amsterdam with participants from many European countries, including some from behind the Iron Curtain. Men and women are being trained for these activities, either within the official church structures at both local and diocesan level, or within the Base Movement. The training helps them to work within the context of the peace movement, the women's movement, movements for social and pastoral care of foreign laborers, and other movements. The Dutch Council of Churches, of which the Roman Catholic church is a member, plays an active part, and the Base Movement has an observer status within this structure.

NORTHWEST EUROPEAN SITUATION

There is a continuing problem concerning the distinction between the pastoral worker, male or female, and the ordained priest within a parish team. Sometimes it causes friction. We must learn not to think of the qualifications of one as "higher" or more important than the other. Classification into high or low derives from a hierarchical way of thinking and is not evangelical. I preach in the student parish in Nijmegen every two months, lead the Service of the Word by myself, and conduct the Service of the Table with the students' chaplain. These liturgies are always prepared by a group of young people and adults. I have experienced that, at least for young people, it is hardly relevant whether the person leading the service is ordained or not, provided she or he is trustworthy. In this student parish we have had a number of "women liturgies," the texts of which have been published with many fruitful consequences.

A minister, woman or man, is a midwife, birthing people into new life. Only the ministry of men and women, each and together, can build up a true community of faith and give the church credibility in these times.

What I see arising in northwest secularized Europe, among Christians who want to take society and the gospel seriously, is a great variety of functions and ministries on behalf of people in their "social and spiritual quest." A lot of these ministries are prophetic, inspired by the gospel. Some are more society- than church-oriented; some more structure- than person-centered. Many young theologians tend to see their vocation in this prophetic role while others prefer to function as pastors within parish and group structures.

NEW MINISTRIES EMERGE

Examples of new ministries include taking care of drug addicts; counseling in situations of suicide and caring for the families and relatives of those involved; helping unemployed people; guiding processes of developing self-awareness of women both in themselves and in relation to the changes within the network of their relations; groups on "woman and faith," "woman and church," "woman and theology." These groups exist both at national and grass-roots levels. The media and institutes for adult education play an important role here.

I consider all these ministries and the people in them as missionary, although they stay and work within their own country. As for myself, more and more I experience "doing feminist theology" primarily as ministry and, of course, also as scholarly work. Formerly, I struggled to have women accepted in the priesthood as it was; now I struggle, rather, to change church structures so that a new form of priesthood, based on radical mutuality, may emerge within the community. Together we hope and pray for the transformation of all the ecclesial structures to enable all people to realize their gifts and charisms, gifts of the Holy Spirit.

25

Accompanying Farmworkers in California and North Carolina

Julienne De Wolf, ICM

My work with seasonal and migrant farmworkers brought me face-to-face with a system that is little understood even in the United States. Farmworkers are not employed on small family farms. They are contracted laborers hired by growers and large landowners involved in agribusiness rather than in farming. Agribusiness is frequently based on the idea of getting as much as possible out of the soil while putting back as little as possible, and in getting cheap labor. On the west coast, Chinese, Japanese, Filipino, Mexican, Arab, and Portuguese people are recruited. Mexico is an inexhaustible source of laborers. On the east coast, first there were the slaves; later came the sharecroppers. Today, in both east and west of the country there exists what is known as the "labor contractor system."

In this system the farmer, either directly or through the Employment Security Commission, contacts a labor contractor who in turn recruits people to do the harvest. In the cities of the United States there are always enough American-born black people, desperately poor white people, and other kinds of unemployed people willing to pick pickles, crop tobacco, or dig potatoes just for money, a place to live, and drinks. In recent years, thousands of Haitians and Latin American refugees have been added to this pool of workers.

The farmers usually offer a fixed amount of money to the contractor who provides some dilapidated tobacco barns or old farmhouses for living quarters. All responsibilities are then passed on to a "crew leader." Food, drinks, and transportation are provided by this crew leader who subtracts all expenses from the workers' wages. Rather than earning some money, the workers gradually owe the boss more and more. The rate of tuberculosis, venereal disease, malnutrition, and alcoholism is very high among the workers. Surveillance of the camps is very strict. Although medical care is provided and subsidized by the state, most workers are not cared for because they cannot get away from the camps. Sick people often remain hidden from visitors and crew leaders bring them out only when extremely ill.

IN CALIFORNIA

I have had two very different experiences of farmworkers in the United States, one in California, the other in North Carolina. In California I was with the United Farm Workers. They were already organized. They had just come out of a long and bloody strike that cost the lives of two workers and saw hundreds jailed and beaten. It was a strike that seemingly ended without results. However, the workers, both men and women, had a great sense of dignity. They took pride in their work and had a joy about their lives which I did not find in other places in the U.S.A. They were people whose fear had changed into hope.

They themselves had made an appeal to the churches for help. The appeal was not for clothes or food, but for people—church people who would join them in their struggle. Their expectations of the church were very precise. They wanted people who would do what they themselves could not do, and who would help them with the few things they could do. But the church people had to be just like them, not above them.

After the strike and the passing of the Farm Labor Act in California, my job was to go to those workers who were against the Union and had always opposed it, or who had been hurt by the violence of some Union members. They asked me to be a healer, a person who could listen to the other side and still defend the Union. I felt this as a tremendous sign of their trust in me. I had to listen to their stories about life in the fields before the Union began. At first I could not believe them, but after a few visits to labor camps I realized all too clearly that Californian riches were often won through the pain and suffering of the farmworkers.

Working and living among people who were poor was not easy, but their spirit was enriching. I had to be liberated from a lot of ideas, customs, and attitudes related to my life as a Religious. I also learned the freedom that came with this liberation. Hospitality, for example, has a special meaning when you are already sharing a small room with another person and have to let in two more. You feel the pinch when someone borrows your last $5.00 and you realize she will never be able to return it. I was put to shame when a young woman who had borrowed $5.00 did return it, for I knew she had felt my hesitation when she borrowed the money.

These workers had received very little support from the local church, but they knew very well how to "be church" themselves. They joined with the many other denominations who helped them and still kept their own Catholic faith. They taught us what ecumenism is, what being one is. These simple people taught me about justice, forgiveness, hospitality, as well as gentle endurance.

IN NORTH CAROLINA

I worked next with the farmworkers of North Carolina. They are desperately poor. They are people with very little hope of change, without the courage to struggle, and with a tremendous fear of becoming even worse off—if such were possible.

One of the areas in which I worked covers four counties with a total of about four hundred labor camps, each having from ten to one hundred people. There are some federal regulations concerning water supply, food preparation, overcrowding and toilets in the camps, but there is no agency to enforce the law. Inspections are carried out by the Health Department but recommendations are not followed up.

In addition to the Health Department, the East Coast Migrant Health Association and the federally funded Migrant and Seasonal Farmworkers Association are also concerned about the workers' immediate needs, such as clothes, food, or health care. However, they do little questioning about the "why" of all these conditions, nor about changing them. On the contrary, they sometimes side with the growers. An example: a sister who worked for the East Migrant Health Association spent several years organizing workers and gathering evidence of unjust treatment of workers. Her efforts led to the arrest of three contractors. All three were convicted of having kept workers in slavery. But the sister lost her job.

There are groups and individuals who join forces to try to improve conditions—for example, the Farmworkers Legal Services which is a subdivision of the Legal Services Corporation. It works with the Peace and Justice Office of the Raleigh Diocese and the North Carolina Council of Churches for legislative protection of the workers. Both on the federal and state levels some laws have been passed to make the farmer more responsible for the workers' wages and their living conditions.

Many in these camps are without material goods. Most of them are also without family or family friends. I joined a group of volunteers from the Raleigh Diocesan Peace and Justice Office. We went to the labor camps, talked with the people about their work, the different crops they harvest, the places they have been along the way. We handed out a small booklet prepared by the Farmworkers Legal Services explaining to the people their rights as workers—the right to just wages; to cook their own meals; freedom to buy food and other necessities wherever they want; to leave the camp; to receive visitors. The booklet had the phone number of the Legal Service Offices where people could call "collect" from any place. Many do call the office for help to enable them to leave the camp or to be taken to a doctor. Some have run away and need to be picked up somewhere. These occurrences, however, do not mean that a complaint is filed either about wages or about bad treatment. Experiences in court in North Carolina are very humiliating for black people or for migrant workers in general. Often we can only encourage the workers to make a statement, ask them to keep us informed about their whereabouts, and hope that three or more people with the same employer will file a complaint together.

The experience in North Carolina convinces me more and more that even the most desperate, dehumanized person can turn into a man or woman with dignity and pride. It takes friends or concerned people, however, to awaken this sense of dignity. There is still a long way to go before there will be a Farmworkers Organization in North Carolina. People are only beginning to come together, to talk and discuss, to mention the word "Union" for the first time. They have begun to wonder about the possibility of changing their own situation.

AN ASSESSMENT

Working with desperately poor people has made me aware that I, too, am a part of this oppressive system. It makes me question the "why" of my own needs, the "how" of my relationships with the people. I have to be careful not to make people dependent on me after I have freed them from a labor camp. It makes me realize that I can help the poor more by showing genuine respect and encouraging personal initiative than by giving them food or clothing or money.

In my work, both in California and in North Carolina, I have been with people of different faiths and of none except their faith in people. Our working together has been very enriching for me and for them. Some of them have visited our religious community. We talked about church and politics, liberation and oppression. Evangelization among the poor is not done by words but by actions, and by a great openness to what people themselves have to tell us and show us. It is essential in our work among the poor that we ourselves are willing to be evangelized.

SOME IMPLICATIONS FOR MISSION INSTITUTES

In California, where I worked with the United Farm Workers, I went wherever the workers needed me—from Stockton to Sacramento, from Modesto to San Isidor, to San Luis, to Arizona. Sometimes I was away from my community for up to two months at a time. Sometimes I lived in a house with other staff people, sometimes with a farmworker's family. I could never keep many personal belongings.

COMMUNITY

Life with the workers and the staff members was inspiring but I needed the contact with my community. I believe that without the support of my superiors and sisters I would have had to leave either my work among the farm workers or my religious congregation. I am sure that for those who do not have the support of their religious community the choice will be made in favor of sharing with the poor. The very values that we profess in our life as religious we see lived by the farmworkers, but not in the narrowness of our religious communities' rules.

The North Carolina situation was somewhat different for me in the sense that there I lived in community. It was different, not easier. Irregular schedules had to be fitted into a lifestyle built on regularity, and so the lifestyle of those living in that community had to be adapted. The greatest need I experienced was for openness and trust towards those of us who lived partly in community and partly in the midst of the poor.

SUPPORT

There came a time when the people in our town began to question my involvement with a group of factory workers. Attempts were made to foment division within our religious community. The members of my community never approached me to ask whether I was allowed to do what I was doing. My fellow

Sisters defended my involvement and our unity itself served as a witness to the people in the town. It was a very strong encouragement to me.

GOSPEL VALUES

My involvement with the poor grew out of my reflection on the gospel. It has been strengthened by the fact that I have seen this gospel come alive in the people. Commitment to the poor is for all of us. "Street" involvement is perhaps for the few who feel the call to more radicalism. Missionary involvement has "fashions," like development, schools, and so on, but commitment to the poor cannot be considered a "fashion."

CHOICE

A word to those who have responsibility. Be slow to assign a sister, brother, lay missioner, or priest to work with the poor unless they do want to go out of conviction and out of love for that gospel message. Let them go then and give them your full support. And do not begin a mission among the poor for the sake of your Congregation. You will only exploit the poor. If there are Sisters who see this light, hear this call, and want to make a real commitment, I would encourage them to go and to stay. They will learn to know Christ together with the poor. They will be liberated together with those people.

26

LIVING WITH THE POOR IN BRAZIL

I. "INSERTION": A NEW WAY OF BEING A RELIGIOUS MISSIONARY

Maria Arlinda Rodriguez

INTRODUCTION

My context is the life of the people in Joao Pessoa and the presence of our Sisters in their midst. But first I speak of Brazil in general, a country of 120 million inhabitants. It is a country endowed with rich natural resources but where the situation of the people is precarious: five percent are rich, fifteen percent are middle class, and eighty percent are poor.

HOUSING AND EMPLOYMENT

Economic and political power is in the hands of the five percent who enjoy social privileges. The eighty percent are the poor masses who have nothing and are at the service of the rich. The minimum salary is extremely low and the cost of living high. The land is in the hands of a landowning class and used mostly for sugar plantations and cattle raising. Vast areas are owned by large agricultural firms. Unemployment is a perennial problem. In Recife, 360,000 people out of a population of 1,000,000 are unemployed. Tne situation of many people is subhuman. They live in *barrios* or *favelas* without any infrastructures. The shanty dwellings are made of palms or cardboard with one or two "rooms" for big families. Many of these "houses" are rented to the people.

HEALTH

Food is poor, consisting basically of beans, cassava flour, rice, and a little meat.

Seventy percent of the population lives in hunger. Five hundred thousand children die every year. Eighty-three percent of the children are undernourished. There are 22 million abandoned children. There are 1.5 million children who have no schooling. Most of the children who do go to school go for *merienda* or snacks. In the year 1964 the national allocation for education was 12 percent

216

of the total budget: in the year 1982 it was down to 6.5 percent. Still the budget for the military forces increases every year.

Medical statistics show that 40 million people have tuberculosis; 70 million are sick with intestinal worms; 10 million with neurosis; 10 million suffer a sickness called *chagas*. Medical assistance is very precarious. People line up at dawn each day in order to register for a medical consultation one to two months later. Many die because of the lack of medical assistance.

Various regions suffer from extreme drought. The government appears to have no interest in solving this problem except to exploit the situation in search of votes at election time.

THE CHURCH

Since the beginning of the colonial era the church has been on the side of the powerful, blessing the situation of exploitation and injustice. Slaves from Africa were brought to Brazil for economic reasons but the church at the time, and indeed for a long time, adapted to this unjust situation. Until the Second Vatican Council it was at the service of the twenty percent of the population that was rich and privileged. After Vatican II and the Latin American Conferences of Bishops' meetings in Medellín and Puebla the church took a new direction in favor of the eighty percent of the population who were poor. Religious, too, an integral part of the church, had been at the service of the rich through schools, colleges, and hospitals; to the poor they gave "assistance," often teaching catechetics on weekends. They, too, changed direction.

THE INSERTION OF RELIGIOUS LIFE
IN THE MIDST OF THE POOR

Inspired by the evangelical appeal of the word of God, we Sisters began to live in the midst of the poor. We considered Luke 4:18: "The Spirit of the Lord is upon me and has anointed me to preach good news to the poor," and Exodus 3:9: "And now, behold the cry of the people of Israel has come to me." In the context of this ecclesial, evangelical, and situational appeal, we are leaving the convent lifestyle to live in the midst of the poor. We are living in poor *barrios* in small simple houses similar to those of the poor. We assume the daily domestic chores and we engage in remunerated jobs to support ourselves.

The house where I live is totally open to the people. It is a center of dialogue with the poor. The people have access to our house from seven o'clock in the morning till eleven o'clock in the evening and participate in our life, meals, prayer, and dialogue. The situation is quite different from that of our convent where the poor were kept apart. This process of insertion has changed our social "space" from the midst of the rich to the midst of the poor.

OUR PRAXIS

At first we place ourselves gratuitously in their presence as Sisters, poor Sisters with the poor. We have an attitude of "listening to" and "learning from" the poor in a profound respect for their culture and the reality of their situation. We begin to know them and to create bonds of friendship. We learn to discover their language, resistance, potentialities, customs, organization, and leadership. More profoundly we discover the "seeds of the word" present in them.

They have their own religious expressions or popular religiosity. They have a great devotion to the passion of Christ because they identify themselves and their sufferings with those of Christ. They also have a great devotion to the mystery of the incarnation. They like to pray the rosary and to take part in novenas and processions. They have a felt need to express their faith through pilgrimage. Every region has its own sanctuary; the northeast has the sanctuaries of Padre Cicero, San Francisco de Caninde, and San Severino do Ramo of Pernambuco. The poor usually save enough money to visit one of these sanctuaries once a year.

We then begin to unite the people and help them to form different groups for dialogue. We help them to discover together what their situation is and what are its causes, to become aware of their rights and to claim their rights. In this context we try to discern the will of God.

Different groups exist, such as basic ecclesial communities where children, the young, and adults gather together to celebrate their faith and their life; youth groups and the Friendship Movement of Children (MAC) which help them to reflect on the plan of God out of their own concrete situation; community councils and *barrio* organizations whose main apostolate is to press for the social needs of the community like the provision of water, light, transportation, garbage collection, upgrading squatter areas, postal services. We help the people to be responsible and to take on different services and ministries in the community. There are ministries for the preparation and administration of baptism, communion for the sick, and the organization of religious celebrations.

PROPHETIC MISSION

Our mission is a prophetic one. Together with the people we try to announce the Reign of God, the Reign of justice, equality, truth, and fellowship. At the same time we denounce the evil of sin—injustice, oppression, lies, marginalization, hunger, and ignorance. We do this in search of a new society based on the values of the Reign of God.

Prayer is fundamental for us. In this way of life we make a new experience of God. Formerly, in the convent, the experience of God was often centered on oneself—an experience of God who leads, loves and pardons one. In the midst of the people we experience God as the God who is committed to the poor, a God of justice, a God who is present in the history of the people.

We meet at the end of each day for prayer. Once a week in the evening we stay at home for community reflection, studies, and sharing of experiences. Once a month we take time for a two-day retreat in a quiet area where we make an evaluation of our life and work. The content of our prayer is the word of God and the life of the people. As "contemplatives in action" we always try to discern the presence of God in this reality.

Personal relationships are an important element in our community life and are made possible through continuous dialogue, mutual concern, mutual accountability, and sharing of experiences.

We are four Sisters in our community. We live our life in common in accordance with the spirit of collegiality. Decisions are made in common. We have a common fund into which we put our salaries. This is administered on a monthly basis by one of the Sisters. The difficulties in a small community are greater than those in a large one, for the problems of one member affect the whole community. We need to grow and mature in this kind of life which requires a personal option for the poor.

EFFECTS OF THE INSERTION

I summarize the positive effects as follows:
1. We have become open to the world in its historical, social, political, and economic dimensions; there is a constant dialogue with the people in all dimensions of their lives.
2. We are discovering and becoming increasingly aware of the presence of God in the world, in events, and in the poor; the incarnational and contemplative dimensions of religious life find expression together.
3. Our manner of seeing the world has changed radically; where before we saw it through the eyes of the rich, today we see it from the perspective of the oppressed.
4. We are converted and evangelized by the poor. Before, the evangelical values were theoretical; today, we try to live, for example, the values of solidarity, sharing, and hospitality in real situations. Recently the father of a poor family died, leaving behind his wife and three children. Another poor family accepted these into their home and offered them a share of what they had. This challenged us. We have a bigger house but we did not offer accommodation or welcome this widow and her children into our home.
5. The new lifestyle challenges the existing structures of religious life, especially its security. We now try to live the insecurity of the poor in a spirit of continuous evaluation. The vow of poverty for us is to be poor in solidarity with the poor. We live from our own work and salary and do not depend economically on either the Diocese or our Congregation. We try to live our vow of obedience in the search for the will of God through dialogue and discernment with the community and with our superiors.
6. We have gained a profound experience of sisterhood and brotherhood, of sharing within our community and of our community sharing with the people.
7. There is a growth in our participation in the local church; we are integrated with the Diocesan Pastoral Plan and with the local priorities of the parish.
8. Through the action of the Holy Spirit we see a new church emerging in the midst of the poor—a poor, evangelical church.

DIFFICULTIES WE ENCOUNTER

Again I summarize:
1. We feel the profound difference in culture. We were formed according to the culture of the rich while the people among whom we now live have their own popular culture, customs, language, and so on, which we have to respect; there is a danger of imposing our own culture which is foreign to them.

2. We experience a constant danger of assuming the attitude of teachers or professors always ready to teach. We have to re-educate ourselves in the midst of the people; this is very demanding and needs time.
3. The ongoing persecution of the church makes our option for the poor difficult; the rich and the government calumniate and persecute this church.
4. We encounter some problems with other members of the congregation who want to maintain existing works and feel threatened about their own present lifestyle; we feel the need of agreed criteria in assuming this lifestyle with the poor.
5. We recognize there is need to prepare for this kind of life; there is need for a new formation in view of this mission.

II. MINISTERING IN SITUATIONS OF INJUSTICE

Heloise da Cunha, RSCJ

One of the most significant experiences of my life has been that of a direct immersion into the pastoral work of the church in Brazil, in effect an immersion into the life of the poor and oppressed. I was influenced by three factors:
1. The "reality" of the situation which was cruel and full of political oppression, and which gradually penetrated into the heart of the church and challenged each one of us.
2. The church of Brazil which, in order to be true to the gospel, entered into this situation of injustice. It became receptive to the clamor of the vast majority of our population, poor, exploited, and oppressed. Its response was based on the decrees of the Second Vatican Council.
3. Our General Chapter of Renewal as a religious congregation, which was held in 1970 and supported the church's appeal. This led to an important exodus among our sisters but it was a happy exodus. Going out to immerse ourselves in the world of the poor, we rediscovered ourselves as religious and became newly aware of the meaning of our religious consecration. This affected the manner in which we lived our vows, the style of our community life, and our spirituality, all of which were incarnated in a lifestyle founded on the Bible. Mixing with many other religious women and men, priests, and lay people, we redefined the specific charisms of our own congregation and of others at the heart of an ecclesial and missionary community.
Doing pastoral work in Brazil in the service of the poor is a challenge, a painful experience, and certainly a paschal one which brought us back to the gospel and therefore to the focal point of religious life in the church.

THE CHALLENGE OF THE LAND ISSUE

According to the Brazilian bishops the fundamental cause of poverty and oppression is the lack of land for the people and the concentration of wealth and power in the hands of the great landowners. Approximately 68 percent of small plots make up only 5 percent of the available land, while at the other extreme a few large plantations make up almost 35 percent of the land. A great many peasants were or are still obliged to leave land which they have cultivated legally for many years. This exploitation is carried out by expulsions, threats, persecution, and even by killings. Between 1982 and 1984, 236 peasants were assassinated during the "battles for land." Poorly paid workers, as well as a large number of unemployed, have no option but to drift to the shanty towns or slums where they live in subhuman conditions. The result is that the majority of the Brazilian people have been uprooted. Urban land is one of the most valuable assets in Brazil's capitalist system. Behind all this there lies obviously a definite political option.

THE CHURCH'S RESPONSE

Two documents on the land question written by the Brazilian bishops have become famous: *The Church and the Problem of the Land* (1980) and *Urbanization and Pastoral Action* (1982). These official documents of the church are samples and symbols of the church's involvement in this huge problem. Two other church initiatives seem to me to be of great significance:

1. the founding of the Pastoral Commission for the Land (CPT) which is one of the organisms linked to the National Bishops' Conference of Brazil (CNBB)
2. the development of basic rural communities. These have become vigorous expressions of the newly born church among the common people in the interior of the country.

The church expresses its concern and courageous commitment not only through official documents but also in the praxis of these pastoral initiatives. Most of the basic rural communities—"real cells of the church," to use Pope Paul VI's apt description—spring up where the peasants suffer most in the struggle for their rights. The road taken by the Brazilian church in its efforts at evangelization in favor of the poor is now stained by the blood of those who have been killed, imprisoned, tortured, persecuted, and calumnied—lay people, priests, religious, and even bishops.

PERSONAL EXPERIENCES OF "INSERTION"

THE LAND WAR IN VICTORIA

My first immersion in the ways of the people began in Victoria in 1973. I lived in a sort of *favela* with other members of my congregation. Fired with enthusiasm by a well-planned Diocesan Pastoral Program, we often found ourselves confronted by the serious problems of land occupation and the plight of poor families. The pattern of opposition was always the same—repression by the police, violence, threats.

The events of February 1982 will be always imprinted on our hearts and minds. About six hundred very poor, unemployed, hungry families occupied land belonging to the state and built their huts on it. The police intervened. The huts were burned; men, women, and children were struck and beaten to the ground. Our little group had begun to get organized and was being helped by some pastoral agents and by the Diocesan Commission for Lodging Rights. This commission consisted of lawyers and other experts from various fields and some pastoral agents bound by their faith commitment to serve the poor. The families sought help from this commission, the only body able to provide immediate assistance. Our group collaborated as best we could. It was my baptism of fire.

MOVE TO THE NORTHEAST

After ten years in Victoria, we Sisters moved to a town in the northeast of Brazil. Before I share my personal experiences of living there with the poor I would like to give you some background on the area.

It is an immense region of over 1.5 million square kilometers with a population of 38 million—almost a third of the entire population of the country. People are very poor. The infant mortality rate is one of the highest in the world—for every thousand births, more than one hundred die during their first year of life. Sixty-six percent of children between the ages of one and five living in the rural areas suffer from malnutrition. Life expectancy is fifty-two years. In south Brazil it is sixty-five and in Europe seventy-five years. In the northeast fifty-five percent of the population over the age of five have not received any education. There the word "hunger" automatically means sickness, the condition of an undernourished body. Unbelievably, in this critical area, the proportion of land in the hands of the big landowners is even greater than in the national average. The consequence is forced migration of the people to other areas of the country.

THE CHURCH'S RESPONSE

The people of the northeast have not always had the benefit of a liberating evangelization. The contrary was true. The northeast lived a passive Christianity, a Christianity which stressed the passion and death of a people rather than the awakening of their vital forces to life. More recently, the bishops of the northeast inspired and set in motion a pastoral program which was to bring about the renewal of the church in Brazil. It is enough to remember one name: Dom Helder Camara.

The chronic difficulties of the northeast reach a despairing climax in the dry season. In the last calamitous period of drought and hunger the church assisted the poor by every possible means. All the dioceses of the country joined in this exercise of solidarity but it became evident that gestures of generosity and charity no longer sufficed, especially in the face of systemic injustice. The church gradually defined and articulated its position. The bishops published their decision in a document issued at their general assembly in 1983. It was entitled *The Northeast, a Challenge to the Mission of the Church of Brazil.*

LIFE WITH THE POOR IN CAMPINA GRANDE

We decided to emigrate from the suburbs of Victoria, which was an industrial town, to an "occupied" quarter in the middle of northeast Brazil. In doing this we were simply following the new option of the church in Brazil.

We moved to Campina Grande, a city of three hundred thousand inhabitants. One of its suburbs had thirty-five hundred little houses built with the revenue from a special tax. These houses were completed in 1980. They had been poorly constructed of cheap materials and without good foundations. There were no water services, no lights or drains, and no proper streets. In March 1983 the poorest families occupied these houses. They had no houses of their own and could not afford to pay rent. They had been registered at the bank to receive a loan but never received one. It was Shrove Tuesday. The women played the main role. In two days all the houses were occupied. Then the police surrounded the area. Those inside had to stay inside; those who came out could not go back.

The occupied houses became like an island hemmed in by the police. In the face of this tragedy the people named the quarter with grim humor *Malvinas*. The episode became a long, drawn-out affair. The church made its presence visible from the very first days. The bishop and clergy of the region came on Holy Thursday and Good Friday, and without taking any notice of the police began to celebrate Mass and lead the Stations of the Cross. In the end the government had to cede and the families were allowed to stay "for the time being," until further investigations could be made on the matter.

We were a small religious community living in the midst of this crying injustice. We lived in one of these small houses for almost a year. We were determined from the beginning to take the struggle and difficulties of the *Malvinas* to heart. We knew we belonged to another social class and that our formation had been for a different socio-economical-cultural context but we decided to be in communion with these people in their suffering.

We attended the neighborhood assemblies and became members of the Association of Residents of the *Malvinas*. We abided by the decisions of the assemblies. We, too, like the majority of residents, were summoned to appear before the authorities in order to "regularize" the occupation of our lodgings, but we did not respond to this summons — nor did our neighbors. Throughout the long, drawn-out proceedings the initiatives and proposals did not come from us. We attended the discussions of the Association and when they arrived at decisions we went along with them.

IMPLICATIONS FOR A MISSIONARY CONGREGATION

Everyone knows we are religious sisters. They accept us and treat us as equals without any deference. We do not hide the fact that we have definite values and criteria, a certain vision and proposals. Gradually we were able to set in motion a slow movement with very clear proposals for the basic pastoral community. But all this was only just a beginning. Quick results are not our goal. We do not feel alone or isolated, for we are at the center of pastoral work in the diocese. Much patience and attention is required as we consider the steps we should take.

A PLAN FOR THE FUTURE

We drew up a plan for the future which I summarize here.

— We will try to identify ourselves with the cause and struggle of the people by cooperating in their own organizations. We wish to be the salt and the leaven mixed in well with the endeavors of the people.

— We will try to awaken the critical conscience of Christians so that they will be able to integrate their faith with their struggle in practice.

— We will continue to participate in the meetings and in the prayers and festivities of the people. We always try to integrate our prayer and faith into the events of everyday life.

— We will follow up the initiatives proposed by the church of Brazil and our diocese to discuss and deepen our understanding of certain topical questions which affect the life of the people.

— We will foster the awakening of small groups, since the number of *Malvinas*-type situations is enormous. Our objective is to help form basic Christian communities in as a short a time as possible and to ensure that they are active and well organized.

OUR OWN CONVERSION

We religious sisters feel increasingly called to our own conversion. We are evangelized by the very harshness of the life of the people who are under continual threat, and by their innumerable friendly gestures to us. Often we feel very small and weak in the presence of the clearsightedness and the frequent gospel-inspired gestures of the poor. The poor people here possess such a capacity for resistance that we believe it can only come from God. They have shown us a thousand proofs of friendship, of solidarity, and of an immense desire to go on living and to overcome these obstacles. They are poor but they are intelligent and full of ideas, and they are well aware of the burden of sin which weighs upon them.

We are happy; we know we are at the beginning of a new mission, which means for us conversion, sacrifice, and hope, because something is about to be born. I know now that good intentions are not enough; that we need criteria; we need proposals based on biblical and spiritual foundations; we need to have ecclesial communion for an evangelization that liberates. We are one with the brothers and sisters with whom we work and pray. We evaluate our progress and we plan our projects together with the wider community.

Our intention is not to keep decision-making in our own hands. The decisions must be approved by the basic groups and widened to enable these basic groups to assume their role and place in history. Unless we have prayer, study, evaluation, objective mission criteria, submission to both an objective external critique and an internal critique, we will run the risk of remaining on the plane of personal, even ingenuous actions.

We move forward with joy and hope, seeking to collaborate in the evangelization of the poor of our country. We are convinced that the people amongst whom we live are the heirs to God's chosen people, the people of the Bible, poor, landless, always at the mercy of powerful neighbors. We firmly believe that one day the light, peace, and joy of these good people will triumph. Our faith in the liberating God of the Bible, the one and true God illuminates our frail and poor itinerary.

In today's Brazil we are experiencing religious life within the context of the church, a church which, in turn, has found itself in the midst of the poor and of the common masses. It is here that both Religious life and the church itself are called to conversion. They are called to take a courageous stand in the face of real persecution and increasing massacres linked to the growth of wealth and luxury of a privileged minority.

FOUR QUESTIONS

There are four questions which trouble me and which I believe we must try to answer in view of our experience.

1. How can so much oppression be explained in a Catholic country?
2. What is the significance of the Brazilian experience for other churches, especially the church of Rome? How should it be considered, assessed, judged in its particular circumstances?
3. What is the extent of the engagement of religious men and women in the struggle against injustice?
   —Is it a secondary, optional commitment?
   —Is it a purely tactical engagement?
4. What does the Christian commitment to evangelize mean in situations of deep injustice?

27

RESPONDING TO INJUSTICE:
A MISSION SOCIETY'S DILEMMA

Ronald Larkin, MSC

In the late 1960s and early 1970s missionary communities had little social consciousness. Like many other groups, their main work was typical of parish missionary stations—routine office work, visits, and administration of the sacraments. In the mid 1970s, however, they began to become more aware of the situation of injustice in which they found themselves and of their own relationship to it. They began to feel they should do something to change the situation in which the people to whom they minister are caught: underpaid, with no chance of a better future and no one to whom they can appeal against injustices.

Missionaries began to feel that their "traditional missionary presence" was not doing much to help change the desperate situation. They wanted to have a more specific kind of presence, a new kind of presence. They began to help the people to form cooperatives, to build basic communities, to teach people about their own national constitutions, to understand the rights given to them by these constitutions, to value themselves as human persons, and so on. They began to support the people, to encourage them to protest openly, to march, to demand to be heard.

The typical reaction set in. Threats were made against the missionaries, against the people, against the leaders. Repression followed, properties were destroyed, scare tactics began. Then came the killings—brutal, bloody, and many. Six missionaries were among the slaughtered.

The missionaries discussed among themselves what they should do. They eventually decided to leave the country, feeling that they were unable to do anything. They would be killed and, perhaps worse still, cause others to be killed on their account.

They moved to a neighboring country, but there they had no new, distinct missionary task. They began to question their decision to leave the first country. They began to argue among themselves about what they should be doing now. What course of action should they take? Their superiors left the decision to them but the group was split, with contrasting ideologies. A sense of hopelessness set in and there were feelings of frustration due to their inability to do anything to correct the situations of injustice in the first country which some feel they have deserted. They did not seem to be able to get others, including members of their institute and its superiors, to comprehend or "feel" the situation like they do. They cannot understand how so many people can allow the situation to continue, how they can be so indifferent.

Today two of them went underground. . . .

THE QUESTIONS

There are many. How do you help prepare religious to confront, or simply cope with, such a situation? What kind of "tools" can you give them to help them deal constructively with such situations? What kind of formation?

WHO ARE INVOLVED?

The situation involves a military regime which has "national security" or simply its own continuing in power as its basic stance, its fundamental justification for all kinds of repressive measures.

It involves a local hierarchy of bishops who do not live in the abject surroundings of most of their people and who in many ways are closer to the government than to their own people. The bishops do not really seem to understand what is going on, nor do they want to risk open criticism of the government. They are often, in the beginning at least, critical of the work of the missionaries.

It involves religious superiors who sincerely want to help the missionaries but who are far away geographically, psychologically, intellectually, and emotionally. Recognizing this distance, the major Superiors often think it best to let the missionaries themselves make decisions about whether to stay or leave the beleaguered country, or about what kind of new apostolate they should take up when they arrive in a new country.

And it involves the missionaries who have a sense of being alone in their struggles, of being unsupported at times by their superiors, and of being misunderstood by their fellow Religious.

A HYPOTHETICAL CASE?

How do you help prepare women and men religious to deal with and function in such situations? These are dedicated missionaries. How do you help them to cope? The situation is not a hypothetical one. It has happened to us in our missionary society and most likely will happen again.

28

APARTHEID: THE HISTORY OF A STRUGGLE

Archbishop Denis Hurley

HISTORICAL REVIEW

This historical review deals with developments from June 1976 to June 1987. It is divided into two periods: 1976 to 1984 and 1984 to 1987.

JUNE 1976 TO SEPTEMBER 1984

The crucial events of this period can be described as follows:

STUDENT REVOLT

The first event of importance was the student revolt that began in the township of Soweto on June 16, 1976. The students were mainly high school students and the revolt grew out of resentment against the imposition of the Afrikaans language as the medium of instruction for certain subjects. A demonstration in Soweto was violently suppressed by the police. This triggered off a student revolt that spread through many parts of the country and resulted in seven hundred officially recorded deaths. The security forces could not manage to contain it until well into 1977, but even after that it continued to flare up spasmodically. Obviously, it was a revolt not only against the imposition of Afrikaans but also against the poor quality of African education in general and the apartheid policy responsible for it.

Other influences that contributed to unleashing the revolt were the collapse of Portuguese colonial power in nearby Mozambique and Angola and the accession to independence of these two countries, the liberation wars in Rhodesia and on the northern border of Namibia, and above all the Black Consciousness movement which in the late 1960s had been initiated by Steve Biko, who met his death in detention in September 1977. The student revolt of 1976–77 established the pattern of vigorous youth participation in the liberation struggle. Though active unrest was quelled in 1977 the consequences of student revolt took several forms.

Revival of African National Congress. An immediate effect of the youth revolt and its suppression was the exodus of great numbers of young people across South Africa's borders and their absorption into the liberation movements, especially the African National Congress (ANC). Quite a few, after training abroad, were infiltrated into South Africa as guerilla fighters and contributed to the progressive increase in incidents of sabotage and other acts of aggression. The popularity of the ANC expanded rapidly, and it regained its position of leadership in the liberation struggle.

Youth and Community Organizations. The suppression of active unrest did not result in a falling off in organizational expertise. A nationwide youth movement, the Congress of South African Students (COSAS), came into existence in 1979, and out of the ranks of rebellious youth emerged the young adults who began to share their expertise with the people of the townships. The result was the rapid growth of community organizations. With unemployment becoming more widespread, the more creative spirits among the unemployed dedicated their talents to these community organizations. The scene was being set for the United Democratic Front (UDF).

Trade Union Movement. At the same time, throughout this period there was a consistent growth in the black trade union movement prompted especially by the Federation of South African Trade Unions (FOSATU), which had adopted a nonracial stance, and the Council of Unions of South Africa (CUSA), which professed a Black Consciousness orientation.

Inkatha Movement. The province of Natal with its patchwork of KwaZulu areas experienced its own kind of development. The Inkatha Movement was called into being by Chief Mangosuthu Gatsha Buthelezi in the early 1970s to promote an African cultural identity. In fact, it quickly became a Zulu national movement. It moved progressively away from the ANC and later came into conflict with the UDF. It opposed the ANC option for violence and the call for economic pressures on South Africa. It has collaborated in the formulation of a special multiracial two-tier constitution for Natal through what is termed the Natal KwaZulu Indaba. It has endeavored to set up its own trade-union structure to counter FOSATU. It is authoritarian and monopolistic, and when it clashes with other organizations it shows little practical respect for the nonviolent attitude it professes.

THE NEW CONSTITUTION

In the other provinces the youth revolt, the growth of trade unions and the emergence of local community organizations set the scene for the next act. This took the form of vigorous black reaction to an attempted constitutional reform by the South African government.

Prime Minister P. W. Botha came to power proclaiming the need for reform. His slogan was "adapt or die." His dilemma was to promote a reform that would satisfy blacks and would not antagonize whites, a kind of squaring of the circle. After discussions and reports dating back to 1977, the government presented a draft of the new constitution to Parliament in May 1983. It was duly adopted at the end of August and submitted to a referendum of white voters on November 2, 1983. The result was a two-to-one vote in favor.

The new constitution provides for firmly entrenched white power and a subordinate role for representatives of the so-called colored and Indian populations. It distinguishes between "general affairs," common to all populations, and "own affairs," special to white, colored, and Indian populations. The structures created by the constitution include the office of Executive President, a President's Council, and three chambers of Parliament: the House of Assembly for whites, the House of Representatives for so-called colored, and the House of Delegates for Indians, each with a council of ministers. There is also a cabinet named and presided over by the president, as well as joint standing committees providing for interhouse consultations. The president is given "control and administration of black affairs," and Africans generally are supposed to find their political aspirations satisfied in homeland government and in local councils in white areas.

Opposition to the constitution and to the elections to the Houses of Representatives and Delegates called into existence the United Democratic Front (UDF), which brought together a loose federation of about six hundred black community organizations with a sprinkling of white support. The UDF did not prevent the implementation of the constitution, but its vigorous campaigning reduced to a farce the elections to the two satellite houses of Parliament. What was more important was that it served as a catalyst for a huge groundswell of black extra-parliamentary opposition strongly representative of black rejection of the apartheid policy and its institutions.

Another much smaller liberation movement came into existence at about the same time, namely, the National Forum or Azanian Peoples Organization (AZAPO), which differs from the UDF in its adherence to Black Consciousness principles.

SEPTEMBER 1984 TO JUNE 1987

Countrywide Unrest. The occupation of the Sebokeng township by troops and police on October 23, 1984, was a clear sign that a political upheaval of major dimensions was occurring. Beginning in September 1984, it rolled over the country like a tidal wave for two years. It was a time of protests, demonstrations, and boycotts; of violent police repression and popular reactive violence which resulted in many deaths and injuries; of funerals and memorial services that became occasions for political protest and further police repression; of ongoing detentions and treason trials; of the banning of organizations; of threats and sometimes the application of economic sanctions; of loss of confidence in South Africa, leading to a dramatic drop in the value of the rand.

The unrest was accompanied by an increase of insurgency. Guerilla incidents included hand-grenade and rocket attacks; car bombings; land-mine explosions; assassinations or attempted assassinations and skirmishes. The ANC had threatened attacks on soft targets and the unleashing of a "people's war." A further dimension of the violence was the outbreak of conflict between the UDF and AZAPO in the Eastern Cape, between Inkatha and UDF affiliates in Natal, and of attacks and counterattacks involving vigilantes. The gruesome specter of "necklacking" made its appearance.

1985 State of Emergency. By July 1985 it was calculated that 450 people had died in political violence and that over 1,500 had been injured. The government decided that urgent action had to be taken to bring the situation under control. On July 21 it imposed a state of emergency in thirty-six magisterial districts. In October the state of emergency was lifted in five districts but imposed in seven others. However, unrest and violence continued with over 500 political deaths in the last six months of 1985 and 569 between January and August 1986. Despite this, the state of emergency was lifted in stages and terminated on March 7, 1986. Media and especially television were relaying the tragic story of South Africa to a horrified world until the South African government decided to clamp down on press, radio, and television.

Visits to ANC. The second half of 1985 was marked by important developments, including the inauguration of a series of visits by delegations of business persons, politicians, church personnel, and academics to ANC headquarters in Lusaka. It had become clear that the role of the ANC in South Africa was crucial.

Formation of COSATU. November 1985 saw the formation of the Congress of South African Trade Unions (COSATU). Though certain trade union groups preferred not to join, COSATU brought together an imposing array of worker organizations, including unions affiliated to the Federation of South African Trade Unions, the National Union of Mineworkers, and thirty-two other unions. At its inauguration, COSATU made it clear that it intended to play a political role, and among other things pronounced itself in favor of disinvestment.

KwaNdebele. During the first half of 1986, unrest became particularly intense in the Transvaal, north of Pretoria, where the South African government was trying, against the wishes of the inhabitants, to force independence onto an area called KwaNdebele and to manipulate borders. The so-called government of KwaNdebele, set up by South Africa, created a force of vigilantes to crush the resistance.

Eminent Persons Groups. At this time, a party of representatives from the British Commonwealth countries known as the Eminent Persons Group visited South Africa with a view to promoting the dismantling of apartheid and the holding of negotiations for a peaceful settlement. The project was aborted when South Africa launched attacks against what it alleged were ANC centers in Zambia, Zimbabwe, and Botswana.

School Situation. The school situation was constantly on the boil, with great numbers of pupils missing out on education in keeping with the slogan "Liberation before Education." The students were reacting to the poor quality of education, the presence of troops in the townships, the banning of student organizations, the high-handed actions of the Department of Education in regard to student representative councils, the transfer of teachers, and the closing of schools without consultation. Beneath the antischool activity was the deep, flaming resentment of the young people against apartheid. Parents and community leaders tried to take the situation in hand. They formed the Soweto

Parents Crisis Committee. Planning began for a more relevant curriculum of education entitled People's Education.

GENERAL STATE OF EMERGENCY—JUNE 1987

The situation grew more tense as the tenth anniversary of Soweto approached on June 16. The government decided that there was only one way to quell the unrest and imposed a general state of emergency on the whole country, to take effect at midnight on June 11.

Hundreds of people were detained and a few deported. Detentions multiplied during the rest of the year to the extent that it was calculated that about thirty thousand people, including thousands of children under the age of eighteen were affected for longer or shorter periods. The leadership of "progressive" organizations was profoundly affected as all the members of the National Education Crisis Committee were detained. Church personnel did not escape the attention of the security forces. At one time or another the Catholic church was represented among the detainees by twelve priests (including Father Smangaliso Mkhatshwa, Secretary General of the Southern African Bishops Conference), three deacons, four Religious Sisters, twenty seminarians, and seven lay persons active in church work. Besides bannings, restrictive orders were issued against persons and organizations.

Stricter control was imposed on the dissemination of news and dissent. The definition of "subversive" was broadened and information connected with the unrest or with the security procedures could be released only with the authorization of the Bureau for Information. Later the control of such information was vested in the Public Relations Division of the South African police.

All reading material except that approved by the Department of Education and Training was banned in classrooms. Parents and other persons were prohibited from entering any school without prior permission.

The UDF was declared an affected organization. An investigation was launched into the finances of many organizations, especially those of extraparliamentary opposition.

Though some points were scored in the law courts against the emergency regulations, the government reacted with new legislation, and when it reimposed the state of emergency on June 12, 1987, it had effectively sealed off all legal loopholes.

Continuing to impose its will is obviously placing an enormous strain on the South African government. Meanwhile the pressure from outside also continues to grow, mainly in the form of economic measures. These have not yet reached the stage of seriously dislocating the economy, but they are causing uneasiness and insecurity in the white population. The whites are reacting in two ways. Some are leaving the country, and no doubt many more would do so if it were possible. The great majority of those who remain see their security in supporting the National Party and even the more extreme right-wing Conservative and Herstigte Parties. This was clearly borne out in the white election of May 6, 1987.

THE BEGINNING OF REFORMS

The reforms which the National Party is considering are marginal, concerning marriage and morality and even group areas. The great pillars of apartheid remain untouched, such as the constitution ensuring white supremacy; the Land Act of 1913 which was amended in 1936, allocating eighty-seven percent of the surface of the country to white ownership; discrimination in education; the Population Registration Act. The move to establish a National Statutory Council for consultation with black "leadership" offers little hope for any significant change. In the meantime, parliamentary rule diminishes continually with the establishment of new state structures. Provincial responsibilities are being suppressed in favor of Regional Service Councils with state-appointed membership. The military has an important say in the National Security Council and the so-called Joint Management Committees operating at the local level.

Control by the security forces, police and military, has been expanded by the creation of auxiliary police, *kitskonstabels,* who receive a mere six weeks' training. Vigilantes are also encouraged.

The destabilization of neighboring countries continues in order to discourage support for the ANC and SWAPO and to maintain the economic dependence of these countries.

After centuries of colonial rule and discrimination, and after decades of apartheid, the African people have taken their destiny into their own hands. Fired by the vision and vigor of the ANC and galvanized by the youth revolt and the UDF, they strain forward to the goal of a nonracial, unitary, democratic, one-person–one-vote South Africa of the future. For the liberation movements this vision is not negotiable. For white South Africa, particularly the Afrikaaner nation, white control is not negotiable. This is the present impasse.

How to resolve this impasse is the great question facing us. The liberation movements see the answer in multipronged pressure from all quarters: guerilla infiltration and activity, trade union activism, internal unrest promoted by youth and community organizations, diplomatic and economic pressure.

A new endeavor aimed at changing white attitudes has just come into existence under the name of the Institute for a Democratic Alternative for South Africa (IDASA). In July it sponsored a group of sixty delegates to travel to Dakar in Senegal to consult with representatives of the ANC. Whether it will be allowed to function and how it will function remains to be seen.

THE ROLE OF THE CHURCH

The question of the role of the church, or, in a multidenominational society like South Africa, the churches, in the political sphere is a vast one. All that can be offered here are a few relevant and salient items of information.

For many decades the leadership of the so-called English-speaking churches, including the Catholic church, has commented and taken stands on the South African situation, but it has exerted little influence on political developments.

The weakness in church policy has been the failure to translate declarations into education of church membership in the principles proclaimed. Recent times have seen the emergence of an increasing number of religious groups operating at the local level to promote changes in Christian attitudes. In these times the sharpest religious reflections have come not from church leaders but from groups and assemblies of other church representatives. In this matter the South African Council of Churches is conspicuous.

The South African Council of Churches. It has come out in support of the Harare and Lusaka Declarations calling for comprehensive sanctions against South Africa, support for liberation movements including their armed struggle, and denunciation of the South African state as illegitimate. This does not mean, of course, that the churches that are members of the South African Council of Churches express the same views or do very much about implementing the resolutions and recommendations referred to them. This is the glaring weakness of the Council of Churches.

The Catholic Bishops. They too started by issuing declarations. Under the influence of Vatican II and the Synod of Bishops of 1974 the South African Catholic bishops became more realistic and saw the need for action. But it was only in 1976, after four years of discussion, that the white and black seminaries were integrated. Multiracial schools were set up. The government did nothing to stop it, although it was illegal. In 1977 the bishops made a commitment to work against all forms of apartheid. Then in 1981–82 they visited Namibia and drew up their Report on Namibia. Again they protested strongly against the constitution of 1983 and they published an effective protest against police violence.

The Government has lost its moral legitimacy, but the bishops ask if it is wise to make a public statement to this effect. The real challenge is to move from prophecy to evangelization. This will be done through community action and a program of education in Catholic social doctrine, showing how this doctrine applies to the South African situation and in particular to ethnic community relations. To this end a specific pastoral plan has now been elaborated by the Bishops' Conference.

The "*Kairos* Theologians." Another body that has been sharp in its comments is the group known as the *kairos* theologians. The main thrust of *The Kairos Document* is that the churches should denounce the South African state as a tyranny, side unequivocally with the oppressed, and support the liberation struggle. The issue of armed struggle is dealt with somewhat ambiguously in the document.

The issues raised by these bodies are legitimate ones and must engage the attention of the churches. For this reason the Commission for Justice and Peace of the Southern African Catholic Bishops' Conference has launched a serious effort to prepare reflections for submission to the Conference on the following issues:

1. the present situation in South Africa and the response of the church
2. in collaboration with the Theological Commission the Commission is dealing with the question of unjust war in Namibia and the use of military force to maintain apartheid in South Africa.

29

DOING THEOLOGY IN THE SOUTH AFRICAN CONTEXT

Albert Nolan, OP

People sometimes ask me, "What do you do in South Africa?" and my answer is, "I do theology." They ask again, "But what do you do about apartheid?" My answer is again, "I do theology." When they insist, "Yes, but what do you do to get into prison?" my answer remains, "I do theology."

I do theology in the Institute of Contextual Theology (ICT) in Johannesburg. The ICT was founded in 1980 to develop a truly South African theology, a theology not imported either from Europe or the USA or Latin America, a theology which starts from our situation of oppression and conflict. The Institute is independent of any particular church tradition, yet it is Christian. This gives us the freedom to explore whatever we want and in whatever direction we want. It is this freedom which made *The Kairos Document* possible. The ICT was created to allow people to say what they really believe.

The ICT is not a teaching institute. It is an office with an office staff. Its members go out to people and groups of all kinds—theologians, priests and ministers, youth, women, trade unionists, development workers, and others, helping them to do their own theology. We do not come forward with a theology based on a set of doctrines which we then teach with a precise methodology. The kind of theology that emerges is of various kinds: black theology, feminist theology, youth theology, a workers' theology made by the workers themselves, a theology of ministering in crisis situations, a prophetic theology, the *kairos* theology. . . .

WHAT IS CONTEXTUAL THEOLOGY?

In its origin all theology is contextual, as are the various theologies of the Bible. Historical circumstances gave rise to different faith questions and the answers to these questions produced the different theologies of the Bible. Biblical studies began to use textual criticism and to become aware of cultural elements in the Bible. Various contexts in biblical times produced various theologies—wisdom literature, priestly, prophetic, court, or monarchical thinking. Different contexts produced and were seen to have produced different theologies—Johannine, Pauline, Marcan. The contexts were not just the local communities. The contexts placed the Bible texts in life situations which included social, political, and economic backgrounds. I shall give you some examples of the contextual origin of various theologies.

Patristic Theology. The context, particularly that of the Greek Fathers, was monasticism. It started from the theological questions of monks, celibate men. Even if afterwards they became bishops and faced the problems of rich and poor people, they still looked at these from the point of view of a monastery, not from being themselves inserted in "the world."

Augustine was preoccupied with the situation created by the fall of the Roman Empire into the hands of the "barbarians." His theology is permeated by this context, as can be seen in *The City of God*.

Scholastic Theology arose within the context of the medieval university which faced the problem of accommodation to the philosophy of Aristotle. The questions which this problem posed are not our questions anymore.

The Theology of the Manuals (Neoscholasticism) had as its context nineteenth-century seminaries and the questions for clerics brought up by the Tridentine seminary system of clerical education. The manuals tried to equip the future priest with all he would need in terms of dogma for preaching and catechizing, and all the moral theology (casuistry) he would need for the confessional. It was a theology centered largely on the sacraments.

European and North American Theology starts from the question of how to live in a secularized society. This is not the question I grapple with in South Africa. Ours is how to live in a racist society.

These few examples illustrate the point that all theology is contextual in its origin. Unfortunately, not all theology is aware of this. Hence problems arise when we take a theology which arose in one context and teach it in another. Students are given answers to questions they did not ask, while the questions which they do ask in their own context are largely ignored.

IS THERE A UNIVERSAL THEOLOGY?

If we lose the awareness that all theology is contextual in its origin, we develop the illusion that a particular theology is universal. Let me give some examples.

Black Theology is contextual because it is conscious of the fact that it is an attempt to do theology from a context of a black experience of oppression. Most other theology is "white," starting from a white experience, but it has the illusion of being universal.

Feminist Theology is contextual, starting from the experience of women in a world dominated by men. All other theology is in fact masculine, constructed by men, answering questions posed by men, from a perspective of men, in the context of a world of men. But men are oblivious to this fact and think that their theology is universal, applicable equally to women and men alike. They would not dream of calling their theology a "masculine theology."

African Theology, arising from a context of African experiences, faces the problem that Western theology is oblivious of the fact that it is Western and assumes that it is the only possible way of doing theology.

Contextual Theology is one in which the theologian is fully aware that he or she is facing faith questions out of a particular context. Those who do theology or have done it without being aware of the context which conditions their thinking always imagine that they are engaged in a universal theology.

Syncretism. To what extent is contextual theology syncretistic, that is, mixing the gospel message with local cultural elements which are often and erroneously referred to as "pagan"?

The word "syncretism" is loaded and Western. It presupposes that it is possible to have the "pure gospel" without any cultural elements. The problem is that we do not want to mix our Western cultural faith with African or other cultures. We have so identified the faith with our Graeco-Roman background that we cannot see how it can accept elements of another culture on an equal footing. As long as we identify "Catholic faith" with our culturally determined theological package, it is indeed impossible.

Independent African churches are accused of syncretism by Western theologians, but are these theologians aware of how much syncretism exists within the Western churches? Is not Western theology syncretistic? Are there no "pagan" cultural elements from a pre-Christian past mixed in with the gospel message? The illusion is that I can deal with Christian ideas as though they dropped out of the sky free of any context—"revealed." All ideas originate in some cultural context, and all words used to express ideas are similarly products of a culture which determines their meaning.

HOW DO WE TEACH CONTEXTUAL THEOLOGY?

We start from life instead of from ideas, from practice instead of from theory, from a context instead of from abstractions.

We try to teach the skills to do one's own theology. We help people in their own context to ask faith questions and to grapple with them. Our method does not consist of teaching theology as if we were giving a kind of "bank deposit." It does not mean that this theology involves less study, research, and reading. Rather it demands more. The student must study the Bible to understood how the prophets, Jesus, and the apostles theologized, and study tradition to understand how the Fathers of the church and theologians theologized.

One need not be an academic to do theology. All that is required is faith and a mind. We must convince people that they can do their own theology, that they are not constrained to ask professors for questions and answers. As they go further into it they may well need resources, to consult experts.

Priests and lay ministers can only do their pastoral work effectively if they can do practical theology. I shall illustrate this process with just two examples.

Sacrament of Penance. How do I teach the Sacrament of Penance contextually? We begin by asking what exactly happened with regard to confession after Vatican II. Why did people stop going to confession? What kinds of sin do people confess, and what kind do they never think of confessing? Why do people feel the need to go to confession? The experience which most people had of confession was of something frightening. What ought it to be?

The next step is to go back to the origin of confession. In what context did auricular confession originate? Is it well known that auricular private confession emerged in the Irish monastic context?

Only then come the practical questions: what do people need? What can we do to meet those needs?

Sin. How do we do theology around the topic of sin? The first step is to ask the questions: what do people understand by sin today? Why do people not use the term "sin" to speak of evils that they feel strongly about, such as sexism, authoritarianism, injustice, and oppression? Why, on the other hand, has sin become almost synonymous with sex, as is clear from expressions such as "living in sin" and "loss of virtue"? Why is it enough to mention the word "sin" to bring conversation about any topic to an end?

The next step is to go back to the original meaning of sin in the Bible and in early theology, and find out how sin came to be connected almost exclusively with sex, murder, and telling lies.

Then comes the question: how can we use it today in a way that makes us aware of what God has always wanted to tell us?

SUMMARY

Our aim is to help the student do theology rather than simply learn the theology that someone else did in a context different from that of the student himself or herself.

We must help people to acquire the skills needed for doing theology. One good starting point is to learn from the way in which others before us did their theology in their own contexts: The prophets, Jesus, Paul, Mark, and so on.

The prerequisite for doing theology is to have faith and to have an average mind. Theology is within the reach of ordinary Christians. They should be taught how to do it, how to think theologically about questions which arise from their own particular context. In South Africa our special context is apartheid.

30

A SPIRITUALITY FOR CONFLICT
AND VIOLENCE

Thomas Cullinan, OSB

For the last two and a half years I have been involved, with others, in building a house. One of the many things my hands have taught me — as my head could never have done — is that to participate creatively in life we must first make an act of profound humility and obedience before the given reality. You cannot use tiles creatively and beautifully if you pretend they are slates, or even want them to be. You cannot learn from concrete blocks how to be a craftsman, as long as you want them to be bricks. You cannot afford to use pinewood without learning its own distinct nature — it is not oak. We come to a singular freedom of action, unselfconscious and free of fear, only by listening to and searching for the truth that is given and present. This calls for humility and obedience before a truth which will set you free.

We are artisans in God's world, artisans whose primary and only task is a loving and total response to truth. "For this I came into the world, to bear witness to 'the truth.'" Sadly we slip in the definite article "the." Bearing witness to the truth, then, leads us to think of Jesus bearing witness to the creed, or dogmas, or academic theology! No! "Truth" is the present reality of peoples' present lives, what is happening to them, among them. And in this reality what does the divine love affair called "God's Reign" look like?

I need hardly comment that the arrogant, independent, Western come-of-age mind has quite a specific approach to freedom. It is a freedom which keeps the self intact and demands the right to choose as one likes. It knows *hubris* but not *humus*. It is self-concerned, not self-forgetful. It seeks to be free from reality and relations. It does not receive freedom and peace as bonus and gift.

CONFLICT

As we reread and reponder the gospel it is clear that if our primary call is to a loving response to truth, born out of an original obedience and humility, then we cannot avoid conflict. It is an inherent part of living for truth; it is conflict unsought but freely accepted. The infancy narratives of Matthew and Luke are not childish sentimental nursery stories but tough-minded summaries of the main themes to be worked out in detail in the life story which follows. They are like the initial "statement" in a symphony, highlighting and clarifying what is to be told more fully in the work as a whole.

Read the story of the massacre of the Innocents from your knowledge of El Salvador or of any contemporary fascist regimes, or past effete royal regimes. There is the appearance, at least rumored, of a new subversive alternative; an initial response of recognizing and working with the new; the discovered inability to do so and then the reaction, the vicious overkill. Read again Matthew's contrast between the inability of the royal regime to have compassion, to know grief, over against the Lamentation of Rachel, the essential voicing of grief. Blessed are those who mourn! Witnessing truth, responding to truth means naming the grief, sharing the suffering at the deep gut level of agony and anger expressed in the Greek word "compassion" so often used in the gospel. This is a necessary part of prophetic liberation, of demystifying the dominant illusion that all is well with the people.

Read again the Magnificat with its terrible proclamation of the divine intention for, and warning to, the social and political order. The powerful are removed from their godlike seats of power, and the powerless, the voiceless, raised up, but not onto those same seats. The poor find blessing in the good news, but not by becoming rich in turn. The hungry are fed. We all want them to be. And the well fed go hungry away. But does God want that? What God are we dealing with?

The gospel is not merely about private virtues and individual spirituality. It is about living in the public forum in the light and truth of God's love affair with people; it is to understand why Jesus passed through noncomprehension, conflict, and finally death. I want to focus on one aspect of the gospel, one that I think we are not too clear about. I believe it would enable us to reread the gospel and to cope with conflict in our own times. This leads me back many years!

WHO ARE THE SINNERS?

When I was thirteen years old I was taught that the sinfulness of sin depended on it being "Serious, Intended, and (k)Nown. SIN." That was good teaching — I still remember it! And since at that age scrupulosity can be a great problem, it was wise to warn us that we could not sin seriously over trivial matters, nor if we did not really intend to, nor by accident. We could not "fall" into sin, only jump. Since the time of the Jansenists that has been standard moral theology in the church. It tends to divide our own lives and our view of society into the naughty and the nice, the badly behaved and the virtuous. As time went on I began to see that most of the evil in our world is perpetrated by high-minded people who see themselves as virtuous. As we prayed and sang the psalms in our community I began to wonder why "the virtuous" were so often those who actually crushed and destroyed others, whether they knew it or not. As we read and tried to hear the gospels I wondered: if being well-behaved or consciously naughty were the significant issues in life, why did Jesus seem to favor the naughty and be in collision with the well-behaved? No doubt you will have pondered similar questions. We must pursue them further—else the church may become even more identified with the middle class than it is at present. I will share a little of my pursuit.

THE MAN BORN BLIND

I have been worried, off and on, about the question at the beginning of John, chapter 9. The disciples ask about the blind man: who sinned, this man or his parents that he should be blind? How primitive to assume that sickness or affliction should be linked with personal or family guilt! I dismissed it as a prejudice that we "moderns" had grown out of ... until, in my few honest moments, I noticed a deep defense mechanism in my own psyche when I met people afflicted, not just sick but silly, not just handicapped but lazy. Only by saying "Raca" somewhere in my psyche could I keep myself intact in the presence of suffering people. I recall a lady once saying to me, "You know—there are no really poor people in our country, only fickle ones."

This brings me back to John chapter 9. The story of the blind man is bracketed between two crucial questions. Both are based on standard assumptions:

Rabbi, who sinned, this man or his parents, for him to have been born blind?

Some Pharisees said, "We are not blind, surely!?"

To these questions, Jesus answers:

Neither he nor his parents sinned.

Blind? If you were, you would not be guilty, but since you say "We see," your guilt remains.

Between those two questions John tells the superb and witty story of the blind man's liberation and his vigorous, fearless confrontation with the authorities. His challenge to them would be like saying to our British defense minister: why are you so fascinated by the Peace Movement? Are you going to join it? Many details of the story resonate for us today: for example, the man's parents not wanting to disown their son, yet not wanting to be counted among the subversives.

TWO DOMINANT IDEOLOGIES

Jesus' confrontation with the dominant religious culture was not a conflict with the Law, the Torah, as such. It was a confrontation with the treatment of the Law as an ideology. The word "ideology" has had a varied history over the last hundred years. I am not using it in the neutral sense, the set of ideas which any culture or class has with which to interpret the world. I am using it in the pejorative sense, referring to a set of ideas, theories, and principles which have ceased to be a relative tool for understanding reality and have become an absolute, a machine, into which reality is fitted. In our own day there are such ideologies, Russian Marxism and Western individualist consumerism. There is a third ready to emerge—Islamic fundamentalism.

If we can clarify why and how Jesus confronted the ideology of his day, I think we would find the origins of the overt conflicts that many Christians are meeting in violent forms in Latin America, parts of Africa, the Philippines, South Korea, and elsewhere. We would find, too, that these overt conflicts are already latent in and originate from the less overtly evident conflicts in Western society. In other words, if the church discovered its prophetic imagination and its call to confront the domination of standard ideologies in the West, it would be in conflict there in ways that our niceness can hardly picture.

CHARACTERISTICS OF DOMINANT IDEOLOGY

May we then feel our way through a number of the characteristics of dominant ideology?

High-minded. Ideology comes out of high-minded and usually long-cherished thinking. Western individualism, Marxism, the Law, each is at root not bad or careless thinking, but careful thinking about real values. It is therefore plausible and mentally attractive, even addictive.

Limited Criteria. By taking limited criteria to assess reality, criteria which today are usually economic, ideology reduces what is perceived as truth, to a limited realm, which can then afford to be extremely forthright and tend to be totalitarian, even in the name of democracy and freedom!

Simplifying Criteria. Having simplified the ambiguities, varieties, contradictions, and mystery of human reality, ideology is able to set up the world scene in a strictly two-camp way, a Manichean division of the world into those who subscribe and those who cannot or will not subscribe to the dominant ideology.

Righteous. For those who subscribe to the ideologies this provides a great sense of righteousness and frees them from any sense of their own guilt. And it makes the misfits guilty by choice of circumstance. In Jesus' time it was impossible for many people, especially Jesus' associates in Galilee, to keep the Law. They were therefore "accused and outside the Law," and in some way guilty.

In my own country (England) a right-wing ideology of self-improvement, effort, and wealth creates a horrible righteousness in the dominant culture and places an unvoiced, at times loudly voiced, blame on those who do not better themselves. There are thousands of homeless families, but recent housing laws imply that this is normally the fault of the homeless, apart from a tiny minority who are the "deserving poor." Similarly much blame for the great enemy, inflation, is placed on wage increases. Wage-earners are seen as blameworthy while executive salaries, expense accounts, business cars are all righteously innocent. The same attitudes appear whenever overseas aid is mentioned—if those people "over there" chose to work and better themselves, they could do so.

Guilty Misfits. For the misfits and the afflicted, the dominant ideology not only sees them as guilty, but they themselves come to think of themselves as being so. They gradually develop a self-image of being under a bondage of fate which is somehow a bondage of sin. This is because the ideology generates a language that is extremely plausible and pervasive. Jesus liberated the blind man not only from being called "a sinner through and through from his birth," but above all from believing himself to be so.

Today, when our dominant ideology projects a constant image of material wellbeing as salvation, those who know they cannot aspire to that see themselves as blameworthy nobodies. The role of prophetic imagination, a Good News of hope, must be able to lift that bondage of sin and fate, not by praying it into "the nobodies," but by releasing them from illusions of the ideology. In a culture of "death by bread alone" people cannot discover themselves as people by more and more bread.

No Oppositions. "Who is not for us is against us." A strong ideology, having set the scene as a simple confrontation between two adversaries, has no place for third parties. Everyone is either Loyal or the Enemy, or a dupe of the Enemy. Any criticism is subversive. This we have seen in a most vicious form in the USSR, regimes based on "national security" in Latin America, and in other forms in Mozambique, Iran, the Philippines. Ideology legitimizes extreme nationalism in a high-minded way, so that it is obvious that it is better that one man (or ten thousand or thirty thousand) should die for the sake of "the people."

But the two-adversary view of the world also means that anyone who is not one hundred percent for us must be simply, and one hundred percent, in the enemy camp. So there is no room for a marxist socialism to create alternative forms, for example in Central America. The irony is that by being so treated the dominant ideology leaves Nicaragua, or Angola, or Ethiopia or wherever, nowhere else to look for support except in the "enemy" camp. Ideologies are self-justifying. "We told you so!"

Perversion of Language. Because a dominant ideology is primarily concerned with proving itself right, it is ready to pervert language to its own ends. A conviction of being right is quite the biggest stumbling block to seeking truth and perceiving what is really taking place. Being right is an attempt to keep one's autarchic ego intact by means of keeping one's right thinking intact. It can never lose face nor admit to changing its mind. It cannot make the basic acts of humility and obedience which alone admit it to perceiving truth and responding with self-forgetfulness. It is willing to interpret history and every contemporary event to prove itself right and to evolve jargon to keep the ideology pure.

The USSR evolved a whole philosophy of the use of language as support for its ideology and not as communication of truth. But the same perversion happens in our Western countries. I think of the way the word "communist" is used, even by Catholics who delight to celebrate the feast days of dead saints, many of whom today would be called subversive communists. A few years ago a confrere and I published a small anthology of the Church Fathers' teaching on the nature of ownership. It was subversive stuff! And looking at the present rhetoric about nuclear armaments, one wonders by what process of righteous thinking can anyone come to the point of saying, in the name of Christianity, that we can only be peacemakers from a position of power? Is that not the ultimate denial of the cross?

WHERE WE STAND AS CHURCH

My suggestion is that we try to understand more clearly what ideologies do to people, and especially how they cast the vast majority of people, the poor, into being dispossessed and fated outcasts. Then we could appreciate what liberation and hope Jesus lived for, and also where we, as church, should be standing today. It would be along these lines, and not along moralistic lines, that we should see Jesus as being counted among the sinners; and that we should understand the Lamb of God who takes away sin.

It would help us appreciate why Jesus' Good News seemed so ambiguous to many of his contemporaries, even his own followers. And it would help us to cope with similar misunderstanding and ambiguity in our day. It would, of course, be a Good News that divides the hearts of many, a Good News that would confront much that is accepted uncritically, a Good News that would divide us even from our own brethren. But he did not come to bring peace at any price. To live the peace that he gives is to learn the art of being vagabonds, displaced persons, fools. Can we do it? – and then not be righteous ourselves?!

"BUILD THE KINGDOM"

As we ponder all these things in our hearts, as we pray the psalms, as we reread the gospels, as we seek to open ourselves to the great questions of death and evil in our contemporary world, as we sense that much of our privatized, spiritualized, and moralized spirituality cannot interpret the scenes we are in, and then as we begin to sense the futility of God and his Reign, and ourselves as part of that, we ask ourselves, how do we cope? What can we do?

One reaction is a yearning to set up an alternative and effective program for God. Shortly before John Paul II left Britain he was at a large youth rally in South Wales. As he boarded the helicopter to leave, he turned, opened his arms, and said, "Young people, young people, build the Kingdom, build the Kingdom." That phrase is common enough today; it appears in some of your new Constitutions and Rules and even in liturgical prayers. But my naughty mind wondered as I watched the television screen, whether Jesus would ever have used it and if not, why not? And then I recalled that it was from near that same corner of Wales by the river Severn, that a British monk, who had lived many years before, went to Rome to tell the loose-living Romans that they should get themselves organized, try harder, and save themselves. Was it perhaps his ghost, the ghost of Pelagius, which managed at that last moment to whisper in the Pope's ear? The Anglo-Saxons and Celts have never needed another heresy. That one has lasted well for fifteen centuries.

GOD'S REIGN

Jesus spoke of God's Reign being near at hand, among us, yet-to-be but already here. He told people they could, or could not, enter it, but never said they were in it. Only one man was said to be "not far from it." God's Reign was in history, yet it was always more than ever expected. It was always appreciated as gift, as grace, but it was never magic. It demanded all the preparation and predisposition that gift-receiving demands, the social justice required by the year of the Lord's favor, and yet it was never merited. Like all love affairs God's Reign was enigmatic, better talked of in stories and in celebration than in books and theses. And like all love affairs it was recognized only by those who knew it by experience. You could know it but not know about it.

I have come to think that the main thrust of all Jesus' preaching was to persuade people to accept this antecedent reality of God's presence and creativity. It is the love of God in people's lives, his antecedent Reign, which urges us.

It is not the building of something on his behalf. He is not this spectator-God waiting for us to do great things in his name.

WHO LIGHTS THE LAMP?

Last year I spent some time with some Medical Mission Sisters discussing a favorite quotation of their foundress: "No one lights a lamp to put it under a tub. ... Your light must shine in the sight of men. ..." Was Jesus saying that you must see to it that your light is effective? be a searchlight? or a lighthouse? Or was he saying that since it is God who is "the one" who lights the lamp, if we are truly alight, then we cannot but be effective? In the context of the Sermon on the Mount, of the Beatitudes, and in particular of the images of salt, and of leaven, he must have been saying the latter. Do not be anxious and worried about how and whether your life is being efficient and effective for the Reign of God. Your focus must be on being true to your calling, a candle burning truly. If you are, you will give light, whether, or how, or when, or to whom, you know not. And in addition you will not draw attention to yourselves as great patrons of God, but will become transparent signs pointing beyond yourselves, signs of the Reign of God. "Seeing your good works, they will praise your Father in heaven."

THE LION IS GOD

The same reflection occurred to me as I was reading Vincent Donovan's *Christianity Rediscovered*, the account of his mission among the Masai in Tanzania. A Masai elder is speaking to Father Donovan. He says, "A person who really believes is like a lion going after its prey. Its nose and eyes and ears pick up the prey. Its legs give the speed to catch the prey. All the power of its body is involved in the terrible death leap and single blow to the neck with the front paw, the blow that actually kills. And as the animal goes down, the lion envelopes it in its arms [Masai refer to the front legs of an animal as its arms], pulls it to itself, and makes it part of itself. This is the way a lion kills. This is the way a person believes. This is what faith is."

"I looked at the elder in silence and amazement," says Donovan. "Faith understood like that would explain why, when my own faith was gone, I ached in every fibre of my being. But my wise old teacher was not finished yet.

" 'We did not search you out, Padri,' he said to me. 'We did not even want you to come to us. You searched us out. You followed us away from your house into the bush, into the plains, into the steppes where our cattle are, into the hills where we take our cattle for water, into our villages, into our homes. You told us of the High God, how we must search for God, even leave our land and our people to find God. But we have not done this. We have not left our land. We have not searched for God. God has searched for us. God has searched us out and found us. All the time we think we are the lion. In the end the lion is God.' "

And Donovan continues. "The lion is God. Of course. Goodness and kindness and holiness and grace and divine presence and creating power and salvation were here before I got here. Even the fuller understanding of God's revelation to humankind, of the salvific act that had been accomplished once and for all for the human race, was here before I got here. My role as a herald of that gospel, as messenger of the news of what had already happened in the world, as the person whose task it was to point to 'the one who had stood in their midst, whom they did not recognize' was only a small part of the mission of God to the world. It was a mysterious part, a demanded part: 'Woe to me if I do not preach the gospel.' "

It was a role that would require every talent and insight and skill and gift and strength I had, to be spent without question, without stint, and yet in the humbling knowledge that only that part of it would be made use of which fit into the immeasurably greater plan of the relentless, pursuing God, whose will on the world will not be thwarted. The lion is God.[1]

THE STILL POINT OF ENDEAVOR: UNION WITH GOD

When we first set out to work for God the chances are that we are all more or less Pelagian and have a reasonably clear ideology. We set out "to do God's will," and God is indeed lucky to have us around to do it. We are the actors, God the spectator. For some, that state of affairs lasts until middle age tempers it and they slide quietly and sadly into mediocrity.

But what should happen, and what I believe is the normal progress in any walk of life for Christians who have remained alert, seeking, and prayerful, is a transition from being in dialogue with God as neighbor, with all the demarcation disputes that this involves, to being in union with God. The mystics talk much to us about this, but we should not think of it as proper to a privileged few. Most of the church's contemplatives are not in "contemplative" communities. And there is no doubt that mission in areas of conflict or crises in life, such as imprisonment, the destruction of all we have given our lives for, serious illness, being present to scenes of irrational violence as in our recent riots in Liverpool—these moments which remove any clarity about what we can or ought to do are demands from God to step into a quite new type of presence and communion.

These call us to a conversion which we cannot program or achieve, but which God's Spirit will work in us if we are open to God's Spirit and persevering. We recognize this by hindsight. It is, I believe, the transition from the "coming to do God's will" of the psalmist, to the seeking truly "that God's will be done in us" of Mary; from moral endeavor for God, to contemplative union with him.

CONVERSION

We have died already. Or as Paul sings at the end of that chapter: I am sure that neither death, nor life . . . no "power" . . . can come between us and the love of God.

This conversion should happen in all our lives, this conversion from active endeavor to contemplative union. It may happen dramatically, it may creep up on us softly, softly, but it is not an oddity reserved to a mystical few. On the other hand, it can easily be missed because it feels like a loss of certainty, a loss of faith, a leap into the dark. It is like a ship leaving the security of navigation lights and finding itself in open sea. There is need for mutual encouragement in this. When you are afraid of "going around the bend," having friends to go around the bend with is precious—or even guidance from those who have already gone around!

ASPECTS OF CONVERSION

This conversion ushers in an intense solitude of communion. We discover that the heart, of itself, is not in the end an ultimate aloneness but a radical solidarity and communion with all God's beloved people. Missioners will know that this communion is a living conversation with the poor, the forgotten, the voiceless, the wounded, the dispossessed. So we carry in ourselves, wherever we are, a deep suffering, perhaps the social equivalent of that wound of love that St. Teresa and the other mystics speak of. We bear wounds of love which never heal, the wounds of the risen Lord.

But also we carry an intense joy because the Christian is not merely a striver for liberation yet to come, but a bearer of a liberation of which the down payment, the pledge, has already been made. It is an enigmatic coexistence of suffering and joy which makes our lives, especially our community lives, living signs. From being patrons of God's Reign, we are called to be instruments of that Reign. In society today there are a thousand patrons of peace to every one instrument of peace. We are called from Jesus' initial "Follow me" to Peter by the lakeside, calling him to work for and preach the Reign of God, to his second "Follow me" by the lakeside after Peter had lost any self-assurance other than loving the Lord!

When you were young you girded yourself and went where you would; but the time comes when you will be girded by others and not go where you choose. Follow me. *Domine, quo vadis?*

It is a conversion, from living out of duty and thereby keeping our self-image intact, our autarchic ego respectable, to abandoning that entire game of "being somebody" before God and others.

It is the conversion which Paul talks of so often in Romans, and which is beautifully worked out in chapter 8. God's Spirit releases us from loving through moral endeavor, to being able to love freely, as it were, naturally.

The conversion always involves a death. Indeed, this side of the grave, it involves a constant dying, but only that a new life and freedom may be released in us. We learn what it is to constantly carry the dying of Jesus in the body (our community of faith) so that his risen life may be manifest. And, surprise, surprise, this freedom from fear makes us invincible. You cannot kill me for I have died already.

MISSIONARY ENDEAVOR

All our work and missionary endeavor is surely, in the end, enabling the daily things of peoples' lives to give glory to God. It is the experience of a number of people I know that the conversion I have tried to speak of enables us to live far more fully in the present, and to savor all things.

Thomas Merton in *Seeds of Contemplation* reminds us: in practice the way to contemplation is an obscurity so obscure that it is no longer even dramatic. There is nothing left in it that can be grasped and cherished as heroic or even unusual. And so . . . there is a supreme value in the ordinary routine of work and poverty and hardship and monotony that characterize the lives of all the poor and uninteresting and forgotten people in the world.

We are not really artisans in God's world, are we! We are "God's work of art" (Ephesians). All the time we think we are the lion. In the end, the lion is God!

NOTE

1. Vincent Donovan, *Christianity Rediscovered* (Maryknoll: Orbis Books, 1978).

31

INTEGRITY OF CREATION: A MISSIONARY IMPERATIVE

Bernard Przewozny, OFM Conv.

The world and humanity are at risk from the environmental crisis created by the industrial revolution unleashed two hundred years ago. Alarming signals of this danger reach us from all directions: industrial accidents which release various pollutants into the environment, depletion of the ozone layer, loss of biological diversity, urbanization, and so on. Environmental problems are rightly perceived as pervasive of all facets of human activity. It is becoming clearer that the environmental crisis which humankind must face and solve is the ultimate problem. On the other hand, it is also clear that an all-embracing institutional structure capable of dealing with the crisis—to ensure the correct identification of its causes and to implement effective remedies—does not yet exist. Difficulties inherent in the very analysis of the crisis are further exacerbated by its complexity and by the widespread uncertainty about its precise nature.

Many factors perpetuate and aggravate the problem: the global interdependence of development and underdevelopment, the negative cultural value of consumerism; social factors, demographics—each one of these elements as well as many others have to be examined in detail in order to acquire even a simple understanding of the extent to which the integrity of creation is endangered.

A Christian definition of integrity of creation must also include the kind of reconciliation of humankind within the biosphere which is described by the New Testament: human beings can become new creatures (Gal. 6:15), and can continually be changed into Christ's likeness from one degree of glory to another (2 Cor. 3:18). Integrity of creation must therefore be based on the truth that a dynamic new order has already begun and now waits with eager longing for the revealing of the sons and daughters of God ... because creation itself will be set free from its bondage to decay and obtain the glorious liberty of the children of God (Rom. 8:19, 21).

Wa Kalemba Malu of the Pontifical Academy of Sciences recently pointed out that in the last forty years, as never before in history, we have been facing six different kinds of explosions:
— the nuclear explosion of matter
— the explosion of life in demographic expansion and in the prolongation of life
— the explosion of scientific and technological knowledge
— the explosion of intelligence or of the application of knowledge to society
— the explosion caused by insufficient participation in management decisions which concern the use of intelligence information and scientific research
— and, finally, hunger.

All six, as accelerated processes endemic to the last generation, exacerbate the environmental crisis and render difficult its solution. In one generation we have passed from light generated by fossil fuels to light produced by nuclear energy; from the rifle to nuclear missiles; from mail delivered on horseback in some parts of the world to intercontinental communications via satellites; from simple animal husbandry and breeding to genetic engineering. And, scientists tell us, there is no end to what else humankind may invent or do in the next generation. But we have not matured, nor are we maturing rapidly enough in our use of what science and technology make available to us. We can, therefore, safely say that scientific and economic development does not always produce full human development.

THE EXTENT OF THE CRISIS

It is estimated that some thirty-five thousand vegetable and animal species will be lost by the year 2000.

Tropical forests are shrinking by 11 million hectares per year. For example, some 30,718 hectares of forests were damaged in Europe in 1986 alone.

An estimated 26 billion tons of topsoil on croplands are lost annually in excess of new soil formation.

Some 6 million hectares of new desert are formed annually by land mismanagement.

Underground water tables are falling in parts of Africa, China, India, and North America as demand for water rises above aquifer recharge rates. Some fifty pesticides contaminate groundwater in thirty-two American states. In 1980, some 140 acidified lakes devoid of fish were found in the Canadian province of Ontario.

Some 2,500 U.S. toxic waste sites need cleaning up. The extent of toxic contamination worldwide is unknown.

1.7 billion people lack access to clean water, and 1.2 billion to adequate sanitation. Every year 60 million persons in developing countries must be offered the possibility to earn a livelihood.

A person in an industrial country consumes much more and places much greater pressure on natural resources than a person in the developing world.

GROWING AWARENESS OF THE PROBLEM

The first warnings of the growing environmental catastrophe came from scientists; the first public outcry was emotional, apocalyptic, and, at times, ideologically inspired. Various organizations, both governmental and private, have contributed to our awareness of the extent, complexity, and seriousness of the environmental crisis. Prominent among these were the International Union for the Conservation of Nature and Natural Resources (IUCN), the World Wildlife Fund (now, World Wide Fund for Nature), the Club of Rome, and so forth. On the negative side, it should be noted that in many cases, even today, conservationist organizations tend to decry the effects rather than the causes of environmental degradation. Furthermore, they are often oriented toward single issues (the protection of endangered species) or point to single causes of the environmental disaster (demographic expansion).

Some of the initial outcry was tainted by an antiscientific and even antihuman mentality. The human being, it seemed, had become the only destructive element in the biosphere. So-called natural disasters and calamities were considered to be benign. That nature's "violence" more than human activity has destroyed countless species in the biosphere was forgotten. Many suggested, and some still do, that humankind should return to a primitive agricultural past.

At best, these reactions implied that the model of humankind's relation to the environment needed revision; at worst, they denied the human being's innate and distinctive creative ability. It should also be noted that, because of the interdependence which exists among all entities in the biosphere, it is almost impossible to distinguish between "nature" modified by human activity and "nature" in its so-called pure state. Furthermore, to return to a primitive, "uncontaminated" past is not only impractical, or impossible, but even harmful. For example, properly farmed soil is subject to rapid degradation only when human beings abandon it. In other words, ecologically sound use of soil is good ecology. And, with the Gubbio document, written by environmentalists and Franciscans for the 1982 International "Terra Mater" Seminar, we can say that "technology, one of the most distinctive expressions of humankind and of human creativity, is not harmful as such but it can satisfy human needs only if used in a way which respects human dignity and the natural processes of Planet Earth."

The first statements of the church to show an awareness of the problem date back to the Vatican II *Pastoral Constitution on the Church in the Modern World*, promulgated in 1965. In Part I, Chapter III, "Human Activity in the World," the Constitution defends scientific and technological progress (34) but insists on the regulation of human activity: "Here then is the norm of human activity — to harmonize with the authentic interests of the human race, in accordance with God's will and design, and to enable persons as individuals and as members of society to pursue and fulfill their total vocation" (35).

In 1971, in his Apostolic Letter *Octogesima Adveniens*, Paul VI wrote rather forcefully that "by an ill-considered exploitation of nature humanity risks destroying it and becomes in turn the victim of this degradation" (21). Furthermore, he noted that "flight from the land, industrial growth, continual demographic expansion and the attraction of urban centers bring about concentrations of population, the extent of which is difficult to imagine" (8). And John Paul II, in his first Encyclical *Redemptor Hominis* (1979; 8, 15,16) and in his recent one, *Sollicitudo Rei Socialis* (1987; 34), and in numerous discourses, has taken to heart humankind's need to improve its relation to the environment.

The concern of the World Council of Churches for the environment has become clear since its Sixth Assembly, held in Vancouver in 1983. Some of its earlier documents also show an awareness of the problem.

THE PROBLEM: MULTIDIMENSIONAL

The environmental catastrophe is multidimensional. Some problems are worldwide, global in nature; others are related to particular geographic, climatic, or developmental conditions. The causes of environmental degradation, as we suggested in the introduction, are legion and their interdependence is not clearly understood or easily manageable. Let us illustrate some of them.

REGIONAL PROBLEMS

Today, many countries experience great difficulty in solving environmental problems on their own. This is partly due to the transboundary nature of the problems, such as acid rain and the management of international river systems. In some cases, individual countries may have little or no control over what is exported to their territories by the atmosphere or water ways. Nevertheless, their forests, surface and ground waters, soil, and even the health of their populations are thus exposed to grave risks. Furthermore, countries may not possess the economic or political strength to protect themselves against such damage.

Some examples of these problems can be readily cited:

When the British noted that emissions from chimneys at steel mills were polluting the immediate countryside, they built taller chimneys. But then the Swedes complained about tree and soil damage caused by acid rain which was produced by fumes from British chimneys.

Cleaning up the pollution of the Rhine required the cooperation of the countries through which it flows. It is encouraging to note that corrective measures of this sort are increasing. The Mediterranean Action Plan to save the sea has been established within the framework of the political realities of the countries bordering on the Mediterranean Basin.

GLOBAL PROBLEMS

Beyond the rising concentration of carbon dioxide, which may lead to the greenhouse effect and the depletion of the ozone layer, the pollution of the environment by chemical substances is a serious concern. Chemicals present a risk to living organisms and may also create global problems such as climate change. Once a risk is characterized, it should be managed. Some of the appropriate measures may require the setting of standards for effluent streams; development of "clean technologies"; testing of new chemicals prior to marketing;

restriction of exports of hazardous chemicals; waste minimization and waste detoxification; prevention and mitigation of chemical accidents; and so on. The scientists are confident that the problem is manageable if appropriate action is taken. The Montreal Protocol of 1987 to protect the ozone layer is an important step in such global management of an ecological problem.

BIOLOGICAL DIVERSITY

The conclusions of the 1987 Study Week of the Pontifical Academy of Sciences on "A Modern Approach to the Protection of the Environment" remind us that the unsustainable and destructive use of the land and other common resources is causing the extinction of a high proportion of the world's species of plants, animals, and microorganisms. Since human societies are based almost entirely on their ability to utilize other species for their own benefit, the irreversible depletion of the earth's biological diversity is extremely serious. Some species are important sources of medicines. For example, certain plants possess medicinal qualities which may help cure leukemia. Thus, depletion of biological diversity is a great loss from the economic, aesthetic, moral, and scientific points of view, and will greatly limit future human potential.

The current deforestation of the Amazon is harming the soil, endangering the earth's ability to produce oxygen, destroying native populations and their rights to ethnic and cultural identity, and depleting one of the earth's biologically richest areas.

ECONOMIC PROBLEMS

The management of the environment is also an economic problem. According to the document *Gubbio 1987: Toward the Third Millennium*, prepared for the Second International "Terra Mater" Seminar, "the economic growth of human communities must (sooner or later) encounter the insurmountable limit to the endurance and regeneration of environmental resources." An essential condition to environmental protection, therefore, is a more equitable sharing of capital and natural resources, that is, a globally more just economic system.

The international debt has been shown to contribute to environmental destruction. Thus, one of the more difficult adjustments that humankind will have to make is the following: sooner or later, it must recognize that income is an insufficient indicator of progress. Furthermore, whole countries will have to accept the costs that the defense of the environment involves. When they do, such costs may even provoke lesser rates of growth or, indeed, a decrease of income. But a drastic reduction of these costs can be achieved by investing in the research and development of new technologies, which, from the initial phases of their planning, should be oriented toward the conservation of the environment.

The production system must, therefore, be subjected to the common sense rule that it cannot produce substances or be involved in manufacturing processes which are injurious to health or the environment. Finally, if basic needs are to be satisfied everywhere in the world, then certain lifestyles in the more affluent parts of the world must be reconsidered in view of a more equitable enjoyment of goods by all populations.

DEVELOPMENT AND UNDERDEVELOPMENT

The environmental issue is bound up with the nature of development or progress. Since natural resources are limited and since they belong to all of humankind, then development cannot be unlimited or without social obligation according to the moral demands of solidarity and social justice. For a number of years now, environmentalists have been trying to define progress. Last year, they invited an interreligious group of Catholics (represented by Franciscans), Greek Orthodox, Waldensians, Buddhists, and Hindus to help them formulate a new concept of progress. The document of that Seminar, *Gubbio 1987: Toward the Third Millennium*, states:

> We must, first of all, distinguish between material and spiritual progress, safeguarding nonetheless the constant tendency toward their dynamic equilibrium. Indeed, should not material progress have as its goal spiritual growth? In fact, history teaches us that merely material progress can carry us far from spiritual progress, reducing itself to egocentrism, conflict, conquest, exploitation, profiteering and discrimination. Merely material progress, destructive as it is of the human–nature relation, ends up destroying itself.

Progress, therefore, should be understood in an integral sense, that is, in relation to all human and social values in their environmental context. In this vision of progress, even if it requires noteworthy self-denial and great discipline, men and women rediscover themselves as simply the custodians of the goods entrusted to them and thus regain their freedom from the slavery of greed. We are therefore convinced that it is necessary to form people according to this meaning of true progress.

Progress should not impede openness to an absolute future which transcends the history of humankind. The future depends on a new consciousness, culture, and formation, capable of creating a new appreciation of nature as the place where we live our religious experiences. We cannot forget that the environment belongs also to future generations and not only to the present inhabitants of the planet. Contemporary consumerism, by wasting natural resources and human energies, closes the doors to a better future. Our Common Future of the Nations United World Commission on Environment and Development, chaired by Gro Harlem Brundtland, also takes this stand on the dangers of consumerism.

MORAL AND CULTURAL PROBLEMS

The solution to the environmental problem is not merely scientific, technical, political, or economic; it is also a moral and a cultural issue. Some of the moral issues are already implicit in what we have been saying so far. They are reiterated in *Sollicitudo Rei Socialis*:

> When it comes to the natural world, we are subject not only to biological laws but also to moral ones, which cannot be violated with impunity . . .

A true concept of development cannot ignore the use of the elements of nature, the renewability of resources and the consequences of haphazard industrialization—three considerations which alert our consciences to the moral dimension of development. (34)

Furthermore, sin and structures of sin must be overcome so that interdependence ... be transformed into solidarity, based upon the principle that the goods of creation are meant for all. That which human industry produces through the processing of raw materials, with the contribution of work, must serve equally for the good of all. (39)

The lifestyle of the Kung Bushmen of the Kalahari desert in Botswana shows how intimately related are environment, culture, and development. According to reliable anthropological studies, these gatherers and hunters work only two and a half days a week in order to maintain a satisfying level of livelihood. They are able to do so because of the influence of their mythologies, social institutions, and rituals, and because of their precise knowledge of the environment, animals, and plants on which their survival depends.

René Dubois described consumerist values of industrialized societies rather well when he wrote: "In present parlance, a society is civilized when it is affluent enough to move its outhouses indoors, to do away with physical effort, to heat and cool its homes with electric power, and to own more automobiles, freezers, telephones, and gadgets for leisure-time than it really needs or can enjoy. Gentle behavior, humane laws, limitations of war, a high level of purpose and conduct have disappeared from the concept."

I remember how a professor of moral theology commented on President Johnson's declaration of war against poverty. "That is an unjust war," my colleague observed. "The poor do not have the means to defend themselves!" The poor cannot defend their cultural values against the greed and wastefulness of an affluent and consumer society, a model frequently and uncritically used as a yardstick of what the poor should desire to become.

DEMOGRAPHIC EXPANSION

Demographic expansion is often cited as the main cause of environmental degradation. *Our Common Future* points to the demographic expansion as one of the most serious causes of the problem, but it admits that "the population issue is not solely about numbers. Poverty and resource degradation can exist on thinly populated lands, such as the drylands and the tropical forests. People are the ultimate resource" (p. 95). And *Sollicitudo Rei Socialis* reminds us: "Just as it is incorrect to say that such difficulties [as development] stem solely from demographic growth, neither is it proved that all demographic growth is incompatible with orderly development" (25).

Recent studies have pointed out that "population pressure" is not always at the root of environmental problems. It does not play a leading role in determining the instability of ecosystems, but it is an aggravating factor in catastrophic situations, the roots of which can be found elsewhere. Population pressure has been often used as a "scapegoat" to distract attention from a serious analysis of socioeconomic and political conditions in many parts of the world. Although this does not mean that population pressure is not becoming a serious problem, other demographic factors should not be ignored. For example, in some parts of the world populations are aging; in others, populations are distributed in areas where their access to necessary resources for quality of life is minimal or limited.[1]

One should be cautious in evaluating statistics about the earth's global carrying capacity or limit in sustaining population growth. According to The Global 2000 Report, issued in 1980 by the American Department of State, the world population should reach 10 billion by the year 2030 and should come close to 30 billion by the end of the twenty-first century. What these statistics fail to consider are many other factors.

Very few countries in the developing world (four, in fact) have the population density of Holland or Belgium.

Three thousand years ago, Egypt suffered from famine when its population could not have exceeded a million. Today, Egypt has a population close to 50 million and it is self-sufficient as far as food production is concerned.

Canada could sustain a population of 300 million within a one-hundred-mile strip along the American border, stretching from the Atlantic to the Pacific.

THE ROLE OF RELIGION

The study of the religious and cultural roots of the contemporary ecological crisis began in a polemical vein with the address of Lynn White, Jr., to the American Association for the Advancement of Science on December 26, 1966.

According to White, although modern technology and modern science are distinctively occidental, their use has been marked both by Jewish and Christian monotheism, which desacralizes nature, and by the uncontrolled dominion over all creatures enunciated in Genesis. Thus, "by destroying pagan animism, Christianity made it possible to exploit nature in a mood of indifference to the feelings of natural objects." In 1973, the late Arnold J. Toynbee also criticized the Jewish and Christian understanding of the Genesis account of human dominion "over every living thing that moves upon the earth" (Gen. 1:28). In Toynbee's words,

> God had created the world; the world was God's to do what he liked with; God had chosen to license Adam and Eve to do what they liked with it; and their license was not canceled by the Fall ... monotheism, as enunciated in the Book of Genesis, has removed the age-old restraint that was once placed on human greed by awe. Humanity's greedy impulse to exploit nature used to be held in check by pious worship of nature. This primitive inhibition has been removed by the rise and spread of monotheism. Moreover, the monotheistic disrespect for nature has survived the weakening of the belief in monotheism in the ex-monotheistic part of the world, and it has invaded that major portion of the world in which monotheism has never been established.

More recently, environmentalists have come to admit that Christianity can contribute through its theological, scientific, and cultural heritage to the solution of the environmental problem. The Pontifical Academy of Sciences concluded its study week on "Agriculture and Quality of Life: New Global Trends," and participants agreed that the technologies already exist to conquer hunger within the next twenty years, provided that the proper economic, political, and cultural measures are implemented. As far as the cultural measures are concerned, they paid particular attention to education in agricultural areas of the developing countries.

A MISSIONARY CONTRIBUTION

Convinced that religion has a vital role to play in education and in creating a new model of development, progress, and human solidarity, missionaries can support local efforts to build and administer educational, medical, and cultural facilities for promoting the integrity of creation. But not all missionaries are versed even in simple agricultural practices and techniques. Their professional formation should include basic agricultural principles, practices and techniques, all of which ought to be shared with the populations in which they work in total respect for local needs and values.

It should be noted that the introduction of simple technologies into certain areas of developing countries can mean the difference between life and death. Furthermore, only education can lead to the kind of increase in agricultural productivity which will be ecologically sound, economically viable, socially acceptable, and politically feasible.

Missionaries have the possibility of developing and implementing a new model of humankind's relation to the environment and natural resources. They can form new cultural models of community and relating to offset the abuses of a consumer society.

ST. FRANCIS

As a Franciscan, I cannot ignore the personalized relationship that St. Francis established with all creatures. In his Canticle of the Sun, he called all creatures his brothers and sisters. He did this for three reasons:
1. they share with humankind a common origin and therefore the same God or Parent
2. they share with us the gift of existence and the same destiny
3. they are symbols and bearers of Christ.

In other words, creatures are our brothers and sisters because they are God's gifts and signs of God's providential and reconciling love: they belong to God alone, they bear God's likeness. In God's name Earth feeds us. Francis gladly recognized his duty to reciprocate divine love with human love and praise, not only in the name of creatures but with and through them.

For St. Francis, work was a God-given grace to be exercised in the spirit of faith and devotion. All human activity in the biosphere must therefore lead to a mutual enrichment of human beings and other creatures. Our symbiosis with nature reminds us that we are microcosms that "incorporate" the world within themselves. How we understand our relation to the world will depend on our self-understanding; and how we understand our stewardship over all creatures will depend on our self-mastery.

In the thirteenth century, St. Bonaventure exhorted the readers of his *Itinerarium Mentis in Deum*: "Open your eyes ... alert the ears of your spirit, unlock your lips, and apply your heart that you may see, hear, praise, love, and adore, magnify, and honor your God in every creature, lest perchance the entire universe rise against you. For because of this, the whole world shall fight against the unwise."

NOTE

1. See R.V. Garcia and P. Spitz, *Drought and Man*, vol. 3, *The Roots of Catastrophe* (Oxford: Pergamon Press, 1986).

32

THE CHALLENGES OF JUSTICE

Reflections of Participants at the SEDOS Conference

SOLIDARITY WITH THE POOR

Justice, the building up of right relationships, makes special demands, particularly in relationships with the poor. An option for the poor is of crucial importance in evangelization. All members of our mission institutes are called to work for justice as an essential part of evangelization. This is not a marginal issue. Clearly it challenges the whole community, but it is not at all clear how the whole community can be involved.

The terminology used is important. "Preferential option for the poor" has acquired such overtones of implied exclusiveness that it effectively marginalizes many. "Solidarity with the poor," both affective and effective, may more accurately describe the commitment called for in an entire community.

There is now a widespread realization that the poor are not only the object of evangelization or the promotion of justice; they are above all the subject of their own liberation. In them we meet God who expresses a predilection for them; they are a *locus theologicus*; they have a profound human dignity; they evangelize.

SHARING THE LIFE OF THE POOR

Mission institutes cannot stand apart from "the poor," judging them from the perspective of their own institutional structures, uninvolved in action for and with them. Solidarity with the poor dictates another perspective entirely. All are called to solidarity; some are called to express this in a deeper commitment by working with the poor; still others are called to share the life of the poor.

This is a special calling, not to be undertaken lightly. Not all can respond. This sharing is not a strategy. It is a way of life for some. The experience of those who share the life of the poor should touch the decision-making process of the whole community which is called to communicate with them, learn from them, and be in solidarity with them.

REMAINING NEUTRAL

Situations occur more and more frequently in which mission institutes find it difficult to remain neutral, in which not opting for the poor and oppressed will mean, in effect, opting for the oppressor. The credibility of institutes may well depend on their taking the side of the poor.

Discernment in these situations can lead to tension and even conflict within communities. Mutual support and love does not exclude the possibility of tension and conflict in the religious community any more than it does in family life. The implications for mission institutes are many.

POLITICAL INVOLVEMENT

Solidarity with the poor and commitment to justice inevitably mean more involvement in "political situations" which, in turn, touches the local, regional, and central authorities of institutes. The need to "take sides" will arise more often.

What constitutes political action or involvement is not easy to discern. "Political" for some is "solidarity with the oppressed." For others, even assisting someone in a court of law may be seen as "political," assuming that there is the possibility of recourse to law, which is not always the case. The possibility and extent of reprisals against those with whom we wish to stand is a constant menace.

Mission societies, too, need to evaluate continually their own institutional wealth and administrative structures which involve them in the exercise of power and control. We have no monopoly in regard to justice any more than the lay people with whom we are often slow to collaborate.

DIALOGUE

In our efforts to promote justice we need to be people of dialogue: firstly within our own communities; with other missionary communities; especially with people of the business and marketing world; with people in the media; with those who exercise power; with those of other faiths than our own; and with people of no faith.

This dialogue implies an understanding of and respect for others, an openness, and a readiness to allow time for change to take place. It is not helped by judgmental and condemnatory attitudes. It always begins with an attitude of "Physician, heal thyself!"

It demands that we are clear about our own identity as "missionaries in solidarity with the poor"; that we are clear about our message at a given time; that we do communicate it, first to ourselves, then to the media, and to the world.

It forces us to examine the "split level" often seen in our Institutes, the painful gap between word and action; between the theory and practice of our solidarity with the poor; between the statements emanating from religious and church leaders and what is actually done.

SELF-CONVERSION

We tend to look outside ourselves when discerning the causes and extent of injustice in the world, to blame others, the rich, multinational corporations, administrative corruption, local governments, and local churches. The first challenge is to convert ourselves.

Missionary institutes need to make serious and continuing analysis of the administration of justice within their own institutes and institutions, and of their own attitudes to justice and solidarity with the poor.

This means making clear choices, not being content to live with uncertainties which arise from procrastination rather than from a humble, sincere search for solutions.

It means being deeply conscious of the prejudices, biases, and inbuilt resistances to change that arise from cultures, our own included.

Look for the causes of world poverty where they really are, not only where we prefer to see them. They are often in our own backyards, in the Northern Hemisphere, in the First World. We avoid dealing with them there, while we go off to tilt at windmills far away.

World population growth has a considerable bearing on poverty, yet we do little to examine what "solidarity with the poor" means in practice in analyzing this problem and working toward realistic proposals for dealing with it.

COMMUNICATIONS

Missionary institutes are international organizations, "multinationals" in solidarity with the oppressed. Part of their challenge is precisely to use their internationality to good effect, but their own decision-making bodies often appear powerless.

A significant part of their role is communicating, but they fail to develop media skills; they fail to communicate. Sharing information with one another, networking, collaborating are very significant, yet isolationism still characterizes much of their activity.

There is need for concerted community action based on solidarity, yet there is persistent individualism. The importance given to values of unity and harmony in communities often waters down the real issues.

INSECURITY

There is no way back for our communities from our commitment to justice, but it would be foolish to pretend that there are not many fears and uncertainties. Moving away from situations of comparative stability into situations of insecurity through commitment to justice is a constant challenge.

Thus there is need for sustained dialogue between members; for solid contextual analysis to support theological reflection and pastoral action; for dialogue with the "official" church and with "popular" churches, and for the wider dialogue.

QUESTIONS REMAIN

To what extent is it possible to follow the call to solidarity with the poor and oppressed to the extent of sharing their work and life while remaining within the present structures of religious missionary life?

Can institutes respond to new challenges while retaining all previous commitments? If not, can they withdraw from some activities in dialogue, in an ordered and systematic way?

Is there a basic opposition between opting for solidarity with the poor and the declared aims of some Institutes written into their constitutions?

When we respond to the challenges of justice and solidarity with the poor, can we, while respecting the need for inculturation, use the same terminology, the same linguistic framework, in Africa, Asia, Latin America, North America, and Europe?

SOME IMPLICATIONS FOR FORMATION

Formation for mission must take account of:
— solidarity with the poor
— dialogue with and inculturation in the lives of the poor
— the basic need to communicate with the world in a language it understands
— lived experiences with people who are immersed in situations of poverty and the struggle for justice
— openness to new theological insights coming from the poor.

A new "spirituality for violence" is needed in view of the increasing possibility of encountering institutionalized violence. Archbishop Romero is well known. But consecrated sisters, brothers, priests, and an increasing multitude of lay people have died and are dying, because of their solidarity with the poor and oppressed and their commitment to full human liberation in Christ. This is a challenge as old as the gospel, but manifesting itself in new ways today.

33

A LETTER FROM BANGLADESH

Bob McCahill, MM

(This letter is one of a series we have received from Bob McCahill over the years. Bob lives in a village in Bangladesh where he is the only Christian in a totally Muslim population. His ministry is one of presence. Eds.)

Dear Friend,

It is reported that the Prophet of Islam, Mohammed, once said, "What actions are most excellent? To gladden the heart of a human being, to feed the hungry, to help the afflicted, to lighten the sorrow of the sorrowful, and to remove the wrongs of the injured." I am daily and deeply grateful to God for having given me one more year of life (number 47) with its many opportunities to gladden, to feed, to help, and to lighten the sorrows of others.

Probably this year's most surprising discovery has been that blind people, of whom Bangladesh has hundreds of thousands, wish to have their photographs taken. Ayub came to get his photo the other day. I had a nice one to present to him. He smiled broadly when I placed it in his hands. His companion, the boy who leads him around the town and villages, exclaimed, "Fine photo!" Ayub chuckled and squirmed with pleasure as others gathered to view his portrait. He cannot see it, of course. But others do see it, and offer their comments about it. That photo indicates to Ayub something about his value. It's as if I had told him, "You're important; I like you." Sometimes a photograph is like a hug.

It's easy to admire blind people. They instruct me by their good example. Every few days, I pass by Banu who sits at the roadside begging. Her three-year-old daughter, Fori, plays in the dirt beside her. Last week I greeted the blind mother and her seeing child. Banu responded in her customary, cheerful way. Then she called my attention to the torn sharee she was wearing. I cajoled her: "Listen, Banu! Already it's the hot season; torn clothing is advantageous; you'll be cooler and more comfortable that way." Banu's face lit up. She giggled merrily. Such a good-humored lady. Blind since birth, owning nothing, and always ready to laugh.

Some persons are so grievously ill that the best way I know to help them is by speaking a word of truth. Last month I admitted Bilayed to a hospital, but within one week they released him. They could not treat him; he should return to the village in order to die at home. Bilayed draped his arm over my neck while we descended the stairway, and sighed, "I'm so weak . . . couldn't eat all week long." I spoke of Allah's love for him, assured him that Allah knows what he's going through, and that he is a good person. Among those truths the latter one was the most astounding for him to hear. No one ever tells a black, illiterate, threadbare, shoeless, physically broken villager that he is a good person. Although Bilayed was beyond smiling, I believe he treasured until the hour of his death those three little words: "You are good."

You may have read about the floods in Bangladesh this year. Recently I was slogging through thigh-deep waters in order to visit Amena, an ailing mother. It was slippery going. A crowd of onlookers watched expectantly for me to fall. I didn't disappoint them. As I lurched backwards into muddy water do you imagine that I heard expressions of sympathy or even politely muffled laughter? Not so. I heard, rather, guffaws and observed that even the sick lady was grinning. I'd touched her funnybone. Sometimes the good I accomplish is not the good I'd intended.

Multiply the above-mentioned incidents by a few hundred or thousands and you'll have an accurate enough idea of what one Catholic missioner priest in a Muslim-majority country has been doing. I try not to exaggerate the joy God gives me through the sick-poor. But, as a matter of fact, I'm truly happy, in love with persons who suffer without grumbling, and more in need of them than they are in need of me.

Praise belong to Allah!

Your brother,
Bob McCahill

Postscript for fellow pilgrims: Sometimes I accuse myself: "When are you going to start helping to change structures that oppress people? You're so wrapped up in people's lives that you haven't the time or energy to grapple with the big issues." Then I beat my scrawny chest, admit my deficiencies, and view myself with calm amusement. Anyway, I say to myself, "Who knows? Maybe God uses even my wee efforts to help transform oppressive structures."

Helping the poor is a work recommended by all the great religions. "Helping the poor" is also an expression so trite that I used to think it described just one among many laudable human activities. No longer do I underestimate that work. The promise of another Great Prophet is fulfilled: "When you give a party, invite the poor, the crippled, the lame and the blind. They have no means of repaying you. That way lies real happiness for you."

34

DIALOGUE OF LIFE WITH MUSLIMS IN THE PHILIPPINES

Desmond Hartford, SSC

The history of Muslim Christian relations in the southern Philippines has been one of conflict resulting in a deep sense of distrust and prejudice toward each other. The roots of the conflict are complex, ranging from land, socioeconomic, and political problems to cultural and religious ones. By the early 1970s the conflict had developed into a war in many areas. In the mid-1970s, under the inspiration of Bishop Tudtud, the Prelature of Marawi was set up. The mission vision of the new Prelature focused on the Christian community becoming a sign of reconciliation for their Muslim brothers and sisters through a dialogue of life and faith. The vision was beautiful; the problem was how to live it. What I would like to share with you are a few lived experiences which highlight some dimensions of that vision.

When the Prelature of Marawi was set up I was working in another part of Mindanao and did not feel any special attraction to dedicating my life to Muslim-Christian dialogue. However, following a thirty-day retreat in Ireland in 1977, I felt a strong conviction that I should engage in this life of dialogue, and so on my return to the Philippines I joined the Prelature of Marawi and was assigned to a small town named Karomatan. The town had a mixed Muslim-Christian population, but as you moved in one direction the area was almost totally Christian and as you moved in the other direction it was almost totally Muslim. It was to some extent a frontier situation. Some Christians had crossed the frontier to seek land or to work in logging operations in the Muslim area. "Christian" soldiers, carrying their arms and machine guns, crossed the frontier to protect the interests of the rich in the area.

DIALOGUE OF LIFE

In an effort to understand more deeply the Maranao Muslim people, I moved to a large village about fifteen kilometers inside the Muslim area. I lived with a Muslim family and from the beginning I was received with typical Muslim

265

hospitality. Considering the difficult circumstances, the trust they showed in accepting me was to grow over a period of two years into a deep sense of friendship. The family was composed of the parents and eight children who ranged in age from four to seventeen. There were also four teenage girls staying at the house who were studying in the local Madrasa School and considered part of the extended family. During my early months with the family, when I spent nearly all my time in the study of the local dialect, relationships began to grow on the human level. I was impressed by the deep concern of the parents for the children. I also began to relate to the family on the basis of human needs, and I came to realize that the ultimate basis of all dialogue is the single humanity of all people.

I told myself that as a basis I must start thinking in terms of "we humans" rather than we Muslims or we Christians. Reflection on the creation covenant helped me in this respect.

In the Maranao culture the word *pagari* has a deep significance. It means brother or sister, and it is also applied to those who are accepted into the extended family as brothers or sisters. After some time I noticed that this term was being used for my relationship to Muslims and the family. I realized that I had indeed been accepted as a brother, when on a few occasions I was left alone at night in the house with the teenage girls. It is nice to be accepted as a brother, but brotherhood has two sides. It means giving as well as receiving. In this respect I found that what I had considered "my" radio or "my" room was being freely used by others. For me the dialogue was liberating, and it was in this dialogue that God was manifested. Put in Islamic terms, we could say "Allah is . . . the source of Peace" (Koran 59:23). My presence among them had become for me a sign of hope.

DIALOGUE OF FAITH

I would not like to give the impression that the dialogue was purely human-istic. When Muslims and Christians of deep religious conviction enter into a dialogue of life, they can only do so as Muslims and Christians. In other words, in the dialogue of life there is also a dialogue of faith. One of my deepest impressions in this respect was that for the Muslim, God is the One Who Is. God is alive and pervades every aspect of human existence. This realization is deeply felt when one observes Muslims at prayer. God must be worshiped in deep submission.

There was an occasion shortly after I arrived in the village when I was praying in the evening in a very comfortable chair, resting my legs on a small coffee table. Just as I had finished, some members of the family present reminded me that it was time for evening prayer. They had not recognized that I had been praying. A Christian cannot fail to recognize that Muslims are performing their prescribed prayer. Muslims have taught me the importance of worship in prayer and the need to express this sense of worship in my bodily gestures.

Just before Ramadan, the month of fasting, I asked some of the women in the house if they were going to fast. I myself was bracing myself to fast for a few days as a sign of solidarity. They simply replied that they would fast if God willed it. They reminded me that we have to live within the plan of God for our lives. The religious Muslim also manifests his or her deep submission to God through their profound respect for God's word in the Holy Koran. The word is proclaimed; received by the believer in his or her heart; ruminated on in the remembrance (*Dikr*) and returned to God in worship and acclamation. There was an occasion when I experienced this process deeply. I was invited to a celebration of the Prophet's birthday. A young girl chanted the Koran with great depth and feeling, and the community present accepted the word and returned it to God in the acclamation "Allah-Allah." The dialogue of faith goes side by side with the dialogue of life. It is through experiences like these that the freedom comes to move forward. God is already present and calling us into a new future where the values of God's Reign will be lived.

Brother to the Poor

For a Christian man living with a Muslim family in rural Mindanao it is not sufficient to become brother to one particular family; one must also reach out in an effort to become a brother to the poor. Sometimes it is easier for a priest who is a foreigner to reach out to the poor than it is for others as can be seen in the following incident. Some Muslims from near the village where I lived took part in an armed robbery of six passenger buses passing through a remote area. The robbers were surrounded by the army and several of them were killed. Two from near my village were taken captive by the army. Everyone in the village suspected that they would be either tortured or killed and no one was willing to find out because all feared the army. I decided to look for them because it is easier for the army to "salvage" people if nobody follows them up. Eventually I found them one hundred kilometers away in Pagadian City. They had been beaten, but not badly. One of them said simply to me, "If you help us in this situation you are our brother."

Brotherhood and sisterhood is for all, but it must first be offered to those in the greatest need. It is in stretching out our hands in dialogue to the poor that we are enriched. It is they who know the meaning of generosity and sharing. This was brought home to me on an occasion when three poor Muslim children came to the house selling vegetables. I had just had some visitors and on the table were some cakes and candy which I gave to the children. They stayed to talk for a while and I noticed that one of them was not eating her candy or cake. I asked her why and she replied that she was bringing them home to her little sister who was not feeling well that day. I have failed to find generosity of this nature among the children of the rich.

Yearning for Justice

The Muslim poor of Mindanao are yearning for justice. Genuine dialogue of life between the Muslim poor and the Christian poor can give hope to that yearning. The Christian community must become a sign of hope that this dialogue is possible. For dialogue to have long-term results in Mindanao it must be a dialogue of life between the ordinary members of the Christian and Muslim communities. However, people with special callings or charisms may have a role in initiating this dialogue.

My understanding of dialogue is that Christ lived and died proclaiming the values of the Reign. He died so that men and women might have the fullness of life. In the global village of today the Reign cannot come because of the great divisions among people. In our times God is calling men, women, and communities to cross those divisions and in a dialogue of life to share the richness of their humanity, their faith, and their resources. The hope is that through this dialogue God will bring about the Reign of justice, reconciliation, and peace.

35

A CHRISTIAN AMONG MUSLIMS IN BANGLADESH

Eugenia d'Costa, OLM

Islam in Bangladesh is eight hundred years old. It was brought by the missionaries from Arabia and is a distinct form of Islam—Sufism. This Sufism is found in the poems and songs of the Bengali people. Christianity is three hundred years old—brought by the Portuguese missionaries.

The population of Bangladesh is 87 million. Seventy-five percent of the population are illiterate poor farmers. Less than one percent are Christians; over 85 percent are Muslims. The area is politically and economically very unstable. I would like to share with you my experience of living with Muslims.

VILLAGE LIFE

I was born in a village in which there were only eight Catholic families. In the vicinity were ten Muslim villages, mostly rich, each of which had about four or five Catholic families, mostly poor. Our Christian faith was passed on to us by our ancestors. My parish priest is Italian. Christians enjoy his support, friendship, trust, and material help. He is involved in all kinds of good works.

By degrees Muslims came to know me and my father. My father is a God-fearing, praying person, just and honest, helpful and sympathetic. His home is open to all at any time. His life has been one of dialogue. He has been a man whom people trust completely. Although a Christian, he settles quarrels about property or any other social injustice with the help of the village chairman (a Muslim) and other prominent leaders of the village. These cases have been heard in our Christian home. All the litigants are Muslims and could be very aggressive in quarrels related to property.

When I grew up, I went away from home to become a religious. When my Muslim friends saw me during my holidays I was different, and they could not accept my choice of such a rigid life. It was a mystery to them. People meet God, serve God in any state of life. "Why this extra austere life?" they asked. I answered, "I can pray more for you all." At this they were happy. I tried to explain the idea of the great commandment of love taught by Jesus and how we teach all the children in our schools to be like him. I felt this greatly five years ago when for the first time in our history we celebrated eucharist in the University Hall. How respectful and helpful all the students were while the word of God was being read, and throughout the service! I felt no division among them. Our convent is attached to the mosque. The school has 1,250 students, only 50 of whom are Christians. I meet the parents monthly. They have so many questions! "Is it enough to pray once a week, on Sunday?" they asked. "What is your fixed time for prayer? Why can't you come and pray with us? And like us? Why do you use the word Jesus more than God (Allah)? He is only a prophet and messenger. Why don't you allow us to pray with you? All of us will become Muslim one day!"

Sometimes I am able to satisfy them with my answers but at times I am unable to satisfy their hunger, especially that of the religious leaders and government officials who are educated and have a different outlook.

THE IMPORTANCE OF PRAYER

I do not give enough time to prayer and the scriptures. I look at my family, my people, my parish, and I ask the question, "Do we really walk in the presence of God? When? How?" My Muslim friends pray five times a day, recite the beads with the ninety-nine names of God, and recite the Koran. We will conquer the world, they say, the day our "Imam" (faith) and your "love" become one. Yes, I, a Christian, have to be a woman of prayer. Is my light strong enough to shine before them? I ask myself too, how can I give them my own personal experience of Jesus? My own relationship with Jesus? How can I show them who Jesus is?

THE POSITION OF CHRISTIANS

I have discovered the negative aspects of living among Muslims. There are injustices under which local Christians suffer. The poor are exploited, and we Christians are mostly poor. We live in fear of losing our faith. This has happened to a number. I myself felt frustrated when, although my examination results were excellent, I did not get a scholarship. It was given to a Muslim. There is little regard for the needs of the poor. There are so many courses and seminars for Muslims. On Sundays our school must remain open, yet, on the death of an Islamic leader anywhere in the world, all schools will be closed.

There are very few Christians attending college or university. All those who attend are continually harassed and tempted to lose their faith. Wealth has a lot to do with this. If a Muslim boy or girl wants to become a Christian they will encounter great hostility, anger, and suspicion. The person will be cut off from the family and even from the country. Women suffer from many prejudices. There are also the evils of a caste system.

There is also the great scandal of middle-caste Christian families who keep Muslim girls for domestic work in a situation akin to slavery.

GOD AMONG THE POOR

I share a lot with the rich, educated minority, but I see little results from this sharing. I do not find the presence of God among these people. What sort of image of God do they have? A God far away? Do they really worship God as the poor are doing? I see my role as asking these questions. We held a seminar for youth on the topic "Who God is to me." There was a great response. Some found a personal loving God. But I really find the presence of God more easily among the poor, simple, uneducated, suffering people of the villages than among those who live in the towns where there are more rich people.

I am convinced that I and my people and my church need to see the many good and holy values of the Islamic religion and to see God's love for Muslims. The seed is planted and growing in my village.

A New Church

The church will take a new and different shape because of its involvement in the dialogue of life in Bangladesh. I believe it will develop through more sharing; more silent contemplative prayer; the witness of consecrated religious life and the witness of austere monastic living; the witness also of our work for peace and justice and for dialogue. These are seeds. Hopefully, they will bring about inner conversions among the people.

I am happy to have been born in a Muslim country and to be living a challenging life of faith with them. I am continuously reminded by them of the presence of God, whereas in Catholic countries I see religion taken for granted. I do not wish to snatch away the faith of Muslims through religious conversions. The presence of God in any man or woman is a great thing. I would like to see them come to closer personal contact with Jesus, whose face is still hidden from them. Maybe I can achieve this by living a life of dialogue. It is more difficult for me, a Bangladeshi, than for a foreigner, but perhaps it is more important that I do it.

Lastly, a word about fear. When I am confronted with problems it is at times difficult to stand up for the values of the Reign of God. I am afraid. If I am to continue it is important for me that I have the support of my congregation which sent me and the support of the Christian community in which I live.

36

THE PEACE OF ISLAM

Armand Garon, MAfr.

The title "The Peace of Islam" was chosen quite deliberately. Had the title "Peace and the Muslim World" been chosen instead, it would have conveyed a different meaning, not altogether devoid of political overtones. When I use "The Peace of Islam," I mean peace as understood within the framework of Muslim teaching. Before proceeding any further, I should mention that Islam, according to a classical saying in Arabic, is *dîn wa daula*, which means, "Islam is both religion and state together." Keeping this in mind, we will now examine the meaning of peace in Islam from a primarily religious point of view.

SALÂM

The Arabic word *salâm* is usually translated as "peace" in English. We note its similarity to a biblical Hebrew word, *shalom*. In fact, both words have a common root and they are closely connected not only in form, but also in meaning. The semantic content of *shalom* extends far beyond the mere absence of war. It is a very positive word and is pregnant with all the benefits that peace conveys: order in society, friendly relations with other nations and understanding between the people of various clans and tribes. It also connotes general prosperity, plenty of water and rain, a plentiful harvest, and food for everybody. It is crucial to understand that this *shalom* is a blessing from God.[1]

SALVATION

When we analyze the word *salâm* in Arabic, its fullest meaning is best conveyed in English by the term "salvation." The *Encyclopédie de l'Islam* states: *"Nom verbal de salima, être sauf, intact, puis comme substantif au sens de salut, salutation."*[2] In the *Encyclopédie de l'Islam* the word *salâm* is never translated "peace," nor does the *Encyclopédie* use the word "peace" in connection with *salâm*. For instance, the phrase "house of salvation" is given for *dâr as-salâm* and "the paths of salvation" for *subul as-salâm*.[3] The word "salvation" can be used as a form of greeting, as in *as-salâm 'aleykum*, or in Latin *Salve!* or in French *Salut!* Translating *salâm* as "salvation" does not mean that the idea of peace is absent, since the word includes salvation from the plague of war. In this case *salâm* as peace is one of God's most precious gifts, so much so that in the Muslim faith it has become one of Allah's beautiful names.[4]

RELIGIOUS CONTENT

From these short remarks, we may conclude that the cluster of consonants *s-l-m*, in Arabic, Hebrew, and other Semitic languages carries a religious content. This is quite in keeping with the sacral character of those early cultures. In other words, the benefits implied by such words as *salâm* and *shalom* are understood primarily as blessing that comes from God. This appears in Arabic even more clearly, since in the older passages of the Koran *salâm* is the eschatological blessing par excellence. Those who will enter Paradise shall hear the one word *salâm*: "They shall not hear therein vain or sinful discourse, except the word peace, peace."[5]

In an article in *Se comprendre*, Father Cuperly states, "This word (salam) may be rendered by peace, security, preservation, salvation, exemption, rest."[6] He prefers to translate it as "peace," but is obliged to couple it with "salvation" in order to convey the full religious import of *salâm* as used in the Koran. Muslims themselves seem to bear this out when, to Christians greeting them with *as-salâm 'aleykum*, they prefer to reply, rather disobligingly, with a quotation from the Koran: "Peace (*salâm*) is on him who follows the guidance" (20:47) — as indeed happened to me in the Sudan. The Muslim peace not only comes from God, it is a blessing which, properly understood, belongs only to those true believers who follow the right path.[7]

HOUSE OF PEACE AND HOUSE OF WAR

In cultures where there is a division between the sacred and the secular, the word "peace" naturally suggests the absence of war. The Western word "peace" can have a religious meaning, and so we use it in our Christian liturgies. The word "peace" may belong to both the worldly and the spiritual realms, but in the Western mind these are not necessarily linked. In the Muslim way of thinking, it would be difficult to conceive of *salâm* without some religious connotation. In fact, the very opposite of peace, which is war, rendered in Arabic by *harb*, is not without a religious ring. In Muslim parlance, the world is divided into two camps: the "House of Peace" (*dâr as-salâm*) and the "House of War" (*dâr al-harb*), the first expression referring to the Muslims and the latter to non-believers.

Consider, for instance, the patently religious coloring of the following verse from the Koran: "So when the sacred months have passed away, slay the idolaters wherever you find them, and take them captives and besiege them and lie in wait for them in every ambush; then if they repent and keep up prayer and pay the poor rate, leave their way free to them; surely Allah is Forgiving, Merciful."[8] This call to war is not simply directed against enemies and foes, but against polytheists, that is, against pagan non-believers. This quotation from the Koran makes it quite clear that from a Muslim perspective war may have a sacral dimension, but it would be wrong to take such passages out of their historical context.

Jihâd

Modern patterns of thinking in the West do not make it easy for us to understand the attitude of Islam towards war and its corollary peace. It is more facile simply to lump all Muslims together and think of them as freely resorting to violence. This tendency is enhanced by the fact that a number of terrorists claim to act in the name of Allah. The word *jihâd*, which newspapers have made familiar to us, is often translated as "holy war," although this interpretation must be explained and qualified. The *jihâd* is something sacred in the sense that it is a duty rendered to God—a meaning which can only be understood within the framework of a sacral society, such as Islam, where religion and state are inseparable. However, the word "war" does not translate *jihâd* adequately. It should be interpreted as a strenuous effort towards a holy goal for the sake of God.[9] This effort may well mean war, and it is quite likely that *jihâd* first evokes the idea of a holy war in unsophisticated Muslim minds, as is evidenced by the merciless conflicts now taking place involving a number of Islamic countries. It may be mentioned here that some Muslim commentators have felt the need for spiritualizing the *jihâd*. They appeal to a saying of Muhammad in order to draw a distinction between a small *jihâd* and the greater *jihâd*, the latter being the fight against one's own evil inclinations.[10]

In an article entitled "L'Islam et la violence," Professor Abdelmajid Charifi contends that in the teachings of the Holy Book a distinction must be made between eternal truths that are of divine origin and other considerations arising from historical situations that are only of limited application.[11] It is indeed true that Islam had to fight against unbelievers in order to ensure its survival as a religious group. This fighting was soon seen as a struggle for the propagation of the true faith, a holy duty to be carried out for the sake of Allah.

Military Conflicts in Sacral Societies

It is important to remember that in sacral societies military conflicts are seen in religious terms as well. The wars that opposed Protestants and Catholics at the time of the Reformation no doubt had political foundations, but they were fought in the name of religious truth. During the French Revolution, when Vendée rose against the central government, people went to the combat singing hymns and canticles. The temptation is always great to drag religion into what are basically political confrontations, territorial ambitions, or mere expressions of racial hatred. Considering that official Islam is still, according to the classical phrase, religion and state together, the danger in its case is even greater. An Egyptian film on the 1973 October War depicted their soldiers rushing to the Israeli defense line with shouts of *Allâhu akbar* (Allah is the greatest). If one remembers all the implications of the phrase *dîn wa daula*, one should not be shocked to find the Pakistani jurist Muhammad Hamidullah writing in his 1968 edition of *Muslim Conduct of State*: "Islamic polity being based on a community of co-religionists, it is unthinkable to contract a treaty of perpetual alliance with non-Muslims."[12] Or again, "Muslim jurists conclude that treaties of friendship should not be concluded with non-Muslims for perpetuity."[13]

A Religion of Peace?

Should we conclude from these statements that Islam considers all non-Muslim nations potential or latent enemies to be fought against whenever there is a possibility of victory? This would not do justice to history, nor would it be representative of all schools of Islamic thought. If asked the direct question, "Is Islam a religion of peace?", all Muslims would undoubtedly answer in the affirmative. But where they will differ is how this peace should be secured. For traditional jurists, such as Al-Mâwardî (973–1058) and Ibn Taymiyya (1263–1328), Muslim peace depends primarily on the faithful application of koranic law. The modern writer Abû al-A'lâ al-Mawdûdî (1903–79) belongs to that school of thought, as does the fundamentalist group known as the Muslim Brothers and the Wahabite Movement which originated in Saudi Arabia.[14]

At the other end of the spectrum, one finds Muslim thinkers and mystics who interpret the Koran in a spiritual sense. They try to uncover the hidden and deeper meaning in what is explicitly stated. These Muslims advocate the example set by the prophet and a behavior that takes as its guidelines the divine attributes as they are expressed in the beautiful names of Allah: God is peace, justice and light; God is the merciful, the holy, the generous, the patient, and so on. In Muslim literature there are doctors of the spiritual life who can be taken as guides, the Sufi writers, for instance. There are also numerous Muslim brotherhoods or confraternities founded to help members develop a life of union with God through various forms of meditation.

A MIDDLE WAY

Between a narrow literal interpretation of revelation and a largely spiritual interpretation, a growing number of Muslim thinkers are proposing a middle way in which the koranic teaching on justice and peace could be summarized in a few major principles that would take into account the new realities experienced by modern Islam in the field of social relations, economics, and politics. A number of well-known writers such as Muhammad Iqbal, Sayyid Ahmad Khan, and Muhammad Arkoun Hasan Hanafi take this approach. There is, however, little uniformity to be found in the practical applications of such middle-of-the-road interpretations. The governments of Turkey, Syria, Libya, and Morocco could, with some justification, all claim to base the political life of their society on this middle-of-the-road interpretation of koranic revelation.[15]

PEACE IN ISLAM

What kind of peace does Islam offer to all those who do not belong to the "House of Peace"? Islam is a missionary religion which has set itself a definite goal, that of bringing the world to submission to Allah. Will all the Muslim believers described above agree to accomplish this task only through peaceful means? One can only hope that Muslim leaders and thinkers, in full awareness of the God-given equality of all human beings, will finally strive after a peace that does not discriminate between Muslims and non-Muslims. The greeting "Peace be upon you" would then become an ecumenical invitation rather than being reserved exclusively for Muslims.[16]

To the question, "Is Islam a religion of peace?", there may be only one answer, and that, again, is another question: "Which Islam do you mean?"

NOTES

1. Whatever light a study of the Hebrew word *shalom* may throw on the Arabic word *salâm*, one must bear in mind the proviso that words hypothetically derived from a common root may assume different meanings in the history of related languages. Before appearing in Muslim literature, the three-consonant element *s-l-m* occurs in Phoenician, Assyrian, Aramaic, Sabaean, and Ethiopian, in written or epigraphic documents; cf. Brown, Driver and Briggs, *Hebrew and English Lexicon of the Old Testament* (Oxford: 1959), 1022. Cf. also "Peace," in John L. Mackenzie, *Dictionary of the Bible* (New York and London: Macmillan, 1974), 651–52.

2. *Encyclopédie de l'Islam*, vol. IV (1934), 92–95, art. of C. van Arendonk.

3. Compare, however, the article by the same van Arendonk in the *Shorter Encyclopedia of Islam* (Leiden: Brill, 1974), 489–91, where the author translates *salâm* as peace, health, salutation, greeting.

4. Compare in the Bible Micah 5:4: "He himself will be peace."

5. Koran 56: 25–26. Translation of M.H. Shakir, *Tahrike Tarsile Qur'ân* (New York, 1983).

6. "La paix—*al-salâm*," in *Se comprendre*, 86/06 (July 21, 1986).

7. Muslim commentators have debated whether Christians and Jews should be greeted with the *salâm*. See "*al-salâmu 'alaykum*," in *Etudes Arabes* 69, 1985-2, PISAI, 19–37.

8. Koran 9:5, translated by M. H. Shakir.

9. Cf. Emile Tyan's article "*Djihâd*" in *The Encyclopaedia of Islam*, 1960. According to the *Quranic Vocabular* (in Arabic) of Muhammad Fou'âd 'Abd al-Bâqî, the word *jihâd* is found four times in the Koran, but the corresponding verb and its derivatives recur thirty-one times.

10. The fact that this interpretation gets only a passing mention (within brackets!) in Tyan's article (cf. note 9) is not without significance. See also Pierre Crépon, *Les religions et . . . la guerre* (Paris: Editions Ramsay, 1982), 131ff.

11. Abdelmajid Charifi, "L'Islam et la violence," in *Se comprendre*, 129, (April 29, 1975): 2. This article (13 pages) reproduces Professor Charifi's talk at the *Colloque islamo-chrétien* held at Tunis in 1974. When Prof. Charifi writes (p. 10) that "*tous les révolutionnaires refusent formellement la violence gratuite, anarchique et aveugle*," one cannot help feeling that the truth of that statement hangs rather precariously on the sole adverb *formellement*.

12. Muhammad Hamidullah, *Muslim Conduct of State* 5th ed. (Lahore: Sh. Muhammad Ashraf, 1968) (5th edition, revised and enlarged), art. 565: 268.

13. Ibid., art. 568: 269.

14. These and the following observations are a summary of Prof. Maurice Borrmans's analysis "Justice et paix dans le monde à la lumière de la foi musulmane," in *Se comprendre* 78/8 (October 5, 1978): 11 pp. Al-Mâwardî and Charles J. Adams in Andrew Rippin, ed., *Approaches to the History of Interpretation of the Qur'ân* (Oxford: Clarendon Press, 1988), 307–23.

15. For more on this, cf. "Justice et paix dans le monde," 5–7.

16. This talk was given in October 1986. There has since appeared an interesting article on the *jihâd* by Biancamaria Scarcia Amoretti, "Bellum pium et justum: il jihàd," in *Islàm: storia e civiltà*, Accademia della Cultura Islamica, no.18 (vol. 6, no.1), (January-March 1987): 5–11.

37

Preserving Africa's Traditional Religious Values

Archbishop Jean Zoa

It is not easy to find examples of real dialogue between the church and traditional religions. Today these religions are in danger of disappearing in Africa. Traditional religion has no written documents or archives. It simply possesses tangible traces of sacred things like trees, places, sacred animals, and sacred times. Beliefs have not been codified. Cults themselves have not been organized on an extensive scale. Life in the forest resulted in the isolation of clans and militated against extended cults. In this context the missionary sought to contact the chief or elder of the group, whose welcome and accord generally brought with it that of the group as a whole. By contrast the peoples of the savannahs or grasslands, where historical and geographical factors permitted a solid and widespread socio-politico-economic organization, have at times presented effective resistance to missionary activity. Examples of these contrasts can be seen in two dynamic African ethnic groups, the Ibos of Nigeria and the Bamilekes of Cameroon.

Values of Traditional Religions

I believe the church has a duty greatly exceeding the simple task of dialogue in their regard. The church in Africa, in a spirit of profound dialogue, appears to me to be the only safe repository for these traditional religions. I would see the church as safeguarding the traditional cults not so much as organized religious structures but understanding them in such a way as to:
– save, preserve, develop, and fulfill, totally or partially, the authentic values inherent in them
– retain and give expression to the deep aspirations of individual Africans and of African society manifested in certain beliefs, practices, rites, attitudes, prohibitions, laws, and ethical regulations of these cults.

Through the Christian communities which are now emerging from the Africa of traditional religions the church must plan and organize a mission to assume and transform these religions. In fact, many of the catechetical manuals now being used by the new generations of Africans attempt to reread and interpret the answers which the traditional religions tried to give "to the enigma hidden in the human condition and which, yesterday, like today, deeply troubles the human heart" (*Nostra Aetate*, 1). Thus, for example, our Ewondo catechism contains an initial compulsory section *Nyebe be tara* about the questions which concerned our parents in their traditional religions. Examples of these are:

—What is the meaning and aim of life?
—What is "the good" and what is "sin"?
—What is the origin and the object of suffering?
—What is the path to attain real happiness?
—What are death, judgment and reward after death?

Traditional religions were and still are deeply concerned with understanding what exactly is "the mystery behind the ineffable which surrounds our existence, from which we draw our origin and towards which we tend," as the Second Vatican Council expressed it. Doubtless, these fundamental questions are common to all religions, but not all the early evangelizers in Africa clearly realized that our ancestral religions sought answers to those same questions.

When we assess the results, however, we must recognize that, despite omissions and even errors which may be attributed to prejudices and to colonial and cultural distortions of the time, missionaries made much progress, at times perhaps unconsciously. Many recognized from the outset in African peoples "a constant sensitivity to this hidden energy which is present in the course of things and in human life." The missionary was often even a part of "the avowal of the supreme Divinity" (*Nostra Aetate*, 2).

Christian missionaries found solid values already present in traditional religions, even if they were unclear to many. I would mention specifically:

—respect for life
—family solidarity
—hospitality and welcome
—belief in life after death
—the meaning of immanent justice
—veneration of the elders as people of wisdom endowed with specific powers, permitting them to bless and curse effectively
—a religious respect for nature.

These values, even today, constitute a universal religious ambience omnipresent in black Africa.

THE CHURCH—PRESERVER OF TRADITIONAL RELIGIOUS VALUES

Today there are many groups and individuals having what my people call *Beg Bekalara*, the "wisdom of the book." They mean that they have been to school and even to university. But these same people may not know the Good News of Jesus. If the church is to dialogue with them it is essential to keep in mind the above values. One must never forget that the modern African who has to a greater or lesser extent experienced village life remains in the depths of himself or herself a practitioner of, and at times an unconscious witness to, his or her traditional religion. This is not an unhappy possession! Today, when a large number of African Christian communities are entering the second phase of their evangelization, that of deepening their faith, the church must safeguard the traditional values. They constitute a real asset for the church as it deepens the faith of the people, and they will help to ensure an African face on the church in our continent.

If in the early stages these values were recognized only intuitively by missionaries through the guidance of the Holy Spirit, today it is necessary to make them explicit in order to elaborate a true kerygma, a meaningful theology, an appropriate catechism, an inculturated theology.

Over and above the normal processes of dialogue, the traditional religions of Africa today ask the church to lend them its voice. Otherwise they may become extinct and their values be lost forever. That would be a great impoverishment, an irreparable loss to the young churches of Africa.

38

DIALOGUE WITH BUDDHISTS IN ASIA

Marcello Zago, OMI

INTRODUCTION

The term dialogue should not be understood merely in a colloquial sense, but should include every kind of positive and constructive relationship with individual Buddhists, with Buddhist communities of lay people or monks, with institutions and societies which recognize themselves as Buddhists.

Dialogue with Buddhists has unique characteristics because it deals with an essentially anthropocentric religion which has transcendental perspectives. There is not just one form of Buddhism. Buddhism is lived by peoples who have distinctive national and cultural histories.

PRINCIPAL FORMS OF DIALOGUE TODAY

Doctrinal dialogue consists in the sympathetic and respectful encounter of the two faiths and doctrines in order to:

— grasp the existential values sought by all Buddhists, be they spiritual leaders, learned or ordinary lay people
— identify what it is that Buddhists understand by the gospel message and by Christian life
— reformulate kerygma, catechesis, and theology.

This type of dialogue is being pursued in different centers such as that of Aloysius Pieris, SJ, in Sri Lanka. It is also happening in Japan. It is a dialogue which is laborious, specialized, and necessary.

Experiential religious dialogue consists of sharing the prayer and meditational experiences of one's spiritual journey in order to understand the other from the inside and to progress together. There are many examples, including the Zen Center of Fr. Lassalle in Japan. The visit of Benedictine monks to Japan where they will stay in Buddhist monasteries is another example. Many Christians and Buddhists have already lived such experiences. It is a delicate dialogue, demanding preparation and discernment.

Dialogue of human-social cooperation promotes development, justice, education and service to refugees, to the handicapped, and so forth. This service is based on common religious values and motivations. The Center of Fr. Tissa Balasuriya, OMI, in Sri Lanka is one example.

This is an important form of renewal for the various religions in the service of humankind. Although more widespread than the two preceding forms of dialogue, it is still the domain of religious professionals.

Existential "lived" dialogue is the ordinary day-to-day living together with "the other," motivated by and illuminated by their respective faiths. It can and should be practiced by all, and is the basic form which makes possible all the others. It is possible when the different communities are progressively more respectful of each other and conscious of each other's separate religious identity.

In a local church these various forms of dialogue are not mutually exclusive but complementary.

MOTIVATIONS FOR DIALOGUE

In church-related motivation:

• the survival of many Christian communities depends on positive relations with the surrounding milieu, and on a conscious approach to the Buddhist people;

• inculturation, an urgent need of the local churches, is impossible without dialogue in its diverse forms, otherwise inculturation remains at the "laboratory" level and will perpetuate a Christian ghetto;

• both the passing on of the message and presenting the meaning of the church will become relevant only in a climate of continual encounter;

• encounter with Buddhism, according to Romano Guardini, is the greatest challenge to Christianity; it demands a deepening at both the experiential and theological levels.

In world-centered motivation (focuses on the coming of the Reign of God):

• the church has the role of supporting unity and progress among peoples. Mutual understanding is the necessary condition for this;

• dialogue helps religions become better paths of salvation for their respective believers. In this sense we can say that the aim of dialogue is to make Buddhists better Buddhists and Christians better Christians;

• dialogue fulfills the specific role of the church in view of salvation, which is realized fully and definitively in the eschaton. Dialogue then becomes cooperation towards achieving the salvation which God wills and brings about for all humankind.

PERSPECTIVES AND REQUIREMENTS FOR THE FUTURE

We are at the beginning of a new era in mission. The SEDOS Research Seminar on the Future of Mission held in 1981 has already indicated some directions. One of these is dialogue. Dialogue not only reaches the great religions remaining untouched, but also reveals the nature of mission itself. Dialogue becomes a modality of mission to such an extent that it characterizes all missionary activity and at the same time has its own place as a specific form of mission.

Difficulties in dialogue will crop up: certain antireligious governments, a possible theological retrenchment in the church, superficiality and lack of preparation on the part of those engaged in dialogue both at individual and community levels. The requirements for making dialogue more effective and workable concern the whole missionary endeavor (personnel, resources, community support) as well as the professional, spiritual, and theological preparation of missionaries themselves.

THE SITUATION IN SOUTHEAST ASIAN COUNTRIES

There are common characteristics to be found in Burma, Cambodia, Laos, Thailand, and Sri Lanka. While their cultures show an Indian influence, the ethnic specificity of each country gives it a particular identity. The official religion, which is also that of the majority, is Theravada Buddhism, which has been deeply influenced by ancestral animism. Throughout this area, Christians are few and come mainly from minority groups, often of foreign origin. Sri Lanka, where the number of Christians reaches 8 percent is an exception to this.

There have been contacts between Christians and Buddhists going back three centuries. In the seventeenth century Jesuits such as Fathers Le Blanc, de la Breuille, and Du Bouchet who were working in Thailand "attempted to familiarize themselves with those inhabitants and to adapt themselves to them." They came to the realization that "in terms of customs and habits a Christian could not teach anything more than was already prescribed by the Buddhists' own religion." In Burma the Catholic bishops of the seventeenth and eighteenth centuries, like Percoto, Mantegazza, and Bigandet, have left us many tracts on both canonical (official) and lived Buddhism. In Cambodia Fr. Maldonado attempted to "assimilate himself as far as possible to the bonzes with their yellow dress, in order to sow the seed of salvation in the Buddhist convents themselves." In Sri Lanka Christianity showed less respect for local traditions in the early period under the Portuguese (1505–1556) than under the Dutch (1656–1796) and English (1796–1954).

Missionaries, despite a real sympathy for the culture, the sociophilosophic systems, and especially for the peoples among whom they lived, did not achieve either a sympathetic objective vision of Buddhism or any in-depth dialogue with Buddhists. They were prevented not only by the prejudices of the time, but especially by the theological standards by which they judged other religions, considering them as human aberrations and diabolical deceits. Colonization accentuated the difficulties of mutual understanding. In Thailand the Catholic school system promoted mutual esteem between the believers of both religions.

Following the arrival of independence, various factors have promoted contacts between Christians and Buddhists: for example, the emergence of Christians from their ghettos in the villages, the progress of urbanization, the need for social collaboration, international and interconfessional meetings, and finally a new view of other religions, particularly among Catholics following Vatican II.

BURMA

Burma seems to be the country where dialogue remains a low priority. Some advance has been made, as can be seen from the studies of Pasquale Anatriello and Winston L. King, but dialogue has not been promoted either by religious leaders or by the faithful. Memories of British colonization, the struggle to make Buddhism the state religion, the attitude of the present government, socialist and secular, have prevented the Buddhists from opening their horizons to dialogue. On the Christian side there was initially a feeling of being under attack from the Buddhist and then they lost the majority of the foreign missionaries. This latter development forced the remaining church leaders to concentrate their efforts on service to the Christian communities who, for the most part, consisted of non-Buddhist ethnic groups. Limited foreign contact and the reduced number of indigenous clergy have hampered any direct promotion of dialogue.

CAMBODIA

Christian-Buddhist dialogue in Cambodia took place between 1970 and 1975. Before this period any genuine encounter was impossible, despite the efforts of clergy like Monsignors Ramousse and Tep Im. Most Christians were considered foreigners. After the coup d'état of March 1970 only three or four thousand of the seventy thousand Catholics remained in the country. The rest either departed for Vietnam or were confined in camps for foreigners. Finding themselves alone and without any proper social support, especially without schools, the Khmer Christians felt both obliged and encouraged to enter into dialogue with their Buddhist compatriots.

Beyond individual dialogue, to which they had been progressively introduced through ordinary pastoral direction and special courses, Christians in the cities became involved in the care of refugees whose numbers grew continually because of the war. Such charitable service brought with it increasing contact with the authorities and with Buddhist leaders. Other contacts were organized between Christians and qualified lay Buddhists to promote reciprocal understanding. Courses and discussions took place at Pnom-Penh and elsewhere.

The presence of Benedictine monks seemed a favorable and promising element. The monastery at Kep had long remained a place of prayer quite removed from Buddhist monastic experience, as had the convent of the Carmelite Sisters at Pnom-Penh. The war brought the Catholic monks into contact with the Buddhists. Some bonzes found asylum in the monastery, and some young Buddhists joined the monks, not to become Christians, but to live that type of religious life. Reciprocal influence was great, not only for mutual understanding but also for adaptation. Buddhists began to accept the Christian monks as true religious and acted on this understanding, organizing, for example, the traditional offering of religious dress (*kathina*).

The liberation of Pnom-Penh in April 1975 signaled the end of all religious structures, Christian and Buddhist. Manual labor in the jungle, constant movement, courses of political indoctrination, and suffering took their toll on the Khmer. The majority of the hundred thousand monks was massacred between 1975 and 1979.

LAOS

In Laos dialogue was well planned and supported by the leaders and faithful of both religions. It has been a catalyst and example for neighboring countries. Thanks to a national office and diocesan coordinators which were instituted and maintained by the Episcopal Conference, all those engaged in pastoral work have been helped to renew their vision and their methods. Meetings between Christians and Buddhists have multiplied on the levels of friendship, mutual understanding, sharing of profound experiences, and collaboration. In-depth research on Buddhism as it is lived and on special questions such as the concept of the divine, as well as research on Christian and Buddhist ethics and religious language, has been carried out. This dialogue has also produced some official recognition, as can be seen in the visit to the Pope by a delegation of Buddhists led by the Buddhist patriarch of Laos himself.

The depth and sincerity of this dialogue could be measured when the foreign missionaries were expelled by Luang-Prabang in August 1975. The Buddhist patriarch did his utmost to change the Party's decision, but without success. He then wished to demonstrate the attitude of the Buddhists by organizing a solemn farewell ceremony in his monastery and personally seeing the missionaries off at the airport. The antireligious measures which the government has taken with increasing intensity both against Christians and Buddhists have not wiped out the benefits of the dialogue. The fact that in some cities small groups of Christians are still permitted to meet for prayer is probably due to the good will towards them developed among the Buddhist population as a result of earlier dialogue.

THAILAND

In Thailand the prospects for dialogue are good, even if at the moment the situation remains stagnant despite the valiant efforts of some pioneers. Catholic schools, which are attended by Buddhists, have prepared the terrain and influenced opinions.

In this case it was the Buddhists who took the initiative. In 1958 a Buddhist university in Bangkok requested the Catholic bishop to provide a professor of Christian religion. The director of the Department of Religion, Col. Pin Matukan, organized a day each year when the religions would meet and present themselves. He also opened a permanent exhibition on religions in a hall of the Ministry of Education. The most widely known bonze in the country, Buddhadasa, became interested and so was able to influence Buddhists in a positive way. The Buddhist patriarch of Thailand visited the Pope in 1972.

Protestants, who generally feel uncomfortable when faced with the question of dialogue and often create obstacles because of their rigid positions and methods, have contributed considerably through the annual "Sinclair Thompson Memorial Conferences" held at the theological seminary of Chiang Mai.

Some Catholics have promoted dialogue through good human relations, such as Msgr. Carretto and especially Fr. Ulliana, who has become one of the best known and influential people at the national meetings organized by the Department of Religion. Collaboration on social questions has also made a contribution. Others, such as Fr. Pezet, have studied the significance of Buddhism by living in Buddhist monasteries and practicing meditation in specialized centers. The Thai bishop Msgr. Ratna of Chiang Mai is involved in the dialogue, both on the theological and the practical levels.

However, in 1982–83 a Buddhist movement caused some concern by denouncing the Catholic church for a presumed plot to replace Buddhism and Thai culture by the year 2000. Such accusations of expansionist intent are based on frequent reports about the church transmitted by state television. At present, relations are good and dialogue is progressing.

SRI LANKA

The situation in Sri Lanka is unique because for centuries it has been the home of four great religions: Hinduism, Buddhism, Islam, and Christianity. The national Catholic seminary of Kandy initiated an openness to Buddhism in 1955 by offering special courses. Various specialized centers promoted awareness, encounter, and reciprocal collaboration. In some areas festivities are celebrated together. Some interreligious groups collaborate in aiding the handicapped, in development programs, and in resettling Tamil refugees. Unfortunately dialogue is not a living dimension of church communities, and some of the pioneers in the field find themselves marginalized by the institutional church.

The hierarchy, after years of hesitation, now seems prepared to lead the dialogue. In 1982 the bishops organized meetings in the various dioceses aimed at formation for dialogue. The Secretary of the Pontifical Council for Inter-Religious Dialogue took part in these.

THE SITUATION IN FAR EASTERN COUNTRIES

JAPAN

Experiences of dialogue in Japan are unique. Buddhist initiative is considerable, both at home and internationally. In this industrialized and secularized society, religious people seem driven to meet together in order to verify and confront their own identity and common values. The populace is sensitive to a certain type of dialogue as personified by such people as John Paul II, Mother Teresa of Calcutta, and Chiara Lubich of the Focolare Movement. Their visits to Japan in 1981–82 received national attention. The Japanese communications media play a significant role in developing awareness and reciprocal esteem, thus creating the basis for interpersonal and interreligious dialogue. Even if an attitude of dialogue has not yet filtered down to the clergy or the laity, and remains the work of religious elite, it is in Japan that dialogue is most developed on several levels.

The "Institutional" Level. The Commission for Non-Christians is studying the relationship between Catholic faith and the traditional ancestor cult. This is also being done in terms of the inculturation of Christianity in Japan. One might expect more collaboration from the better-known Catholic writers, such as Endo, Yashiro, Miura, and so forth.

The "Academic" Level. Symposiums, seminars, courses, and publications on

Japanese religions are sponsored by three major institutes for the study of religions:
- The Institute for Oriental Religions at Sophia University, which produces various publications.
- Nanzan Institute for Religions and Culture at Nanzan University and its publication, *Japanese Journal of Religious Studies*.
- Oriens Institute for Religious Research in Tokyo, which publishes the famous review *Japanese Missionary Bulletin*.

The "Social" Level. There is collaboration with non-Christians for social improvement, especially in the two interreligious organizations created for this purpose:
- World Conference on Religion and Peace (WCRP) founded by Mr. Nikkyo Niwano, President of Rissho-Koseikai, a new lay Buddhist movement. It is a worldwide interreligious movement to promote peace and has a good number of Catholic members. In Japan a number of the bishops have been active members.
- Japan Religious Committee and World Federation, founded by the late Zen master, Sogen Asahina. It has collaborated with the Pontifical Commission for Inter-Religious Dialogue.

The Level of "Experience." There is an exchange of religious experiences and spirituality. In this regard two initiatives deserve special mention:
- Zen-Christian Colloquium, which takes place every year since the famous Oiso Conference of 1967. Christians and Buddhists live together the contemplative experience of Christianity and Zen.
- Spiritual Exchange between East and West: an ambitious project in which in 1979 fifty Japanese Buddhist monks, scattered in twelve Benedictine monasteries in Europe, experienced the monastic life of the Western Catholic tradition. Such exchange between Benedictine and Buddhist monks is continuing today.

"Grassroots" Level. This is no longer just a dialogue between specialists, but dialogue in day-to-day life. It is the "dialogue of life" which is the more important. In this area there is still a long way to go. The only venture showing any success is the annual Inter-Religious Youth Encounter in which young people of various religions meet to live, pray, and discuss together. The inspiration for this and its implementation are both due to the late Cardinal Pignedoli.

KOREA

In Korea the twelve million Buddhists belong to eighteen different sects. Contacts and reciprocal attitudes are good and the Buddhist monks are trusting and open. However, the majority of Koreans consider Buddhism to be inadequate as a religion in the modern world and incapable of meeting its challenges. Catholics do not seek out dialogue because four-fifths of them are converts and are more interested in deepening their knowledge of their faith than in engaging in dialogue with the former persecutors of Christianity.

CHINA

In continental China Buddhism is reorganizing. Collaboration with other religions takes place on the political level, under the guidance of the Party, and only between those patriotic religious associations approved by the Party.

TAIWAN

In Taiwan, as in China, Buddhism is one of the many traditional religions, and dialogue is consequently multilateral. There are two important institutions: the Association of Official Religions, created through the initiative of Cardinal Yupin, and the Institute of Spirituality of the Far East in Taipei under the patronage of the Federation of Asian Bishops (FABC).

CONTINENTAL LEVEL

On the continental level FABC has a Commission for Ecumenism and Dialogue with five members and a permanent Secretariat. In almost all Asian countries there is an Episcopal Commission for Dialogue, and in some cases this same Commission is responsible for ecumenism. In these Commissions the president is a bishop and the members are drawn from among clergy and specialists. The roles of these commissions vary: animation, study, meetings, proposals for inculturation, and so forth.

WESTERN COUNTRIES

In recent decades Buddhist presence in the West has become more consistent. Western countries where Buddhist influence is greatest are the United States, England, Germany, France, and Italy. Tibetan and Japanese Zen forms are the strongest. Adherents in the West are mostly middle-class youths. Many more adopt Eastern forms of meditation.

Dialogue with Western adherents is nonexistent or difficult. This is partly due to the anti-Christianity of many of them and their hybrid religious-cultural attitudes. Until now, Christianity has given little attention either to Buddhism or to the new religions and sects. We should be paying more attention to the values that people are seeking in these sects.

39

AUTHENTIC DIALOGUE TODAY

Reflections of Participants
at the SEDOS Conference

Participants at the SEDOS Research Seminar on Mission in March 1981 identified two forms of proclamation of the Good News:

The first is concerned with extending the visible communion of the Church, a "centripetal" purpose, leading people directly into the Church. The second is concerned with recognizing and furthering the values of the Kingdom, a "centrifugal" purpose, allowing the power of the Gospel to encounter and move humanity in its struggles and diversity. . . .
   This second model is achieving more prominence today and may be directing us to what will become the priority in future missionary proclamation. The first is concerned with conversion, the second with dialogue, inculturation and liberation.[1]

The following reflections summarize further aspects of dialogue which emerged at SEDOS conferences and seminars since then.

ASPECTS OF DIALOGUE TODAY

1) Dialogue presupposes a strong faith in God, a deep hope in the continuing action of the Holy Spirit in all men and women, and a fidelity to prayer. It is often exercised in a dynamic of "faith supporting faith."
   2) It is a fruitful "locus" of theology. The reflection of the church on situations of dialogue and the practice of dialogue is itself a valuable source of theology. Theology should not only underpin dialogue but should arise from it.
   3) A dialogical attitude is an absolute necessity for all engaged in mission today. There is a sense in which dialogue can be described as constitutive of mission, as an integral part of proclaiming the gospel. Nevertheless it is not an end in itself. The coming of God's Reign is the goal of dialogue.
   4) The love of Christ leaves us no option but to dialogue. Questions like

"How? With whom? Where?" call for practical approaches as a consequence of this love.

5) Unless one goes to meet the other in life situations, one may never become involved with him or her in dialogue. It is necessary to risk taking the first step in breaking what is often a vicious circle of misunderstanding.

6) Dialogue is multifaceted: there is interreligious dialogue with people of other faiths, as for example the great religions of Asia; dialogue with people of ancestral religions in Africa, Asia, and Latin America; dialogue with "post-Christians"; with non-believers; with followers of secular ideologies; and there is dialogue between the followers of the great Asian religions themselves which Christians can only observe and accompany sympathetically.

7) Recognition and acceptance of legitimate pluralism in interpreting the Christian message is essential for Christians entering into dialogue. So also is the self-understanding of other faiths—how they themselves understand their religious beliefs.

8) Discerning the values of God's Reign is of paramount importance in dialogue which often begins in a common search for these values in particular contexts. The pursuit of these values can bring about solidarity, understanding, confidence and trust, mutual enrichment, communion, and participation. These values transcend the confines of different religions; it could be said that the soul of dialogue is "disinterested" communion.

9) Dialogue has an ecclesial dimension for Christians. This implies communion with, support of, and encouragement by the appropriate church institutions. Members of Mission Societies have an analogous relationship with the appropriate authorities of their Societies to whom they look for understanding and encouragement.

10) The quality of dialogue within the church itself affects the wider dialogue. It is difficult to participate in dialogue and to emphasize the need for and values of dialogue, if within the institutional church itself there is lack of dialogue at appropriate levels and in appropriate situations.

11) In dialogue with ancestral religions, the church is called to be a real and significant protector of these religions and of the values of God's Reign found in them.

12) The experience of dialogue can be one of great joy, but when dialogue is rejected or made seemingly impossible by one party, the experience is closer to that of the "suffering servant." One must be able to absorb criticism and suffer pain in dialogue.

13) Christians in dialogue seek to find Jesus Christ already present in the other person, in other institutionalized religions, and even in ideologies or secular realities. This search, in honest and respectful dialogue, involves risks on both sides.

14) Any kind of dialogue is rooted in a "dialogue of life" which supports more formal exchanges and brings about a growing together in closer communion. This often effects a kind of conversion in both parties by a deeper submissiveness to the truth.

SOME CRITERIA FOR IDENTIFYING AUTHENTIC DIALOGUE

The following emerged as criteria for an authentic dialogue.

1) Dialogue cannot take place from a position of power. There is "power-lessness" that is empowering, the powerlessness manifested in the life of Jesus. Dialogue requires this powerlessness. It is not contrived. It does not seek to dominate or to pressurize.

2) Dialogue is not a technique or a process necessarily bringing about results. When there is an impasse it may continue only as a dialogue of life or a dialogue of prayer, but these are not alternative or further steps undertaken because dialogue at the level of mutual conversation has ceased.

3) Basic to dialogue is an understanding of oneself, of one's values, attitudes, and prejudices. Without this inner or intradialogue and centeredness, dialogue with others is extremely difficult. Growth in self-knowledge is not only a prerequisite but also a consequence of dialogue. It is part of the wider requirement needed in order to understand the other and to understand the situation in which dialogue is taking place.

4) Dialogue of life frequently involves sharing poverty and insecurity, and being involved in a search for justice and integral liberation. In many of the situations of dialogue "the option for the poor" is crucial. Such an option frequently brings its own rewards: a deeper awareness of the bonds of human-ness which unite all women and men, a deepening of one's own faith, and liberation from a ghetto mentality.

5) Without a certain simplicity of lifestyle dialogue is difficult, often meaningless.

QUESTIONS THAT EMERGED FOR FURTHER DISCUSSION

1) "God wanted all perfection to be found in him and all things to be reconciled through him and for him" (Col. 1:19–20). On the basis of this and similar texts the "fulfillment" theory has been developed: the Good News of the gospel is to subsume the values, fill the lacunae, and overcome the negative or evil dimensions of the culture it encounters. This theory is intolerably patronizing for many, not least many Hindus. It does not recognize that the Good News is necessarily conveyed through a cultural medium, a contextual situation. Is the church not always a searching church, always seeking to reform itself regardless of the culture in which it is incarnated, even Western culture? Does the "fulfillment" theory effectively block dialogue?

2) When one partner is clearly unwilling to remain open, dialogue cannot lead to mutual enrichment. How can dialogue continue in the face of such an impasse? By praying? Living in hope? Learning to ask the right questions? Hearing the answers and simply trying to understand the significance of the answers?

3) The difficulty of dialogue from a position of power raises questions for professional experts in mission. The exercise of a profession in mission even in a spirit of service can place one in a position of quasi-dominative power. What is the effect of this on dialogue?

4) Does the possibility of conversion militate against sincere dialogue? What are the criteria for sincere conversion?

5) Dialogue leads to an even more fundamental question: what is the nature of the Christian presence in the world today? How can we distinguish the essential from the nonessential elements in the church? The Christian was "the soul of the world" for some of the Fathers of the church. What relevance has this in the dialogical approach of today?

6) Is aptitude for interreligious dialogue a special charism which should be given consideration in formation programs and in assignments?

NOTE

1. *Mission in Dialogue* (Maryknoll: Orbis Books, 1982), 630ff.

40

THE WORLD COUNCIL OF CHURCHES' ECUMENICAL AFFIRMATION: MISSION AND EVANGELISM

Dr. Emilio Castro

(Address of Dr. Emilio Castro, Director of the Commission on World Mission and Evangelism of the World Council of Churches, to the SEDOS General Assembly, December 9, 1982, at Rome. This affirmation is the agreed statement on Mission and Evangelism by the Member Churches of the World Council of Churches.)

Why did the World Council of Churches need to have this Ecumenical Affirmation? First, it was an institutional need. The Roman Catholic church had its Synod of Bishops with a very good document on evangelization, *Evangelii Nuntiandi*. The Evangelical Conservatives, one particular branch inside the Protestant family, had its Lausanne Covenant. "Mission and Evangelism: An Ecumenical Affirmation" was an attempt to state where we, the World Council of Churches, stand and what our contribution is to the total conversation around mission and evangelism.

The second reason was less institutional, more dynamic. The World Council of Churches has a solid reputation for being a social-political animal. Anywhere in the world where there is a problem, be it in relation to racial issues, minority issues, justice issues, women's issues, you will find somehow, somewhere, a statement, a presence, of the World Council of Churches! The accusation developed that we had become a kind of religious or Christian version of the United Nations. If you eliminated the Christian element, what remained was not quite as efficient as the United Nations but covered the same territory. There was also the accusation that we had become "horizontal and secular." So the questions arose. Is all this activity undertaken in the name of Jesus Christ? Is all this involvement in the human rights struggle not simply a "Red Cross" exercise? Do we state clearly our basic Christian position? What undergirds the whole life of the Council? Why do churches come together to take such strong positions about certain regimes? What does this have to do with the proclamation of the Reign of God, or with personal faith in Jesus Christ? It fell to me to integrate the underlying convictions, to articulate them, and to show the Christian religious basis for social commitment.

GROWING DICHOTOMIES

EVANGELISM AND DEVELOPMENT

There has been a gradual and dangerous specialization of our Christian ministries in the world. Perhaps this was necessary for the sake of efficiency. However, the Western churches have evolved highly developed instruments, sometimes with the money and support of their respective governments, for sharing in world development and world relief. But we do not seem to know the relationship between our money sharing and our gospel sharing!

I would like to tell you about an interesting example that occurred in the late 1960s just after the civil war in the Sudan. Peace was negotiated to a great extent through the World Council of Churches. Reconstruction began and rural hospitals and schools and other institutions were being built. One day we were contacted by an official of the Islamic government. He asked, "What is going on in your sector of the country? You are not rebuilding your churches!" We answered, "Our money is money for development." He responded, "We are rebuilding all our mosques and sacred centers because we believe that strengthening the spiritual life of the people is the fundamental basis of all national development." It was a challenge to the spiritual dimension of our work and from a Muslim government official.

Later the Mekani-Jesus, a Lutheran church in Ethiopia, wrote an open letter to the Lutheran World Federation. A similar challenge appears:

> Brothers and Sisters, we are very thankful for your cooperation with us, but do not disturb our total ministry, do not oblige us to become an agency for the economic development of our people when we have the responsibility to look after the totality of the life of our nation. Give us a chance to be the Church of Jesus Christ that is trying to participate fully in the building of the nation but not reducing ourselves to being a branch of your development concern.

CHURCH GROWTH

Among other Protestant communions the dichotomy was also growing. Friends in the Fuller School of Mission in the United States developed a very interesting theology of church growth. They bring people inside the church first in a kind of first conversion, and then entrust them to those responsible for Christian education to make "real" Christians of them. It is a kind of double-movement theology. First you convert to God and then later to your neighbor. The strange thing is that you can be so happy with your conversion to God that you have no time to lose in concern for your neighbor. They preach that the gospel is free, but when you come forward to become a Christian there is an envelope for your offering on the following Sunday. This kind of approach trivializes the gospel in the name of church growth.

Rapid church growth which proceeds without challenging the human divisions based on caste-groups, racial groups, ethnic groups, or other social groups makes a mockery of the gospel in the name of proclaiming it. So there was not only an over-secularization on one side, but an over-spiritualization on the other. The need was felt to integrate theologically all these dimensions of the gospel of Jesus Christ. The Affirmation is an attempt to articulate this integration in a holistic way.

EVANGELISM

Finally, the document was necessary to enable us to speak unashamedly of evangelism, to give an instrument to the churches for instruction, inspiration, or correction. It was not to be defensive in tone. In the ecumenical movement among the churches of the Reform tradition there is a tendency to develop a critical attitude vis-à-vis the other churches. We know what the churches are doing wrong; the difficulty is to propose what could be done better. It is easier to criticize than to propose alternatives. And so a certain impatience was expressed:

> You are able to speak with Paolo Freire about new approaches in education, why can you not do the same with regard to the evangelistic and missionary outreach of the church? You go on criticizing the mass rallies of Billy Graham and the mechanics of converting without forcing yourself to consider how you fulfil the Great Commission, or how seriously you take the injunctions of the New Testament to carry the gospel to the whole world.

All of the elements we have just examined led to the attempt to develop this affirmation.

THE PROCESS

It was not an easy process. There were strong voices against the attempt. It took us at least three years, that is, three sessions of our commission (CWME) to convince people that the exercise was worthwhile. Why this resistance? First, there was mistrust of the Western conceptual style of doing theology. We might ask whether the West has even yet developed a nonconceptual way of doing theology. In an attempt to overcome this difficulty a proposal was made to make the report a "collage," a collection of stories of what is going on in evangelism, how mission is actually being carried out. Those experiences and stories would convey inspiration, conviction, and perhaps even some concrete suggestions, without trying to analyze and categorize them. We would simply share what was happening and let the stories speak for themselves.

Second, we thought that liturgical or poetic language could be used in a document to suggest or evoke more than what was actually said. A good example of that is the Report of the Bangkok Conference in 1973. Much of the report was written in poetry. But it is one thing to want to be poetic and another to have the inspiration and the capacity to be poetic, and then to steer the poetry, intact, through the mill of the Commission and its committees.

So the document which you have before you is not juridical, but it is more conceptual than was expected. It should not be handled as an ontological affirmation. It points to certain common convictions that can be affirmed conceptually and intellectually, but also with passion.

We cannot speak to the whole church, to the whole world, with one document. We know today that theology is made in a given context and in an interplay with that context. The gospel comes alive in discussion with African, Latin American, Asian, and other traditions. The mission of the church today is defined in relation to a specific context. Still we do not hesitate to speak together on matters, for example, of apartheid, that belong to a specific context, or on matters of peace, militarism, human rights, and so forth. It is important to see every local struggle in the perspective of the whole Reign, in the perspective of the global purpose of God, and to see the contribution of my church in Uruguay and your church in Italy as part of the total economy of God's Reign. The document does not replace my duty and privilege of theologizing in terms of my missionary commitment in my local situation, but it enables us to address global issues together. There is much to be said on the interplay between the local and the global. In my local commitment I can reflect on catholicity and be enriched, challenged, and provoked by the particular testimonies coming from local experiences.

Taking all these viewpoints into consideration, you can see that six years was not too long to produce this document. Admittedly it was not a full-time job, but there was full-time pressure during that period.

KEY ELEMENTS OF THE DOCUMENT

CHRISTOLOGICAL FOCUS

I will highlight three dimensions of "Mission and Evangelism." First, in the introduction there is a christological focus. The mission of God is the overall concept. The mission of God concentrates itself in the sending of God's Son to live, to die, to rise. In Jesus Christ we see clearly manifested our own struggle to overcome sin, misery, and death. We are familiar with the traditional scheme that in the cross of Jesus Christ sin is defeated and death is overcome. We know that he has brought the power of the Reign to bear against the Reign of Satan, and through his resurrection we have been given eternal life. That is well known and invoked in our funeral services, and in our pastoral ministry of forgiveness, reconciliation, consolation, and so on.

Political-Historical Dimension. In the last thirty years, we have seen the strong reaction that comes from the discovery, or rather, rediscovery of a political-historical dimension of the gospel. Jesus has been rightly reintroduced to us as the Liberator, the man who dies as a political criminal, "King of the Jews," the man who confronted the establishment, the status quo and the imperial powers of Pontius Pilate. Reading the gospel in a political perspective is a fascinating exercise. In the infancy narratives we rejoice in the celebration of the coming of the Son of God, but we forget that the soldiers sent by Herod into Bethlehem are there to remind us of the brutality of the world in which we live. Jesus Christ died for us, but we forget that before he died, many children died for him. That is the interplay between the historical and the incarnational. So he took the road to Egypt as a political refugee. This historical dimension has come as a cry, challenging us to recognize that we have tamed Christ. By concentrating on the individual, the personal problem of sin, and the overcoming of death, the final enemy, we have forgotten the actual historical struggle of Christ with historical sin and death manifested in the oppression of the poor and downtrodden of the earth.

There was the danger of having not only two different christologies but two different gospels. What we are trying to do in the christological focus in this Affirmation is to rediscover that these three enemies—sin, misery, and death—are together overcome by the sacrifice of Jesus Christ and by his resurrection. In Salvador people are confronting the reality of sin, misery, and death and bringing this confrontation to the worshiping table of the Lord, asking, "How long, O Lord?" That "How long?" is not a pious "How long will I be living until you will take me into your eternal kingdom?" It means, "When are you coming to overcome the factors of oppression in our historical situation?"

The Struggle To Overcome Poverty Is the Gospel. Sin is seen in the reality of social situations. Poverty is an indication of the oppression prevailing in society. Death is at work in both personal and social sin. The call to struggle comes from the depth of our faith. It is not a reductionism of the gospel. The three elements are clearly present in Jesus' ministry. So to struggle to overcome poverty is not just social gospel, is not just social ethics, is not just a consequence or fruit of the gospel. The struggle to overcome poverty is gospel. Without that struggle there is no gospel at all. The struggle to announce victory over death is gospel, and without that announcement there is no gospel. Otherwise, we are depriving people of the knowledge of a fundamental promise in Jesus Christ. The entry point of the announcement of the gospel could be any one of those three dimensions—sin, death, misery—but ultimately, through our denouncing of sin and announcing of forgiveness, we should be inviting people to accept the gift of eternal life through commitment to the struggle of the poor. By calling people to enter into the struggle of the poor we are calling them to realize that sin, both personal and collective, should be purified, and that we are assured that in that process, whether in life or in death, Jesus Christ is our friend. So, the circle is complete in this christological focus.

OPTION FOR THE POOR

The second dimension I would like to highlight today is the preferential option for the poor. This option is meant to include the totality of one's life. Justice to the poor is included in the knowledge of God's preference for them. When, in our struggle for justice, we forget to tell the Good News to the poor, we are robbing them of real justice. If God is for them, who am I to decide that what they need is a higher standard of life, but not the revolutionary knowledge that God is for them, that God is with them? So there is no Christian social justice that does not include the proclamation of the gospel invitation to personal faith. If we try to develop social service or to participate in national development while taking away this dimension of announcing the personal gospel of Jesus Christ, we are making the poor who are the victims of injustice even poorer still. We are robbing them of something that primarily belongs to them. There is no involvement with the poor in total social justice unless it includes the bringing of the gospel. At the same time, there is no such thing as the announcement of the gospel that doesn't include justice as due to the poor. Some people ask: where does this concentration on the gospel to the poor leave the rich and the middle class? It includes them insofar as they recognize that the invitation to join Jesus Christ is an invitation to be on the side of the poor, to struggle together with them, to overcome death and misery and sin. In fact, here we have a concept of justice that includes what traditionally was called proclamation, because the gospel we proclaim is God's preferential option for the poor.

THE UNREACHED REGIONS

A third key dimension in the Affirmation concerns the unreached regions and the people who have not had a chance to come to know about Jesus Christ. We develop plans to go to them, but a glance at the world indicates to us that those who are unreached are the poor of the earth, basically the masses of poor people in China, India, and the more remote regions of Africa. The poor of the earth are the unreached. If we understood our mission in terms of justice, we might see that in working together with the poor, we point like John the Baptist towards Jesus Christ.

Put in another way, the call to a personal conversion to Jesus Christ should not be cut off from the poor. They are called by God to a protagonist role. They have the right to say yes or no to God's invitation in Jesus Christ. Our paternalistic approach pretends to be a respectful approach; we just help the poor or give them something instead of speaking to them of Jesus Christ. This paternalism is depriving the poor of the right they have to say no to Jesus Christ. Who are we to say, a priori, that the gospel is good for us but dangerous for them?

Our document also makes clear the tension between the planting of the churches (the expansion or multiplication of the churches) and the priestly-servant role of the church in a given place. The motivation to plant churches does not mean the selfish salvation of a small group of people that will gather around word and sacrament, but rather the building of a living community, bringing before God in daily intercession its dreams and tragedies, its plights and hopes.

TWO CONSEQUENCES

THEOLOGY OF RELIGIONS

We must develop a clearer theology of religions. If Jesus is the hidden source of all life, then what role do other religions play in God's Reign? What is their interplay with the historical revelation in Jesus Christ? Maybe it will be difficult to advance the debate beyond the classical statements, but today we renew the question in the context of religious pluralism everywhere. The churches of India and Sri Lanka, for example, are realizing that they cannot expect everyone to become either Catholic or Protestant. So the question of "other religions" has to be put again. Is God in Christ defeated? Are there other ways of relating to this situation?

THE LIFE OF THE WORLD

Finally, our ecumenical affirmation should remind us of the missionary urgency of proclaiming Jesus, the Life of the World, for we are the first generation of humankind that can create life in a laboratory, manipulate and change it. The theoretical possibility that you can order a child to your own specifications will soon be a practical possibility. This is also the first generation that has the privilege of being able to create a world culture. It is urgent to ensure that in the shaping of this world culture the values and vision of the gospel will not be absent.

41

A CATHOLIC RESPONSE

Bishop Basil Meeking

This is not a Catholic evaluation nor an analytic critique of the document "Mission and Evangelism: An Ecumenical Affirmation," but a few personal reactions by a Catholic who has followed the development of the document in the Commission on World Mission and Evangelism (CWME). It is an attempt to assess the usefulness of the document in the current discussion on mission and in promoting ecumenical awareness.

1. Common discussion. Today it is possible to speak of a common discussion or debate on mission. This is made possible and stimulated by, for example:

a) common mission studies. There are common sources, as one can see by looking at the bibliographies in the *International Review of Mission. Evangelii Nuntiandi*, the Evangelicals' Lausanne Covenant, and the many World Council of Churches studies are more and more becoming common property. People from all confessional backgrounds are members of missiological societies. There is the growing Catholic presence in places such as the Selly Oak Colleges in Birmingham, England.

b) the Catholic presence within the Commission on World Mission and Evangelism. Four mission-sending Catholic institutes have consultative status in the commission and there is a considerable Catholic impact. This was evident in the preparation for the Melbourne World Missionary Conference and in the work of the task force.

c) the consultation on mission organized as a Catholic contribution to the sixth Assembly of the World Council of Churches, Melbourne.

d) the new "tradition" of Christians from different confessions, including the Catholic church, giving witness together in all sorts of situations (see the Joint Working Group study, "Common Witness," n. 14).

2. The possible role of the document. Like the CWME itself, it provides a context, a framework, a forum for a continuing discussion. The document is in a sense itself the field of dialogue, attempting as it does to hold together diverse elements and positions. It does this with a certain success. It is in light of this that its positive statements ought to be assessed.

It is not to be judged in comparison with *Evangelii Nuntiandi*. This would hardly be fair. There is a difference of source and authority. There is the different nature of the CWME constituency which is necessarily less specific and less magisterial. Rather, it is itself a witness to the growing together of a broad spectrum of Christians.

3. The ecclesiological thrust of the document is already indicated by this quote: "Christian mission is the action of the Body of Christ in the history of humankind." This awakens Catholic interest at the same time as it helps dispel the stereotype of the Protestant discourse on mission as the simplistic preaching of an individual relationship with Christ. Instead the document can refer to the church's "mission of mediation" and for Catholics, Orthodox, and others puts the discussion on a new level. Still, the ecclesiology is only indicated. It must be developed in future discussion. It should be noted that the publication of this document coincides with the publication of the Faith and Order Report on Baptism, Eucharist and Ministry in which Catholic theologians have been involved. Here one sees a common vision of the church beginning to emerge. The two studies must interact and support each other.

4. The theme of mission and social action which is also an actual one for the Catholic church is a question which runs throughout the document. It is part of the more fundamental question, "What is mission?" to which elements of a reply are given in the section of the document entitled "Proclamation and Witness." There it is recognized that the church's life of worship and prayer, its advocacy of the poor, its stand for human rights, its lifestyle and the way it acts, are all part of the proclamation. Simplistic solutions are ruled out and the dimensions of the problem indicated when the document says, "A proclamation which does not hold forth the promises of the justice of the Reign of God to the poor of the earth is a caricature of the Gospel; but Christian participation in the struggle for justice which does not point towards the promises of the Reign also makes a caricature of a Christian understanding of justice."

5. Conversion. A sentence in the first chapter of the document, "The call to conversion should begin with the repentance of those who do the calling," relates to a similar call in the Second Vatican Council's *Decree on Ecumenism*:

> Christ summons the Church as it goes on its pilgrim way to that continual reformation of which it always has need insofar as it is an institution of people here on earth. (6)

The last decade has been marked by just such repentance, both of the short-comings in mission, and of the separations which had hardened among Christians. This document speaks for Catholics as well as other Christians when, in a tone of realistic, humble confidence, it calls for a repentance that does not look like loss of nerve but is an openness to truth and therefore to a conversion of heart, understanding, and mentality.

The churches are responsible for a truth that is greater than themselves—God. But it is a truth that has first to be shown forth in themselves, as has the unity, both present and to be accomplished, which is the transcendent destiny of the human family. This demands real and costly conversion to overcome the resistance in our hearts to the gospel demands for reconciliation, justice, and peace. Our ecumenical solidarity in mission perhaps begins here as we have to face the demands of faith and of unity that come to us even as we respond to the call to mission. Mission and unity combine as the powerful impetus to our common conversion to the gospel, a conversion much greater than we can at this moment envisage.

6. Witness among people of living faith. I have tried to suggest that the document not be regarded as a complete and final statement; it can be an invitation to common effort just where it is needed most. The chapter on relations with other faiths is such a one. It is rather cautious and only begins to broach the issue. Perhaps in the Roman Catholic church we are pressed more strongly by our teachers and theologians from Africa and Asia and the Pacific? In any case, relations with other faiths is a prime question in any Roman Catholic discussion on mission. The church is called to announce the Good News of God for every human being in the world. Already the Good News, manifested and accomplished as the gospel of Jesus Christ for the life of the world, is like a ferment present in the world religions, working in human hearts and calling them to the search for truth and life.

The paschal mystery climaxing in Pentecost is the gift of the Spirit spread abroad upon all flesh so that the visible history of salvation is the powerful sign and pledge of a broader history which the Word and the Spirit of God are writing with the whole of humankind, even beyond the visible frontiers of the church. For the church of Jesus Christ, as the body of those who are saved, extends beyond the visible church which is the sign and indispensable means in witnessing to the accomplishment of salvation. Thus it becomes even more urgent to announce the gospel to all peoples for the fullness of life they seek and to enable the process of conversion to the justice of God. We need to find ways of continuing this discussion together.

7. The church and its unity in God's mission. The third chapter, which has this title, rests on the common understanding that mission is not simply one activity of the church but that the church is itself a function of the mission of God in the world. By the gift of the Spirit which it receives, the church is established as first witness of the gospel and Reign of God with its mission to sow everywhere the seeds of the risen life of Christ and to be his instrument for healing the wounded flesh of humanity. Itself founded in unity, it is called to grow in unity in order to be the prophetic sign of the unity and reconciliation of humankind. The discussion at Melbourne took up something of this in a most promising way and it is reflected in the document. Yet it is only a beginning.

Perhaps it is time in the Roman Catholic discussion with the Commission on World Mission and Evangelism to take up again the opening words of one of the early studies of the Joint Working Group, "Unity in witness and witness in unity," to develop our understanding that the passion for unity is a fundamental service of mission. A point of entry to this discussion is suggested when this chapter speaks of the eucharist as the place for the renewal of the missionary conviction at the heart of every congregation. The emphasis on the eucharist as bread for a missionary people was one of the insights of Melbourne which awakens an immediate response among Roman Catholics, rooted as it is in Catholic spirituality and touching the heart of our understanding of the church.

PART THREE

PEOPLE IN MISSION

42

A Question of Identity

Donald Nicholl

When I am invited somewhere to speak I refer the question to the Holy Spirit.

About a year ago I was invited to go to Lomé in Togo to take part in a conference there on The Role of the Laity. I referred this request to the Holy Spirit and did not get any answer at all! So I decided I would not go to Lomé. I felt, at the same time, I had to understand why I was not being encouraged to go there by the Holy Spirit. I think that when I got the invitation I was immediately very unhappy about the title of the conference—The Role of the Laity.

Metaphors are very revealing about the way our minds work, and it seemed to me that this title was a sort of ecclesiastical jargon. The word "role" is used of plays. You are cast in a role and are expected to say the words that the playwright and the producer have fixed for you. So it seemed to me that going to Lomé to hear what the ecclesiastics would say about my role as a member of what is called "the laity" was not something I particularly wanted to do.

Apart from anything else I find the expression "the laity" a curious one. It reminds me of the time people would talk about "the unemployed" as though they were a kind of tribe on Mars. There is no such body as "the laity" of which one could be an organic member. The opposition of clerics and lay people reminds me of the foolish Bull *Clericis* of Pope Boniface VIII in 1300, which began by saying that the whole of history taught that lay people had always been opposed to clerics. That seems to me to be a historically unfounded statement, a half truth.

Lay/Cleric Dichotomy

More important, perhaps, is the fact that as soon as you begin to use the dichotomy "lay and cleric" you introduce a dualism into your thought which means you can never bring them together again. Once you get "lay" on one side and "cleric" on the other, it's a bit like Humpty Dumpty—all the King's horses and all the King's men couldn't get Humpty together again.

Soon after I received the request to go to Lomé there was a meeting on the role of the laity in preparation for the Synod on the Laity. I was there for about an hour towards the end of the meeting. What so saddened me was that my expectations arising from the title were realized. Commissions were starting their report just as we arrived. I heard constant complaints by the lay people about the clergy, which is such a boring and useless kind of activity. I also heard the report of the Commission on the Spirituality of the Laity, and was much comforted by the remark of Bonino who was present at the meeting. As far as Latin America was concerned, he thought that to talk of spirituality of the laity was a really strange and a funny thing to do. He compared it to talking about the spirituality of the goal-keeper as opposed to the spirituality of the center-back on a football team! And I agree with him. It is not just church people who make these kinds of misleading dichotomies. You notice that political philosophers like Locke, Rousseau, Hobbs, and all those people with their various forms of social contract, talk about the individual on one side and society on the other and they can never get them together again. They never really manage it because they have made it impossible for themselves from the beginning.

CHURCH/WORLD DICHOTOMY

We do the same sort of thing when we talk about the church and the world as though they were completely separate. In fact the whole discussion, as far as I have followed it, makes me grateful for the discipline that I received in my younger days when I studied St. Thomas and used to read the writings of Etienne Gilson. One of the things that always impressed me so much about Gilson was that when he came to a question such as we are addressing today, he would write an article of maybe ninety-five pages, and bring into it this consideration and that consideration, this and that quotation, this and that example. You would read page after page and ask yourself, when is Gilson going to get to the point? What was happening was that he was steadily working through numerous options and cutting out various possibilities until eventually, by the time you got to page 90, he had posed the question so precisely that the answer emerged in about three or four pages, almost by magic. All the work had been done really in posing the question exactly.

It seems to me that what people are getting at, if they are not misled by using this ecclesiastical jargon "lay/cleric," "church/world," is that our task today is ministry which the church is called upon to exercise towards the whole of creation, particularly of course towards suffering beings. Eventually we shall all have collaborated in that condition to which St. Peter in the Acts of the Apostles refers, "the restoration of all things," where all beings will be illuminated at the end of time and there will be no more suffering.

I think that once one puts it that way, one's horizon becomes completely different and horizon is crucial in this. In a way, what determines one's attitude toward most issues is one's horizon. If one's horizon is simply one's family, or the church, then this is rather narcissistic. Horizon has to be the whole of creation—what our Buddhist friends call "all sentient beings."

A WAY OF MYSTICISM FOR ALL

Throughout the world there is a whole way of mysticism not only in the Christian churches, but also in other faiths. For example, take our Jewish brothers and sisters. Whereas mysticism was regarded by them almost as a swear word even thirty years ago, nowadays young Jews are not discouraged by any means from studying their mystical treatises. The same is true to a lesser extent in Islam, and it is also true of Hindus. Amongst the Native Americans the elders who know their mystical teachings are now saying they are so afraid for the human race that their teachings, once confined to the small body of elders, must now be made available to everyone because the earth requires a mystical teaching for all members of the human family.

It is very striking that perhaps the most successful series of books being published at this moment in England by Darton, Longman and Todd is a series which contains selections from the great mystical teachers such as Lady Julian of Norwich, St. Francis de Sales, the Methodist John Wesley, and the Anglican William Law. It is interesting also that there is no distinction of different denominations, because this is a genuine ecumenical way. We find the same in the school of prayer which George Bibway, a Coptic priest, and I have initiated at Selly Oak Colleges. It is easily the most successful course we have given there. At the end of each meeting, without any difficulty, we meditate for half an hour in silence. In the same way, for example, the Religious Experience Research Unit at Oxford has discovered that for many so-called ordinary people (I have never met an ordinary person!), like butchers and fire fighters and tailors, mystical experience is much more common than was thought in the past. People who have had these experiences are always reluctant to speak about them because they fear that others will think they are a bit odd. And again, at Oxford, we do not know to what Christian traditions the different people belong.

So there is this tremendous search for interesting mystical things throughout the world. In order to illustrate this, let me tell you of an incident that occurred to a very good friend of mine. He came from a very devout Presbyterian family from the north of Scotland, one of those for whom the things of God were constantly in their hearts. He became a Catholic. About a year later when he was in practice in Nottingham he went to his parish priest and said, "Father, I have been a Catholic now for a year and feel at home, but I do feel that I need some help in deepening my spiritual life." To which he got the reply: "Now don't you start worrying your head about that kind of thing, laddie! What you need to do for us is to get yourself onto the local Council and make sure we get a Catholic school!" He was much older than I was and he told me of this incident many years later when he and I had become friends. I listened to this and I thought about it, and one day I took him a copy of the fourteenth-century mystical treatise *The Cloud of Unknowing*. He never looked back after that. For the last ten years or so of his life he was constantly reading *The Cloud of Unknowing* and he would tell me something he had found. So the last ten years of his life were enriched by this mystical teaching from the fourteenth century.

Nevertheless, old habits do persist and give the impression that this teaching is not for everyone. If you look at the 1984 Bulletin from the Secretariat for Non-Christians which was celebrating twenty years of its existence, you will find in many of the documents, and especially in the Pope's speeches, a pattern of how dialogue should proceed. There are the ordinary encounters between theologians, and then, as the Pope says, at a deeper level there is a meeting between the monks of other faiths and the contemplatives within the Christian community. I find it very strange that this "deeper level" should be confined to monks! In a sense, this specialization, this role, so to speak, for this special group of people is actually a danger to them also. Many of the people who are engaged in this East-West encounter are friends of mine and I sometimes ask them, "Is your identity first of all to be a monk and then a Christian, because it seems to me sometimes that you behave as if being a monk is more important than being a Christian."

In fact it is not I who am saying this. It is the scriptures which say that the deep things of God are meant for all. In the second Letter of St. Peter he speaks about the promises God has made to each of us—we are called to be sharers in the divine nature. Friends hold everything in common. Sometimes when I am giving a retreat or a conference I quote this phrase and I ask people, "After you have become sharers in the divine nature, what do you want next? Do you want a biretta? Do you want a good career? Do you want to do a more advanced spirituality course—with the Carmelites? What is there beyond sharing in the divine nature?" And this sharing is for all. I don't really see how anyone can speak of the deep things of God not being for all people. We are told in the first Letter to the Corinthians that the Spirit investigates, researches, penetrates into all things, even the deep things of God. We are tempted to believe that we know more than the Spirit. Notice that in the next verse it says the Spirit alone is able to search into the depths of God.

Here I am reminded of an incident in the life of the great Russian saint, Seraphin of Sarov. He was a great counselor and one day he was busy seeing people for many hours. The local priest who was sitting in the corner said to Seraphin after all the people had gone away, "Father Seraphin, the human heart is open to you. You know what is in the hearts of all these people who come here." Seraphin said to him, "The human heart is open to God alone. When people come to me I instantly refer them to the Holy Spirit and if I do so, and the Holy Spirit tells me what words to use to them, then those are the words that they need. If I do that, I get it right. If I start trusting in my thinking, my own reasoning, I always get it wrong."

THE HOLY SPIRIT

That story of St. Seraphin ought to be a warning to us not simply to invoke the Holy Spirit as a kind of trick for injecting enthusiasm into our own desires, especially in our missions. Here I think it is very sad to read the story of what happened at Edinburgh at the great Protestant missionary meeting in 1910, and more recently what happened at Nottingham in 1964. Take Nottingham first. The Protestants, Anglicans, and Free Church people at Nottingham made a kind of contract—they would be united by 1980 or 1984. When I heard that declaration, I thought, "My goodness, who are they that they think they can preempt the work of the Holy Spirit?" None of us can tell the Holy Spirit what has got to happen. Unity is, of course, the work of the Holy Spirit.

The 1910 Edinburgh meeting was such an historic occasion, but it makes me wonder. The Assembly there sent forth a cry that they were going to "win the world for Christ in one generation!" Now I understand the enthusiasm but at the same time, isn't it terrible arrogance to talk about "winning the world for Christ" and "in one generation," as if one could direct the Holy Spirit oneself? Recently I have been reading a good deal of the literature from that period. Some of the things said about other cultures and other religions are absolutely breathtaking. The arrogance with which they spoke about others! Maybe we do the same in our own way, but it is salutary to notice it.

I think at that time they had a special hope that China was going to become Christian in one generation. On the whole the missions were going well in China, at least considering the numbers who were coming into the Christian church. But we all know what happened in the revolution of 1949 when the Christian missionaries were driven out. Although at the time I was very distressed, as were other Catholics, at what was happening to the missionaries, nevertheless, I began soon afterwards to ask myself whether we shouldn't interpret those events in the light of what is said in the Acts of the Apostles, "They were prevented by the Holy Spirit from preaching the Word in Asia."

I began to think of the position of the church before and after 1949 in China. I thought to myself that before 1949 the church was free to preach the gospel but the ordinary people were hungry, they had virtually no health services, they were subject to local warlords, they were illiterate. The ordinary Chinese people were in a terrible situation. After 1949 things changed and became better than before. And I wondered whether, in the long run, those events might not have been good also for the church. Suppose the church had triumphed—and it was a triumphalist church—what kind of Christianity would we have had in China? Would it have been a very perverse form? Perhaps also it might have infected the rest of the church. It might have become a model of what the church was not supposed to be.

It began to seem to me that it was perhaps comparable to what happened to Paul when he was prevented from going to Asia; he was called to Macedonia, after which he began the evangelization of Europe. I ask myself also whether maybe the work of the missionaries in Latin America which resulted from the fact that they could not work in China was not comparable to the evangelization of Europe by Paul. In other words, the Holy Spirit blocked one way and that meant that people had to search for another way.

UNITY IN THE CHURCH

I am trying here to raise this question of what it means when the Holy Spirit prevents us from doing something. The Holy Spirit does not direct us, because that would turn us into puppets. The Spirit prevents or blocks us from doing certain things and that gives us the scope to find, in freedom, what way we are supposed to go. As a result of my work in Tantur I became especially interested in the work of ARCIC, the Ecumenical Commission of Anglicans and Roman Catholics, and the other Commissions—Catholics and Lutherans, Lutherans and Methodists, and so on. They produced various statements about agreements between the churches and theologians coming together. It does seem, however, that the work of theologians is not going to lead to any direct movement towards reunion. Generally speaking, one feels it has been a failure. I think there is a different way of interpreting these efforts. It is formulated by Therese Vanier, who has worked for many years among the mentally handicapped. She said not long ago, "I do not believe that the different churches will ever drink from the same chalice until all of them learn to drink from the chalice of the suffering of the poor and oppressed."

What is happening through the blockage and frustration of ARCIC is that we are being told, "No! If you were to unite at this level it would be a superficial union for middle-class intellectual people. If there is to be a real full union in the church, you have to go deeper and deeper and we are pointing you in a different direction."

THE LESSON OF FAILURE

Many of you will have read Vincent Donovan's *Christianity Rediscovered: A Letter from the Masai.* You may remember that for Donovan the most important moment in his life as a missionary was when the group of Masai whom he had been instructing for a year said to him, "Father, we are grateful for your having come here, but we do not believe in your Jesus. Thank you and now we will go away." Donovan said it was the most isolated moment of his life, and also the most important moment. He learned more from that than from anything else. So he owes a great deal to those Masai—a blockage led to some kind of revelation.

As I was thinking of Donovan a week or two ago, I recalled what I heard from an engineer on the radio. Speaking of engineers he said, "We learn more from one failure than from a thousand successes." We theologians should try to do the same. We, all of us, are reluctant to learn this lesson. The reason, I think, is that every failure represents a threat to the identity which we have set up for ourselves in our own minds. That is why we are often afraid of what is coming in the future, because we are losing some part of our identity which we have established for ourselves.

We come then to the question which I wish to pose to you. It is this: can we, through the blockages we are experiencing, discern those deep things of God towards which the Holy Spirit is drawing our attention? Here is my own attempt at an answer. I hear from all ranks of the faithful about "the crisis of identity." Only a few weeks ago the Pope himself used this phrase, when he said that the laity were experiencing a crisis of identity since the Second Vatican Council. The same is happening to missionaries who have this experience as a result of their encounter with other faiths. If people are capable of achieving salvation through their own faiths, what is specific about being a missionary? Priests are also having a crisis of identity. Many of their traditional tasks are taken over by lay people and so they ask, "What is left for us? What is it that constitutes our specific identity?"

A QUESTION OF IDENTITY

I first began to experience how crucial this issue is about six years ago at Strawberry Hill College when I was giving a three-day conference to university chaplains. What seemed to be troubling them was: "How can we define anything as specifically Catholic? We seem to have lost all the things that differentiate us from Protestants, from others. We don't have the Mass in Latin. We don't have abstinence on Fridays. We don't go to confession so often now. We don't seem to believe in the infallibility of the Pope. Birth control and contraceptives are not 'out.' What is left that is specifically Catholic? What identity do we have left?" My answer to them was: "First, if what you are looking for is an identity based on inflexible difference from others, then perhaps you should better go and imitate Ian Paisley and Ayatollah Khomeini!" They have that kind of identity more surely than anyone I can think of. In this respect, at least, they are like the worst of the Pharisees who kept on congratulating themselves that they were not as other people.

That reminds me of an incident in the life of Thomas Merton which is so illuminating. You may remember that Merton as a young man wrote *The Seven Storey Mountain* which is a kind of hymn of praise to himself for not being as other people. Then one day he goes into Louisville and sees all the people around and he realizes they are good and beautiful, and he is glad now that he is as other people. Does it not strike you that in many respects during the last days of his life Jesus seems to have had his identity called in question by the events of those days? In Buddhist terms we would say that during those days Jesus passed through the great doubt in order to set the seal on his final identity.

Why do we instinctively seek to establish our identity through marking our difference from others? There are probably two main reasons for this: first of all, as humans we have inherited a tribal or national way of establishing our identity. The tribe occupied a particular territory. You were who you were through not being the other people, through being different from the other people, and often, of course, at enmity with them. That way of defining oneself leads inevitably to tribal or national warfare. Here I would call your attention to a recently published book by Wilkinson, an Anglican priest, in which he shows that the present weakness of the Christian church in Britain, and its progressive weakening over the last seventy years, can be traced almost entirely to the failure of the church to get beyond this tribal identity. The church's attitude, when it came to the First World War, was a kind of sanctification of this tribal identity. I would suggest to you that we are more or less wasting our time on evangelism as long as we are not working against this form of identity which is renewed in tribal warfare.

The second cause of our establishing our identity through difference from others is through scarcity. We believe we can only be distinguished from others if we have more than others in some way, or have some form of distinction which others do not share. In the days when I used to teach Celtic history, for example, I would tell the students about the wonderful Welsh legend which reveals that every person is a secret prince or princess. It was interesting to see the reaction of students. Some rather grumpy ones would say, "If everybody is a prince or princess, no one is." The more generous-minded students were delighted to discover that at the end of the day it would be revealed that everyone is a prince or princess. As tribal definition in an historical way leads to tribal warfare, so the definition of one's identity by scarcity inevitably leads to class warfare. And so I would again ask the question whether we are not wasting our time on evangelism so long as we do not work against the scarcity in the world which leads to this hostile form of defining oneself.

OUR TRUE IDENTITY

What I want to say now is what I believe to be the true identity for all. There is ultimately only one identity. It is to be seen through the text in Galatians where Paul says, "God forbid that I should boast in anything but the cross of Our Lord Jesus Christ." And that, I think, is the true identity. It is an identity which transcends all other claimed forms of identity because those other forms of identity belong to a different order. So long as those other forms are kept at a certain level, say, like being an Englishman, or a Maryknoller, or whatever, so long as they are kept in proportion and are not claimed to be identity in the strict sense of the word, but simply stages on the way to identity, then they are all right. If they take over and we think of them as our true identity then they become idolatrous.

How crucial this is was illustrated lately in an article by the Irish theologian Enda McDonagh, who put the question whether we ought not to stop baptizing in certain parts of the world, as for example in Northern Ireland, because existentially we do not baptize into the body of Christ. We baptize into a tribe or a sect, and if that is treated as a final identity it is a form of idolatry.

In determining our identity there are two questions we need to ask ourselves. The first is a personal one. I think that, in trying to determine whether we have a true identity or not, all of us ought to ask ourselves, "In what do I glory? Do I glory in anything other than the cross of Christ Jesus our Lord?" The second is, "Do I think of myself as God's favorite against others?" Most nations seem to do this and are therefore idolatrous. Is it not true that our Lord revealed this was not his way, because he says that God treats everyone the same and God's rain falls on the just and the unjust?

Finally, I would like you to consider this text from Paul's second Letter to the Corinthians: "When they measure themselves with one another they are without understanding." In other words, to establish one's identity, or boast of it, by comparing oneself with other people is to be without understanding.

And the last word I will give to you is a word from the great patriarch Athenagoras who said, "I renounce the category of comparison." To which I myself add—"Comparison is death to the spiritual life."

43

THE STORY OF DEIRDRE AND DERMOT

Deirdre and Dermot McLoughlin

Dermot. Deirdre and I met in the hospital in Dublin where we were both in training—she as a physiotherapist and myself as a doctor. We became engaged a year after meeting. After qualifying we went to Nigeria with the Medical Missionaries of Mary and the St. Patrick's Society in the then Diocese of Ogoja. We planned that I should go out for six months to see if we could work there together. If we thought we could, Deirdre would then follow.

Deirdre. We were married in the small convent chapel in the leper village where we had gone to work. We first came in contact with primary health care in Nigeria through my work as a physiotherapist. There were many leper villages and many children at school in these villages. Deformities were widespread. As I could not be everywhere I brought one or two children from each village to the central village. I held classes for them there for three weeks, during which time they could also attend school. They learned about the care of hands and feet, what exercises to do, how to warn other children about not walking on sharp objects, hot coals, and so forth, and encouraging them to wear sandals. As sensation was often dead in their feet the leper children compounded their illness by not taking these precautions. Then I called to supervise them when they had returned to the villages. Dermot was also involved with "leper attendants"—people who had six months' training and were in charge of leper villages, dispensing medication, and so on.

Our first son John almost died during this time. I remember traveling with him between Abakaliki and Anawa. He was a baby of twelve months and had malaria. Halfway to Anawa he seemed to have stopped breathing. We stood with him on the side of the road and cried. It was an isolated place. He began breathing again and we carried on to Anawa. He was still a very sick baby and eventually we had to take him to Dublin.

We did not go back to Nigeria. We wanted to, but because of John's health we were advised not to. We went instead to Glasgow in Scotland where Dermot specialized in radiology. Financially we were poor. Dermot earned less than $2,000 a year from which he had to buy books, travel to London for his examinations, and get affordable accommodation there.

We were lucky to get a ground floor apartment in a tenement in Glasgow. We knew we would only be there for a couple of years, but the woman who lived across the hall from us with her husband and seven children continued to live there for many years after we had left, although it was a condemned tenement. She taught me something about life. We went to Ireland for Christmas one year. It was freezing on our return. There was no central heating in the apartment and I dreaded returning there. The morning we arrived back was foggy and cold, and we were miserable when we got to the house. There was a light on, a fire burning, the place was warm, the table was set, and breakfast was half prepared. With all their problems our neighbors had stayed up for a good part of the night to make sure things would be comfortable for us when we got back.

When Dermot finished his radiology he was told by the head of his Department in the Royal Infirmary in Glasgow, "You will have to leave Scotland; we have our full complement of staff; there are no prospects here." It was then that we decided to go to Canada.

Dermot. We were there only a couple of years when I got a very good medical appointment with four other radiologists in a small city. I was soon able to set up a very successful medical group. It was a far step from the condemned tenement in Glasgow. Soon we were, in North American terms, "leading the good life." We were members of the country club and patrons of the arts in the city. Deirdre was a member of the guild for the local theater. I was chairperson of the Catholic High School Board and a member of the Knights of Columbus. Deirdre was president of the Catholic Women's League. We had a very beautiful home and, as Deirdre used to say, half of our religion was filling this home with antiques. We "had it made," were living in "the fast lane," working hard, playing hard, having a good life. We were good, decent, rich people. And had five healthy sons. But I did not find that I had achieved happiness. When we stopped to think, which wasn't often, we thought that perhaps we had been happier in the Glasgow tenement where we had more time together ourselves.

Our beautiful house had over an acre of land overlooking a lake. There was a window trimmed with stained glass on the stairs. Sometimes at night I would go there to pray. I thanked God for the beauty of the place we were in. If I prayed for a considerable time, feelings of guilt came to me. I kept getting the same message: "I showed you the slums of Glasgow and rural conditions in Nigeria. What are you doing with your life here?" I would feel uncomfortable and raise this with Deirdre.

Deirdre. But I did not agree at all! I thought we had done our bit. I was enjoying life. I was involved with the community, doing good things, and so I am afraid I left Dermot to his guilt feelings!

Dermot. About that time Deirdre's teenage sister Maureen, who was very attached to her, came to visit. She had a fatal blood disorder and was with us for the last months of her life. Deirdre took her body back to Ireland for the funeral. While she was away I did something which was not really fair, considering how upset she was at that time. There was an Institute where about seventy-five lay members lived in a very simple fashion. About fourteen priests had joined them. They organized interests in the summertime for families who would live on the grounds of the Institute in simple log cabins. Most days there were conferences with one of the priests. I reserved places there for our family for a date about six weeks after Deirdre's return.

Deirdre. I was not at all happy about this! I felt he should have asked me. I was going through a very bad period, feeling very empty. I had to work through Maureen's death. The idea of going with the family to a family retreat week was the last thing in the world I wanted. That week was one of the most difficult weeks of my life.

Dermot. On the other hand, I felt that this was just what we needed; but obviously there was a lot of friction between us. The group of families with us was middle class. Babysitters took care of the children and we spent most of the day with the priest who helped us examine our material lifestyle. This had never happened before. I thought of our local parish where we were honored by the priest for helping him. We were taken out to dinner and entertained profusely. Now it was quite the reverse. We were being challenged on how we were living. Even though this is what we had come together to consider, it was interesting that when we were in fact challenged, we defended our lifestyle. It developed into a debate between the ten families and the priest. Ten against one! So we left feeling we had won the debate. Six months later, however, we were all obviously troubled and . . .

Deirdre. . . . I was the one who suggested we go back again! I had been thinking things over and recognized how empty my life was. I felt that Dermot was right — it had to change. I suggested that we talk again to Bob Wilde, the priest with whom we dealt at the Institute. I thought he would give us some blueprint to follow. The first thing he said was, "Are you praying?" "Well, I go to Mass on Sunday," I said. But he asked again, "Are you really praying?" And I thought: probably not. When I was a child I used to chat constantly with God. But that seemed to have gone, and apart from routine things like Sunday Mass or church devotions I really hadn't been praying or giving time to prayer. "Well," he said, "become a little less active and spend some time just sitting in the presence of Jesus."

I started and liked it and became very inactive. I gave up most of my activities and spent most of my spare time praying. Dermot pointed out that he felt this was not really the way things were supposed to be. We might have been on a treadmill before, but spending all my spare time praying was not the solution either. I began to realize that contemplation without action was just as wrong for me as action without contemplation. Both of us had come to realize that we needed to change our lives, and so we set out on a search.

CHANGING OUR LIFESTYLE

Dermot. Just about that time I was asked to give a talk on World Leprosy Day. My audience was made up of seventy-five young people, fifteen from the city where we lived, the remainder from other towns. I gave my usual talk and was winding up with the observation that people of North America should share with peoples of the other half of the world to help especially the 15 million people suffering from leprosy, only one-third of whom were getting medical treatment. We should be generous, gift-giving, and so forth. I looked into the audience. There were two teenagers who knew me and our lifestyle. They said nothing, but I could see in their eyes, "You are a total hypocrite!" Their challenge was the challenge of the priest on the retreat. I still remember the look in their eyes. When I got home I realized I could never again talk publicly about leprosy.

We discussed our search with many lay people, sisters, and priests. I vividly remember talking with one of Cesar Chavez's workers, from the migrant workers' organizations in California. The boycott on buying grapes and lettuce from California was in force. She spoke about nonviolence. I had a great idea and told her what I intended to do. At the supermarket I would fill my handcart with groceries, put some of the Californian grapes and lettuce on top, ask at the check-out if these came from California. I would then leave the handcart there, declaring that I would buy nothing from that store.

"But," she said, "that is being violent! Some worker in the store now has to go to the trouble of putting everything from that cart back on the racks." "I thought that was nonviolent action," I expostulated, and asked her what she saw as nonviolent action. In California she said she had stood outside supermarkets handing out leaflets and asking people not to buy Californian grapes. A woman came up to her and spat in her face. She said, "Thank you." Again the next day the same woman came by. She handed her the little leaflet again and asked her again politely not to buy the grapes. Again the woman spat in her face and went into the store. Three or four days later the same meeting took place—except that this time the woman looked into her face and burst into tears. "That is nonviolent," she said.

In our search we met two young nurses who had started a house of prayer. We met a number of young men and women who worked half the year for a salary and worked as volunteers for the other half. We met many interesting people—one of them being Jean Vanier. He said he thought our role was to walk between the two worlds of the rich and the poor and be fully a part of neither. This in fact has become true in our lives. The poor we work with regard us as rich, which we are, and our well-to-do friends now regard us as eccentric and uncomfortable to be with. Our way of life challenges them. We have lost a lot of our close friends. We seldom get any invitations, even from those with whom we work, and they almost always decline invitations to our home.

That year we received an invitation from the Provincial Superior of the Holy Spirit Congregation to their Pentecost celebration. The Superior recalled that I had some missionary experience. He told me that at their recent General Chapter they had discussed the question of new forms of membership in their congregation. "Would you be interested in exploring this with us?" he asked. I said no, as I presumed we were going another way.

A few months later it became very clear to us that we were to go back and talk with the Superior of the Holy Spirit Congregation about his invitation to become lay missionaries in their congregation.

Deirdre. Thus we bought a house in Toronto and moved there as a family. I sold my mink coat, antiques, Waterford glass, and other trappings. We opened our house to all and left it open to needs as they arose. The "needs" started to appear. People stayed for a while, some just for a meal, some just to talk. Others asked to join us. "Aisling Community" was born. Some of those in the community became Lay-Spiritans, others remained in our community as committed Christians but without becoming Spiritans.

FAMILIES IN MISSION: WORKING FOR PEACE

Deirdre. Three or four years ago a number of us were involved in working for peace in different organizations, but we felt the need for more contemplation, more prayer. We seemed to be always going to meetings which were very busy and action-oriented. So thirty-three of us got together to decide upon a time when we could meet to pray as well as to talk about peace. We were all busy people, and the only time we could decide upon was 6:30 on Thursday mornings.

The group included some who were unemployed, a carpenter, the moderator of the United Church, the Provincial of the Sisters of Sion in Toronto, one or two priests, a Mennonite minister, and others, quite a number of whom were professionals. We came together to pray for an hour and then to discuss and discern for an hour what action or initiatives we should take.

We were called "Christian Initiative for Peace." After some months we decided to ask Litton Industries in Toronto—the company making guidance systems for the Cruise missile which Canada was testing—to cohost a conference with us. We would ask Lucas Industries of England to come and tell us how they had moved from making machines of war to socially productive and useful merchandise. Litton Industries refused our invitation. Some time later we decided to send groups from our membership to Moscow, Washington, and Ottawa to promote peace. Six of us would present letters and messages from the people of Canada to people in Moscow. Two other groups would go, one to Ottawa, the other to Washington. We thought we would get a few hundred letters when we put the notice of our intention to go to Moscow in the newspapers. We ended up with between ten and fifteen thousand.

To Moscow

Meanwhile Litton Industries wrote to us saying they would be interested in seeing how a group like us would be treated in Moscow—probably, they suggested, "like dissidents, as you are dissidents here." We accepted their challenge. We got in touch with Helsinki-Watch and they gave us the names and addresses of some of the people in Moscow involved in trying to develop trust between the USSR and the USA. We arrived in Moscow the week after the downing of the Korean Airline plane and were not really welcomed with open arms, because Canada had just closed its airports to Aeroflot. We visited the Religious Affairs Department—quite a funny visit, really, because it was a department staffed entirely by atheists, one of whom said, "You know, I was baptized—my Grandmother insisted!" We had a good meeting with the people of this department. They suggested we go to the service in the Baptist church, which we did. Our group was made up of the Provincial of the Sion Sisters, a Catholic diocesan priest, a Redemptorist, a Mennonite minister, two United Church ministers and myself. The two United Church ministers preached at the service.

One of the highlights of our visit was trying to find a group known as "Develop Trust," particularly the couple who were directing it. When we eventually found them we were a little concerned that they might get into trouble because we went to visit them. They welcomed us with open arms, however, because, they said, "You have come at the right time. Moscow is totally isolated now and by your coming you are going to save us being harassed and persecuted by the KGB in a lot of ways. When they feel no attention is being given, they move in." We visited them twice and then the KGB did move in on us and told us we were not being good tourists and that we had to behave. Olga and Uri, her husband, had told us, "Don't be afraid, stand up to them. Half the problem is that people get scared. Just don't be afraid; they are not going to do anything to you." So we decided it was more important to go and visit them than to pay too much attention to the KGB. We did visit them again, but then the next time three of us were stopped as we entered the building. We had quite a confrontation and eventually had to give up our attempt to continue visiting. However, one of our group, Mary Jo Leddy, the Sion Provincial, did succeed in visiting our friends again and she got from them a taped transcript of a peace seminar they were holding on the conversion of arms factories to useful productivity.

BACK TO CANADA

When we got back to Canada we phoned Litton and told them we had something we would like to share with them. They did not answer. We wrote; they did not answer. We telexed and said that on Ash Wednesday we would come to their gate; we would be praying from seven until eight and we would stay until such time as they decided to make an appointment for us with the president of Litton to discuss our original proposal and our Moscow transcript.

It was forty degrees below zero when we arrived at the gate. We prayed for an hour and then a personnel officer from the factory came with the police to meet us. He told us he was very sorry, but the president was out of the country. We said that was all right, we would wait until he came back. He said, "But he is in Europe!" and we said we would wait. He said, "Well, wait for a little while," and he sent us out coffee on silver trays. So we waited. For the first few nights we stayed in cars, and after that we set up a tent. Somebody was there all the time. As most of the people had jobs, those who worked during the day took a watch at night, and those who were too busy during the week came during the weekends. We stayed outside Litton for forty days and forty nights. It was extremely cold, but it was a wonderful experience. The temperature hovered between thirty and forty degrees below zero for most of the forty days.

We changed shift usually every four or five hours. We had philosophy seminars and we had prayer every four or five hours. We had discussion groups too. The police, who monitored our conversation by remote radio, were very concerned, and used to check on us at night to make sure everyone was all right. People we did not know would come in their cars to bring us coffee. We continued like this until we were told we were a health hazard, which we were not. We said we would not move the tent until we were officially told to do so. We had to appear before the Mayor and the City Council and argue our case — we told them we were waiting to have a meeting with the president of Litton and we would wait until such time as we got it. The Mayor could not get over this, so he got in touch with Litton and insisted we have a meeting, but insisted also that our tent be removed. We did not resist his decision. We did have our meeting, the date being Holy Saturday. So for the whole of Lent, from Ash Wednesday to Holy Saturday, we had kept vigil. Very little came of the meeting with the president, but the whole process was deeply religious and ecumenical for all those involved. It also gave all of us time to reflect, pray, and fast.

OUTREACH TO CANADA'S NATIVE PEOPLES

Dermot. When Helder Camara was on one of his visits to Canada, he was asked, "What should Canada be doing for Brazil?" His comment was, "One of the first things you should do is clear up the awful scandal of the way the Native Peoples live within your own country." Here are a few statistics:
— Natives are only 1.9 percent of the population but they are seven times more likely to be imprisoned than people of the general population. In two provinces, Manitoba and Saskatchewan, Native People are 40 percent of the jail population.
— Suicides among the Native Peoples are three times the national average. As a medical person I know that suicide amongst Natives is often unreported, and so in reality the average is much higher. In the fifteen to twenty-four-year age group it is six times the national average of reported cases.
— Native children are two and a half times more likely to die before the age of twelve months.
— Canada is supposed to have one of the best medical services in the world, yet the statistics for Native health are similar to those of many third-world countries.

I proposed to the Holy Spirit Congregation (Spiritans) that we should look at the possibility of becoming involved with the Native Peoples, and in 1978 a priest and I went on a tour in the north. We visited several communities, spent some time with Native chiefs, and went to a Community Medical Health Conference. On our return, the priest reported to the Provincial Council of the Congregation that it was not an appropriate mission at that time. I reported back that I thought it was very appropriate. So the lay people decided to investigate further to see if it were possible to develop a lay mission program there. I had offered to do some work in one of the University of Toronto hospitals in the north while I was there, as I am a radiologist and a general medical practitioner. There was one reservation, New Osneburg, which was not yet under the medical care of any hospital, and so about 1979 I went there as a general practitioner.

I was shocked at what I found. There was a lot of violence. Many houses had boarded-up windows. I thought these were not lived in, but I found that there were up to twenty people living in some of those two-bedroom houses. I did not realize, as most Canadians do not, the amount of squalor and poverty amongst the Native Peoples. Being mindful of the charism of the Spiritan Congregation to go to places where others are unwilling to go, I felt this was just the place for me. I offered my services as a part-time general practitioner, and the following summer our family came up and stayed there. One of the difficult things about staying on a reservation like this is that the people live in very poor housing.

In that particular reservation there were no water or sewage facilities for any of the Native homes, yet the staff houses for the federal workers had hot water, showers, and tubs, as well as washing machines and dryers.

INSERTION

As we began to get to know the people it became extremely embarrassing to live in these privileged conditions and to be friends with the people who lived in poor housing on the reservation. We asked the chief of the reservation if we could have a place where we could live on the reservation in a house like everybody else. He was a little suspicious at the beginning. After we got to know one another he said, "Why don't you come and live with us? Stay with us as often as you can. We know you cannot be here all the time, but get to know us and let us get to know you and trust you. When we trust you, if we want you to do something we will ask you; if we don't have anything we want you to do, don't do anything. Just be here and get to know us." That was how we started to move out of the Nursing Station into the community.

The first summer we stayed there the bishop had given us the use of an old church. In back of the church there was a small apartment which we used as our living quarters. Gradually we got to know the people on the reservation. During the winter the church burned down. Then when we went up we went as individuals and stayed in people's homes. In the summer of the following year we were asked to supervise a program for the children. We agreed willingly, but insisted that it would have to be run by the older teenagers. And so things developed.

During this period I went up to the reservation four or five times a year and frequently ended up sleeping on the floor in one of the homes of the Native Peoples. They are phenomenally generous in their sharing. The home where we stayed had two bedrooms, and often there were two families staying there, but whenever I went there they would find a place for me. Nobody would ever say there was no room because the house was too full! They would apologize that there was no bed to sleep on.

Deirdre. Pecking order is important too. I remember once when I was the last to arrive I got the spot beside the stove. It is the worst spot because you melt and then you freeze, and you are also responsible for putting wood on the stove in the middle of the night. I was sharing the living room with a number of other people — somebody had the sofa and I think three of us had the floor, but being last in, I got the worst spot and that is the accepted approach.

Dermot. As well as doing medical work, we were asked by the bishop to teach catechism in the summer. I felt very uncomfortable about this, and so I talked to one of the chief negotiators of the Native Peoples about it. There is a great religious and cultural revival going on among the Native Peoples at the present time, and although he had once been a minister in the United Church he had gone back to his Native religion. He said that he would tell me what he told another community that wanted to come in and preach. "Go to the nearby town, and if you convert the so-called Christians there so that they treat Natives as normal human beings and overcome racism, then you will be welcome to come into our community and open a Christian church." Because of this and other comments I was hearing from the Native Peoples, I went to the local bishop, Msgr. Liguria, and told him we would be happy to do development work and respond to requests from the people on the reservation but we did not feel comfortable teaching catechism. He agreed to this, and in succeeding years has continued to support us in our endeavors in development work.

But even though we are not directly catechizing, something has happened. One of the senior women, a councillor, came to us and asked us if we could find training for her as a lay person so that she could run a small Christian community on the reservation. Arrangements are being made for her to go to a Jesuit training center for Native deacons and Native lay people who wish to do ministry. The Spiritan Congregation asked us if we would facilitate their students' field experience in the reservation. We were happy to do this, and arrangements were made with the Toronto School of Theology so that Deirdre and I could be the field supervisors for the students.

Three seminarians spend the summer there under supervision. One result, I believe, is that the people of the reservation have selected one young seminarian whom they want to come back as their priest. This is an interesting development, because at present when a priest comes on Sundays about once every six weeks, only ten people attend church although about 40 percent of the people on the reservation were probably born Catholic. The people move from church to church on Sunday as we do too when we are there with them. We go to the Anglican church in the morning and to the Catholic one if there is a Mass, and then to the Pentecostals. "We will come back," say the Catholics, "if we are well serviced." Hence, the significance of their interest in a seminarian.

I also spend a lot of time with the elders and hear their reactions to the white people and to the Catholic church. We have taken away their lands, they say, and what has been left to them is polluted by acid rain. There are two reservations near us where so much mercury has been put into the river system that the Native People will not be able to fish there for another seventy-five years. A Finnish scientist first discovered that this mercury was coming from a paper mill in Dryden. Despite protests the government took no action for six years, and now it is too late to do anything about it. I was called into another reservation in northern Saskatchewan to look at the uranium mining in the area (Canada is the biggest uranium supplier in the world), and already there are three lakes near the mines where the fish are inedible because they are radioactive.

INCULTURATION

One of the most beautiful customs in Native religion was the "vision quest," what Fr. John Haskell, an Ojibway priest, calls "confirmation." When the child reaches the age of twelve or thirteen the parent, usually the father, organized the "vision quest" for his son, and sometimes, too, for his daughter. The young persons were taken to meet the medicine man. They fasted for some time and then went to the sweat-lodge, a small log building in which there was a fire. There they were subjected to extreme heat and then, when the fire went out at night, to extreme cold. After this they usually went high up into the hills where there was a smooth, flat rock, much worn from all the people who, over hundreds of years, had lain on it. The youngsters lay on this rock, but before they went up, the Native medicine man had explained to them that while they were there they would dream and their dreams would help them in choosing their career in life. He would visit them every four or five hours, day and night, to see that they were not totally terrified and unable to continue with the experience, which usually went on for about three days.

I have spoken to Carl Brandt, who is a Mohawk Indian psychiatrist, about what was actually happening. He explained that their blood sugar count dropped in this situation and they began to get controlled hallucinations. So they dreamt, and since they had been prepared to look for a career in those dreams, something significant happened. At the end of the three days they came down and shared their dreams with the Native medicine man and were helped to choose their career.

This is only one of the many experiences within Native religion which I might call almost sacramental. When the missionaries came they looked upon these experiences as the work of the devil. The Native medicine men were condemned, and there are very few of them today.

The Native People are now beginning a cultural revival. One Canadian bishop I spoke to told me that he had gone to the sweat-lodge himself and taken part in the ceremony. He lit the fire and blessed the lodge because he saw the importance of molding Christianity with the good things that were in Native religion. But there was turmoil when he emerged. A lot of the people in the community were scandalized. "Bishop, you told us thirty years ago," they said, "that this was devil worship, and now you go in there yourself!" It is a very difficult stage in inculturation. We need to be sensitive in whatever we do.

I find that one of the most important times for contemplation is when I lie on the floor in a home on the reservation. I do not sleep too well, and so I am awake a lot of the night. I can go over what is happening in my life, the way I live, and the way the people there live, the simplicity of their life, and what it is calling us to do. I find it a precious time for examination of conscience.

In return for their receiving us we started welcoming Native Peoples into our own home. They have told us often that many people want to visit them to "have a look at the Indians" as they say, but few invite them back to their own homes. So we began the reverse process. Deirdre and I were counting the other day and realized that we have had over fifty people from the reservation in our home during the past twelve months. We have only two guest rooms, so we have begun to follow the Native way—when the beds are full there is plenty of floor space and plenty of sleeping bags and pillows. In fact we always have some Native People living with us now.

44

THE LAYWOMAN'S MISSION
IN LATIN AMERICA TODAY

Ana Maria Tepedino

The role of the laywoman in Latin America today is quite similar to the one she must have played in the primitive Catholic church. Small groups formed with faith in the Lord where women and men toiled side by side and witnessed even unto martyrdom.

With the advent of Vatican II, the church once again paid special attention to the poor, an option confirmed by the conferences held at Medellín and Puebla. Since the 1960s many movements in Latin America sought social change, but they failed, and military governments took over power in many countries. In Brazil in 1964 the military government closed down all the normal institutions of civil society or put an army general in charge of them. The only institution that could not be directed by the military was the church, which became a privileged space where people could still meet to discuss their problems. It was during this time that faith came to be understood as having social implications.[1] God was seen as a God of life who could not bear to see any of God's children having less life than the others.[2]

The religious experience which then began was based on solidarity, since the pain of one's suffering brother or sister was a challenge to the Christian conscience. Some priests and university students became involved in social problems, and some actually went to live in the urban slums or in poor rural communities. Living close to the poor, they came to understand that religious salvation was to be obtained through their commitment to the here and now of the suffering "other."

Bible study groups began to appear, reflecting on the word of God and comparing it with their own lives. The members gradually discovered ways to aid themselves on their journey along the road of faith towards the building of God's Reign. These Bible study groups were also the germinating seeds of the basic ecclesiastical communities (CEBs)—a new way of being for the church on our continent.

It was precisely in the CEBs that women began to exercise a new and important role by assuming leadership positions, stimulating and promoting many services such as works of charity, teaching catechism, organizing liturgy, spreading the word of God. The predominantly male face of the church began to change. Women are generally more religious than men. They experience God in their day-to-day lives and in their hope for a better future.

Traditional catechesis taught that a person who suffers now will have a better life eternally, but with Vatican II we began to understand that we have to struggle to transform this present life into a better and more dignified one according to the loving plans of God. We appreciated the Council's view that "earthly progress is highly important for the Reign of God, in the sense that it can contribute towards organizing human society" (*Gaudium et Spes*, 39).

A NEW UNDERSTANDING OF THE REIGN OF GOD

The Spirit that "breathes anywhere and does not say where it came from or where it is going" (John 3:8) calls for constantly renewed forms of service to the gospel according to the times and the needs of different communities. With the biblical renewal inspired by Vatican II, a rereading of the sacred scriptures was undertaken in the concrete reality of each region. In this manner, the Reign of God came to be understood not as something realized after death, but something that begins here and now to the extent that we seek to live in more sisterly, brotherly, and egalitarian relationships with each other.

The Reign of God is something dynamic. It is the intervention of God in the reality of the world in order to transform it. It is a free gift, but seeking it is a task that depends on each one of us. This change of axis in understanding reality is based on a more biblical, less dualist, less Greco-Roman understanding of faith. Instead, faith is understood in a more integrated and integrating way. We saw that we had to demonstrate our faith in God by transforming unjust reality and struggling to provide more dignified living conditions for all God's children. God's maternal instincts (Isa. 49:15, Jer. 31:20) cannot bear the idea that her most unfortunate children who are also her most beloved children, suffer so much.

Thus the church in Latin America—a continent which is so rich and yet so exploited and so full of misery—has made a preferential choice towards the poor. This is the fruit not just of ideological considerations but also of the need and desire to suffer along with, to feel with, to have compassion for those who suffer. Considering the reality of the misery and death which surrounds us in Latin America, our theological discourse wishes to serve life. The God of Life, of Mercy who is Love, challenges each one of us to take up a position in the face of the reality of suffering, death, naked exploitation, and structural violence.

It is women who suffer most from violence and exploitation. Hence the clamor of women emerges from within the cry of the oppressed, imploring the heavens for a place, for a space. The difficult task of building the Reign of God involves the concrete struggles of women, blacks, Native Americans, urban and rural workers—in short, of all kinds of persons marginalized from society.

WOMEN'S CONCRETE STRUGGLE TO BELONG TO GOD'S REIGN

The gospels tell us of the egalitarian relationship Jesus had with women: he gives them refuge (Mark 5:25–34), converses with them (Mark 7:24–30, John 4:4–42), gets to know their sufferings (Matt. 15:21–28), becomes involved with their problems (Mark 5:21–24, 36–43), values them (Luke 10:42), restores their dignity as the beloved daughters of God; in short, they are persons just as important as men for the mission of building his Reign.

This experience of equality is fundamental for women who are traditionally oppressed. It enables them to participate in the process of becoming full-fledged human beings and, together with men, transmitting the image and likeness of God which indeed they are (Gen. 1:27). This important discovery is taking place in the grass-roots movements. Many women, oppressed just for being women, for being poor, and many times for being black, discover themselves as people who can think for themselves and express their own opinions.

The grass-roots movements began in the community centers of the churches. The organizational form that became the most important was the Mothers' Clubs.[3] In these clubs, by sharing experiences and relationships the women discover that they share the same problems and can mutually help one another. A strong bond of solidarity arises among them. It is as if a new world is opened before their eyes, enriching their lives beyond the household environment. This awakening of consciousness is a truly liberating process which makes women lose their timidity and expand the horizons of their little family world. Some of the most dynamic movements that have arisen since the 1970s had their starting point in those Mothers' Clubs—for instance, in the struggle for community day-care centers in São Paulo, the fight against high prices, and the battles for health centers.[4]

There has been a highly successful experience also with the organizing of community ovens, where the mothers get together to make bread and divide it according to the needs of each one of them. A new type of working relationship is created based on the dictum, "To each according to their needs." And while the dough rises, they reflect on the word of God which gives them strength and inspiration and Good News on which the whole community can feed. In other parts of Brazil, similar experiences are lived out in the preparation of community soap used by poor women who wash clothes to earn their living.

From these communitarian experiences women discover the strengths of being united and organized and begin participating in people's movements.[5] Having discovered themselves as people, they begin to struggle for a better life for all, in this manner following Jesus Christ who came to bring "life and life plentiful" (John 10:10). At this point, when they open themselves up more to the world, they feel the crushing weight of male chauvinism. Going to church and community meetings is one thing, but getting involved in social movements is another. After all, home is the proper place for women—the men claim. Thus the women have to struggle not only against their husbands at home, but also against other men at the union hall, in the associations, and at political meetings. These struggles are undertaken together with others for better living conditions. The first demands are for better health conditions, then for schools, for better transportation, and for a place where they can plant and live — in short, for the basic elements necessary to be able to live a proper human existence.

Their struggles have not always led to victories. Many have been taken prisoner, tortured, killed. But female resistance is a hidden force which they have. Their lives, which have been marked by oppression and marginalization, have given them fiber, "guts," and the will to struggle, anchored in faith and in hope. This strength emerges especially at moments of crisis, such as widowhood (Ruth, Gen. 38) or war (Judith). So they continue courageously the struggle to build a better world for their children and grandchildren.

Movements of women from among the working classes of Brazil continue to emerge today. They are sustained by faith and by the churches, and make their presence felt particularly with respect to social questions. Their struggle has profound consequences because it questions deeply embedded structures and types of relationships regarding the family, the ecclesiastical hierarchy, and working traditions.[6]

SCULPTING FEMININE FEATURES ON THE FACE OF THE CHURCH

One practice that has given enormous courage to women in the churches is the study of the Bible, especially of what their sisters accomplished in the history of the people of Israel and in the primitive church. In spite of the patriarchal context they made their presence felt through their struggle on behalf of the people. Women in Brazil today want to recover and revalue this experience. This redemption of the past provides energy to face the present situation and to struggle for a better future. They find, for example, that even before the world knew of the existence of Jesus of Nazareth, certain women had already had intimate contact with him — Mary his mother and her cousin Elizabeth. The meeting between them made their hearts leap with joy and hope (Luke 1:39–55).

In much the same manner, before the basic ecclesial communities (CEBs) became well-known in the Latin American church, some women had already been involved in them. It was not only the Bible study groups but also the grassroots educational movement (MEB) which benefited from the contribution of the catechist-laywomen of Barra do Pirai (RJ), or the parish vicar-sisters of Nisia Floresta (PE). In order to deal with the situation arising from a shortage of priests, these women became involved with the people in a way that contributed enormously to their unity and organization. They called reflective groups together, they prayed, and moved by their faith in God and their confidence in life and in love, they did not give up in the face of any difficulty.[7]

These pioneers were followed by many others so that one can affirm today that women are actually a majority in the CEBs. They participate as simple members or are involved in coordination, inspiration, catechism, liturgy, Bible study groups, helping the needy, and so forth. Little by little these women came out into the open and are now a vast contingent sculpting feminine features on the face of the church. They are assuming once again the activities that were habitual in the primitive church about which we are told in the New Testament: announcing the Good News (John 4:42 and 20:18), serving the community's table (Luke 10:38, John 12:2), spreading the redeeming word of Jesus (John 11:26), teaching the faith, and inspiring the communities (Acts 18:26). The Acts of the Apostles, furthermore, tell us that they met on the outskirts of the cities (Acts 16:13–15) to listen to the word of God, to reflect, and to pray. They invited others to join them. One cannot possibly keep to oneself such a great joy; the discovery has to be communicated so that others can likewise participate in it.

Many have discovered that failure to read the holy scriptures produces a hollowness in a person; reflecting on them produces a critical spirit with regard to one's own rights. This frequently leads in practice to persecution and the threat of death.[8] And so we have our women martyrs—Margarida Alves, Sister Adelaid, Sister Cleuza and others. The participation of women in society leads them to expose their very lives in the struggle for better living conditions for all. In the communities the women draw on the Bible and find that they too have citizenship in the church due to the rights conferred upon them by the sacrament of baptism.[9] It is through these experiences that they discover their space in the church as beloved daughters of God. In the CEBs they are no longer just a passive presence; they discover new ecclesiological values and bring up new questions for theology.

RELIGIOUS WOMEN

Another feminine feature that has appeared is the experience of the religious women who migrate to the poor peoples' areas where they rethink their vocation and their mission.[10] They set up their communities on the outskirts of town, and share the challenges of other migrants. They take on a triple workday— domestic, religious, and professional, like the majority of women who live in the poor areas. Some of them take responsibility for parishes, assuming the functions previously reserved to the clergy. This new practice, besides questioning the mode of their consecration, brings them closer to the people. Such living experiences involve them in problems previously known to them only theoretically, problems of marriage, abortion, sexual relationships, violence against women, motherhood, educating and raising children, the drama of the unwed mother, and so forth. All this leads the religious woman to a new discovery of herself as woman.

The presence of these religious women has also brought about a rereading of the Bible as the history of a people linked to the poor by religious tradition, and from whom they can learn faith in day-to-day life. There is a rediscovery of the image of a God committed to the liberation of the oppressed; of a more approachable Jesus who chose his friends and followers from among those on the fringes of society; and a new image of Mary, closer to the problems of women, not as a passive and subordinate woman but as active and participating and having a prophetic dimension. She is an inspiration for those who, throughout the Latin American continent, participate in the struggles and aspirations of the poorest members of society, in the people's movements, in the CEBs, on the streets and in the churches.[11]

CATECHISTS

Another feminine feature is sculpted on the face of the church by the women catechists who are responsible for the most systematic initiation into the Christian faith, mainly of children and adolescents. Eighty percent of those dedicated to teaching catechism are women. The fact of being involved in the selfsame realities experienced by those who are being taught catechism is highly important. They participate in the same problems and the same solutions. They share joyfully in the progress of the group, build bonds of friendship which never become untied and which may be most helpful at some future point when problems arise in the life of the child or adolescent.

The evangelical strength of the catechists is tremendous, not in the sense of memorizing, but in developing an impressive dimension of creativity. Today in Latin America we can speak of many catechism teachers having "revolutionary tasks." They are open, in an effective and shared manner, to the problems of their people. They are capable, not just of militant activity in the people's movements, but also of transmitting to children a Christianity marked by the struggle for justice, by the valuing of life, by the importance of sharing goods — in short, by an alternative to our consumerist and hedonistic society.[12]

As a result of these diverse pastoral activities, a woman — whether as a religious in the midst of the people, or as a catechism teacher, or as a lay person engaged in a movement or religious activity — begins to feel the need to reflect on her faith. Reality raises so many questions for the Christian faith. And in trying to respond to these challenges, the woman begins to study theology in order to have an improved pastoral participation.

THE INSPIRATION OF MARTHA OF BETHANY

Martha of Bethany is a very inspiring figure for women. According to the gospels she managed to combine domestic chores (Luke 10:38, John 12:2) with religious commitment and also theological reflection. Luke and John present her as deaconess, a technical term used to designate service to the community. Jesus makes his supreme revelation to Martha. "I am the Resurrection and the Life." He explains precisely what type of Messiah he is. And he asks, "Do you believe in this?" Martha responds with a magnificent declaration of faith: "Yes, Lord, you are the Christ, the Son of God who came into this world" (John 11:25–26). She is thus the spokeswoman of the community's faith of the Fourth Gospel, just as Peter is the spokesman of the Matthean community (Matt. 16:16). She adds to the christology of the synoptics, represented by the titles *Kyrios* and *Christos*, the heightened christology of the messenger which characterizes the Gospel according to John.

Until now theology has been the exclusive sphere of men. Today women are perceiving their own way of creating theology where the elements of daily life are intimately mixed with talk of God. A new awareness is arising out of the liberating fecundity of reading the Bible, taking into account the female experience of oppression and poverty, of resistance, and also of hope. One begins to hear the echo and resonance of texts of scripture in the hearts of those who are on the side most diametrically opposed to power and domination. A woman who knows intimately the fragility of life, the need to shelter and protect it, has also an original point of view regarding the creator of life, that same God who, through the Bible, speaks to us of the fullness of life of human beings.

Still another characteristic of a feminine approach to theology is the integration between sensitivity and scientific strictness, between experience and serious research, thus helping to overcome the gap that arises between a spirituality which involves devotional practices and a theology frequently reduced to cold and spiritless speculation. This is because a woman's way of being, thinking, and living has never learned how to be compartmentalized.

It is vitally important in this process that women doing theology in academic centers should be in close contact with their sisters from the poor classes. A woman's theological thoughts and deeds should be in solidarity with the situation of others, and be the fruit of her compassion and of identification with them. Through her theologizing the life experienced by all of God's daughters and sons will be seen as dignified.[13]

COLLABORATION IN THE BUILDING OF NEW CHURCH AND A NEW SOCIETY

The world today is witnessing the phenomenon of women beginning to speak up. Moving away from being the oppressed, the complainer, the forgotten, the little remembered, women today are starting to be heard. In all areas of society, in all segments of the labor market, in all fields of knowledge, she is constantly making her presence felt, taking on more and more jobs and functions, carrying out tasks of responsibility and explaining in a new discourse her new ways of being and doing.[14]

After having rejected the place assigned to her by men, of being passive, inferior, emotional, irrational, and sinner par excellence, she has discovered the new face of her identity, becoming increasingly visible and speaking up in society and in the church. This is her new historical moment, a time fecund with future promise, a propitious time for announcing the Good News that is here and is still to come.[15] Like Mary Magdalene, women today are being called upon to bear witness to the resurrection and to deny the final triumph of death over life. They must be the witness of life in the midst of despair and defeat, proclaiming the opening up of new roads of hope.

NOTES

1. This is the moment of greatest strength for Catholic Action in Brazil.
2. Cf. Jon Sobrino, "A manifestaçao do Deus da vida em Jesus de Nazaré" (The manifestation of the God of Life in Jesus of Nazareth), in *VVAA A luta dos deuses* (São Paulo: Paulinas, 1984), 96–103.
3. These are weekly meetings of women in a church hall to learn how to sew

and to join scraps of cloth together to make clothes and quilts, where they also reflect on the word of God. They work together and begin to trust in each other and see their lives from a common perspective.

4. I. Fiorotti, "A irrupçao do novo Clubes des Maes" (The eruption of the new in the Mothers' Clubs), mimeographed text (Rio de Janeiro Pontifical Catholic University, Institute of Theology and Religious Sciences, 1985).

5. The struggles for land, unions, slum-dweller associations, community home construction crews, community clean-up and garden projects, pro-black and pro-Indian movements, and so on.

6. Cf. the editorial in *Tempo e Presênca* 214 (November 1986), CEDI (Ecumenical Center for Documentation and Information, Rio de Janeiro), 3.

7. Cf. T. Cavalcanti, "Sobre a participaçao das mulheres no VI Encontro Intereclesial das CEBs" (On the participation of women at the Sixth Interecclesiastical Meeting of the Basic Ecclesial Communities), REV (*Brazilian Ecclesiastical Review*).

8. Ibid.

9. Ibid.

10. Cf. M.J. Rosado Nunes, "Vida religiosa nos meios populares" (Religious life in the midst of the people) (São Paulo: Paulinas, 1985).

11. Cf. C. Mesters, "Maria mae de Jesus" (Mary, mother of Jesus) (Petropolis: Vozes, 1981).

12. Cf. Y. Gebara, "A mulher faz teologia" (Women make theology), in REB 46 (Petropolis: Vozes, 1986).

13. Cf. María Clara Bingemer, "Mulher e Teologia" (Women and theology), in *Tempo e Presenca* 214 (November 1986): 19.

14. Cf. María Clara Bingemer, "E a mulher rompeu o silencio" (And woman broke her silence), in *Perspectiva Teologica* 46 (September/December 1986).

15. Y. Gebara, "A mulher faz teologia."

45

THE VOCATION AND MISSION
OF THE LAITY

Sean Fagan, SM

Fishermen tend to exaggerate when describing their successes. I recall a newspaper cartoon which showed, under the water, two rather small fish. On the river bank two fishermen with arms outstretched showed the size of the huge fish they almost caught. One little fish says to the other in amazement, "You know, that's us they are talking about!" I can't help thinking that the reaction of many lay persons would be somewhat similar if they could listen to some of the possibly unreal things said about them at meetings of clerics and religious. No doubt many beautiful things were said at these meetings about their unique dignity, their sacred destiny, and their responsibility for furthering the Reign of God. Indeed, the Vatican Council documents and even the Code of Canon Law have said it all already. But many lay people will say that the "felt" reality, the lived experience, is rather different. A major problem is how to bridge this credibility gap.

About five years ago I was lecturing at a symposium on "Moral and Psychosexual Problems of Handicapped People." One of those present, a very talented businessman who had been in a car crash, was in a wheelchair, paralyzed from the waist down. His wife was behind the chair at the coffee break, and one of the other participants, who was kindly pouring coffee to give to the invalid, asked the wife over her husband's head, "Does he take sugar?" She simply said, "Why don't you ask him?" The moral of the story is fairly clear, and also its relevance to the laity. So often, the vocation and mission of the laity is not the subject, but the object of the discussion among clerics. If we really believe in the dignity, maturity and responsibility of the laity, why do we speak about them rather than with them?

CHURCH TEACHING AT VARIANCE WITH PRACTICE

Just as God is revealed more in deeds than in words, so too the official or hierarchical part of the church teaches as much through its actions as through its pronouncements. It can ignore in practice what it preaches in theory. To say this is not necessarily a criticism. Even the human authors of sacred scripture were not always aware of the full implications of what they wrote. St. Paul was quite absolute in his insistence that there is no difference between slaves and free persons, that all are equal in Christ (Jews and Gentiles, men and women), yet at no stage did he question, much less condemn, the institution of slavery, or object to the inferior status assigned to women by the culture of his time. It took nineteen hundred years for the church to recognize the intrinsic evil of slavery, and judging by its attitudes and actions even now, its assent to the basic equality of women and men is still more notional than real. In terms of basic principle, the church has some magnificent teaching on the laity in the documents of the Second Vatican Council and in the new Canon Law, but some of its structures, administrative decisions, and attitudes seem to be at variance with that teaching. Indeed, they deny it in practice.

DIFFERENT ECCLESIAL MODELS

How the laity is seen depends on one's ecclesial model. The church has been slow to follow the lead of Cardinal Newman, who in 1859 wrote an article "On Consulting the Faithful in Matters of Doctrine." Msgr. Talbot, agent of the English bishops in Rome at that time, was more typical of the general attitude of the church when he said, "What is the province of the laity? To hunt, to shoot, to entertain. These matters they understand. But to meddle with ecclesiastical affairs they have no right at all." When the bishop of Birmingham asked, "Who are the laity?" Newman replied, "The church would look foolish without them." The official church at the time, and indeed even today, could smile at this as a facetious remark and fail to realize its implications. Part of the reason for this is the fact that until Vatican II the dominant model in our ecclesiology was the juridical one. Any reference to the church as sacrament of Christ, community, servant of the world, herald of God's Reign, could be treated as pious metaphor. Everybody knew that the church was the perfect society, hierarchically constituted from its foundation.

Since the Second Vatican Council the laity are told that they are the church, the holy People of God, but they are more conscious of the clergy/laity distinction which has become, in practice, almost a division between two classes of people: one with power, status, privilege, dispenser of grace, and often identified as the teaching church, and the other passive, obedient, receptive, the object of pastoral care, and frequently considered the learning church. Many of the laity have been conditioned to feel that their role in the church is to pray, obey, and pay. When they are now told of their true role in the church, some are confused, not having been prepared for it, but others are impatient, frustrated, even angry. "Words, words, words," they say. "Show me!"

Friederich von Hügel, Jacques Maritain, Frank Sheed, Maisie Ward, Frank Duff, Dorothy Day, and Jean Vanier are just a few of the outstanding lay people who in recent times have enriched both the church and the world by their Christian activity. Movements like the Legion of Mary, Young Christian Workers, Focolare, Cursillo, Movement for a Better World, and the Charismatic

Renewal Movement encouraged lay people to play an active part in the church's mission. Since Vatican II large numbers of lay men and women have taken degree courses in theology and scripture, and many of them are more highly qualified in these areas than most clergy. In various parts of the world new roles have been opened up for the laity in parish life, education, ecumenism, and church finance. Parish councils, diocesan committees, and national pastoral councils have involved them to some extent in the decision-making process in the church.

THE EXPERIENCE OF THE LAITY IS A GENUINE SOURCE OF THEOLOGY

It all looks so beautiful on paper, and it is true that a great deal is happening in reality. But many of the laity feel that although the old authoritarian voice has gone and we now hear words of invitation and encouragement implying partnership, the authoritarian spirit lives on in the subconscious and continually shows up in Freudian slips. At the 1980 Synod Cardinal Hume said that the experience of Christian married people is a genuine source for the church's exploration of the theology of marriage. Does it not follow that the experience of the laity is a genuine source to be listened to for a theology of lay people in the church? Their experience includes their fears, confusion, and anger, as well as their devotion, commitment, and intimacy with the Holy Spirit in prayer and daily living. An Irish woman recently wrote: "As a lay person I have the impression that the official leaders of the Church often speak for me and sometimes at me, but rarely or never with me. If the official Church doesn't listen to the feelings of the people of God it will lose the emotional allegiance of its members."[1]

Consultation is simply not enough, no matter how professionally it is carried out. Those consulting decide the topic, its scope, degree of detail, duration, and timing of the consultation, and then filter and summarize the results to fit a prearranged procedure, perhaps sometimes a predecided conclusion. Very little of the original response gets through or is really heard, certainly not the depth of feeling. In this situation, the laity can hardly be blamed if they become cynical or alienated. The call to dialogue, to understanding, to respect, is a call to a recognition of the basic equality of all Christians, so clearly expressed in the Vatican II documents and in the new Code of Canon Law.

DIFFERENT THEOLOGIES OF LAY LIFE AND MINISTRY

Since neither the Council nor the Code was able to arrive at a satisfactory theology of the lay person's life and ministry, the confusion of the past twenty years is understandable. In *The Lay-Centered Church*, Leonard Doohan has traced the different theologies that emerged in the last few decades, and has shown how they operated in practice. First there was the theology of instrumental ministry with its emphasis on Catholic action, lay activity mandated by ecclesiastical authority. Then came the theology of ecclesial presence to the world, recognizing that earthly and temporal realities have a value and goodness of their own, and the role of the laity is to be present to that world, developing and perfecting it. A development of this, namely that the lay person is not only to be in the world, but for the world, led to the theology of world transformation, with the laity as agents in the consecration of the world.

RESTRUCTURING THE CHURCH

A fourth theology could be described as laity and ecclesial restructuring. Yves Congar, whose 1957 book *Lay People in the Church* marked the beginning of serious study of the topic, came to the conclusion twenty years later that a meaningful theology of the laity now calls for a restructuring of the church. The reasons for this:

1. Study of the New Testament and early church history shows that some of our understandings of ecclesial structure are oversimplified, local, and relative.
2. Vatican II values experience over structure, emphasizes the functional dimension of ministries, and calls for decentralization and collegiality.
3. Ecumenical dialogue is forcing the church to review the laity's role in church decision-making and structures.
4. Many scholars are now questioning the relationship of authority to Christian community.
5. Finally, there is a theology of self-discovery for laity. This means that laity are discovering their role through experience, responding to needs as they arise, and only later reflecting critically and theologically on that experience.

These last two trends would seem to be the path for the future. If these trends are not taken seriously by the hierarchy then they will be open to the same devastating critique Michael Winter applied to the English bishops because of their response to the Report of the Liverpool Pastoral Congress: "Basically what was missing was any sign of a willingness to make institutional changes. . . . Resolutions were answered with platitudes, and the whole apparatus of Church organizations and institutions went on as before without any modification being introduced. Four years after the event, nothing of major significance has emerged from its deliberations and the exercise must be considered frankly as a failure."

REDISCOVERING BASICALLY CHRISTIAN ATTITUDES AND PRACTICES

It would be so easy to dismiss these critical warnings and seemingly radical comments as an attempt to have the church imitate the democracies of the Western world. But in fact it is a question of the church rediscovering some of the basically Christian attitudes and practices it had before it allowed itself to be shaped and influenced by the status, power and structures it acquired when it began to compete as a superpower with the Roman Empire and the various European nations.

In the early centuries the laity were involved in the decision-making process, were consulted on major issues, and were present as full participants at synods, regional meetings, and even ecumenical councils. Pope Boniface VIII decreed, "Whatever affects everyone must be approved by everyone." St. Cyprian, bishop and martyr in the third century, convoked many synods to which the laity were always invited, and worked on the principle that, in his own words, "no decree can be established which does not appear to be ratified by the consent of the plurality."

WOMEN IN THE CHURCH

Pope Paul VI called for "a re-reading of Church history while paying particular attention to present needs" (*Evangelii Nuntiandi*, 73). Have we done that yet? The Council document on priestly life says: "Priests should be willing to listen to lay-people, give brotherly consideration to their wishes and recognize their experience and competence." Leaving aside the patronizing tone of that statement, is this listening really taking place? Perhaps we should reread and listen again to the resolutions formulated by the Third International Congress of the Laity held in 1967—twenty years ago! There were three thousand participants and, among other things, they asked that "a serious theological study be undertaken on the place of women in the Church and in the sacramental order." Furthermore, they asked that "competent women be appointed to all papal commissions," and "that women be consulted in the revision of the law concerning them, so that women's dignity would be fully recognized and they would be given the fullest possibility for service in the Church." This was twenty years ago!

WOMEN AND POSITIONS OF AUTHORITY IN THE CHURCH

It is true that the new Code of Canon Law recognizes equal rights for women and men except in relation to the sacrament of orders. What happens in practice? How many lay women have been appointed to positions of authority in any of the Vatican Congregations since that request of twenty years ago? Is it still the rule that ambassadors or ministers accredited to the Holy See by secular states must be male? The Congregation for Catholic Education has been assessing United States seminaries for the past five years, and in its interim report expressed particular concern about the use of lay people and nuns as teachers of "sacred subjects" and as spiritual directors for seminarians. One wonders, if Teresa of Avila were to apply for a teaching post, would her status as a canonized saint and Doctor of the Church outweigh the major disability of her female sex? At a conference on Women in the Church, held in Washington last October, attended by twenty-five hundred people, women expressed what they think, what they feel, what they experience. They cannot be blamed for wondering, asking (and I am surprised that they are not shouting), "Is anybody listening?" So often I hear clerics complaining of the stridency of the feminist movement in the church. What surprises me is that the women are not more angry. One needs a lot of patience to hear mountains groaning for twenty years only to produce an anemic little mouse.

LEARNING FROM FEMALE EXPERIENCE AND FEMALE CULTURE

What of the other request of the International Congress held more than twenty years ago? Has there been a really serious theological study done on the role of women in the church? Even apart from the special questions of the ordination of women, the whole church could benefit from taking women more seriously. The Vatican Council in its Decree on Missionary Activity, and Paul VI in *Evangelii Nuntiandi*, spoke of the need for "inculturation." Inculturation is learning from the philosophy, wisdom, customs, and experience of people, so that the gospel may become a living tradition enriched by, and incarnate in, their culture. Is the same not true of female experience, female culture? The New Testament writers were all men, heavily influenced by their male-dominated culture. It would be interesting to have a gospel written by Mary of Nazareth or "the woman who was a sinner," or a letter from one of the Roman matrons who hosted a domestic eucharist. In time, of course, the big question of the ordination of women will have to be faced. Bishop Remi de Roo of Victoria, British Columbia, told the Washington conference that "evading this issue would endanger ecumenical relations and cause irreparable harm to the credibility of the Catholic Church." Many theologians and scripture scholars hold that there are no convincing theological arguments against it; it is more a question of sociological factors.

WOMEN'S ROLE IS A CENTRAL ISSUE FOR THE CHURCH

This reference to the church's attitude to women is not a light-hearted digression. The women's question is already a central issue for the church. It is not true that it is simply a middle-class, first-world phenomenon. I have met many third-world women who feel equally strongly about it.

THE MEANING OF THE WORD "LAITY"

At this point it may be of interest to note the ambiguity of the word "laity." There is no definition of it either in Vatican II documents or in the Code of Canon Law. Insofar as it comes from *laos*, "people," all members of the church are laity, the People of God. But when the code speaks of "lay members" it means "non-clerics." Therefore, in principle, it includes non-clerical religious, Sisters and Brothers. These are "lay" religious. Plain laity are therefore defined by a double negative, non-clerical, non-religious. Is it any wonder that our laity feel second-class?

But what of the in-between group—the lay religious? Are they on the side of "management," with the clerics? I hope I will be forgiven for raising the question of "sensitivity," which in some cases may also involve principle. When the Union of (male) Superiors General elects a group of their members to represent religious at a Synod of Bishops, only clerics are eligible. I know this rule is not of their making. But if a Synod is serious about laity participation and responsibility, it ought to ask itself what kind of impression is thus created. But then one would like to ask: what does "representation" mean? If these questions are not raised at some stage, synods may be going through the same motions for another twenty years.

On the question of "sensitivity" I would like to make a personal comment, in parenthesis. I have been to hundreds of meetings of religious over the past thirty years. When all present were priests, concelebration of the eucharist made a lot of sense. But I could not help feeling that when it is a mixed group, of Sisters, Brothers, and priests, concelebration is less appropriate, because if we meet specifically as religious what we have in common is far more important than what divides us.

NEW INITIATIVES IN LAY MINISTRIES

What is actually happening in the church? The diocese of Kinshasa in Zaire has had lay ministries for eleven years, beginning in 1975 when Cardinal Malula entrusted eight parishes to lay people. The whole experiment has been evaluated by a special commission and pronounced a success. There are similar initiatives in other parts of the world. In 1982 a survey of seventy-eight parishes in the United States showed that thirty-three of them did not have resident priests and another fourteen said they would be without priests in five years. The gap is being filled by nonordained pastoral administrators, usually religious Sisters, who function on a full-time basis, reside in the rectory, and do everything except celebrate Mass and hear confessions.

The shortage of priests has forced some bishops to overcome their hesitation about laity, but they have moved only to the halfway house of religious. When religious can no longer fill the gaps will they finally turn to the rest of the laity? To tease out the implications of all this could force us to take a fresh look at our ecclesiology and raise questions about clerical celibacy. Have we not got our priorities wrong when our only response to the millions of Catholics who are deprived of the eucharist because there is no celibate male priest available, is to pray for vocations — to the celibate male priesthood?

LAITY — THE SLEEPING GIANT

There is a great need to look at the various ways in which lay involvement can be developed and made meaningful, from the acceptance of new ministries to structures enabling the laity to share in decision-making. Likewise, preoccupation with ministries and structures should not distract from the laity's essential role of Christian living in the secular world. But too much concentration on the laity as such can confuse the issue, because the clergy/laity division has set up so many false problems for the church already. The role of the laity, the sleeping giant, the holy, priestly people, the plain People of God, will remain confused until we get some meaningful light on that other piece of unfinished business left over from the Second Vatican Council — the role of the clergy and the meaning of the ministerial priesthood. However, we must first recapture the vision of the whole church as the "People of God," from among whom some are called to the ministry of orders, without losing their "lay" status as members of Christ's body. Without that vision, and without a real conviction of the basic dignity and equality of all Christ's faithful women and men, we lack the proper context for any fruitful discussion of roles in the Christian community.

NOTE

1. Ben Kimmerling, in *The Furrow* (September 1986).

46

WOMEN AND MEN: PARTNERSHIP IN MISSION

Matilda Handl, OSB and Paul Van Parijs, CICM

MATILDA HANDL. Leading women of our day such as Benazir Bhutto in Pakistan, Cory Aquino in the Philippines, and Britain's "Iron Lady" Margaret Thatcher, are proving Pope John XXIII a credible prophet. Already in 1963 he listed the rise of women in society among the signs of his time.

Exploring the topic "Women and Men: Partnership in Mission," I invite you to use the imagery of "Pillows and Pillars of the Church," unlikely partners as they may seem to be. Let me share with you a few thoughts and experiences that led me to this imagery.

Some years ago in New York City an exhibit of women's art featuring beautiful blankets, pillows, and other functional items bore the title *Pillow of the Church*. In Rome I have seen many pillars—ancient and modern, graceful and sturdy, intact and broken—reminding me that even hard and durable things can crumble. Pillows and pillars can be either functional or ornamental. Both support and connect but in different ways—pillars by separating top from bottom, pillows by softening edges to allow for contact and ease; pillars more durable, pillows more flexible; pillars more visible when they function, pillows hardly visible when they function, providing support.

If the People of God are to be at home in the church, then the unique gifts of women and men must serve both as pillows and pillars as the needs of people require. Women and men are needed to serve as partners and equals in the mission given us by Jesus, to go out and make disciples of all nations, uniting them in the conviction that God loves, saves, and calls them; that history is alive with the presence and action of God who delights in the diversity in creation; that God can heal and make whole what human sin has broken and separated. The triune God whom Jesus made known to us and in whose image we are made wants us to work with Jesus in partnership. In the Advent Antiphon of December 22 we call on Jesus as the cornerstone who makes the two into one.

Paul Van Parijs and I will try to model partnership in mission as we integrate our presentations, using the pillars of our expertise and the pillows of our experience. He will begin by sharing the fruits of his Old Testament scripture background, the partnership of Israel with God, and I will follow with reflections from the New Testament.

THE BIBLICAL BASIS OF PARTNERSHIP IN MISSION

OLD TESTAMENT

PAUL VAN PARIJS. In presenting the topic "Women and Men: Partnership in Mission," Matilda and I have chosen to start from the brief look at the contemporary scene in the church, its pillows and pillars, before turning to an analysis of the biblical basis for partnership in mission.

In searching to establish a biblical basis for the topic of partnership in mission there is a certain temptation in Christian circles to highlight the impressively positive attitude of Jesus towards women in the gospels by contrasting it with some of the more negative attitudes in Judaism. An example of such a negative attitude is the prayer composed by a man of the Talmudic tradition: "Praised be God that he did not make me a Gentile. Praised be God that he did not make me a woman. Praised be God that he did not make me a fool!"

It would be just as easy to turn the tables on the Christian tradition and show the superiority of the Jewish tradition by selectively quoting texts from the New Testament. However, I prefer to start from the positive elements in both traditions, keeping in mind that Jesus, a Jew, in proclaiming his message and in living his mission, brings out the best in both the Jewish tradition and in the Christian tradition he founded.

The Jewish tradition, and more specifically the Old Testament tradition, finds its roots and basic religious impulse in the exodus experience of the people of Israel's liberation from Egypt, the wanderings in the desert, and the covenant as a lived reality. The exodus shaped the destiny of the Chosen People and for us Christians, the exodus continues in our walking with Jesus of Nazareth, in our discipleship and partnership in his mission.

Any human language or experience used to express our relationship with the living God is inadequate; so also is the covenant language. But the covenant language is part of our Jewish and Christian heritage, and it may still be one of the most felicitous ways of reflecting on our call to partnership in mission.

We find the covenant language prominently used in the Torah and in the prophetic literature, less overtly in the wisdom books. The covenant language is a central theme of the Torah: "I am your God, you are my people." The prophets are the watchdogs of this covenant relationship in times of stress. The wisdom literature tries to implement it in everyday life. This paper will not attempt a survey of the history of the relationship between God and the people of Israel from Moses to Jesus. We will focus instead on a limited part of the rich Old Testament tradition.

GENESIS: THE CREATION STORY

I chose the opening chapters of the Bible, Genesis 1 to 3, to illustrate the ideas, convictions, expectations, and visions that were alive among the people of Israel during the major part of their Old Testament history. A double reason has guided my choice. In the first place, Genesis 1, the creation story, and especially Genesis 2 and Genesis 3, the Paradise story, can only be properly understood against a background of covenant thinking, a thinking in terms of partnership between God and the people of Israel. Secondly, these chapters figure prominently in the reflection on the dignity and vocation of women in the Apostolic Letter of Pope John Paul II.

Still, it may surprise you that for our reflection on the partnership of women and men in mission, we have opted to go back to Old Testament society. It was rather notoriously patriarchal and male-dominated, notwithstanding some shining examples of female figures playing important roles in Israel's history. We have made our choice, aware that "the road is made by walking," and that the Old Testament is a great teacher showing the gradual growth of new ideas into established values and eventually into societal structures. Often the road is rough, at times even interrupted, but somehow the seed of an idea or insight develops and grows and establishes itself. Such a basic insight is the fundamental equality and dignity of human persons, male and female, covenanted in freedom and responsibility to the living God, Ruler of the universe, Father and Mother of us all. The first three chapters of Genesis speak about this with an amazing force and conviction.

Genesis 1 is the younger Priestly account of creation, well structured, systematic and clear. Its major statement about humankind is: we are created in the image and likeness of God, female and male, willed for our own sakes and called to be like God, called to act like God. Moses, the great figure in the history of Israel, was called to be like God to his brother Aaron in the Burning Bush episode; in other words, he was called to empower his brother to speak responsibly and courageously for the liberation of his people. "In the image and likeness of God" has therefore to do with "empowering the other," with the "gift of self" for true self-realization.

The gift and the call are addressed to men and women with equal force. It is difficult to misunderstand Genesis 1 on this point; it is difficult to use it to defend a position of dominance of men over women or vice versa. Both women and men are created in the image and likeness of God, and both are invited to a responsible stewardship of the earth, partnership in a mission.

GENESIS: THE PARADISE STORY

The trouble starts with the Paradise story in Genesis 2 and 3. It is an older and more colorful presentation of basically similar insights. Actually, the Genesis 2 and 3 story deepens and clarifies Genesis 1 by going beyond the vision in Genesis and by sharing insights based on the historical experience of success and failure in the pursuit of the grand vision of the opening chapter. The Genesis 2 and 3 story enriches the reflection of Genesis 1 by stressing the steadfast love and mercy of the living God who patiently walks with humankind in their pursuit of covenant harmony. This covenant harmony, after much struggle with the forces of evil (represented by the serpent), must ultimately lead to equality and dignity for all and to a new heaven and a new earth where the wolf and the lamb shall graze together and none shall hurt or destroy.

Unfortunately, both the underlying historical background and the covenant theology of an author living in the early Kingdom period have been lost sight of in the course of Jewish and Christian reflection on the colorful story. This has led to interpretations that come close to contradicting the fundamental insight we started from: the equality and dignity of human persons, female and male, covenanted in freedom and responsibility to the living God, Ruler of the universe, Mother and Father of us all.

The Image of Eve. Pamela Milne states that there is no biblical story that has had a more profoundly negative impact on women throughout history than the story of Eve in Genesis 2 and 3.[1] Eve is usually depicted as secondary and inferior to Adam because she was created after Adam and from Adam. She is also regularly portrayed as weak, seductive and evil — the one who causes Adam to disobey God's command.

At the same time, Eve came to be regarded not only as the mother of all living things but as a paradigm for all women. A unique exception would be Mary, the mother of Jesus, who later became for Christians a paradigm in her own right for idealized womanhood. This combination of the negative image of Eve with the idea that she is the model of what it is to be a woman provided an important basis for the development of depreciatory patriarchal theologies of woman. Pamela Milne asks the question: can this story be reclaimed for women? Can feminist analysis recover it from centuries of patriarchal interpretation and make it a spiritual source for women?

My answer is: it has already been done by contemporary exegesis and as a result it can be used as a spiritual source for both women and men. Contemporary exegesis, by a keener awareness of the historical context (early Kingdom period), by a clearer insight into the underlying covenant thinking, and by a greater sensitivity to the figurative language used as building material for the whole story, has recovered the Paradise story as a vivid illustration of the profound conviction of the author regarding the equality and dignity of human persons, male and female, covenanted in freedom and responsibility to the living God.

The Covenant Lived or the Covenant Broken. The first part of the Paradise story, Genesis 2, is the vision of what happens whenever and wherever a man and a woman live the covenant with God, whenever and wherever they walk before God, naked and not ashamed, accepting the "givenness" of their lives and responding to the call of responsible stewardship. What happens is that they live in Paradise. The garden, the river, the abundant fruits are all images of blessing and happiness, and this picture is crowned by the ultimate image of human blessedness and happiness: the partnership of a woman and a man, accepting to walk before God, naked yet not ashamed. Their relationship with the living God is the source of their strength and their joy.

The second part of the story, Genesis 3, is the reversal, the other side of the coin. It is the vision of what happens whenever and wherever the covenant relationship with the living God is broken. What happens is that man and woman live in hell. And hell is most visibly and most deeply felt in what was the foremost image of blessing and happiness: a man and a woman walking together before the living God. Broken partnership with the living God leads to hell on earth and it makes mission difficult. Hence, the images of bringing forth new life in pain and cultivating the soil in sweat. What used to be a joy and a glory becomes a painful burden.

Genesis 2 is all positive, Genesis 3 is all negative. The stories are premised on fidelity to the covenant with the living God or on a broken covenant. The relationship, the partnership between a woman and a man, has potential for heaven and for hell. We can choose.

In none of the images used is there any statement about the superiority or the inferiority of one of the human partners. They are either equally good or equally bad. And when they walk together "in the fear of the Lord," they are irresistible.

Doing Theology Together. How is it that such a positive and rich statement about the human partners has been so often interpreted both by Jews and Christians in such a depreciatory way for the woman? I think that one fundamental reason for such a development has to be sought in the fact that in the course of our Jewish, and of our Christian tradition too, we, men and women, have not done theology together, we have not walked together, we have not ministered together. Or maybe it is fairer to say that male theologians and male church leaders have lived too much of their daily lives separated from half of the human family and from the community of people at large.

A Jewish rabbi wrote: "The Shekinah [the presence or glory of God] cannot dwell where male and female do not dwell together." We may have forgotten the wisdom of partnership in mission.

NEW TESTAMENT

MATILDA HANDL. I agree with Paul that we may have forgotten the wisdom and the importance of partnership in mission even while we were working well as partners. This was brought home to me forcibly last week as I checked out some articles on our Benedictine East African missions in the *Dizionario degli Instituti di Perfezione* (1973). They were written by brethren and friends of our Benedictine Congregation with whom we Benedictine Sisters have served for over a century. Hundreds of our Sisters have worked in partnership with the Benedictines of St. Ottilien in Tanzania. Pillars and pillows of the mission, we cooperated in trying to build up the now flourishing churches of Tanzania. Together we braved the unknown, the dangers, tropical illnesses, early and sudden deaths. Even to this day we are spreading the gospel as partners. But as I read those articles I was shocked to discover that they did not even mention the Missionary Benedictine Sisters! The Germans have a descriptive word for it: *totgeschwiegen*, killed, obliterated by silence. Innocent readers of later ages would never guess from these writings that women and men had worked as partners in the mission.

How remarkable, then, that accounts of women's roles in the life of Jesus and in the early church have survived at all in the New Testament, considering that the gospels were recorded, collected, and edited by men in a patriarchal culture decades after Jesus' time. How profoundly Jesus must have affected his partners and disciples, even shocked them by his utter freedom from the patriarchal taboos of his time against women, and by his valuing women and men alike, treating them as equals. Let us take a brief look at some gospel passages.

PARTNERSHIP IN JESUS' TIME

Jesus accepted both women and men as disciples and apostles. Mary of Bethany, "having chosen the better part," "sits at Jesus' feet," terms used for enrolling as disciples of a rabbi and for becoming an adult Jew; all four gospels relate that the women who had followed Jesus from Galilee stood by the cross; Mary Magdalene is the witness of his resurrection to the male apostles who were in hiding on Easter morning.

Jesus enjoyed the company of both women and men. He engaged both men and women in theological dialogue: Nicodemus and the unnamed Samaritan woman at the well who was told of Jesus' messiahship and became an apostle to her townspeople; he spoke with women in public, obviously enjoying the quick-witted Syro-phoenician mother and conceding she had made her point by healing her daughter.

Jesus related with freedom and compassion to the women he met: even to those who were ritually or morally "unclean," and to those oppressed by illness and social injustice; he accepted service from women, material support, loyalty to death, and messianic anointing (Mark 14:9).

Jesus freely used feminine imagery in his teaching. He compared God to a homemaker, himself to a mother hen; he manifested a sensitivity and gentleness but also a fearlessness that his disciples could neither forget nor neglect to record; he lived a new relationship of equals in the new family of God which he himself proclaimed (Mark 3:31–35); he looked around at those sitting in a circle about him (no hierarchy, but equals) and said, "Here are my mother and my brothers; anyone who does the will of God, that person is my brother and sister and mother"; there is not one recorded word or action of Jesus which hints at inferiority of women in relation to men — evidently because there were not any to record.

This freedom of Jesus to embody in himself the full human response of an integral personality in God's image served also as the pattern of relating among his first disciples. All of them received his Spirit and went out in pairs as Jesus himself had sent them, to bear witness to him and to continue his ministry of bringing the Good News of God's love for all people to all people. His life and his example are the pillars of the early church.

PARTNERSHIP IN THE EARLY MISSIONARY CHURCH

Jesus wrote nothing, but entrusted his disciples with the message to be spoken. They went out, pillars and pillows, to fit into the situations they encountered. They went out in pairs and they supported and encouraged each other in building up the church. Few but eloquent indications of these early missionary partners are preserved in the New Testament. We can only guess at the thousands of others who, traveling together and afire with Jesus' love and spirit, spread the Good News over amazing distances.

Prisca (or Priscilla) and her husband Aquila are mentioned three times in the greeting sections of the epistles (Rom. 16:3–5, 1 Cor. 16:19, 2 Tim. 4:19) and three times in Acts 18. In four of the six passages, Priscilla is named first, which is unusual for the times and shows her as possibly the more prominent or zealous of the pair. Perhaps Aquila made the tents and Priscilla did the teaching. This couple may have been among the Jews from Pontus mentioned in Acts 2, since Aquila hailed from there and was therefore a Christian since Pentecost. They preceded Paul as missionaries and gathered believers in their home at Rome, at Corinth and at Ephesus. They were mobile, but more stable than Paul, risking their lives for him and his life-long friends, yet quite independent of him. Priscilla instructed the famous preacher Apollos, a full-time apostle and well-known among the believers of different churches.

Andronicus and Junia are mentioned only once, in Romans 16:7, where Paul greets so many other missionary pairs. They are called Jews and fellow prisoners of Paul, "outstanding apostles" who became Christians before him.

They were possibly among the five hundred disciples who had seen the risen Jesus in Galilee, as Paul carefully guarded the title of apostle for those who had seen the risen Jesus. Junia is the only woman in the New Testament who is explicitly called an apostle. (Rhabanus Maurus termed Mary Magdalene *apostola apostolorum* for proclaiming Jesus risen.) Since about the year 1300 her name has been rendered masculine in translation (also by Luther), though Junia was a common woman's name and not a man's. We know nothing about the imprisonment of Andronicus and Junia with Paul, and nothing of their work. We can only guess from Paul's tone of love and admiration what "outstanding apostles" they must have been.

Phoebe is commended to the community in Romans 16:1–3 as "our sister, a deacon of the church at Cenchreae," the port city of Corinth (the masculine *diakonos* denoting the office). Paul asks the Roman community to "give her, in the Lord, a welcome worthy of saints, and to help her with anything she needs, for she has helped a great many people, including myself." When Paul wrote to the Romans, church offices were fluid, still evolving, and obviously held by women as well as by men.

Paul knew an amazing number of Christians in Rome by name, eight of the twenty-five being women. We can surmise that Phoebe, not of Jewish origin to judge by her name, was an influential lady, prominent for her service to the faith. She was not an assistant to Paul, but a missionary and leader (perhaps single or widowed) who used her means and influence for the church, helping itinerant missionaries like Paul. Anyone obtaining visas for missionaries today would appreciate her!—both a true pillar and pillow of the early church.

Lydia, an independent businesswoman, was a cloth merchant from Asia Minor (probably having a different name, as Lydia indicates her origin). She was converted by Paul's preaching in Philippi. She was a prominent "God-fearer," not yet a convert to Judaism (perhaps not ready yet for keeping the details of the Law?), but familiar with the Lord and open to the gospel. She provided support for him and the other believers. Exegetes wonder whether she might have been either Evodia or Synyche, the two women with whom Paul in Philippians 4 pleaded so earnestly "to be of one mind in the Lord," and who with Paul had "fought for the gospel," possibly by speaking. The disagreement of the two women, if over issues in ministry, must have been hurting the church to make Paul so concerned.

Other missionary partners too "toiled for the Lord" or gathered the believers in their house churches: Mary, Tryphaena and Tryphosa, Persis, Nympha, Apphia, Philologus and Julia, Nereus and his sister Chloe, and Mary the mother of John Mark. Their very listing occurs in relation to others—pillows and also pillars of the faith!

HISTORICAL ASPECTS OF PARTNERSHIP IN MISSION

MATILDA HANDL. What has happened since the first generation of missionary partners lived as equals proclaiming that for all those baptized in Christ, "there are no more barriers between Jew and Greek, slave and free, male and female, but all are one in Christ Jesus" (Gal. 3:27–28)?

The new freedom and equality of women and slaves in the Christian community was a revolutionary development in the patriarchal culture of the first century. There must have been considerable tension and strain for newly baptized Christians in non-Christian households. Church leaders began to urge loving accommodation to the patriarchal culture for the sake of peace and order, perhaps also to lessen persecution. First Paul, then the writers of the later epistles, and finally Luke in the Gospel and in Acts, tried to defend the Christians and to show them as law-abiding and submissive citizens. Good order and propriety were valued more highly than freedom and equality as the church grew and developed structures of government. The Christian communities became both victims and carriers of a patriarchy whose fundamental organizing values were separation and division. In order to create and maintain order, there was judgment as to comparative worth, separation, exclusion, even domination and suppression of values that were different—thus the devaluing of women and nature.

Men and women prophets spoke in the spirit of Jesus in the first generation and spread the gospel in partnership. Then revelation was declared to have ceased with the death of the apostles. The written words and teachings of Jesus were codified and fixed in the canon of scripture. Teaching authority was institutionalized in the bishops. When Christianity became the official religion of the Roman Empire in the fourth century, Christ's rule over the earth became identified with the new Christian emperor and with the dominant society. God came to be seen as male, and male as normative. Would Jesus recognize his now hierarchical, patriarchal church?

Twenty-five years ago, Cardinal Suenens looked around at the 1,600 Catholic bishops gathered for the Second Vatican Council and asked, "Where is the other half of humanity?" Where, indeed?

THE FEMINIST MOVEMENT

There have been feminist movements which aimed at equality in Christ throughout church history. Though women came to be considered inferior, no longer equal partners, and though they were marginalized and deprived of a share in official ministries, there are still glimpses of situations where partnership was realized.

Monastic women, for example, enjoyed considerable personal freedom and a measure of equality. Anglo-Saxon missionary Benedictine women of the eighth century were renowned for their learning of the scripture and their prudence in counsel which was sought by both bishops and emperors. They worked as partners of St. Boniface in consolidating the faith in Germany. Abbesses governed double monasteries of men and women in England, Germany, and other European countries.

CONTEMPORARY FEMINISM

Rosemary Ruether in her book *Sexism and God-Talk* describes three basic forms of contemporary feminism:

Eschatological feminism was a countercultural movement in the first two centuries. Strongly mystical and ascetical, it saw in Jesus the new androgynous Adam. It aimed at equality in the final age (and therefore in the church), without attempting to change the patriarchal structures of society.

Liberal feminism holds that men and women were created equal, but injustice has distorted society. This situation needs to be changed by revolution; marxist feminism is derived from this thinking.

Romantic feminism sees women and men as complementary opposites and ascribes to women deeper spirituality, intuition, altruism, refinement of feelings, and moral (sexual) purity. This is developed in Mariology. It nearly inverts the patriarchal mind frame and holds that men need a pure and good home and a wife and mother who provide it as a counterbalance to dealing with a sinful world of power and selfishness. It extols the virtue of self-sacrifice, but blocks women from true equality and participation in improving the structures of society.

You will recognize this type of thinking in church documents in language referring to "women's nature" (is it really different from men's?).

Contemporary feminism is heir to both the liberal and romantic types of feminism, seeking the truth in a synthesis of these two. The goals of wholeness for both men and women, of bonding and strengthening society by accepting and treasuring diversity, of creating a just and peaceful world by alternative structures, seem remarkably gospel-like. They are akin to Pope Paul VI's "to affect, and as it were, upset, through the power of the Gospel, humankind's criteria of judgment and determining values" (*Evangelii Nuntiandi*). The Catholic church itself needs the power of the gospel to renew its traditions and structures. True partnership in mission is not yet a reality, and the effectiveness of evangelization is thereby diminished.

PARTNERSHIP IN MINISTRY: NEW INITIATIVES

The recent Pastoral Letter of the U.S. Bishops, *Partners in the Mystery of Redemption*, acknowledges that sexism, like racism, militarism, and economic oppression, is sinful. Conversion of the heart is required, but so also is the changing of sinful patriarchal structures. The document calls men to be partners with women in the responsibilities of sexuality, procreation, and parenting; it invites the insights of women theologians, spiritual directors, and experts in human sexuality—though the writers of the document failed to use available works by women! It recommends that the admission of women to the order of deacon be studied. Patriarchy as a way of life is losing ground, but it will not be overcome by words. A change of attitudes, values, and structures is necessary.

New initiatives in ministry in which women and men work together in true partnership are signs of hope and indicators for the future. Some examples:

Deacons. During the past six years, the number of permanent deacons in the USA has doubled to about 8,000. They are developing new forms of partnership since their spouses also receive spiritual training. Thus they can support each other. Are they not like the pairs greeted in Paul's letters? Perhaps not yet, but they are moving in that direction.

Teamwork in pastoral ministry is increasing and involving women and men, laity and clergy. Sisters serve on pastoral teams in small communities in the USA, Korea, Brazil, the Philippines, and in several African countries. They instruct converts for baptism, consolidate the faith of the people by Bible studies, encourage consciousness-raising among oppressed workers, women, the imprisoned. They also minister to people in priestless parishes and foster basic Christian communities in which men and women freely share their gifts of the Spirit and their living of the gospel in love. One pastor in the Appalachian Mountains of eastern Kentucky requires as a qualification for Sisters on his pastoral teams that they are both able and willing to challenge their pastor! It is a new spirit of partnership and it is transforming the priestly ministry itself.

Retreats/Renewal Sessions. Other areas in which women and men fulfill Jesus' mission as partners are spiritual renewal and retreat movements; marriage preparation by teams that include couples, clergy, and religious; liturgy planning and celebrations; youth and social justice ministries.

Pastoral Councils. The leaders of the Archdiocese of Omaha, Nebraska, in the midwestern USA have listened for the past fifteen years to the People of God who have participated in setting directions for that church's course. The Omaha Archdiocesan Pastoral Council comprises over four hundred Catholics coming from every parish and ministry. They gather on the parish, deanery, and diocesan levels. People said that a group of this size would be unwieldy, that it could not be done, but the creativity and skill of persons working as partners and being supported by the Archbishop resulted in an inclusive process. The ongoing programs initiated by the Archdiocesan Pastoral Council are monitored by an executive committee. Priorities for action were chosen—the renewal of family life, social justice, the pastoral care of Hispanics, youth ministry, and rural life. When "evangelization" was first chosen as a priority, many

Catholics had to learn how to say and understand the word! Then they began to seek out their unchurched neighbors and people alienated from the church, and to invite their participation. The pillows and pillars of the church are functioning well together in Omaha.

The Impact of Women on Ministries. Sandra Schneiders in her book *New Wineskins* describes the impact that women, unfettered by official administrative responsibilities in the church, have on ministry. I have seen it happen. Sisters who staffed hospitals and nursing homes and who were no longer sufficiently numerous to serve as a labor force have initiated comprehensive pastoral care programs, working as partners with priest chaplains. Perfunctory sacramentalizing of the faithful gave way gradually to gentle, considerate conveying of Jesus' love. The families of patients, especially receptive during times of crisis, have experienced new gospel awareness. Employees, who may at first have applied for work because of the salary alone, are oriented to Christlike service. I see such ministry as the leavening of society by men and women being true partners in mission.

The Funding of Formation of Women. Two months ago a Catholic service organization offered to fund the formation of young women in my community. Traditionally the Knights of Columbus had provided stipends for seminarians. Now they seem ready to support women as partners in mission for a fuller service to the church of the future. This practical help was timely, as several of our novices had student loans before they joined us and had to repay these before they could enter the novitiate. Perhaps one day the Catholic church might even pioneer equal pay for equal work? There is much harshness and hurt in the world and it will always cry for the "pillows" of volunteer service to the brokenhearted. But this does not free us from the duty of striving for just salaries when the resources are at hand, thus setting up the "pillars" of just structures.

FORMATION FOR PARTNERSHIP IN MISSION

PAUL VAN PARIJS. In March 1985, Pope John Paul II made the following statement in a discourse in the Netherlands:

> For Christians and for all who believe in a Covenant, that is, in an unbreakable bond between God and all human beings, no form of discrimination—in law or in fact—on the basis of race, origins, sex, or religion can ever be acceptable.

Forms of discrimination have to be challenged, therefore, in the matter of partnership of women and men in mission. Ways have to be explored to bring the lived reality closer to the vision of the scriptures. For most of my life I have worked in formation work and training. I have been engaged in seminary teaching, Sisters' formation work, the training of catechists and lay leaders, and ongoing formation of priests and religious. I have been a scripture professor but also an organizer and administrator of a school of theology. My experience has been mainly in the Philippines. Upon my arrival there in 1970 I was struck by the rich potential of the women for ministry. I noticed plenty of talent and willingness to participate. Most of the lay leaders, catechists, and teachers were and still are women. There is a large and growing number of women religious in these roles as well.

However, I found that very few theologians or scripture professors were women. Not many superiors of women religious were eager to give talented Sisters the prolonged training in theology required for a master's or doctoral degree. Short courses and weekend seminars were eagerly followed for immediate short-range purposes but rarely anything beyond that. I also found many Sisters were servants of the priests and also worked in seminaries in kitchen, laundry, reception, and secretarial work. This is not something negative in itself, but it often creates a distorted picture of the potential role of women religious in a common mission.

PERSONAL EXPERIENCES AND A VISION OF THE FUTURE

Elaborating on the Jewish prayer I quoted during my first intervention I would like to add: "Praised be God that God did not make me an only child but put me in a family with six brothers and six sisters!" I received a lot from all of them, both male and female. And I am convinced that the large family context with its "give and take" and its intimate relationships is a good preparation for partnership in mission in an atmosphere of mutual respect and healthy nonexclusive friendship. Much can be said in favor of an open coeducational school system to prepare for a common mission later in life. I also consider myself fortunate that as a young religious, after a traditional novitiate in holy isolation from the world, I was able to continue my formation in the coeducational environment of a university. I learned that, inasmuch as my own life option was clear and publicly acknowledged, relating to my female costudents was easy, pleasant and enriching. I share these more personal experiences because they have influenced my approach to formation work.

I believe that in seminary training an open environment with the presence of women both on the staff and as fellow-students is a very positive asset in the maturation process of men religious and seminarians. It prepares them for workable and meaningful partnerships in pastoral work. In order to give structural expression to such a conviction, a number of obstacles had to be overcome in the Philippines. Introducing women staff members into the theology faculty of a diocesan seminary was and still remains difficult, as does accepting Sisters or lay people, especially lay women, as students. Some superiors of women religious are still convinced that serious theological studies are dangerous for their Sisters.

From 1970 to 1987 I participated in the gradual development of a training program for ministry offered to both women and men. The religious groups took the lead. A major step forward was the setting up of a school of theology recognized by the government. It had no boarding facilities as in the traditional seminary. This school functions as an academic training center for a wide variety of religious houses of women as well as of men. My own experience at the

Maryhill School of Theology has taught me that this formula eases the way for more participation by lay people, especially women at all levels. The addition of an evening program and summer courses intensified the presence of women. There are now two women Religious with doctorates on the staff. A good number of Sisters and lay people who teach religion are attending the M.A. program.

In my experience the women staff members and students have a positive influence on the seminarians and young men religious who attend the school. At the Sisters' Formation Institute a similar effort to bring women and men together at the formation stage is being tried. The problem of finding qualified women for the staff is gradually being overcome, but it remains difficult to convince religious superiors of women to send candidates for a protracted doctoral program. Many superiors find the master's degree level more than enough. This is a loss which the church today can ill afford. I am convinced of the need for fully qualified women for the future church where partnership between women and men will be a reality.

NOTE

1. *Bible Review* 4, no. 3 (June 1988).

47

FORMATION FOR MISSION TODAY

Reflections of Participants
at the SEDOS Conference

Elements of Formation

Three important elements emerge in formation for mission today: preparation for inculturation, dialogue, and justice. These three elements should be inserted realistically into any formation program. Some suggestions follow:

Inculturation. Arrange periods of "internship," in the actual conditions of a mission situation. These situations are to be found in all parts of the world, from Appalachia in the USA where Catholics are 1.8 percent of the population of nine million and where poverty and exploitation are endemic, to Belfast in Ireland, Recife in Brazil, Madras in India, Mombasa in Kenya, and so forth.

Dialogue. Arrange meetings with brothers or sisters of another religion in prayerful dialogue. It is difficult to sensitize those in preparation for mission to the richness, beauty, and goodness of other religious traditions without experiencing this richness personally. Formators should inculcate attitudes of listening, of appreciating, of seeing the other as he or she is. One's view of the other is often a caricature based on prejudices and historical inaccuracies, whether the other be a Muslim, a follower of an ancestral religion, a Christian, Hindu, Buddhist, or whatever. Sincere dialogue within the formation community itself and with the local wider community, including the poor, will help to inculcate this attitude.

Justice. The "missionary" can no longer evade the responsibility of trying to understand how world politics and economics operate. The gospel is not preached in a vacuum. Historically the gospel message was frequently proclaimed in association with movements of empire, colonialism, and nationalist struggles for independence. It is not surprising, then, that preaching the Good News today may be involved in movements for liberation, systems based on capitalism "national security," Marxism or new colonialism.

Social analysis is important. The missionary must be aware of his or her place in the world. The search for the values, options, and methods that are most in harmony with Kingdom values in such situations demands a balanced social analysis of the context in which the missionary in serving.

FURTHER ELEMENTS OF FORMATION

VIOLENCE

It is particularly important to be aware of the scope, actual or potential, of structural violence even on one's own doorstep, and in the structures of human institutions even in the "divine-human" institution of the church. A theology which is too "spiritualistic," too individualistic, cannot deal adequately with such situations. Programs of formation should incorporate a communitarian aspect of spirituality. They should acknowledge the danger of, and prepare people to deal with, situations of conflict such as: structures of injustice whose origins often lie in the Northern Hemisphere; control of information; commerce in armaments; destruction of primary natural resources; economic imbalance between North and South; discrimination against women; racism; and so forth.

Being a missionary calls for courage, sometimes heroic commitment if one is to resist the temptation to abandon work in difficult circumstances arising out of attacks from the "left" or the "right." Not all are capable of such heroism, but the possibility, if not probability, of living in such situations should be part of the formation process. Honesty in acknowledging these difficulties is essential in the periods of formation.

MODELS OF INSERTION

It is easier for the rich to go to the poor than for the poor to return again to the poor after having experienced a higher lifestyle. The truth of this dictum is increasingly recognized. In some countries the accepted "Western" seminary model is being reassessed. Men and women, trained in an institute or system which took them away from their cultural roots and style of life, encountered serious difficulties in their reinsertion among the poor.

There are new models of formation which acknowledge the challenge of pluriformity, inculturation, and incarnation. Some missionary societies of men have moved away from central novitiates and theologates to regional novitiates and training centers in small houses, sometimes in villages. Theologates are being rearranged so that students can be trained largely in the areas where they live or work. They can thus integrate an understanding of the local people's experience of God into their reflection and study. In some cases, periods of study at central theologates, where academic courses are provided, are followed by periods of reinsertion in village life.

Pilot schemes in Latin America include the formation of local leaders who are chosen by the wider community. These receive special training for ministerial responsibilities with a view to possible ordination. "Academic" standards are waived in some cases. The reality of pluralism is illustrated, however, by the experience that in a country in West Africa, a similar type of experimental formation was resented by the local clergy because courses which led to degrees or academic diplomas were omitted. The problems and opportunities which appear in these experiments apply equally to the formation both of men and women.

LAITY

Missionaries of the future will come from the First, Second and Third worlds. They will be missionaries from everywhere to everywhere. The whole world is "in mission" and the proportion of lay people involved in mission will be much greater. Lay ministries will be much more developed and diversified. This change of emphasis must be reflected in formation programs which involve lay people both in the processes of formation and as missionaries needing ongoing formation.

SUGGESTED QUALITIES TO BE SEARCHED FOR IN FORMATION PROGRAMS

Participation in noninstitutional ministries demands certain abilities and qualities in the ministers. We believe that discernment of these should begin at the initial formation stage. They include:

1. an ability to learn local languages and willingness to take time to do so
2. maturity to be able to live and act independently, to be self-reliant
3. flexibility and adaptability to cope with material difficulties and to accept the temporary nature of some new apostolates
4. ability to work in a team
5. formation of leaders and communities that will be self-reliant, avoid attitudes of superiority and ethnocentrism, able to "let go" and "move on"
6. awareness of the value of one's own culture; awareness likewise of the need to contextualize the gospel message. One excellent school of inculturation is to become aware of the acceptance, understanding, and toleration of local peoples
7. ability to live with frustration, to become conscious of the limitations of the "efficiency" syndrome which permeates Western culture
8. readiness and ability to share the life of the poor
9. "cool nerves, perpetual optimism, trust in human nature" summarizes many of the required qualities.

FORMATION FOR SPECIAL SITUATIONS

1. "Respecting the value and dignity of the human person" and "rejecting anonymity" are two characteristic features of society today. Formation, therefore, should encourage people to develop their own talents, discover the talents present in others, and encourage the development of both.

2. New developments in ministry demand a solid basic spiritual formation. The development of new ministries need not and should not cause a confrontation between old and new formation programs.

3. Mass communications media as well as the various levels of nonverbal communication are increasingly significant. Those in formation must be introduced to this modern development.

4. It is vital to prepare for basic communities; to recognize their spontaneity and the different forms which they take according to local needs; to become aware that great flexibility of adaptation is required to guard against the ten-

dency to control them; to avoid authoritarian relationships.

5. The demands of new ministries today call in question many of our traditional patterns of formation which still lack any experience of "noninstitutional ministries."

6. Programs of continuing education should integrate younger and older persons. The deeper challenge in these programs is not just intellectual achievement but a change of heart.

7. Formation is preparation for situations special to today:
   —where there is much change, mobility and insecurity with potential frustration and tension
   —where interpersonal relationships are valued and one needs the ability to be at ease with oneself in various kinds of communities or groups, crossing boundaries of age, race, sex, nationality
   —where one must depend on local financial resources rather than on "aid" from abroad.

COMMUNITARIAN AND ECCLESIAL DIMENSION

Formation should include exposure to different situations in which one is helped to discover one's personal charisms. This ongoing search will always be in dialogue with one's Religious Institute and with the local church. It does not exclude situations of conflict that may exist within the local church or between the local church and the Religious Institute. This entails a truly communitarian formation.

The ecclesial dimension cannot be overlooked. Uniform models of church structures are giving place to the development of a plurality of forms. The problem arises of ensuring continuity for new ways of presence at the mission level. Continuity is a value that must be considered. The missionary does not fulfill only his or her personal vocation, but is also the instrument through which the mission of the church is implemented. Hence the importance of teamwork, of communitarian projects, of personal individual efforts remaining in contact with the wider community, of entry into the pastoral planning of the local church. Part of formation and preparation for mission is to acknowledge that the missionary's prophetic role may not necessarily be accepted or recognized by the local church; that the local hierarchy, local clergy, or local people may have different priorities; and that the local people's experience of the missionary of the past may color their current expectations and be an obstacle to their understanding and acceptance of new ministries.

Missionaries have to be prepared also to cope with conflict both inside the church and inside the missionary Congregation or Society of which they are members. They need to be trained to arrive at decisions based on group discernment as well as reliance on individual judgments.

THE INSTITUTIONAL DIMENSION

Central administrations will inevitably face decisions of redirecting personnel and resources towards nontraditional apostolates, especially perhaps towards poverty programs. This will almost certainly involve painful decisions about priorities in training and formation programs. Missionary Institutes which developed over the years may, in fact, have become institutions catering to a privileged group of people. Some of these can be reoriented and become once again a relevant missionary presence. New types of institutions will emerge from new situations. Missionary Institutes should remain open to this possibility. More and more frequently outside circumstances will force them to leave particular situations, sometimes for merely political or financial reasons. There will be an increasing trend towards noninstitutional involvements. It is vital to research and prepare for these. Ministry will include service even in structures which are non-Christian, but where gospel values are present—structures over which missionaries will have no control. Planning for these situations will affect formation.

All members of Missionary Institutes will not be capable of these new ministries. A choice of persons may need to be made at the formation level. The whole Institute, however, should be involved in a certain common process of discernment by

— listening to what is happening at "the periphery"—at the "grass-roots" level
— raising the consciousness of the general membership so that these projects are taken on by the Congregation or Society even if many members cannot undertake them personally
— planning a new style of initial and ongoing formation to prepare for them.

The basic question which the disciple, the bearer of the Good News, faces is, "Who do people say that I am?"—the same question put by Jesus to his disciples. The basic quality towards which all formation is directed is the growth and development of a disciple who is seen to be one who experiences Jesus and who communicates the values of Jesus in her or his life. It is a life lived in faith. This faith is a gift. Formation nurtures it through the action of the Spirit. It is the work of the Spirit.

PART FOUR

MISSION:
FROM VATICAN II
INTO THE COMING DECADE

48

THE CHALLENGES OF MISSION TODAY

Michael Amaladoss, SJ

INTRODUCTION

Crisis can be a time for growth. I think that the theory and practice of mission is in a crisis today. Some speak of paradigm shifts: the focus of mission has changed from the church to the Reign of God. Others are concerned that mission is losing its very center: Christ. Some are asking whether "foreign missions" are still relevant? Missionary Institutes are questioning their identity and revising their methods. This crisis is the result of two related developments: the field of mission, namely the world, has changed; the theology of mission has had a rather rapid development in recent years. A clearer understanding of these developments may help us to grasp the nature of the crisis better.

A POST-COLONIAL WORLD

Since the Second World War, former colonies have been gaining their independence one after the other. This has affected the practice of mission in various ways. The missionary movement in recent centuries has been contemporaneous with the spread of colonialism. While it may be simplistic to say that the faith followed the trade routes and the sword, the colonial conquests certainly facilitated the spread of the missions. While missionaries, here and there, protested against some of the colonial practices, many did profit by the logistics provided by the colonial set-up. In any case, in the mind of the "natives" the faith was linked to the culture and political power of the colonizers. After the colonies became independent, there was a resurgence of local religions and cultures. There was and continues to be a suspicion of all that is foreign—except science and technology.

A desire for a certain autonomy also characterizes the churches: one speaks of inculturation and the local church. Where the church continues to spread among the tribals, the oppressed, and the marginalized, it is as much a cultural and political phenomenon as a religious one. While some may see in these developments only obstacles to mission, what is being challenged is a whole way of doing mission over the past five centuries.

CHANGING THEOLOGICAL PERSPECTIVES

Corresponding to this situational change there has also been a change at the level of reflection. The roots of mission are seen in the heart of the Trinity, in the mission of the Son and of the Spirit. The church itself is seen as mission, so that mission becomes a process that is present everywhere and at all times. There has also been a broadening of the task of mission. Mission or rather evangelization—the change of the term is itself significant—includes not only proclamation with a view to conversion, but also inculturation, interreligious dialogue, and liberation of the poor. At the root of this broadening is, of course, a new way of looking at culture, at other religions and at the poor. The key to this change in theological perspectives is the Second Vatican Council. But the theology has continued to develop even after the Council. A brief history of this theological development will help to illustrate the contemporary under-standing of the challenges of mission.

CONTEMPORARY DEVELOPMENTS IN THE THEOLOGY OF MISSION

BEFORE THE COUNCIL

Before the Second Vatican Council the focus of mission was the saving of souls. Though it was not the official doctrine of the church, it was the popular belief that people who were not baptized would not be saved. So the drive was to baptize as many as possible. A certain anxiety characterized mission. To this anxiety was added a certain aggressivity when the other religions were seen as the works of the devil and erroneous and had to be fought against and sup-pressed. Some, however, questioned this game of numbers. Taking a more institutional approach, they suggested that the goal of mission was to plant the church among a particular people. Once this was done, one must move on to areas where the church was not yet established, trusting the new church to carry on the task of witnessing to the faith. The goal of mission activity in practice is to establish a "mission compound": convert a group of people, build a church, establish a community of Sisters, start a school, engage in works of mercy. Structurally and culturally, the planting of the church was more a transplanting of structures with which one was familiar back home.

In the years before the Council efforts were made to translate the Christian message into the linguistic and cultural categories of the hearers so that they might understand it better. Works of a social nature—schools, hospitals, orphanages, and so on—among the other believers were encouraged so that these services might dispose them to listen sympathetically to the message. They were considered activities of pre-evangelization. When it was realized that these works witnessed in their own way to Christian charity, they were said to constitute indirect evangelization. Mission itself was the preaching of the message of Christ: the stress was on verbal expressions of the Truth. Faith was an intellectual assent to a body of truths. Hence mission was identified as proclamation. Salvation was thus linked to knowledge.

In terms of mission practice, the world was neatly divided into the Christian countries and the missions. Missionaries from the Christian world went out to convert the pagans and bring them salvation. Theologians who were not happy to condemn the majority of humanity to eternal damnation struggled with theories of possible salvation for non-Christians. Some might think that these ideas belong to the past. But they still remain at the back of many people's minds in various forms and become sources of difficulties. Books are still written on crosscultural mission that only speak about how adequately to translate the message. It is against this background that we can understand the radical change of perspectives brought about by the Second Vatican Council.

FROM MISSIONS TO MISSION

The attempt at the Council to find a solid theological basis for mission in the context of the growing de-Christianization of the traditional Christian countries led the Council fathers to discover and stress the trinitarian and christological depths of mission.

The Church on earth is by its very nature missionary since, according to the plan of the Father, it had its origin in the mission of the Son and the Holy Spirit. This plan flows from the "fountain-like love" of God the Father.[1]

Since the plan of God extends to the whole universe, one could say that mission is unique and universal, though its concrete task may vary from place to place according to circumstances.[2] The *Decree on Missionary Activity* goes on, however, to specify missions as "defined territories recognized by the Holy See," where through missionary activity the church is implanted.[3] Commentators, however, foresaw that in the light of the deepening of the idea of mission, this restrictive view of "missions" would not survive very long.[4]

The deepening and the broadening of the project of mission was helped by many other documents of the Council that are also responsible for later developments in the theology of mission. I would like to point to three areas in particular.

1) Universality of God's salvific plan. First of all, there is a strong affirmation of the unity and universality of the salvific plan of God that reaches out to all human beings. The *Constitution on the Church* affirms traditional doctrine when it says:

Those also can attain to everlasting salvation who, through no fault of their own, do not know the Gospel of Christ or his Church, yet sincerely seek God and, moved by grace, strive by their deeds to do God's will as it is known to them through the dictates of conscience.[5]

To this search at the personal level of each one's conscience corresponds God's plan that reaches out to every one.

> Since Christ died for all, and since the ultimate vocation of all people is in fact one, and divine, we ought to believe that the Holy Spirit in a manner known only to God offers to every person the possibility of being associated with the paschal mystery.[6]

The *Decree on Other Religions* stresses further that all peoples make up a single community, which has God as its origin and goal. "God's providence, manifestations of goodness, and saving designs extend to all."[7]

2) Social nature of the human person. A second key affirmation of the Council is the dignity and the social nature of the human person.

> In all activity a person is bound to follow his or her conscience faithfully. ... However, the social nature of people requires that they should give external expression to their internal acts of religion; that they should participate with others in matters religious; that they should profess their religion in community.[8]

Religion should not be viewed in the abstract, as a system of doctrines and rituals. It is primarily a relationship between God and the human person, an interplay of two freedoms. It is God who saves. Religions do not save.

3) The limits of the church. The third series of affirmations concerns the limits of the church. The church is in the world and it is for the world. It has a particular religious function in the world. It shares with humanity its historical condition so that it is a pilgrim church.[9] It is the "seed and the beginning" of the Reign of God which it proclaims;[10] it is not simply identified with it. It is "in the nature of sacrament—a sign and instrument of communion with God and unity among all people."[11] Without being identified with it, the church "stimulates and advances human and civil culture."[12] In the interest of promoting the welfare of the whole human person, "body and soul, heart and conscience, mind and will,"[13] the church wishes to dialogue with all peoples: other Christians, believers in God, and even people of good will who are committed to human values.[14]

AFTER THE COUNCIL

One can easily see how these perspectives of the Council have influenced the later developments in the theology of mission. A brief glance at subsequent history will show this. The Asian bishops, meeting in Taipei in 1974, saw mission as a dialogue with the threefold realities of Asia, namely its rich cultures, its ancient and great religions, and the poor: inculturation, interreligious dialogue, and liberation.[15] Having a living experience of other religions, they accepted them as "significant and positive elements in the economy of God's design of salvation" and acknowledge that "God has drawn [the Asian] peoples to God through them."[16]

In his post-synodal document *Evangelii Nuntiandi*, Pope Paul VI underlined a new vision, which I referred to earlier.

Evangelization has been defined as consisting in the proclamation of Christ our Lord to those who do not know him, in preaching, catechesis, baptism and the administration of the other sacraments. But no such defective and incomplete definition can be accepted for that complex, rich and dynamic reality which is called evangelization without the risk of weakening or even distorting its real meaning. Evangelization means the carrying forth of the good news to every sector of the human race so that by its strength it may enter into the hearts of men and women and renew the human race.[17]

This refusal of an incomplete definition is significant. Taking a broad view of evangelization, Paul VI spoke of what he called first proclamation. This was directed, not only to the followers of other religions, but to all those who had not heard of Christ, to children, and to the people in de-Christianized societies.[18]

Already in 1971 the Synod of Bishops on Justice had declared that "action on behalf of justice and participation in the transformation of the world fully appear to us as a constitutive dimension of the preaching of the Gospel."[19] *Evangelii Nuntiandi* confirms this, saying that evangelization must "deliver a message, especially relevant and important in our age, about liberation."[20] It speaks further of the need to evangelize "human culture and cultures."[21] Unfortunately, it has a very inadequate view of other religions, seeing them as merely natural, human efforts, "with their arms raised up towards heaven."[22]

John Paul II, however, has corrected this, especially in his symbolic gesture when he came together with the leaders of the other religions of the world to pray for peace in Assisi, in 1986. This very gesture gave a legitimacy to the other religions as media of divine-human dialogue. John Paul explained later how what united the different religions is more profound than what divides them.

If it is the order of unity that goes back to creation and redemption and is therefore, in this sense, "divine," such differences — and even religious divergences — go back rather to a "human fact," and must be overcome in progress towards the realization of the mighty plan of unity which dominates the creation.[23]

A NEW PARADIGM

Looking back on this history one can see a new image of mission emerging. The church's mission of evangelization has its roots in the mission of God. It starts with God's plan to communicate God's self to all human beings as an overflow of love. This movement starts from creation. The whole of history thus becomes a history of God's saving act — a history of salvation. The mission of the Son is linked to the mission of God in creation. It is in the Word that the whole world is created. The Word becomes incarnate to bring this mission to its fulfillment. The mission of Jesus has to be understood in the context of the mission of God. Similarly the mission of the Spirit, too, starts at creation as it hovers over the waters. The Spirit is immanent and creative in the world and in humanity. The church continues the mission of the incarnate Word—Jesus. But it does not monopolize or exhaust the continuing action of the Word and the Spirit in the world. The mission of the church is at the service of the mission of God.

The identification of mission with the plan of God makes it at once cosmic and historical. As cosmic, it embraces everything: not only human beings, but the whole of creation. As historical, it not only realizes itself in history, in space and time, and in human life; it is also a dynamic process whose completion is in the future.

Alongside this deepening of the vision of mission in a trinitarian and cosmic perspective, we have a broadening of mission to include inculturation, inter-religious dialogue, and liberation as integral dimensions of mission. From one point of view these are different activities corresponding to different realities of the world. Christians dialogue with cultures, religions, and socioeconomic situations. One could even say that these dimensions come into the limelight from different geographical areas of the world. Liberation is highlighted in Latin America, the other religions are dominant in Asia, and the Africans stress the need for cultural freedom and self-expression. But whatever be the concrete origin of these concerns, once they have been given expression, we see that they are integral dimensions of evangelization everywhere. We also see that they involve each other so that we cannot really do one without doing the others. The gospel cannot really dialogue with cultures without dialoguing with the religions, whether great or popular, that animate them, and without taking into account the socioeconomic and political situation that both conditions and is conditioned by the cultural world views and value systems. The gospel cannot dialogue with another religion unless it shares with it a common cultural lan-guage, that is, unless it is inculturated. Interreligious dialogue will be an aca-demic exercise unless it has an impact on the promotion of common human and spiritual values for the building up of a new humanity of freedom, fellow-ship, and justice. Work for liberation in terms of transforming sociopolitical and economic structures will be ineffective unless it can find inspiration and motivation from the religions and goes hand in hand with cultural transfor-mation affecting peoples' attitudes, world views, and value systems. So we see how inculturation, interreligious dialogue, and liberation mutually involve each other, even though as activities each has its own identity. But authentic mission will have to include all these three dimensions.

Looking at mission as such an integral action with many dimensions, one cannot think of its goal in the narrow sense of building up a new local church in places where it does not yet exist. This corresponds to only one activity of mission specified as "first proclamation" by *Evangelii Nuntiandi*. The focus of mission is really the Reign of God, proclaimed by Jesus. God, through the missions of the Word and the Spirit, is active in the world, building it up. We — the Christians, the church — are called to collaborate with this plan of God through our word, witness, and action. We do this through an ongoing dialogue with the world, its cultures, religions, and sociopolitical and economic situations. In the process of doing this, we welcome and constitute communities of people who, called by the Spirit, choose to share our faith and our commitment. These communities are the nuclei of a people's movement that is vaster than they are. The very identity of these communities is to be on mission — that is, for the Reign of God. These communities in themselves are not the primary focus of mission. They are at the service of the mission of God, the plan of God reconciling all things in God.

The church is therefore for the Reign of God. It is its sacrament, not simply identified with it. It should never be looked at in itself. The church indeed has to be made present and be built up, but not for its own sake. Once we understand this, then we see inculturation, interreligious dialogue, and liberation in a wider horizon. The Christian community can contribute to the transformation of cultures, of other religions, and of socioeconomic situations, even when these do not become institutionally Christian. On the other hand, one cannot really build up an authentic local church except in the process of an ongoing dialogue with the cultures, the religions, and the socioeconomic and political situations of a particular people. This was seen very well by the Asian bishops when they made the building-up of the local church through a threefold dialogue with the cultures, the religions, and the poor of Asia the focus of evangelization. They would have done better to see the building-up of the local church in the dynamic context of the realization of the Reign of God.

Mission is therefore the proclamation and building up of the Reign of God and of the church at its service. Inculturation, interreligious dialogue, and liberation are integral dimensions of mission as proclamation and realization. They are not pre- or pro- or indirect evangelization: they constitute evangelization. This dynamic process includes a specific moment and action that focuses on the building-up of a local community of witnesses. But this should not be isolated from the integral process.

One sometimes speaks of a paradigm shift in the vision of mission. We can see the shift in three mutually involved areas. We move from a Christ-centered vision of salvation history to one that is centered on the Trinity and its mission through the Son and through the Spirit. Salvation is not only of souls, not merely of persons, but of the whole cosmos: it is God's plan to reconcile the whole world to God. The goal of this movement of history is not the church — the visible institution of which we are members — but the Reign of God, of which the church is the servant. The model missionary, then, is not one who goes out to conquer, but one who goes out to give himself or herself that others may live. One must be ready for the kenosis, for the paschal mystery. Looking at mission from this point of view gives us an image of it that is very different from a spreading empire that can be evaluated in terms of numbers and territories.

In the context of this broad vision of mission, we can now look a little more closely at the concrete situation of the world and spell out the various challenges that mission faces today.

THE CHALLENGES OF CULTURE AND CULTURES

By the term "culture" we mean the way of life of a people: their social symbols and rituals; art, language, and literature; social relationships and organization (kinship structures); and finally the ideologies that guide their concrete choices in the field of economics and politics. Culture includes all the meaning systems of a society. In this sense it also includes religion. But one can distinguish religion from culture as that element that is concerned with ultimate meanings, in terms of origins, of ends, and of transcendence.

One often speaks about the dialogue between gospel and culture. While such a discussion may help an abstract clarity, it lacks the concreteness of a confrontation between the church and the world. The gospel comes embodied in a community and its institutions, that is, inculturated. The culture is an aspect of the life of the people here and now. We are not interested in culture in an ethnographical sense, studying its past manifestations in literary, artistic, and social monuments. The dialogue between gospel and culture takes place in the ongoing movement of the history of a people.

The gospel in relation to culture has a twofold task: it must find embodiment—incarnate itself—in a culture to become a local church; it must also seek to transform the culture of the people among whom it is made present by this local church. Taking the case of India, for example, one can say that, though after two thousand years of mission the Christian community is less than 3 percent of the population, Christian values and perspectives have influenced Indian society through its contact with English literature and the British constitutional and legal system, as well as through leaders like Mahatma Gandhi who were themselves influenced by the gospel and Christian friends.

CONDITIONS OF CULTURAL ENCOUNTER

The conditions in which the dialogue between gospel and culture takes place can be quite diverse. I would like to evoke just a few. Owing to the phenomenon of secularization there is a growing differentiation among social institutions. In former times religion provided an englobing meaning system to society. In medieval times every science was part of theology and Galileo could be condemned as a heretic for his scientific views. But today religion has become one meaning system among others. In our pluralistic world there are other systems and ideologies: philosophy, economics, politics, and art. There are autonomous meaning systems, dependent on their own first principles. The Second Vatican Council recognized this. But tension arises, not only from the fact that these meaning systems sometimes seek to make their autonomy absolute and thus compete with religion at its own level, but also because, being autonomous, they do not automatically respond to the values and the moral demands of religion.

Another source of diversity in the situation is the various levels of culture. Very broadly one can distinguish between tribal, folk or popular cultures, and elite or developed cultures. A tribal culture is normally self-contained. There is no clear distinction between religion and culture as institutions, though they are different elements in the totality. Tribal societies are closed in on themselves. A folk culture is the popular form of a developed culture. There is an ongoing mutual relationship between these two forms. An elite culture is one that is not only lived and expressed in symbol, but is reflected upon and systematized. The gospel and the church cannot relate to all these cultures in the same way.

After two thousand years, Christians have not yet learned the art of encountering an elite culture. This is clear if we look at Asia. It is true that Christianity was able to integrate Greek philosophy. But that was at a time when Greek culture was no longer an independent force and the dialogue was not on equal terms. When people who belong to a folk or popular culture become Christian, they tend to hang on to their cosmic symbols and rituals, adding on to them meta-cosmic rituals, scriptures, creeds, and organizational structures. Where they are a minority group, as in India, they lead a double existence: at the religious institutional level they relate to the foreign Christian culture; at the sociocultural level, either they relate to the culture of the people around them, or they try to integrate the foreign cultural elements, thus living as foreigners in their own country. Tribals easily integrate the meta-cosmic religious superstructures of a great religion.

This process sometimes becomes complex and ambiguous. Because the contact between Christianity and the folk and tribal cultures coincided with the colonial period on the one hand and with the spread of modernity from the West to the East and South on the other, what should have been a religious encounter becomes confused with cultural and political elements. In a tribal situation in Africa, the missionary comes as one who is more culturally developed and more modern technologically. In conjunction with political power this becomes a powerful combination to resist. But by becoming Christians, the people not only adopt a new faith, they also adopt a new culture, at once more developed and more modern. Not only the church, but the whole pattern of life is transplanted. This would not only lead to alienation of the people from their own roots. Uprooted from its own milieu, the church can no longer be a community on mission. Of course, it is not for the church either to favor or to hinder the ongoing encounter between cultures or between tradition and modernity that is constantly going on in history. But caught in the middle of the process, the church could unduly delay or even miss its own proper mission. In India, for instance, an option by tribals for Christianity could be as much an option against the dominant culture of the country which is seen as oppressive, and for a culture that is perceived as the bearer of modernity and "progress" as it is an option for the faith. Similarly, Christian schools and hospitals, to the extent that they are welcome as the bearers of modernity, will have little religious impact on the people. These are the cultural factors in which mission has to find its realization. Therefore, the dialogue between gospel and culture is not as simple and straightforward as one might imagine.

MISSION IS COUNTERCULTURAL

Success in the task of building the local church—that is, of incarnating the gospel in a particular culture—depends on the freedom and creativity of the local community and on the spirit of kenosis on the part of the preachers of the gospel. The preachers have so far preferred to transplant, or at best to translate. A certain adaptation in externals would even be encouraged today, but there is reticence with regard to what is considered the essentials. These are not only numerous; one is not even sure of what they are. One has still to evolve criteria to distinguish between the variable and invariable elements in the church. In this atmosphere the local community is neither free nor creative—one could say that, leaving the official structures alone, the people make their own inculturation of rites, prayers, and reflection in popular devotions, practices, and celebrations, so that one could speak of two parallel churches. It is not surprising that for communities which have no clear identity as a group, mission remains the activity of an elite few. Mission resembles more a recruitment drive than a witness of life. I wonder whether the task of inculturation can be really called a dimension of mission. The task of a community to express its faith in its own culture is an element of its life. But one could hardly call the task of becoming a local church mission.

On the contrary, the Christian community is on mission when it tries to convert and transform culture so that it conforms more adequately to the attitudes and values of the gospel. For this the gospel has not so much to be inculturated as countercultural. It is true that the gospel cannot speak authentically a relevant word if it is not inculturated. But it must not be so inculturated as to lose its distance from culture which makes it possible for any religion to be prophetic and critical.

PROPHETIC ROLE

There are two sorts of situations in which the gospel can play its prophetic role with regard to culture. In a largely Christian community the church is the conscience of the community. It has to defend human and spiritual values and to be critical of anything that is not in accord with them. It has to preserve the freedom necessary for this prophetic role. At the same time it has to be involved, especially on the side of the poor, the marginalized, the oppressed. It is from their point of view that the church will see more clearly the evils and the compromises that it has to condemn. There are, however, two problems with regard to this task. In the process of becoming an institution, the church necessarily takes on the symbolic and organizational structures of society. The institutional church must permit the free action of the charisms that arise, especially those that challenge unjust structures. Unfortunately institutions often tend to defend the status quo. This is the phenomenon of overinculturation.[24] It becomes particularly counterproductive when there is a compromise with political power. The church, on the contrary, must be open and dynamic. This is not always easy, because in the dialogue between the church and the world the agenda is set, not by the church, but by the world. Sociocultural or political changes are rarely church-inspired. They come from all sorts of movements external to religion. Unless the church is constantly alive to these movements and their significance, it cannot fulfill its prophetic role. Fortunately, charisms and the Spirit find ways of surviving and doing their prophetic service, even if they have to suffer in the process.

Another sort of situation is when the Christian community is a small minority in society. There may be a number of reasons why the church hesitates to be prophetic in such a situation. Sometimes the church may not be really inculturated. It may remain a "foreign presence" culturally and socially. Therefore, it has no relevant message for society. At other times the church may be self-defensive and afraid. In such a situation it tends to support whoever is in power. It is overconscious of its rights and privileges and is keen on protecting them. In this case the church can hardly be prophetic. But neither fear nor alienation becomes the church. One can be a minority of one and still be prophetic. Of course, in a concrete situation one has to discern well, balance off various interests, protect the weak, refrain from being foolhardy. But prudence is different from fear.

THE CHALLENGE OF SECULARIZATION

The greatest problem that religion has to face in contemporary culture is secularization. Some of the consequences of secularization are good. The growth of science and technology has led to the purification of religion from some of its myths and superstitions. There has also been a growing differentiation between the various social institutions, so that each has gained autonomy in its sphere and has been able to grow and develop freely. Religion itself has become aware of its precise identity as dealing with ultimate meanings, and of its consequent prophetic role in society. Religion has acquired a certain distance from society which is necessary if it is to exercise its prophetic role. Religious belief and practice are no longer merely social phenomena, but freely chosen and adhered to. Religion has become more personal.

But secularization has also had negative consequences. Some of these are just the negative aspects of the positive developments indicated above. Religion no longer has a social presence. The freedom to choose is also the freedom to refuse or simply ignore. The disappearance of social control has also affected the frequency of practice. Those who do practice want it to be meaningful.

The differentiation between religion and other social institutions, especially science and knowledge, has led to negative attitudes toward religion. This seems especially true of Europe. Because of the strong institutional presence of the church, and because of the ongoing conflict between the institutional church and the scientific world, of which Galileo is a symbol, an antireligious intellectual and philosophical tradition has grown up in Europe. It is often more anti-clerical and antiecclesial than antitheistic. This has, of course, affected the prevailing intellectual climate in the universities, as well as the attitudes of the common people through the media and literature. It has also had consequences for religious practice.

We must, however, avoid the tendency to universalize the European experience in the matter. In the United States of America, which is equally modern, the practice of religion has not registered the same decline as in Europe. Among the reasons may be the clear distinction they have maintained from the beginning between church and state, thereby avoiding a conflictual situation such as that in Europe. Philosophically, too, Americans have tended to be more practical and utilitarian rather than aggressively antireligious. The impact of modernity also could be very different in the cultures influenced by Buddhism, like China and Japan. Buddhism is, in a sense, a secular religion that does not explicitly speak about transcendence. Confucianism is more an ethical system than a religion, though it is found in conjunction with Buddhism or Taoism. These cultures react to modernity in a different way. The religions of the Indian subcontinent are supple and are not highly organized. They are also able to adapt themselves to the varying circumstances of culture and history. This means that the challenges of modernity with regard to religion and culture will vary from area to area.

SCIENCE AND TECHNOLOGY

Science is a search for the understanding of nature and its laws. In pursuing this it follows the principle of rationality and immanence. The principle of immanence demands that one does not invoke supernatural causes to explain natural phenomena. The principle of rationality supposes that one can understand nature only if one can see and measure, experiment on, and control it. As long as science is dealing with nature there is no problem. But science may give rise to a general attitude that says that what one cannot see and measure does not exist. Thus science may lead to materialism; but it is not inevitable. Such a step is often taken more by philosophers than by scientists.

Technology devises the mechanical means to use the laws of nature discovered by science in order to control and exploit it. Modern technology gives rise to industrialization and urbanization. Unbridled production, commercialism, consumerism, an unlimited quest for profits, individualism and competition, unjust accumulation of wealth by some at the expense of the impoverishment of others, uncontrolled exploitation and destruction of nature—these are some of the consequences of the abuse of technology. This abuse leads to a crisis of values. It is a moral rather than an intellectual crisis. This crisis is a problem, not of faith, but of selfishness, both individual and collective. People have not become less religious; but either they have no time for religion and go in for easy substitutes, or they do not take seriously the demands of religion on their lives.

The challenge faced by religion in this situation is twofold. On the one hand, because it no longer has a strong or normative social presence, religion must reach out to individuals and small groups and seek to give meaning to their lives through symbol and ritual. A mere repetition of credal statements and traditional symbols and rituals will not be sufficient. We have to seek to persuade, to convince. We have to create new symbols. We have to make religion meaningful to the contemporary world. On the other hand, we must see the crisis as a moral one that yields too easily to the temptations of plenty, which never recognizes when enough is enough. We must preach self-denial and sharing, participation and solidarity. Lack of meaning leads to alienation and discontent with life so that people, especially the young, seek refuge in drugs. Selfishness and the drive to have more lead inevitably to oppression, exploitation, and violence. Showing people how to find meaning in self-giving and sharing is the greatest challenge of religion in the face of contemporary culture.

Even the advances of science and technology not only do not solve, but make more striking and urgent the perennial problems of life and death, of sickness and unmerited suffering, of selfishness and ill will, of the need for love and community, of ultimate meaning and transcendence with which religion is normally busy. That is why the secularization thesis has been contested recently by religious sociologists.[25] Patterns of religious expression and practice have changed. But people have not become less religious. They might find traditional religions less satisfactory so that they become either more fundamentalist or search for new religious movements. How to play a relevant prophetic role in such a situation is perhaps the greatest challenge facing religions and the church today.

THE CHALLENGE OF PLURALISM

A final challenge that I would like to evoke here is that of pluralism. When we speak of the encounter of the gospel with culture, we must speak of *cultures*, in the plural. The plurality of cultures witnesses to the richness of people's creativity. It is a sign of the gifts of God. The plan of God is to gather all these into the fullness of the last day. This is the concrete way in which the universality of the divine plan is manifested. This is also the meaning of the catholicity of the church. Catholicity does not mean simply being present everywhere. It is more intensive than extensive. This means that the pluralism must be gathered into a unity, not by the suppression of differences that leads to a dull uniformity, but by creating mutual integration through a constant dialogue. The church is committed to this unity in pluralism. It speaks of itself as a communion of churches. But it is still some way from making any serious effort to achieve it. Ultimately the principle of unity will not be formulae or symbols or structures or organization. The key to unity is the unity of a community of persons. The Trinity is our model. It is a reality of different persons linked in relationship. Dialogue and relationship are the important things. Basically it is the question of trusting another person, another community and its response to God's call.

Authentic inculturation will never close a person to another. One becomes more fully oneself only in relation to another. Wanting the other to become like oneself is probably the greatest insult that we can offer to the dignity of that person. The dignity of the other person is based precisely on his or her relationship to God. Thus the final principle of unity between persons as well as cultures is God. If the church realizes this, it will be more free and creative in its mission to cultures.

THE CHALLENGES OF INTERRELIGIOUS DIALOGUE

Interreligious dialogue becomes a concern only in two situations. First, existentially, people who belong to different religions are living together in one society. Secondly, ideologically, we have a positive view of and respect for other religions. Let us briefly explore both these situations.

Religion has no meaning in itself, but makes life meaningful in an ultimate perspective, providing inspiration and motivation. As Mahatma Gandhi once remarked, those who say that religion has no role in politics do not know what religion means. But of course we understand this role as one of prophecy, providing basic spiritual meanings and moral values that inspire and determine one's attitudes and behavior. It is because of this close link between religion and sociopolitical life that religious pluralism becomes a problem. The problem is whether people who constitute one sociopolitical and cultural community can draw inspiration from different religious beliefs. At the national level, looking around the world, we see various solutions to the problem. We have confessional states that are linked to a particular religion, though the other religions are given more or less freedom: for example, England has an established church, Italy has a special relationship with the Catholic church, Nepal is a Hindu kingdom, Iran is an Islamic state, and so forth. We have secular states that choose to be areligious, like France. We have a strict separation between the state and the churches in the USA: some would speak of a civil religion. We have states in which there is a positive attitude to all religions, as in India or Indonesia. But whatever the institutional position, where believers in various religions are living together, there is a need to come to terms with this situation at the religious level—unless we wish to opt for a society where religion is strictly privatized.

THE LEGITIMACY OF RELIGIONS

Interreligious dialogue becomes a concern and a challenge only when we have a positive view of other religions. If they are seen simply as wrong or even evil, then the only proper attitude is to oppose them. But even while opposing them, one could always envisage the possibility that God can reach out with grace to individuals in spite of their religious affiliation. Not many hold this view today. Some see the religions as natural (as opposed to supernatural) and human (as opposed to divine) efforts to search for God. Christian revelation will then be the divine, supernatural answer offering salvation. This was the perspective of *Evangelii Nuntiandi*. Theologians even before the Council, taking into account the social nature of the human person, saw in the religions ways in and through which God's saving grace comes to the believer. The Asian bishops recognized in them God's action of drawing all peoples towards salvation. This legitimacy granted to the other religions was confirmed by the event of Assisi October 1986. An authoritative commentator, Fr. Marcello Zago, has said:

At Assisi, the welcome given to the religious representatives present at the prayer service offered by the various religions was in some way a recognition of these religions and of prayer in particular, a recognition that these religions and prayer not only have a social role but are also effective before God.[26]

Recognizing the legitimacy of the other religions is not equivalent to asserting that all religions are the same or that all religions are equal. This is the sort of language that is quite irrelevant in dialogue. One can make such statements only after an objective comparison between religions as systems. Since religions involve personal faith commitments, such objective comparisons are not possible. Many others, however, will see the relationship of the other religions to the church as imperfect to perfect, or partial to full. Some will speak of three covenants, progressively more perfect: God's covenant with Noah, with Abraham, and in Jesus Christ. This depends on a linear view of history in which the other religions become anachronistic, if not illegitimate. This again is an a priori scheme that does not come out of experience. Others affirm a basic unity in pluralism: a unity that is found in God who is the origin of all things. This unity still has to be achieved in history, precisely through dialogue.[27]

THE RELATIVITY OF RELIGION

Religion is primarily a relationship between God and the human person in community. It is not simply a system of dogmas, rituals, and institutions. These only mediate God's call and human response. Here we have an interplay of two freedoms that is the real source of pluralism. This relationship is concretized in symbolic structures. This relationship is always absolute—because it is with the Absolute on the one hand and with the absolute authority of conscience on the other—but at the same time lived in a relative way—humanly, symbolically, and in culture and history. Religions are all relative in this sense, not in relation to each other, but in relation to the Absolute. Religious expression may be more or less developed: we have great and popular religions. But the relationship that it expresses is always deep. It need not be the same, even at mystical levels as some seem to say, because the persons to whom and the conditions under which God relates are different, even if it is the same God. It is always God who saves, not the religions. We are saved in and through, not by a religion. Religions are not representatives of the mystery, but its servants.

All these observations are true of the church too. We have only one mediator, namely Jesus Christ. The church has only a ministerial role. It is only a sacrament that symbolically makes present a mystery that is greater than itself. The Latin tendency to anthologize these relationships is not helpful for clarity in the matter. The mystery that the church makes present and celebrates is absolute and eternal. But the church itself is a historically and culturally conditioned realization and expression of it. In addition, it is also affected by human limitations and sinfulness. The Council sought to express this by talking of the pilgrim church. The saving mystery of Christ is certainly unique and universal.

But this uniqueness and universality do not characterize the historical realization of the church. We should say the same thing also of other religions. Saying that they are legitimate does not mean that they are also not affected by human limitation and sin, and culturally and historically conditioned. Hence a constant discernment is necessary. But I wonder whether any one religion can claim to have all the keys for this discernment. Their encounter and mutual challenge will certainly lead to mutual purification. Mutual compatibility may also be a criterion. But there may also be radical differences that one should learn to live with, without glossing them over. This I think is the real challenge of pluralism.

Such an awareness of the church itself and its limitations makes place for other religions. Words like "prophecy" and "revelation" become not absolutely univocal but analogical terms that have a particular significance in a historical context. That is why theologians in India responded positively to the question of whether the scriptures of other religions can be considered revealed. One could accept that Mohammed had a prophetic word for his people, without necessarily acknowledging that he is a prophet for us, though in the context of history and dialogue what he said is not merely meaningless, but has a challenge for us too. It is from this point of view that one could speak of a complementarity of religions, not in the sense that they are parts of one whole, but in the sense that they represent various experiences and expressions of the relationship between God and his people. This means that we can really learn from other believers.

WHY DIALOGUE?

But our belief in one God and in his one plan for the whole universe implies that this pluralism is not chaotic, but has a structure. The "three covenants" scheme is one effort to discern such a structure. I think not only that it is inadequate, but that it is a mistake to evolve such schemes a priori. It is only through dialogue between religions that the underlying structure of unity can be progressively discerned. Perhaps this structure itself is not something given, but is to be achieved through mutual exchange and influence.[28] The church itself is aware of a call to be the sacrament of unity. As John Paul II said after the experience of Assisi:

> The very identity of the Catholic Church and its self-awareness have been reinforced at Assisi. For the Church—that is, we ourselves—has understood better, in the light of this event, what is the true sense of the mystery of unity and reconciliation which the Lord has entrusted to us, and which he himself carried out first, when he offered his life "not for the people only, but also to unite the children of God who had been scattered abroad."[29]

This is the answer to those who sometimes ask why we should be pursuing dialogue while the other religions do not seem to be interested in it at all. We have a vision of and feel a call to the mystery of unity which other believers at the moment, for whatever reason, may not be aware of. Our own consciousness regarding this is quite recent and may not be unconnected with historical developments that we have lived through. Therefore, interreligious dialogue is not an intellectual operation, but a practical and spiritual one, in which reflection will follow experience. While we approach such dialogue in the context of our own faith, we should be sensitive to the fact that other believers too, especially of the great religions, feel that they are at the center of God's history of revelation and salvation.

DIALOGUE AND PROCLAMATION

One reason for hesitation with regard to interreligious dialogue is that it may be detrimental to the proclamation of the Good News. Much of the difficulty arises because dialogue and proclamation are defined abstractly in themselves. Proclamation is directed at the religious conversion of the other, whereas dialogue is only an exchange of views and experiences. Some would even see dialogue as useful in creating an atmosphere in which one can proclaim. In practice, however, things look very different. Dialogue is not between two religious systems. It is a conversation and sharing between two persons and communities. There is mutual respect for each other, but also mutual honesty with regard to each one's identity. One cannot really speak to the other at the religious level without witnessing to one's own deep convictions, spiritual experiences, and moral options based on values. I do not know what more proclamation can do. In the context of a conversation between persons, proclamation can only be dialogical.

On the other hand one cannot really dialogue unless one is true to one's identity and is ready to confront the other with one's own vision and options. Otherwise, dialogue would become a harmless searching for a common ground that would boil down to the lowest common denominator. If dialogue is no more than exchange of views, then it is not worth wasting time on. That is why I would see dialogue and proclamation as two poles of one action. I feel the urge to proclaim because any true believer feels the desire to share what he or she has discovered and experienced; because the Spirit is calling me to witness to the great deeds of God in my own and in my community's life and history; because I feel that I have something very special to contribute that will give a meaning to people's lives, namely, the love of God as manifested in the cross and the resurrection of Jesus and the gift of new life. I feel the urge to dialogue because I experience the mystery of God in the lives of others; because I see in their experience and expression aspects that enrich my own experience of God; because I am conscious of being at the service of the mystery of unity through which God wishes to reconcile all things.

Dialogue and proclamation are then seen as dialectical moments of one action that builds the Reign of God: we should not subordinate one to the other. If a person is called by the Spirit to become a disciple of Christ in the community, I am happy to welcome him or her. But I respect the mystery of

God's action in the other. Mission without mystery is oppressive. A sensitivity to the mystery will make our proclamation less anxious (since the saving of souls from hell does not depend only on me) and less aggressive (since, besides being a sinner myself, I am not face to face simply with error and sin). We can leave to the theologians the further reflection still necessary either concerning the theology of religions or regarding the significance of Christ in the context of religious pluralism. These reflections may help to clarify our own minds. But such ultimate clarifications are not necessary to engage in the present task of dialogue and proclamation. I would even say that we should not reflect on those questions except in the context of a living and ongoing dialogue with other believers, and that it is our experience of dialogue that will ultimately shed real light on these problems.

THE PROCESS OF DIALOGUE

What, then, is interreligious dialogue of which we have been speaking so much? It is more than living together with tolerance. It is more than mutual removal of prejudices and promotion of understanding through sharing of information and experiences and through theological discussion on common themes. Interreligious dialogue involves interaction and collaboration at two levels: growth in the experience of God in the light of the challenge of the faith of the other, and providing a common moral and spiritual foundation to public life. These two aspects are closely related to each other. The first is at the service of the second; but the second provides the living context for the first. John Paul II brought out both these aspects in speaking to leaders of other religions in Madras, India:

> By dialogue we let God be present in our midst; for as we open ourselves in dialogue to one another, we also open ourselves to God. . . . As followers of different religions we should join together in promoting and defending common values in the spheres of religious liberty, human solidarity, education, culture, social welfare and civic order.[30]

Providing a common moral and spiritual foundation supposes that the various religions agree, first of all, that while they all have a role in public life, this role is not strictly political, but is limited to emphasizing the values and moral principles that must guide options, decisions, and behavior in public life. It is the task of the politicians or businessmen to translate this value system into laws or guiding principles. But the religions also inspire and motivate their own adherents to be loyal to these values and principles. These values and principles constitute a consensus among the various religious groups. These may make further demands on their own faithful, though they refrain from seeking to impose these same demands, through law for example, on other believers who may not agree with them. This does not, however, hinder them from trying to persuade others to adopt their own convictions. This consensus should arise from a serious sharing of perspectives, and neither be imposed nor agreed to merely as a workable compromise. Under these conditions it could be dynamic, ongoing, creative, and mutually enriching. Such a dialogue could lead religions to re-examine and reinterpret their own tradition, not only in the light of new realities and conditions of life, but also responding to the challenges of other world views and faith commitments.

When one speaks of accepting or being open to the experience of God in other religions, one is afraid of syncretism. The legitimacy that we concede to other religions extends also to their scriptures, rituals, and methods of seeking for spiritual experience. To be really enriched by the religious experience of the other is to experience with the other. This togetherness requires solidarity and not merely physical nearness. For instance, it is easy to read the other religious scriptures and interpret them in the context of one's own tradition. It is not then a challenge, though it could be an enrichment. But it will be a challenge if we somehow enter into the other and see the world and God from the other's point of view. The same is true also about the rituals and methods of seeking spiritual experience, like Yoga and Zen, for example. To Christianize them as preparation for prayer is one thing; to experience them under a proper master and integrate or grow through them is another. This is why this experience has been called a baptism. This is a challenge that Christianity has not yet really taken up. The great religions of Asia offer an opportunity for such a deep dialogue. There have been efforts made in this direction.[31] But this requires strong and deep rootedness in one's own tradition, a proper guide, and deep and long search. At other levels of experience one could speak of common reading of the scriptures of various religions, participation in each other's rituals, discovery and celebration of common symbols, and so forth. The Assisi event, when the Pope came together with the leaders of other religions to pray for peace, is an example. At that time it was carefully explained that the leaders did not pray together, but came together to pray. I hope it would soon be possible for them to pray together. However, the real difficulty for this will probably come not from the Christians, not certainly from the Hindus and the Buddhists, but from the Muslims.

The challenges of dialogue will vary according to the religions with which we are dialoguing. Dialogue among the monotheistic great religions may, at this moment, be more difficult than dialogue with the religions of Asia. When we speak of interreligious dialogue we think normally only of the great religions. Recently, however, there has been a move to take also the popular religions seriously. Popular religion is not necessarily a lower form of religion. Living the faith in a human, social way through ritual and symbols is to live it popularly. The people may not reflect on their symbols and verbalize their meanings. This does not mean that they are not aware of or do not experience those meanings. Dialogue at the popular level will mean symbolic participation rather than discussion.

Today one speaks also of new religious movements. Some are offshoots of traditional religions. Some are considered syncretistic. But we must recognize that they respond to the needs of the people today in ways that traditional religions do not seem to. Those who practice them are serious and sincere about them. If our approach to other religions is based primarily not on religions as systems, but on the people who live them, their human dignity and conscience, then we have to dialogue seriously also with the followers of the new religious movements. They could certainly point to areas in which we have ourselves failed.[32]

OBSTACLES TO DIALOGUE

Our exploration of the challenges of dialogue will not be complete if we do not attend to some of the factors that make dialogue difficult. Overcoming them is also a challenge. I shall not elaborate here on ignorance, prejudice, fear, and privatization of religion. I shall speak only of communalism and fundamentalism.

Communalism is basically a political attitude. It believes that people who share the same religious faith also share the same economic and political interests. Therefore, it tries to instrumentalize religion as a political force. It abuses the emotional power and the absolute character of faith. The other believers are not merely not accepted; they are enemies to be fought against. Religion loses its prophetic character and becomes simply a legitimation for political power. One cannot dialogue with a religion which is no longer a religion but has become a political tool.

Fundamentalism is a narrow affirmation of the truth, not only of one's own religion, but one's own interpretation of it. The others are simply deluded, if not wrong. Therefore, one has no respect for them. There is no openness for dialogue. Fundamentalists are so convinced of their position that they often tend to be aggressive proselytizers. But when fundamentalism becomes communalistic, then we have an impregnable fortress.

I think that the challenge of fundamentalism and communalism cannot be met at the religious level. The communalist has a political agenda. Religious emotion is only a tool that the communalist uses. Very often a small group of people in power or searching for power seeks to gain the support of the masses by exploiting their religious sentiment. Similarly, fundamentalists are people who are afraid to face reality. Their absolute certainties are reactions of fear. Faced with rising tides of uncertainties, they hang on to simple and easy solutions to problems. These political and psychological causes have to be met at their proper level. The people have to be made aware, through community experience, of the autonomy of the secular and of the reality of the pluralism of religions. Here again a dialogical approach has greater chance of success than an aggressive one. Aggression only makes the other self-defensive and intransigent.

THE CHALLENGES OF JUSTICE

That the promotion of justice is an essential dimension of evangelization does not need an elaborate defense today. Mahatma Gandhi put it very succinctly when he said that to a hungry person God dares to appear only in the form of bread. *Evangelii Nuntiandi* declared that "there are close links between evangelization and human advancement, that is, development and liberation."[33] The bishops of Latin America, at Puebla, spoke of "liberative evangelization."[34] John Paul II says that in speaking about the various aspects of authentic development "the Church fulfills its mission to evangelize."[35]

The basis for this vision of liberation as an integral dimension of evangelization is threefold. First of all, we have a holistic view of salvation. Salvation is not only for the "soul" but for the whole person. The creative love of God transforms not only the hearts of human beings, but also their lives and the world they live in. Just as sin introduces a disorder not only in human beings but also in their earthly and social existence, forgiveness promises a new heaven and a new earth. The miracles of Jesus are the symbols of this creative and transformative love of God.

Secondly, our vision of history is eschatological. History is not simply the work of human beings. Without detriment to the freedom of human beings, its basis is the plan of God leading all things to fulfillment and unity. History has a purpose. It is the creative self-communication of God to the world. People are called to be cocreators, with God, of this new heaven and this new earth. Though this consummation is in the future, the new creation has already started. It is not a reality that will manifest itself only in the "other world." It is being made present here and now, though as beginnings and first fruits. It is God's gift, but also our task. As the Second Vatican Council's *Constitution on the Church in the Modern World* said:

> Far from diminishing our concern to develop this earth, the expectancy of a new earth should spur us on, for it is here that the body of a new human family grows, foreshadowing in some way the age which is to come. That is why, although we must be careful to distinguish earthly progress clearly from the increase of the Reign of Christ, such progress is of vital concern to the Reign of God, insofar as it can contribute to the better ordering of human society.[36]

Thirdly, our view of faith is no longer that of an assent to a creed, a list of truths. It is a commitment to a person, Jesus Christ. In Jesus, it is a commitment to God and to the other. It is a decision to be a disciple of Jesus: that is, to love the other in service and sacrifice, even unto death. It is a commitment to solidarity and communion, because it is in mutual love and service that we live and experience the mystery of God. Evangelization, therefore, is not the proclamation of an abstract body of truths to believe in, not only a call to a change of heart, but a program of life to which we commit ourselves.

A CALL TO JUSTICE

The call to faith today is a call to justice, because the vision of a new humanity of freedom, fellowship, and justice is confronted with an actual world where there is poverty, oppression, unfreedom, inequality, injustice, violence, and hatred. I need not document this reality very elaborately. There are a thousand manifestations of this in every continent. I shall be satisfied with indicating some elements of a new awareness through which we view this reality today.

The poor have always been with us. Helping of the poor (charity) has been a standard Christian practice. But today we have a new awareness that the poor are not merely poor, but are made poor, are oppressed. They are victims of unjust economic and political structures. They remain poor not because they lack economic initiative, but because this is denied to them by the situation in which they live.[37] The political power is in the hands of the dominant minorities even in the so-called democratic societies, so that the poor are powerless; they have no possibility of participating in community; they are marginalized. They have no fundamental freedoms that are aspects of their human dignity. A diversity of talent and opportunity may be inevitable in any society. But when such inequalities become systematic and structural, based on caste, race, sex, or creed, then they become unjust and causes for concern. Very often these inequalities become cumulative. Poverty, discrimination, and oppression mutually increase each other.

We are aware today that, thanks to the development of science and technology and to the resources, albeit limited, of the globe, no human being need be denied the minimum to live with dignity. If this is not possible, the reason is that the available resources are unequally distributed. The reasons for this unequal distribution are basically human and moral, though they may easily translate themselves into structural ones: individual and collective selfishness, unbridled consumerism, the uncontrolled search for profits, unlimited accumulation of wealth, the hand-in-glove operation of economic and political systems—one could go on adding to the list. The roots of injustice are in sinful choices, which are often not seen as such because they are camouflaged in structural terms. The striking example and sign of such injustice are the poor and the oppressed in the affluent countries—sometimes called the "Fourth World." The human meaninglessness of this unrestrained cycle of production and consumption is seen in the rise of violence, either against the other in destruction and war, or against oneself in drugs. Is it significant of the times that the arms-related industry is the biggest in the world today? How easy is it to condemn war, without condemning the production and sale of arms or the consumer needs that are satisfied by such production and sale? Security, national and international, has become a sacred cow. What does security protect except the privileges of the few?

Another aspect of this problem that is becoming more and more evident today is its global nature. International production and commercial patterns and policies make sure that the rich remain and become richer and the poor remain and become poorer within and among nations. Politics seems to be more and more at the service of commerce. Third-world countries fight proxy wars for the rich and the powerful. Their fate is often decided in the board rooms of multinational companies or in the political arena of the superpowers. One striking example of a global crisis, of which people today are becoming aware, is the plundering of the earth's resources and the consequent ecological destruction.

THE ROLE OF THE CHURCH

What are the challenges that evangelization faces in proclaiming the gospel in this situation? I think that the first challenge is the need for the church to discover its own precise role in the promotion of justice. The church could be torn between two contrary poles. On the one hand, the church has to be involved in the realities of the world in order to bear witness to the values of the gospel. On the other, in the world as it is, with the growing differentiation between social institutions, the church has to respect the autonomy of secular institutions. There is a Christian social doctrine; but there is no Christian economic or political ideology. Even if the church condemns marxist socialism and capitalist liberalism, it does not have a third way of its own to offer.[38]

The problem poses itself differently at different levels. An individual Christian is at once a believer and a citizen. One has to witness to one's faith in one's life situation. This is not easy, given the sometimes impersonal structures one has to contend with. At the other extreme we have the church institution. As such it cannot compromise itself with existing or alternative power structures. Its prophetic voice will be credible and effective only insofar as it keeps its independence. Between these two are the institutions through which the Christian community manifests its social concern: schools, hospitals, development projects, social and political movements, and so on. It is at this level that the dangers of compromise become serious. In order to survive and function, they may come to terms with the powers that be and even be at their service. Because of their very concern to survive and continue to do the "good" that they are doing, they may tend to be silent. The problem becomes worse if the church itself, especially in a minority situation, mutes its prophetic voice to protect its institutions.

This challenge of keeping a balanced approach is particularly difficult in the political sphere. Evangelization cannot afford to be apolitical. Then it will have no relevant word to say to the modern world. But at the same time, the gospel as such has no political solutions to offer. To divide the task between the clergy (prophecy) and the laity (involvement) seems to me to be a superficial solution. Such a separation between the church as institution and the state may be thinkable in Christian societies. Such niceties are more difficult where the church is in a minority. Where the society is Christian, even nominally, as in Latin America, one may not see the challenge in this way. One emphasizes involvement. Where the church is a small group, sometimes still with "foreign" trappings, it becomes a more delicate challenge. I do not say that the church must therefore withdraw from the challenge. I only point to the implications of promoting justice in particular situations. It is a special matter of concern, for example, when the task of evangelization is interpreted narrowly as building up Christian communities and in order to promote this, church leaders keep silent on the social implications of the gospel. On the other hand, at least in some areas, fighting for justice has been one of the reasons for people opting to become disciples of Christ. In these areas the governments are opposed to evangelization, because they are worried not about what people believe, but about its social consequences in terms of awareness, desire for freedoms, and demand for rights.

MULTIDIMENSIONAL CONTEXT

A second challenge is the need for proclaiming the gospel in a context that is multidimensional. There has been a tendency in the past to speak of the promotion of justice, mostly in relation to the economically poor. A certain underpinning of marxist analysis focused on economic and political structures to the exclusion of others. Opponents of this approach often emphasized other forms of "poverty." People could be poor in spiritual or other human goods. Without denying such other needs, I think that calling them poor is a misuse of the term and only confuses the issue. But what I mean here by multidimensionality is that the problems of injustice are wider than economic poverty and political powerlessness.

For many people, if they are not in absolute misery, living poorly may seem less a problem than living without human dignity and a sense of self-worth. People who are discriminated against and denied their rights because of color, race, gender, or caste are made to feel less human. In the past, when hierarchies in society were accepted without question, this may not have posed a serious problem. But today when equality (in dignity) and democracy (as participation) are considered desirable everywhere and proclaimed as ideal, their denial to some people for reasons for which they are not responsible is very oppressive. The church had adapted itself to social situations like slavery and caste too easily in the past. In the church itself collegiality and communion are more talked about than practiced. Still, it has to bear witness to the Good News that in the risen Christ there is neither Jew nor Greek, male nor female, slave nor free.

Another value that is consonant with human dignity is freedom. Everyone would agree that this is a fundamental right. But freedom can be denied in a hundred different ways. What strikes us is, of course, the lack of political freedom for people under totalitarian regimes of the left and of the right. But even in democratic societies freedom is denied in so many subtle ways. Justice is available to everyone, provided one has the money or the influence to secure it. People become slaves to all sorts of idols promoted by affluence. Fundamentalism, communalism, and all sorts of ideologies hold many people enslaved. Others are slaves to the ignorance, disinformation, and prejudice purveyed by the media. Making people really free is a real challenge today. The various schools of counseling may help people to adjust to reality. Only faith and commitment to the Absolute can really bring interior freedom by detaching oneself from and seeing everything else as relative. The success of some of the Buddhist meditation techniques is due to the guidance they provide towards achieving this inner freedom. This is the freedom of the beatitudes. How effective has the church been in proclaiming and realizing it?

A HOLISTIC APPROACH

Another challenge for evangelization in relation to the promotion of justice is the need to be holistic. Seeing justice as an economic and political problem, we may tend to ignore many other aspects of the problem. There is, of course, the economic problem of production and equal distribution. Politically we have to promote the sense of the common good as the foundation of public life and a sense of participation and responsibility in every individual. Psychologically we have to combat individualism and the tensions of a competitive life that lead to disintegration of personalities. Unless we can help toward the growth of integrated human beings, mere sociopolitical changes will not help. Culturally we have to promote new world views and value systems. Religious effort should lead to conversion of heart and the building of community. Religion itself should be prophetic rather than legitimating. Without such a multipronged approach one cannot promote authentic justice.

A GLOBAL CHALLENGE

As I had indicated above, many problems that have to do with injustice and oppression have an international character. They cannot be tackled effectively and adequately only at the local level. We have to raise the consciousness of the local people and help them to take their destiny in their own hands, be self-dependent, creative, and so on. But often favorable conditions for such an effort are not present. The real causes of the problems may be as much outside the country as inside. While it will not be helpful to make the people throw the blame for all their ills on factors outside themselves, in many instances the best way of helping a poor country economically and politically may be doing advocacy work in the first-world capitals or in international organizations. The church, being itself an international community, may be ideally placed for such international efforts through networking, facilitating information flow, effective lobbying, and so forth.

A NONVIOLENT WAY

One of the easy and quick reactions to the experience of injustice is anger. One then speaks not only of struggling for justice, but of violence. Yet violence is not the Christian way. Violence is destructive, not only of the other, but of oneself—one's humanity. Violence also has a way of spiraling. The end does not justify the means. One does not produce peace and fellowship through war. The way of Christ, so well understood by Mahatma Gandhi and others, is a way of nonviolent struggle. One has to struggle against evil; one has to resist it. One does not accept it or remain passive before it. But one opposes evil with good, hatred with love, destruction with creativity. Nonviolent struggle humanizes not only the one who practices it, but also, and much more, the one whom it opposes. By returning good for evil it awakens the other's basic humanity. This is the way of Christ on the cross. This is something specific that Christians can offer, because there is nothing more proper to Christianity than Christ dying on the cross, struggling with evil and surrendering, not to evil, but to the Father, who will raise him up. But such nonviolent struggle is not possible without hope.

A CALL TO LIVING WITNESS

The church is the sacrament of unity to which God has called everyone. In a world broken up by injustices of all kinds, one way that the church is called to witness to the Good News is to show concretely that one can shape one's life in accordance with it. This means building up small or large communities where one can live free and equal, loving and sharing, happy and at peace with each other. The whole church is meant to be such a community. The church of the apostles made some tentative efforts along that line, though we also know the divisions that existed at Corinth. Later the monks and religious took up that challenge, while the church as a whole conformed to the world. Such communities of religious may still occasionally provide a model; but it is more a model to inspire symbolically than to imitate, precisely because one has to leave the "world" in order to create a community like that. Maybe the challenge today is to create similar communities of ordinary people living in the world. This could be a type of basic Christian community. The church can hardly proclaim an ideal to the world, if it cannot realize it in at least a small way.

Many theologians in Asia today speak of the need to go beyond the ideal of basic Christian communities to basic human communities. This would be a group of people belonging to different religions but living together as an ideal community. As a matter of fact, in countries like India there are action groups with multireligious membership who try to live such an ideal. In the previous section we spoke of the need for different religions to collaborate to provide a common moral and spiritual basis for public life. Now we should go one step further and suggest that they can also struggle together for the same values where these are denied. This is not an easy thing to achieve. Gandhi in India tried to do this, with his multireligious prayer meetings. But fanatics made it difficult. Actually, Gandhi was shot dead by a religious fanatic as he was walking to such a prayer meeting.

Even a cursory look at the great religious systems around the world could give us an indication of the richness of resources that each religion can offer, even if its practice by its own followers leaves much to be desired. The tribal religions will stress a sense of continuity with life and community that does not abandon an individual to him- or herself. Hinduism will bring a holistic attitude to nature and the world that transcends the dichotomies characteristic of the Greek tradition: nature-supernature, body-soul, reason-emotion, and so on. Buddhism can offer an inner peace, harmony, and compassion with which to face a world of suffering. Christianity witnesses to a deep respect for the other, to the self-giving love of the cross, and to the hope for the resurrection. Islam has a keen sense of justice in social relationships and of absolute dependence on (or surrender to) God.

Speaking of the challenges of justice to evangelization, I have not spoken much about the poor, though I have been talking around them, so to speak. Oppressive poverty has certainly to be struggled against. In this struggle the church should take the side of the poor. But we must avoid a sort of mystique of the "poor." We opt for the poor because we wish to liberate them from their poverty. Poverty, while it can strongly motivate those suffering from it to struggle to overcome it, is not in itself a guarantee for creativity or newness. The poor, just because they are poor, are not free from desires. They often exploit others poorer than themselves. Their very deprivation may sharpen their consumer instincts and make their consumerism more thoroughgoing when there is an opportunity.

To take the side of the poor in a struggle for justice is to challenge the rich. But a class approach that sees the situation in black and white terms may not be the ideal one. The rich, too, may be prisoners of structures which they have inherited, not created. They too need to be liberated and have their consciousness raised. We should then enlist the collaboration of all people of good will. We should not make the poor the object of an ideology. Gandhi, who had some success as a revolutionary, was a practical man who was able to compromise when necessary. He knew the art of the possible.

Besides opting for the poor, the church should choose to *be* poor. Voluntary poverty is the prophetic sign that challenges the selfishness and consumerism that stand at the root of oppressive poverty in the world. Yet it is a difficult sign to live, as the experience of the Religious orders shows. Maybe in the past the church depended on political power and money to spread the gospel. It was standard missionary practice to seek to convert the king or the chief first, hoping that the people would follow their leader. This may be one reason that Europe was never properly Christianized. Today the practicing Christians are a minority, even in the so-called Christian world. Karl Rahner spoke of the church of the future as the "little flock." It may be time for the church to find strength in poverty and humility, to believe in the power of truth, to be ready to die with Christ, to trust in the creativity of the Spirit, to hope in the plan of God for the world, of which the church is called to be the sacrament and witness.

AGENTS OF EVANGELIZATION

Who are the evangelizers in the world today? Until now, missionaries went from the North and the West to the South and the East. The main paradigm of mission was *missio ad gentes—gentes* here meaning not simply people, but Gentiles or pagans, understood as "foreign mission." Even though one can discern today a little movement from the South to the South, it is effectively North-South since it is animated, guided, and sometimes organized by the North. At least the models followed are those set by the North.

MISSION AND THE LOCAL CHURCH

But in recent years a new awareness has been emerging, even if it has not yet influenced policies and programs. I would like to highlight three elements of this awareness that are relevant to our discussion here. The Second Vatican Council has made us aware that the whole church is on mission everywhere. The growing de-Christianization of Europe and the declared need for a new evangelization have made us aware that it is not merely a theoretical perspective. The Ecumenical Affirmation on Mission and Evangelism, elaborated jointly by the Roman Catholic church and the World Council of Churches, speaks of "mission in and to six continents":

Everywhere the Churches are in missionary situations. Even in countries where the Churches have been active for centuries we see life organized today without reference to Christian values, a growth of secularism understood as the absence of any final meaning. The Churches have lost vital contact with the workers and the youth and many others.[39]

Therefore *missio ad gentes*, in the sense of "first proclamation" as specified by *Evangelii Nuntiandi*, is everywhere.

Secondly, thanks to the efforts of missionaries, especially in the past five centuries, we can say that

today, Christians might be a tiny minority in some places but the Church has been established everywhere. Even if a minority, that indigenous Church is officially recognized and is supposed to be self-governing, self-supporting and self-propagating.[40]

These young and small churches need some help from people who have a particular expertise in one or another area. But they should be left free to grow and mature as local churches, taking responsibility also for their task of evangelization. The free influx of foreign people and funds may be detrimental to such maturing. The foreigner, with all good will, brings with him or her models of church institution that may hinder the natural, inculturated growth of such institutions locally. The foreign funds continue to keep the local church dependent in various ways, not only financially. They also give the local church a foreign image, particularly of affluence and power, much beyond the possibilities of the local community, and this might eventually be a counterwitness to the gospel. Suggestions have been made regarding the possibility of financially helping the poor through channels independent of the local church (including the foreign personnel who may be collaborating with it), so that it can carry on its life and witness credibly and with authenticity.[41] Sometimes one hears of the need to establish the church on a firm basis. One wonders whether they are not speaking with the background of models familiar to them back home which may be little suited to local conditions. Examples are not lacking of local communities tempted or forced to put up institutions or adopt structures that they do not need or are not able to maintain. The example of the church in China that has grown in spite of persecution and without any foreign help is worth reflecting on in this context.[42]

The responsibility for mission of every local church has been strongly and clearly affirmed by the International Mission Congress in Manila, meeting in 1979. It speaks of a "new age of mission" and tries to spell out what this newness consists in.

Every local Church is "sent" by Christ and the Father to bring the Gospel to its surrounding milieux, and to bear it also into all the world. For every local Church this is a primary task. Hence we are moving beyond both the vocabulary and the idea of "sending Churches" and "receiving

Churches," for as living communities of the one Church of Jesus Christ, every local Church must be a sending Church, and every local Church (because it is not on earth ever a total realization of the Church) must also be a receiving Church. Every local Church is responsible for its mission, and co-responsible for the mission of all other Churches.[43]

This coresponsibility can be fully understood only in the context of a new ecclesiology of the universal church as a communion of local churches. It is not necessary to go into problems such as how do we delineate a local church (place, culture, people). But however it is delineated, every local church is open to all the others. It is in this context that one can speak of the relevance of a *missio ad extra*, that is, outside one's own local church. But given the responsibility of every local church for its own mission, such missionaries *ad extra* must not merely be sent, but also be asked for and accepted. The Spirit of God gives various charisms to the people, and one of these can be the desire to go out of one's own culture and people to love and serve others. But attitudes and motivations will have to be carefully examined and the person(s) will have to be well prepared for a new type of mission.

GLOBAL MISSION

In the emerging new context of global mission, I wonder whether we should not stop talking about "foreign mission," and think instead of mutuality in mission or of international mission. Obviously, the traditional motivations for "foreign mission," based on need and urgency, would not suffice to explain international or global mission. We have to develop a new theology. Such a theology is possible and has both a factual base and a theoretical perspective.

The factual base can be quickly outlined. Owing to the outreach of the mass media and the rapidity of communications, the world is said to have become a global village. While I doubt this as a cultural reality, there is no doubt that we are open to all sorts of influences. As I tried to point out above, most of the economic and political problems today have a global character, and one cannot really promote justice unless one acts globally—that is, in each country, but with a common purpose and coordinated action. There has also been a large-scale movement of populations that has made pluralism of religions and cultures a reality everywhere. The resurgence and reassertion of the cultures and religions of former colonies have added to the experience of this pluralism. The impact of the oriental religions on the West and the international character of some of the new religious movements cannot be denied. Not only socioeconomic and political structures, but ideologies too spread across frontiers. Human problems like drugs and social challenges like peace and disarmament demand an international approach. The urgency felt today to protect the environment as the common property of all peoples from the selfish and improvident exploitation of some requires a global effort toward a solution. The spread of science and technology may not result in the emergence of a uniform "modern" culture everywhere. On the contrary, the nondescript sameness of technology seems to be provoking people to search for their roots and affirm their separate identities. But the humanistic and naturalistic attitudes and individualistic selfishness and consumerism have an impact on every culture and people, even if these react differently to this impact. Thus the field of mission that needs the human and spiritual values of the gospel is global, both in a geographical sense and in the sense of their being intricately interconnected internationally.

THE PLAN OF GOD

The theological perspective for international mission can be spelled out in two points: the globality of the plan of God for the world and the demands of the catholicity of the church. Meditating on the life, death, and resurrection of Christ, both Paul and John discover the universal outreach of the paschal mystery. Paul speaks of the cosmic Christ who was at the beginning of creation and who will be at the end as the principle of unification of all things (Eph. 1:3–14). This unification extends not only to the human world, but also to the natural and supernatural universe (Col. 1:15–20). It would transcend merely human differences based on birth, sex, or social position (Col. 3:11; Gal. 3:28). Paul is not unaware of sin that divides. That is why he speaks of a redemption and reconciliation. The human role in this process of gathering up all things, and the role of the church to witness to and serve this mystery, are particularly emphasized. Paul also assigns a particular role to the Spirit in the whole process (Rom. 8:13–17). We see a similar development in John. Reflecting on Jesus, he sees in him the incarnate Word in whom everything is created, who enlightens every person coming into the world (John 1:1–9), and who establishes a community of love and self-giving as a mystery of unity that is the communion of the Trinity itself (John 17:20–26).

This universality of the plan of God is also recognized and emphasized by the church. The Second Vatican Council spoke of God as being the common origin and end of all peoples.[44] It spoke of the church as the sacrament of unity among all peoples.[45] John Paul II has also reaffirmed this basic unity of all peoples which he characterizes as divine, prior, and more basic than the divisions that are merely human. He also affirms the one plan of God to actively realize this unity.[46]

There are, however, differences in the way in which one conceives the role of the church in promoting this unity. Traditional mission theology thought that this unity will be achieved only when everything—the world—became church, so that the church is the form of this unity. The church also had the exclusive task of promoting and actualizing this unity. Today more and more people think of the church as the symbol and servant of this unity which is still to be achieved and whose form is a mystery—it is the Reign of God. God is present and active in the world through the Word and the Spirit in many and various ways unknown to and beyond the limits of the church. The church is called to collaborate in this mystery, which may also be served by others besides Christians. This is the teaching of the Council, as I have shown briefly in the beginning. This is behind the appeals made by the Council and the popes after it, not only to Catholics, but to Christians, to the members of other religions, and to all people of good will.[47]

The plan of God for the world has, therefore, global dimensions, and the church, which is at the service of this mystery, has also to think globally.

THE CATHOLICITY OF THE CHURCH

The second element in our reflection on the internationality of mission with reference to the church is its catholicity. The catholicity of the church is not merely extensive, geographical presence. It is intensive in two ways. As a communion of local churches, each of which is inculturated in a particular culture, it should represent in itself the richness and variety of the different cultures of humanity. The church is not merely present everywhere; but it is called to become rooted there, to become incarnate. The catholicity to which the church is called is intensive in a second sense. An ongoing dialogue among the local churches in communion with each other leads to the mutual sharing of their riches so that all converge together towards a community in pluralism. The Council has said it:

> In virtue of this catholicity, the several parts bring their own gifts to one another and to the whole Church, so that the whole and its several parts grow by the mutual sharing of all and by a common effort towards the fullness of unity.[48]

International mission is, therefore, not a practical tactic for the better placement of personnel and finances, but the expression and demand of the catholicity of the church. This catholicity is only the symbol of the catholicity of the final gathering of all the peoples in God's Reign. I have referred above to the awareness of the Asian churches of this international responsibility. Here is the affirmation of the bishops of Latin America, gathered at Puebla:

> Our Churches have something original and important to offer all: their sense of salvation and liberation, the richness of their people's religiosity, the experiences of the basic ecclesial communities, their flourishing diversity of ministries, and their hope and joy rooted in the faith.[49]

In the concrete, this responsibility for international mission will have to be translated in terms of some people who hear a special call for it. One could work in one's own country, either to promote this international spirit or to do advocacy work in favor of other countries and peoples. One could work with international organizations, especially at the socioeconomic and political levels. One could also go to another country and culture as a bearer of this international, crosscultural mission. What are the conditions for the success of such a mission?

THE CROSSCULTURAL MISSIONARY

It is clear that the local church is responsible for its mission. Therefore, anyone coming from outside is there to help, to play a subordinate role, to go away when no longer needed. One has to get acculturated to the local situation: learn the language, get accustomed to the food and climate, adapt oneself to the way of life and customs, and so on. Besides bringing expertise, he or she has to play a number of roles. She or he is the "other" to whom the local people can relate, discovering their own identity in the process. The other can also play a challenging role to help them realize their own imperfections and limitations and to seek to grow out of them. Secondly, the person from another local church is the bearer of the richness of the cultural and spiritual experience of that church. Through him or her that local church is sharing it with the local church that receives her or him. The person, therefore, has a special role of promoting such an intercultural encounter. The person also has a reverse responsibility of carrying back to the local church from which he or she comes the cultural and spiritual riches discovered in the local church in which he or she is living and working now. Such crosscultural missionaries could be called the catalysts of catholicity or promoters of communion. Only insofar as they can integrate in themselves the richness of the two cultures can they effectively fulfill their role of mediation.

As long as mission was seen primarily as the planting of the church, involving the building of a mission compound with church, school, dispensary, and so forth, the stress was on the priests and Religious women and men as missionaries. But in an international mission conceived in these broad terms, the laity come into their own. Without the institutional trappings they may be even more successful and effective in international mission.

The vision of mission as international will lead us to think of promoting not only a North-South and West-East exchange, and perhaps a South-South exchange which often seems to pass through the North, but also a South-North and East-West exchange. There are already some such exchanges at the level of service ministries: for example, hospitals, old peoples' homes, and liturgical functions. Could it rise to higher cultural levels? I do not know. There may be many practical difficulties. Such difficulties may indicate that our international vision may still remain, after all, unidirectional in practice.

This international vision of mission will pose many questions to the traditional missionary institutes. I hope they will rise to the challenge.

MISSION FOR TODAY AND TOMORROW

I have spoken above about a paradigm shift in the theology of mission. The focus of mission has shifted from the church to the Reign of God, from Christ to the Trinity, from the planting of the church to inculturation, liberation, and dialogue. As I am coming to the end of this reflection I wonder whether we are faced with another paradigm shift in the vision and practice of mission.

In the past, mission theology was done from the point of view of the missionaries. The missionaries, of course, had to find some meaning for their particular charism. This is normal in theological reflection. Someone who reflects on mission from an Indian context thinks of the other great religions and the necessary dialogue with them. Someone from Japan, faced with science and technology, finds interreligious dialogue a thing of the past. Besides, people belonging to the Confucian tradition keep saying that their people have a religious sense, but no religion, only a morality. So what could interreligious dialogue mean to them? Where people are still coming to the church in considerable numbers, as in Korea or among the tribals in India, one would obviously speak about planting and building the church. Looking at China, one sees a land of opportunities and challenges. People in Africa wish to reassert their cultural identity, which they think has suffered during the colonial period. Latin America would talk of mission as the liberation of the poor. People in the First World speak of a post-Christian society and of the need for a new evangelization. One's living and working context conditions one's preoccupations and reflections. One should not be surprised if missionaries and Missionary Institutes seek legitimation for their identity and work in their reflection on mission.

At a second stage, with the Second Vatican Council, the reflection tends to become abstract. The vision of the Trinity in mission is beautiful and awe-inspiring. Mission acquires a depth that is cosmic. It is also good to see that the whole church is mission, that mission is everywhere and that everyone is on mission in one's own way. But when mission is everything and everywhere, it does tend to lose a precise focus. Scholastic theology is at home with such universal concepts. But what is gained in terms of freeing oneself from narrow restrictions is lost in precision and focus. This could result eventually in the loss of a certain dynamism in action.

A DIFFERENT POINT OF VIEW

Without denying the advantages that such approaches have—each approach has a relative validity—I shall try to look at mission from a different point of view. My view may be said to have two characteristics: it is a view from below and it is a view from the periphery. As a view from the periphery, it looks at mission not from the point of view of the traditional missionary but from that of an observer. I cannot claim to be an "object" of mission. My vantage point for vision is India. Someone from Africa or Latin America or elsewhere in Asia may have a different point of view. My view is also from below. I do not start with a definition, or with the Trinity. I start with the reality of the world to which we are on mission.

If I look again, for example, at the three integral aspects of mission, namely, inculturation, interreligious dialogue, and liberation, I have a lot of questions. I think we need to focus more accurately their mission dimension. The Melbourne Mission Congress of the World Council of Churches said:

Proclamation is always linked to a specific situation and a specific moment in history. It is God's Good News contrasted with the bad news of that specific situation.[50]

I think that it is a good criterion for evaluation when we have to discern a missionary situation. Mission is prophecy. It is a call to conversion. When Jesus began his mission, he said, "The time is fulfilled, and the kingdom of God is at hand; repent, and believe in the gospel" (Mark 1:15). His teaching and parables challenged the Jews to a decision. Even his miracles were not just acts of compassion, but a symbolic call to reflection and option. He preached the gospel to the poor; but he also challenged the rich, the powerful, the wise. He proposes the vision of a new world; but in the context of that vision he calls for a change of heart and life. Let us look at what we consider mission today from this perspective.

We say that inculturation is mission. Inculturation is generally defined as the incarnation of the gospel in a particular culture. When the gospel encounters a person and that person is influenced by the gospel, this person's changed attitudes and behavior find expression in that person's culture. This is a natural process. Every local church, every group of people who listen to and live the gospel, if they are not prevented from doing so through imposition of foreign cultural forms, do so in their culture: language, customs, symbols, way of life, and so forth. Conversion of these people is mission. I do not see why their expressing in their culture the gospel they have received should be considered mission. For a foreign missionary witnessing to the gospel in a culture that is different from his or hers this may be a problem. But this is the problem of the foreign missionary, not of mission as such. If the primary agent of evangelization is the local church, and if that local church has been struggling with foreign forms imposed on it and is now to trying to discover more inculturated forms, that is a pastoral problem of the local church, which is a legacy of its history. The local church, in trying to inculturate itself, can hardly be said to be doing mission.

On the contrary, when the gospel encounters a culture, raises its prophetic voice against what is limited, imperfect, or sinful in that culture, then it is on mission to that culture. The gospel is on mission in relation to a culture precisely insofar as it is countercultural. Whenever the gospel has inculturated itself too much in a cultural situation, it has not been true to its nature. Paul proclaimed that in the risen Christ there is neither Jew nor Greek, male nor female, slave nor free person. And yet, yielding to the contemporary cultural situation—that is, inculturating himself—he asked slaves to obey their masters and ordered women not to speak in the church. In these areas Paul has not been true to the mission of the gospel. To his credit, it must be said that he did fight for the equality of the Jew and the Greek. The proper process of mission with regard to culture is therefore not inculturation, but being a counterculture. Looking at it in this way we see that the church needs to be as countercultural in Christian countries as in others—perhaps even more so. It is true that in order to be authentically countercultural the church must first be at home in that culture—that is, inculturated. But that is how it should normally be. If churches in Asia and Africa are not yet inculturated, they should be soon, but I do not see it as a task of mission.

One could make a similar analysis with regard to interreligious dialogue. In talking about dialogue one often implies that the other religions are the objects of mission. When other religions were considered evil and they had to be fought against and abolished, then I can see that any contact with them, including dialogue, could be considered mission. But when we have given the other religions a certain legitimacy in the plan of God for the world and the church calls the believers of other religions to collaborate in the common defense and promotion of human and spiritual values, one can hardly consider them anymore as objects of mission in the same sense. Of course, in relating to other religions it is necessary to get to know each other better to remove prejudices and misunderstandings. In a multireligious society this should be a normal way of life. Encounter with other religions becomes mission when through mutual influence religions challenge each other to grow, when in that process they particularly point to the shortcomings in each other, especially to fundamentalistic trends, and thus fulfill a prophetic function. Religions are in mission, when, in dialogue with each other, they fulfill their common prophetic role in society in the defense and promotion of human and spiritual values. At this level the mission itself is mutual. It is the mission of God expressing and manifesting itself in and through the religions. To a non-Indian, Hinduism may be something different to react to. To an Indian Christian, Hinduism is part of his or her heritage, and any dialogue should be first of all interior and personal before becoming exterior. Interreligious dialogue, therefore, is mission, but under specific circumstances with a special focus.

Liberation is also said to be mission. One speaks of preaching the gospel to the poor. The gospel is indeed a message of liberation to the poor. It assures them that God is on their side. To promise that they will be freed from their misery and will attain freedom and plenty here and now may be a more delicate matter. But it seems to me that the real object of the proclamation of the gospel in such a situation is not the poor and the oppressed, but the rich oppressors. It is they who are to be called to conversion. This prophetic focus is sometimes missed because we speak in the abstract about the sinful structures that have to be changed. I wonder whether we can change the sinful structures without changing the sinners. Should we not say, then, that we have a mission to the sinful situation that creates the poor, rather than to the poor themselves? We have a mission *in favor of* the poor. We make a clear option *for* the poor. But our mission is *against* injustice and *against* the oppressors. If we limit ourselves only to the helping of the poor and alleviating their miseries, we are practicing Christian charity and witnessing to Christian love. Some have to do this, too. Such work may be even urgent in some situations. But there may be a temptation to stop with this. The missionary comes as a *deus ex machina*, with seemingly inexhaustible sources of funds. This may effectively be a counterwitness to the poor Christ on the cross. That is why mere charity does not have the same impact as struggling against the oppressors and their structures.

I feel, therefore, that in speaking of inculturation, interreligious dialogue, and liberation as mission in a general way we are somehow missing our target. Inculturation is a way of being. Interreligious dialogue is a useful means. Liberation as opting to be on the side of the poor is a strategy. But the real focus of mission is something else.

If we look around the world today, the striking problems are the unjust economic structures leading to maldistribution, massive poverty, and the exploitation of nature; offenses to human dignity through all sorts of discriminations based on race, caste, religion, or sex; and violence of all sorts, against countries, against others, and against oneself through drugs. I think I do not have to enlarge on these. I have evoked these problems in the section on justice. But the roots of these phenomena are at the human, moral, and spiritual levels. People have become slaves to all sorts of idols and machines: individualism, competition, and restlessness have turned people into machines. Consumerism and collective selfishness witness to a deep moral failure. They are at the root of economic and political exploitation and oppression. People may still have a religious sense; but they have no time for religion, have little actual sense of transcendence, and are largely indifferent to authentic religion.

Human sin is everywhere, and so is mission that announces the Good News and calls us to conversion. Asia, Africa, and Latin America certainly need the challenge of the gospel today in the midst of situations of violence, poverty, injustice, and religious indifference. But if one can read the signs of the times and talk about urgencies and priorities, I wonder whether we should not look at the world with new eyes—from the point of view of the people of the Third World.

Speaking to a group of Asians in April 1947, Gandhi said:

> If you want to give a message to the West, it must be the message of love and the message of truth. . . . I am sanguine if all of you put your hearts together—not merely heads—to understand the secret of the message these wise men of the East [Gandhi counted among these Zoroaster, Buddha, Moses, Jesus, Muhammad, Krishna, and Rama] have left to us, and if we really become worthy of that great message, the conquest of the West will be completed . . . The West is today pining for wisdom. It is despairing of a multiplication of atom bombs. . . . It is up to you to tell the world of its wickedness and sin—that is the heritage your teachers and my teachers have taught Asia.[51]

I wonder whether the situation has very much changed. Where there is more lack of faith, where there are the roots of contemporary injustice, where people have but would not share, where people have less sense of the sacred, where people are indifferent even to their true selves—there is mission today and tomorrow. I think that if there is any urgency about evangelization, it is with this moral crisis that mission must concern itself. Though this moral crisis is present everywhere in the world in various degrees, I wonder whether the really urgent need for the challenge of the gospel today is not in the First World. The problem is so much the more acute there because as post-Christians their sensitivity to the challenges of the gospel is more blunted. In a sense it is easier to think of the poor in the Third World rather than confront the oppressors who keep the Third World poor, and challenge them to a conversion that will be manifested in a change of the unjust structures. After all, people in Asia,

Africa, and Latin America seem to be much more religious and to have a more actual sense of God than the people in many parts of the First World, where there is a growing indifference to God and religion.

People sometimes speak of the third millennium. I do not know how the world will be in another ten years. Let us look at the world today as it is and ask ourselves what and where are the more urgent challenges that face the witnesses to the Good News. I do not intend here to criticize the theories and choices made by people in the past. They reflected on and discerned their task in light of their awareness and of the reality of the world as they saw it. I have only deep respect for their commitment. I do not either intend to play down the needs of the people in the Third World. I would not dare to criticize the charisms and special calls of the Holy Spirit to persons and groups when they are properly discerned. I am talking of a new point of view, of priorities, and urgencies.

I wonder whether in this age of the mass media a community that really lives its Christian faith may not be a more powerful witness of the gospel even across frontiers among other peoples and religions. When Gandhi and other Indians say that they admire Christ but not the Christians, we might resent this distinction that they make between Christ and the church.[52] But can we deny responsibility for such a distinction? In a world that is said to be becoming a global village will not our witness to the gospel be more credible if the Christian world were really Christian?

I do think that today we should look at the challenges rather than at numbers and geography. I think that the real challenges are of a moral nature. Though this moral crisis is everywhere, its epicenter is the post-Christian world. The political and economic elite of the Third World are involved in it too, but they are supported and encouraged in their roles by the First. We cannot ignore the sufferings and the needs of the poor. We need to do what we can to alleviate them. But to promote justice in the world effectively we have to fight against the causes rather than concern ourselves only with the effects. These causes are not merely economic and political, but also, and much more, moral and spiritual. The gospel does not offer us concrete economic and political ideologies. But it is a moral voice crying against injustice and sin. In this its voice is in harmony with the voices of the poor and the oppressed of the earth.

I am not making a simplistic assertion that the mission field today is the First World. I am pointing to a twofold priority whose elements are very much interlinked. There is a moral and spiritual crisis that needs the challenge of the gospel. This crisis seems particularly evident in the First World so that mission there seems an urgency and a priority.

CONCLUSION

I think that the church is called to be at the center of an international moral movement of people. We are familiar with various images of the church in scripture and tradition: the body of Christ, the temple, the sheepfold, the leaven, the People of God, and so forth. I think that the appropriate image for today would be that of a people's movement that is committed to the building up of the Reign of God in this world. The church is aware of and rooted in its own identity as the body of the disciples of Christ, as witnesses in word and deed of the Good News he proclaimed, and as sacraments of his paschal mystery. But the church is also aware of a call to be the sacrament of unity of all peoples. Therefore, it needs to be a community with open frontiers, ready to dialogue and collaborate with everyone in the service of the Reign of God. It needs to be a community alive and sensitive to the mystery of God's action among peoples and in the world, often in ways unknown to it. It needs to be a community involved in the life of the people, and yet standing apart from it in a role of prophecy. It needs to be a community open to the future of the creative newness of the Spirit. It needs to be a community of struggle ready to die in the cause of justice. It needs to be a community of pilgrims, on the way, walking toward the new Jerusalem in which God will be with the people: "God will wipe away every tear from their eyes, and death shall be no more, neither shall there be mourning nor crying nor pain any more, for the former things have passed away" (Rev. 21:4).

NOTES

1. *Ad Gentes*, 2.
2. Ibid., 6.
3. Ibid., 6.
4. See A. M. Henry, "Mission d'hier, mission de demain," in *L'activité de l'église* (Paris: Cerf, 1967), 434–40.
5. *Lumen Gentium*, 16.
6. *Gaudium et Spes*, 22.
7. *Nostra Aetate*, 1.
8. *Dignitatis Humanae*, 3.
9. *Lumen Gentium*, 48–51.
10. Ibid., 5.
11. Ibid., 1.
12. *Gaudium et Spes*, 58.
13. Ibid., 3.
14. Ibid., 92.
15. Federation of Asian Bishops' Conferences, "Evangelization in Modern Day Asia," no. 12, in *For All the Peoples of Asia* (Manila: IMC Publications, 1984), 29.
16. Ibid., nos. 14–15, p. 30.
17. Nos. 17–18.
18. Ibid., nos. 52, 53.
19. *Convenientes ex universo*, Introduction.
20. No. 29.
21. Ibid., 20.
22. Ibid., 53.
23. Pontifical Council for Inter-religious Dialogue, Bulletin 64 (1987): 56–57.
24. Though St. Paul proclaimed the equality of man and woman and slave and free in the risen Christ, he goes on to forbid women to speak in the church and to tolerate slavery. Cf. Brendan Byrne, *Paul and the Christian Woman* (Homebush: St.

Paul, 1988); Elisabeth Schüssler Fiorenza, *In Memory of Her* (New York: Crossroad, 1986).

25. See Philip E. Hammond, ed., *The Sacred in a Secular Age* (Berkeley: University of California, 1985).

26. Pontifical Council for Culture, *Bulletin* 64 (1987): 150.

27. See M. Amaladoss, "The Theological Basis of Religious Pluralism," in S. Arulsamy, ed., *Communalism in India* (Bangalore: Claretian Publications, 1988), 115–38, and the other references there.

28. I have always been struck by St. Paul's refusal to write off the Jews as "Old Testament" and his agonizing over the significance of God's covenant with them. See Romans 9–11.

29. Pontifical Council for Culture, Bulletin 64 (1987): 60.

30. See *Origins* 15:36 (February 20, 1986): 598.

31. See, for example, Swami Abhishiktananda, *La montée au fond du coeur* (Paris: O.E.I.L., 1986).

32. See Allan R. Brockway and J. Paul Rajashekar, eds., *New Religious Movements and the Churches* (Geneva: World Council of Churches, 1987).

33. No. 31.

34. No. 562.

35. *Sollicitudo Rei Socialis*, 41.

36. No. 39.

37. *Sollicitudo Rei Socialis* calls this the right of economic initiative. See no. 15.

38. See *Sollicitudo Rei Socialis*, 41.

39. No. 37.

40. Emmio Mantovahi, "Missionary Societies of the 80's and 90's," *FABC Papers* 43:16.

41. See G. Gispert-Sauch, "Crisis in the Missions," *The Clergy Monthly* 32 (1968): 533–43.

42. The Ecumenical Affirmation refers to the proposal of a moratorium on missionaries and resources. See No. 38.

43. *Towards a New Age in Mission*, Book I (Manila: IMC Publications, 1981): 24.

44. *Nostra Aetate*, 1.

45. *Lumen Gentium*, 1; *Gaudium et Spes*, 92.

46. Pontifical Council for Culture, Bulletin 64 (1987): 56–57.

47. See *Gaudium et Spes*, 92; *Sollicitudo Rei Socialis*, 47.

48. *Lumen Gentium*, 13.

49. No. 368.

50. *Your Kingdom Come* (Geneva: World Council of Churches, 1980), 195.

51. *From Communal Unity*, 579–80, quoted in Wm. Theodore de Bary, *Sources of Indian Tradition* (New York: Columbia University Press, 1958), 273–74.

52. See *Evangelii Nuntiandi*, 16.

AGENDA FOR FUTURE PLANNING, STUDY, AND RESEARCH IN MISSION

GENERAL INTRODUCTION TO THE AGENDA

This Agenda contains those issues which surfaced during the SEDOS Research Seminar on the Future of Mission on March 18–19, 1981, in Rome, Italy. It is not a statement of agreed facts or priorities, but rather an account of what has emerged from our reflection and study in the ten groups which were an integral part of the seminar process. This recorded syllabus contains those elements that emerged as a more general consensus, as well as those that remained as divergences, both of which call us to develop and deepen our understanding, experience, and perspective of mission.

We, therefore, offer this Agenda so that the points it contains may be taken up and explored further in planning, study, and research in view of choices and actions to be taken in the service of mission in the future.

As we now enlarge the horizon of our prayer, reflection, and enquiry by inviting you to join us in the continuation of this process, we hope that we may move toward an ever fuller realization of the Reign of God.

RESULTS OF THE SEDOS SEMINAR ON THE FUTURE OF MISSION, ROME, MARCH 1981

This Agenda is being compiled at the end of ten days of a lived experience shared together by more than one hundred persons from all parts of the world, priests, religious, and laity of the Catholic church, along with some participants invited from the other churches. Some were persons involved in central administration of missionary institutes and religious congregations, others were in various pastoral activities of the church, while some others were "experts" who had been asked to write preliminary papers for the seminar. This report is not intended to be a blueprint for the future of mission, but it is offered humbly as one attempt by some tired drafters working under a time constraint to catch the spirit of the Seminar by sharing some of the results of much discussion, sharing, and praying together in small groups, in plenary sessions, in prayer groups, in the corridors, in the dining room, in the beautiful grounds of Villa Cavalletti situated in the Alban Hills outside Rome, and in the various groups which formed around particular fields of interest as the seminar progressed.

We feel that it is best to arrange the results of the seminar under three broad headings:

A. The Directions in Mission Today

B. The Central Role of the Local Church

C. The Task for Missionary Institutes

There appears to have been a convergence in the seminar taken as a whole around these three key areas, as new and enriched understandings of them developed. The seminar seems to have entered upon a journey which is far from ended. It may only be just commencing.

A. THE DIRECTIONS IN MISSION TODAY

1. The seminar has not been directly concerned with the reasons why the church is missionary. It is presupposed that the established teaching in the Catholic church, at least since the Apostolic Constitution on Evangelization in the Modern World (*Evangelii Nuntiandi*) published in 1975, is that the whole church is missionary at all levels. It is missionary by that nature intended for it by its founder, Jesus Christ, and in view of which it is given the gift of the Holy Spirit. The concern of the seminar has been rather for the manner in which mission is being undertaken today, the how of mission.

2. Four main activities stand out:

a. Proclamation

b. Dialogue

c. Inculturation

d. Liberation of the Poor

The results of the discussions concerned with these four principal activities in the missionary action of the church will be reported separately. However, the close links existing among them in the actual missionary practice of the church need always to be kept in mind. In each activity, considerations emerging from the Seminar upon which there appeared to be some kind of consensus are first reported, and then questions to be explored further in the future are listed.

PROCLAMATION

Considerations which have emerged:

3. The authentic proclamation of the gospel is a witness by word, by the silent witness of action, or by the even more silent presence of a gospel life lived faithfully among others. At the same time it is a listening to life, discovering the presence of God's word and Spirit among a people, a presence which has preceded the missionary. In this way the light of the gospel can continually illuminate the signs of the times to manifest the language which is to be used by the one who proclaims the gospel here and now (*Gaudium et Spes*, 4).

4. The goal of proclamation can therefore be understood according to two models different but complementary:

a) Extending the visible communion of the church

Proclamation here has a "centripetal" purpose, leading people directly into the church, which in this way becomes a visible communion, implanted within a people in a way that it is capable of growing into a full institutional reality.

b) Recognizing and furthering the values of the Reign of God

Proclamation in this model has a "centrifugal" purpose, allowing the power of the gospel to move out and encounter humanity in its struggles and diversity. It entails, in the one who proclaims, a readiness to seek the Christ he or she announces. This kind of proclamation of the gospel is fruitful when it promotes and furthers the values of the Reign within a culture and denounces and inhibits what is not of the Reign of Christ.

5. This second model is achieving more prominence today and may be directing us to what will become the priority in much future missionary proclamation.

6. There remains a need for "full-time" missionaries who are prepared to leave their own country in order to proclaim the gospel in a foreign land. The "ongoing" evangelization of churches already evangelized should not curtail this need for the primary proclamation of the gospel in places where it has never been heard.

7. Statistics indicate that this kind of "full-time" missionary who goes to proclaim the gospel for the first time in a foreign land is coming increasingly from the young churches.

8. The proclamation of the gospel within a church is an ongoing task which is never completed.

9. The courageous defense of the rights of the poor and oppressed, wherever these are violated, directly or indirectly, is a constitutive element in the proclamation made by the church.

10. An authentic proclamation of the gospel is particularly necessary in our times among immigrants and refugees around the world.

11. Questions to be explored for the future:

a) What are the implications for the proclamation of the gospel when we speak today of mission on six continents?

b) Have religious and lay persons in the church a way of proclaiming the gospel that is specifically their own? Prayer and contemplation? Political and social action for justice?

c) What are the criteria to use in order to evaluate an authentic proclamation of the gospel in different regions of the world today, whether it be by word, action, or silent presence?

d) How does one proclaim the gospel to the rich, the powerful, the privileged classes in a culture? By witness of a commitment to gospel values? By making efforts to enlighten them on the need for transformation of existing institutions and accepted attitudes?

e) How can the proclamation of the gospel by different missionary institutes and by different Christian churches be better coordinated to diminish the scandal of divisions?

f) How can listening, learning, and discovering become more a part of the missionary proclamation of the gospel?

g) Are missionaries sufficiently aware of the two models for the proclamation of the gospel and the criteria for deciding which model is to be employed in a particular situation?

DIALOGUE

Considerations which have emerged:

12. If proclamation is concerned chiefly with presenting Christ, dialogue seeks also to find him already present in a given situation. Dialogue involves the humble discernment of the Word of God in other persons, in the institutionalized forms of other faiths, in various ideologies, and in secular realities. Dialogue can take place on many different levels: chance personal encounters, meetings organized at local or regional levels, in national and international conventions.

13. Dialogue is not a diminished form of mission, an expedient to be used only because direct proclamation of the gospel is impossible. It is missionary action and is implied in all genuinely missionary activity. The immediate goal of dialogue is the deeper recognition of Christ in the other through honest and respectful conversation, which involves risks on both sides.

14. Dialogue is an entry into the true mystery of the other person, fostering a kind of "consciousness-raising" in a "dialogue of life." Authentic dialogue effects a kind of conversion by a deeper submissiveness in both parties to the truth, and brings about a kind of mutual "incorporation" with each other in an experience of growing into closer communion (a kind of nonsacramental "baptism"?).

15. Dialogue is a genuine form of Christian witness. Dialogue transforms persons and through them becomes transformative of society and culture. Authentic dialogue with those of other faiths, and even with those who claim to be of no faith, will be a self-evangelization for Christians. Dialogue with other faiths calls for an accompanying dialogue within the Christian community.

16. Concrete situations should be the focus of dialogue, not merely principles and abstract presentations of positions.

17. Dialogue, when carried on in a spirit of faith, readily becomes a prayer dialogue.

18. It is acceptance by Catholics of the "relativization" of the "Catholic Absolute" that the Catholic church is also a "searching" church. This becomes possible only by understanding the life and mission of the church in terms of the larger realities of the risen Christ, the Holy Spirit, and the Reign of God, all of which, of course, though distinct from the church, are inseparable from its total reality.

19. Dialogue always presupposes a desire for the total liberation of one's partner in dialogue and a concrete involvement, wherever possible, in effecting this liberation. Any form of imposition is destructive of authentic dialogue. The "tactical" dialogue or the refusal to dialogue "without conditions" prevents an authentic dialogue.

20. Interior silence, modesty, a recognition of the value of little gestures, no anxiety for quick results, a willingness to be present for the other, a person-

oriented rather than a results-oriented approach—all these are qualities which greatly assist dialogue.

21. Dialogue is greatly helped by a knowledge of the prejudices in the other, especially the image that is held of us as church, as Christians, and as missionaries.

22. Dialogue often calls for some practical follow-up, for example, Paulo Freire's method in Brazil developed after his dialogue with the poor.

23. As a positive response to China's opening to the world, Christians should foster and participate in dialogue and exchanges in economic, scientific, educational, cultural, religious, and other fields.

24. Christians need to be sensitive to the seeds of a future liberation of the poor growing within a culture, and seek to link these with the first flowering of the Reign already present in the church.

25. Dialogue presupposes faith in the interior action of the Holy Spirit within human hearts.

26. Christian monks and nuns have a privileged place in the church's dialogue with the great religions of Asia.

27. A "dialogue of life" is implied in any real sharing of life and calls for a willingness to give and receive and to take part in life together.

28. Questions to be explored in the future:

a) How can structures within the Christian community be better organized so that the fruits of dialogue with those of other faiths or ideologies can become an effective means of animating the ongoing dialogue within the Christian community at all levels?

b) Can we better structure our missionary institutions, buildings, work, and lifestyle to create an atmosphere more conducive to dialogue?

c) Can the polarizing tendencies often occurring between the methods of analysis and dialogue be satisfactorily reconciled in practice?

d) Is the dialogue between missionaries of different Christian churches, often occasioned and stimulated by a shared missionary concern, given sufficient time and attention by missionaries? Are they sufficiently aware of the strengths and weaknesses in the classically Catholic, Evangelical, and Reformed traditions?

e) Is education for the missionary task of dialogue with those of other faiths and of various ideologies receiving sufficient attention in the formation planned for their members by Missionary Institutes? What formation for dialogue should be given to all? To future specialists in dialogue? (Cf. Asian Theological Conference of 1979. V. Fabella, ed., *Asia's Struggle for Full Humanity*, Orbis, 1980.)

f) Are missionaries sufficiently convinced that dialogue has a solid spiritual basis? That it can be an experience that is genuinely kenotic? That it can become for persons a first entry into the *mysterium tremendum* of God and into the basic experience of all faith, "I am not alone in the world"?

g) Can we accept that the first source of and supreme model for all dialogue, understood as a facing of the other in total honesty and truth, are to be located in the great mysteries of Christian faith: the Trinity (John 1:1), the incarnation (John 1:14), and the Holy Spirit (John 20:22)?

INCULTURATION

Considerations which have emerged:

29. Inculturation has its source and inspiration in the mystery of the incarnation. The Word was made flesh. Here flesh means the fully concrete, human, and created reality that Jesus was. Inculturation, therefore, becomes another way of describing Christian mission. If proclamation sees mission in the perspective of the Word to be proclaimed, inculturation sees mission in the perspective of the flesh, or concrete embodiment, which the Word assumes in a particular individual, community, institution or culture.

30. What is inculturated is the gospel, or more correctly, faith in the gospel. In this sense, inculturation is essential to all authentic missionary action. It cannot, however, be artificially induced, but needs to flow spontaneously from the personal faith of people, expressed within the symbols and institutions of their own particular culture.

31. Inculturation cannot be artificially induced, but occurs naturally when the liberating message of the gospel is joined to the liberative struggles of the local communities.

32. Inculturation of faith in the gospel by Christians of a different culture will mean for the church a new discovery of the gospel which she proclaims authoritatively to all people, and therefore a new enrichment for the life of the church.

33. Inculturation will always bring a new healing, purification and transformation of a culture.

34. Through authentic inculturation of a people's faith in the gospel, Christ becomes concretely alive in that culture.

35. The importance of basic communities in the process of inculturation is stressed, whether these be ecclesial communities confessing and celebrating the gospel, communities of faith socially involved, or communities of solidarity between peoples of different faiths or differing opinions.

36. Inculturation of the gospel remains always the responsibility of the Christian community, of which the missionary is part.

37. With regard to the great heritage of Chinese culture, Christians are encouraged to deepen their appreciation and understanding of its values, in the spirit of Matteo Ricci. A thorough inculturation of the gospel with Chinese ways of thinking and living will enrich the whole church.

38. Inculturation calls for a special kenosis in the missionary who disposes himself or herself for change and participation in the creative inculturation undertaken by the whole Christian community in a particular place. The missionary is called to be a catalyst of inculturation rather than its agent.

39. Questions to be explored in the future:

a) Some believe that inculturation as a process of missionary action should be subordinated to liberation. They argue that inculturation is a by-product of involvement with the less privileged people in their struggles. Inculturation without involvement in liberation results in the institutional church identifying with an elitist culture—which is the situation in many third-world countries.

b) Inculturation implies local responsibility. In what way is this compatible with a centralized organization with common doctrines and a uniform discipline?

c) What are the implications for the universal church of inculturation as a basic missionary principle? For the local church? For the missionary?

d) Is inculturation of the gospel among a particular people possible without its assuming at the same time social and political dimensions?

e) What are the particular implications of the process of inculturation within an Islamic culture?

f) How can the gospel continue to be a challenge to people after it has become inculturated?

g) To what extent should a missionary leave behind his or her own culture?

h) Will the process of inculturation in the young churches inevitably mean successive stages of declericalization, deromanization, and decentralization of the church?

i) Will inculturation increase the participation of the laity within the church?

j) How can missionaries best prepare themselves to identify, use, and enhance the symbols already existing within a particular culture?

k) Are the ecumenical possibilities of the inculturation of the gospel at a local level sufficiently explored?

l) Are missionaries sufficiently prepared to re-examine their own understanding of truth in the light of inculturation experiences in the young churches?

LIBERATION OF THE POOR

40. Liberation as a dynamic of mission today is a thread which has woven itself through discussions of all the challenges we face in mission. To capture the range of discussion and debate on what has become a central concern in missionary activity in many parts of the world is difficult, if not impossible.

While there was not a clear consensus on an exact meaning of "liberation," "poor," "class," yet all the members recognized their importance.

The considerations which follow here from the discussions are grouped roughly into three areas: liberation and the gospel, issues in liberation, and the response of Christians to the struggle for liberation.

Considerations which have emerged:

41. The message which Jesus preached was Good News to the poor, freedom for captives. Jesus' own direction of his message of liberation in a special way to the poor is the basis for liberation theology. Puebla reaffirms this in its preferential option for the poor.

42. The process of evangelization can be seen as the process of liberation of the poor.

43. The gospel as liberation of the poor emphasizes the prophetic aspect of evangelization. It calls for an analysis of the anti-Reign values in a situation and a witness to Reign values, recognizing the seeds of liberation present.

44. The poor should not be understood as objects of our evangelization. Rather, since the gospel is meant for them in a special, even primary way, they understand the gospel message of liberation better than others. Because of this, they are the agents of evangelization.

45. "The poor" refers to those who are deprived in a systematic fashion of the means for the fullness of life by another group. Most commonly, this means deprivation of material means of subsistence and deprivation of basic human rights. It is sometimes used in an extended sense to mean a group of people deprived in some nonmaterial fashion (for example, women—as the poor).

46. Overcoming the deprivation, or oppression, of the poor will ordinarily involve conflict. This overcoming of the oppressive situation involves: analysis of the situation; struggle between the opposing forces (poor and rich); resolution of the struggle.

47. Many forms of social analysis are used. Analysis drawn from a marxist critique of oppressive patterns in society is commonly used, although by no means exclusively. A clear set of tools is needed, since patterns of oppression tend to be interlocked from a local to a global scale.

48. Liberation theology can be understood as a form of theological reflection which is part of the analysis in the process of ending oppression.

49. The struggle between poor and rich usually follows lines of class (as in much of Latin America), race (as in South Africa), or sex (in many parts of the world). The struggle is marked by violent confrontation—either a violence from the side of the oppressor to maintain the oppressive situation, or from the side of the oppressed to counter and overcome the oppressor's violence.

50. Social analysis reveals the widespread, even global character of oppression. For this reason, commitment to the saving message of Jesus Christ entails commitment to the liberation of the oppressed. This commitment means engagement in the struggle for justice and an end to oppressive structures.

51. The struggle for justice reveals in a special way the relation between liberation and other dynamics of mission. Genuine dialogue in a situation leads to a commitment to the oppressed partner and so to justice. Genuine inculturation happens best when it involves first immersing oneself in the liberative streams of the people. Proclamation of the gospel involves a genuine enactment of the liberative message for the poor.

52. More than one pattern of social analysis is needed. Latin America has developed its theology of liberation in responding to the marxist critique. Asia is developing its liberation theology also by identifying the liberative stream in religions and cultures, and joining the Christian experience to this stream. Asia has also noted the power of voluntary poverty, as practiced in the great monastic traditions, for the transformation of society. The Asian bishops have also urged the "dialogue of life" as part of the solidarity of the struggle for liberation:
—which involves working with and learning from the poor
—in the process of participation in the transformation of unjust social structures
—being a "constitutive dimension of the preaching of the Gospel, i.e., the mission of the Church" (Asian bishops are quoting the Synod of Bishops, Rome, 1971).
The tools of social analysis must fit the concrete circumstances of a situation.

53. Even in situations where liberation is proclaimed, as in socialist regimes, new forms of oppression often occur. These need to be criticized and struggled against in socialist regimes as much as in capitalist regimes.

54. In the conflict between poor and rich, both poor and rich need to be liberated from the relations of oppression. Christians insist upon liberation of both. How the rich are liberated is a matter of dispute. Some say through consciousness-raising; others say through the liberation first of the poor.

55. If Christians are to be true to the liberative message of the gospel, they must align themselves with the oppressed in the struggle to bring justice and love. They must take care not to consider themselves the sole liberators; often solidarity with the oppressed means aligning oneself with liberation movements already alive among the people.

56. Just as the net of oppression tends to be global, so must Christians bring their own international networks to bear upon the struggle for justice.

57. Social analysis is an integral part of Christian spirituality. The commitment to justice is part of the response to the gospel.

58. In solidarity with the struggle of oppressed people, the Christian is faced with the possibility of engaging in various forms of violence, including armed violence, against the oppressive forces. How to decide about this is a controversial question. There is a tradition of nonviolence as the response to oppressive power in the gospel. There is also a tradition that permits violence in some circumstances. Depending upon circumstances, Christians may be called to engage in violence in some instances.

59. On responses of missionary institutes to the pursuit of justice, see Part C.

60. Questions to be explored in the future:

a) What has been the effect of our responses to injustice?

b) How consistent are we in our commitments to justice? How is it reflected in our policies and use of resources?

c) Many of our home bases for our missionary institutes are in first-world countries, which are often the oppressors of third-world countries. How have we responded to that situation? Has there been an analysis?

d) What role does justice play in our formation programs?

e) What are the elements of a new missionary spirituality that responds to this mission to the poor?

B. THE CENTRAL ROLE OF THE LOCAL CHURCH

Considerations which have emerged:

61. The church is a communion directed toward mission, a mission whose goal is communion in Christ, among all people. It is a people gathered to be sent, and sent to be gathered. In this perspective the classical description of communion as the planting of the church remains valid. The church is called and sent to be the sign and the instrument of communion and solidarity among all people, a foretaste of the coming Reign of God. It fosters and deepens communion together with its constitutive dimensions of justice and peace, wherever they occur already, and seeks to create them where they are not. A "worthy" participation in the eucharist, summit and source of the church, presupposes a lived communion among people (1 Cor. 11:29). The church must

be ready to recognize true freedom wherever it is emerging and proclaim the reality of this freedom given already in Christ.

62. Not only a conversion of hearts is needed for new churches, but a conversion to new structures which encourage the recognition of the charisms present in the people, foster new ministries in accord with these charisms, and stimulate coresponsibility at the grassroots level of the church. Communion requires firstly interdependence, not dependence. Catholic communion is meant to be a pluriform unity, and such a unity in diversity can only be achieved from below. How can we form "churches of the people," places of human solidarity and Christian communion?

63. In the Catholic understanding it is this communion of all these local churches that forms the universal church — the *ecclesia ecclesiarum* — having as its bond of unity the local church of Rome. It is this universal church which is endowed with the missionary mandate of Jesus. However, for certain historical reasons, the local church of Rome has for some centuries reserved this mission to itself and has, through the Congregation for the Evangelization of Peoples (CEP), extended itself to many territories and has established many churches under its jurisdiction. Thanks to Vatican II, these local churches now recognize their "right and duty" for self-government (Vatican II, *Decree on Ecumenism* and *Decree on Eastern Rite Churches*). They believe they have an equal share in the mission of the church and they have a right and duty to initiate new missions without thereby being accused of encroaching on any "exclusive" rights of the Roman church with which they are in communion.

However, the present structures geared to excessive centralism do not help such missionary initiatives to flower in local churches.

64. This observation in no way implies a disregard for the special charism of Rome as the bond of communion. In fact, it was with pain that we participated in the several sessions on the fate of the Chinese Christians who suffered and still suffer for their allegiance to the faith and the papacy, and we pray that communion be established between all Chinese Catholics so that they may once more become a self-governing local church of China, in communion with Rome and in the service of the Chinese people.

65. The other point we make is that the old distinction between mission-sending and mission-receiving churches is becoming blurred. This is partly because of the vitality of the young churches which generates vocations and a parallel dimension of the number of missionaries in the older churches. This situation should help strengthen the conviction that all are mission-sending as well as mission-receiving churches. The mutual mission to one another thus becomes a further reinforcement of the communion of local churches. One, of course, immediately senses the need for structures that should help exchange of missionaries among the churches, structures that complement the CEP. It is hoped that each local church will, according to its specific charism, produce the type of specialized missionary that other local churches require. Mission institutes have a role to play in this.

66. Besides the exchange of personnel, there is a great urgency for an exchange of information. First of all, in the matter of justice, a communication

system between the poorer churches that are most concerned with it and the churches of the affluent countries would facilitate global consciousness-raising on various issues. A similar network of information on the research, surveys and analyses done in so many centers of theological and pastoral reflection would be useful.

67. Sharing of funds is already done. Organizations like Misereor, Missio, and Caritas are splendid examples. It is normally the receiving church that determines the needs and the modes of spending. Massive development projects in local churches which are found amidst non-Christians can be construed as a form of colonialism if such projects turn the Christian community into an island of wealth and power amidst poverty. Expansion of institutes with no visible improvement among the poor is a clear sign of this. Care should be taken not to compromise the missionary witness and prophetic call to simplicity and poverty in the Third World by indiscriminate use of funds coming from richer churches. The local church must involve the people in the decision-making process if it wants to avoid such mistakes.

68. The fundamental revitalization of local churches takes place through a process of evangelization at the grassroots, through a kenosis by which they shed elitist cultures of dominant classes and appropriate the culture of the poor, the primary addressees of the Good News. It is with such self-liberative acts of kenosis that young local churches can acquire missionary efficacy toward those in their immediate environment and towards other older churches.

69. Coming now to the internal life of the local churches, we realize that it exists at various levels of communion: domestic, parochial, and diocesan. Besides these accepted forms, there has evolved the structure known as basic communities, the ultimate constituents of local church. In our reflections we have assigned to them a primary role in the formation of leaders (missionaries). The following observations have been made:

a) The basic communities are the origin of missionary vocations as well as the locus of their formation.

b) It is vital for basic communities to preserve the principle of subsidiarity whereby what can be decided or executed at the grass-roots level is not to be decided or executed at a higher level. Rather than delegate powers from above, the central authority of the local church should discern, catalyze, and coordinate what takes place below in these basic communities.

c) It is then in basic communities that new leadership is formed and, possibly, that new ministries are born. The restoration of the laity to their missionary role is easier in such new communities. It is there that the lay person becomes a missionary to his or her own people.

70. Questions to be explored in the future:

a) What structures would you envisage as means for furthering missionary exchanges among the local churches? How would such structures relate to the CEP?

b) With the increasing cultural pluralism and diversification of local churches, what new means should we adopt for maintaining communion among them? What role does the exchange of missionaries play in this?

c) What ways are open to members of local churches to venture out across new missionary frontiers (for example, among a particular class of people, religious group, culture, and so forth, outside the churches)? Are lay initiatives subject to Canon Law and episcopal jurisdiction? What relationship does a missionary have towards the local church?

d) For questions on ecumenism, inculturation, and dialogue in the local church, see A, above.

C. THE TASK FOR MISSIONARY INSTITUTES

71. While the future of mission has been the overall concern of this SEDOS Research Seminar, the issue of what this future means for missionary institutes is a focal concern. The kind of future which missionary institutes have, and how to meet the challenges of that future, have shaped many of the discussions during the Seminar.

The considerations which have emerged and the questions for further exploration in the future are presented here in four sections:

— Missionary institutes in the church's mission
— Formation for the future
— Communication between missionary institutes
— Building communication between missionary institutes and the local churches

MISSIONARY INSTITUTES IN THE CHURCH'S MISSION

72. This section deals with the specific role of the missionary institutes in the church's mission, both as to the nature and purpose of such Institutes, and specific areas with which missionary institutes should be concerned.

Considerations which have emerged:

73. There are persons in local churches called to missionary vocations, and missionary institutes provide a vehicle for them to respond to God's call.

74. That vocation often entails leaving one's home church and culture to engage in proclamation of the gospel, dialogue, participation in the life of other local churches, struggle for liberation with the poor.

75. For this reason, some missionary institutes should be international in character.

76. Many missionaries are now coming from countries which were themselves considered until recently as "mission countries"; hence the need for international missionary institutes to mediate these vocations.

77. Evangelization in churches previously evangelized can also be a task for missionary institutes.

78. The aspect of evangelization stressed in the charism of the institute (for example, proclamation, dialogue, struggle for liberation, communion, and so on) may give a special character to the missionary institute.

79. The missionary institutes foster dialogue between local churches.

80. The presence of missionaries from another church and culture in a local church can create a positive tension to stimulate response to the call of the gospel.

81. International missionary institutes can witness to multicultural values within their structures and membership.

82. Missionary institutes can serve as a link in the total network of alliances for the liberation of persons and societies.

83. Missionary institutes can oppose global oppression on the international level and serve as advocates for the poor.

84. Missionary institutes can foster dialogue between the rich and the poor.

85. Missionary institutes should embrace the preferential option for the poor.

86. Questions to be explored in the future:

a) Are our current structures adequate for the future task we face?

b) What role do Contemplative Institutes play in the future of mission?

c) Will decline in numbers lead to amalgamation of some missionary institutes, especially those originating in countries where few or no vocations are forthcoming?

FORMATION FOR THE FUTURE

87. Formation policies and programs commensurate with the future task of mission will need to be decided upon.

Considerations which have emerged:

88. More effort needs to be directed toward searching for those persons who may have missionary vocations.

89. Formation programs should not alienate candidates from the people with whom they are to work, especially the poor, by accommodating them to a more affluent class.

90. Local churches have a large part in forming missionary vocations and in their training for work.

91. New centers for spirituality and social concern, as well as local communities, should be as much a part of formation as traditional structures such as seminaries and novitiates.

92. Formation for leadership of communities should stress skills which facilitate communion, inaugurate social analysis, and empower people in the local church.

93. A new spirituality for mission will be needed to meet the challenges of the future. This spirituality includes not only traditional individual practices of spirituality (private prayer and asceticism, combat of sin and temptations, discernment, and so on), but also the societal dimension of all these practices, particularly as they relate to justice.

94. The new spirituality will need to deal in a special way with formation to justice and to intercultural sensitivity.

95. In the intervening time until such a new spirituality can be worked out, missionary institutes should be especially sensitive to those charismatic persons opting out of current structures and struggling to find new forms of missionary life. They need the protection and support of the missionary institutes.

96. Items to be explored in the future:

a) A kind of checklist needs to be developed of the attitudes and skills necessary in the missionary candidate for the future.

b) Revision of programs may be necessary to ensure proper areas of study.

c) Revision of training may be necessary to include training of candidates in the local community, in a situation outside the candidate's home culture, and so forth.

COMMUNICATION BETWEEN MISSIONARY INSTITUTES

97. This section deals with structures already used and others envisioned to promote communication between missionary institutes. It is also concerned with how these communication networks might promote more effective work in achieving the goals of mission.

Considerations which have emerged:

98. Many structures have emerged since Vatican II to promote contact between religious institutes in general and missionary institutes in particular (for example, UISG, USG, SEDOS). These structures need to be evaluated in light of their effectiveness for mission.

99. The kinds of Justice and Peace Commissions found within religious institutes need to be extended to a network among religious institutes, for example, the Justice and Peace Commissions of the UISG and USG working together with SEDOS.

100. Such new networks for global solidarity in justice should also work with other international networks, such as Amnesty International and that of the World Council of Churches.

101. Such new networks for justice should be concerned with the gathering of information, with the ability to mobilize quick response to pressing situations, and with providing solidarity and support to local communities that are struggling for justice.

102. Networks for other kinds of information exchange, for example, about needs for specific kinds of personnel, and their availability, should be developed.

103. Where possible, structures for communication already existing should serve as the base for expanding these networks of communication.

104. Questions to be explored in the future:

a) Are there other needs for collaboration, particularly in view of the challenges of mission for the future, which need to be identified?

b) Who will take the initiative in beginning discussions which will lead to the new or expanded networks?

BUILDING COMMUNICATION BETWEEN MISSIONARY INSTITUTES AND THE LOCAL CHURCHES

105. This section deals with special activities of missionary institutes in local churches, lines of communication and decision-making between missionary institutes and local churches, and the issue of financial assistance.

Considerations which have emerged:

106. Missionaries can serve as catalysts for dialogue and for inculturation.

107. Missionary institutes' commitment to justice must be manifest in local churches by engagement in the struggles for liberation of the people.

108. The structures of missionary institutes should provide for contact at the

level of local churches, especially to provide information pertinent to discernment of future directions for the Institute.

109. The issues of flexibility and mobility for missionary institutes are most real in the Institute's relation to the local community.

110. The work of the missionary institute in a given area is guided also by the discernment of the local church.

111. The greater part of evangelization may be carried on by the local church since it is already inculturated. There may be instances, however, where it is better done by missionary institutes.

112. Financial assistance from missionary institutes should be used in local churches to enable local people to achieve their genuine objectives.

113. Funding should occur only after thorough consultation with local communities. This consultation often involves helping local communities unlearn patterns of expectation about funding inherited from the past.

114. An important criterion for dispersal of funds is how funded projects will be sustained over a longer period of time.

115. Funding should always have in mind the progressive achievement of self-sufficiency of the local church in the area of finance.

116. Patterns of funding should not result in priests and religious living on different levels and being able to carry out their work with differing levels of resources within the same local area. Moreover, all should be living at the same level as the people with whom they work.

117. Consideration should be given to missionary institutes' sources of funding, e.g., contributors in home countries. Raising their consciousness about how their money is used is important, as well as increasing their awareness of injustice in their own home countries.

118. Questions to be explored in the future:

a) How will these understandings of missionary institutes' relations to local churches affect relations with local leaders, especially bishops?

b) Can there be cooperation between missionary institutes in a given area to equalize the kind of funding provided by their respective members?

c) What will flexibility and mobility mean in this understanding of the relations between missionary institutes and local churches? How will it be achieved?

CONCLUSION

119. In addition to the general themes of the seminar, which were discussed in all the groups and have been listed in this report, a number of groups met spontaneously during the seminar to discuss particular questions. They were the Asian group, the African group, the group on Islam, the group which discussed missionary institutes, and the group on justice and peace. Each of these groups presented separate reports to the Plenary Assembly which are not included in this general report.

Also, each day, consolidated reports on the discussions which took place in all the groups were prepared by the drafting committee and circulated to all.

These contain further material on the themes which is not completely incorporated into this final report.

Finally, the drafters would like once again to confess their limitations and beg forgiveness in advance for contributions that were distorted by us or omitted. In a seminar of such variety, divergences of opinion were plentiful. While presenting what we saw as the main lines of the themes discussed in the seminar, we have tried to respect minority views, although we know that we have not fully succeeded. We trust that the Holy Spirit will further in all of us the work begun during this seminar.

CONTRIBUTORS

MICHAEL AMALADOSS, SJ, is a liturgist and theologian. He taught theology at the Institute of Religious Studies, Delhi, India and was editor of *Vidyajyoti*. At present, he is Assistant to the Superior General of the Jesuits in Rome. He is Vice-President of the International Association of Mission Studies and past member of the SEDOS Executive Committee. He is also a member of the editorial board of *Spiritus*.

MARCELLO AZEVEDO, SJ, was President of the Brazilian National Conference of Religious Men and Women for nine years. He is presently a member of the John XXIII Center for Research and Social Action in Rio de Janeiro. He is author of *Basic Christian Communities in Brazil* and *Vocation for Mission*.

PIERRE DELOOZ was for many years a research fellow in Pro Mundi Vita, Brussels.

ANDREW EDELE is a member of the Society of the Missionaries of Africa. He worked in the city of Lusaka helping to form small Christian communities. He is presently working in Lilongwe, Malawi, where he is parish priest at Kanengo.

JOHN FUELLENBACH, SVD, has been the Director of the SVD Renewal Center at Nemi. He is Professor of Theology at the Gregorian University, Rome.

IVONE GEBARA, CSA, has a degree in Theology from the Catholic University of Louvain and a Doctorate in Philosophy from the Catholic University of São Paulo. She has taught philosophy and theology in the Institute of Theology of Recife for the past sixteen years and for twelve years has been a member of a team which forms young people for pastoral work in the church of northeast Brazil.

BOKA DI MPASI LONDI, SJ, from Kisantu in Zaire teaches Pastoral Theology at Lumen Vitae, Brussels; the Gregorian University, Rome and in Nairobi. He is editor of *TELEMA*.

JOSE MARINS is a diocesan priest from São Paulo, Brazil; **CAROLEE CHANONA** is a Sister of Mercy from Belize; **THEOLIDE TREVISAN, ICM,** is from Brazil. All three form an itinerant pastoral team which emerged in response to the Bishops' Conference of Medellín in 1968. They accompany the church's efforts to implement the Medellín Conference at the grass-roots level.

NGINDU MUSHETE is a diocesan priest from Zaire and former Professor of Theology at the Catholic University of Kinshasa, Secretary of the Center for the Study of African Religions, founding member of both the Ecumenical Association of Third World Theologians (EATWOT) and the Ecumenical Association of African Theologians, and member of the editorial board of *Concilium*.

DESMOND O'DONNELL, OMI, is a clinical psychologist by profession. He studied Modernity and Secularization at St. Paul's, Ottawa. He has lectured in Britain, the USA, Ireland, South Africa, and Australia. He is Regional Councillor for Asia/Oceania for the Oblates of Mary Immaculate.

EFOÉ-JULIEN PENOUKOU was born in Benin and has a Doctorate in Theology and Anthropology and a Masters in Political Sociology; Professor at the Catholic Institute of West Africa (ICAO) at Abidjan in the Ivory Coast since 1979; Dean of the Faculty of Theology there since 1985; consultor to the Pontifical Commission on Inter-Religious Dialogue.

BISHOP SAMUEL RUIZ has been bishop of San Cristobal de las Casas, Chiapas, Mexico, for over twenty-five years. He attended the Second Vatican Council and had a key role in the Medellín and Puebla Conferences. He is fluent in all five Indian (Mayan) languages spoken in his diocese.

JYOTI SAHI is an artist and theologian. He founded the Indian School of Art for Peace (INSCAPE) at Bangalore as a center for reflection on the relation of Christian art to inculturation. He and his wife and children live in a small lay ashram.

SIDBE SEMPORE, OP, is from Burkina Faso in West Africa. In 1986 he was appointed Novice Master in Abidjan, Ivory Coast, and he continues to teach Scripture. He has published articles and studies on Afro-Christian Churches—"Popular Religion in Africa: Benin as a Typical Instance," in *Concilium*, August 1986.

TERESITA WEIND is a Sister of Notre Dame de Namur and has been Liturgical Coordinator for the African American parishes in the diocese of Chicago. She received her Master of Theology degree from Mundelein College in Chicago in 1972. Teresita is Pastoral Associate at St. Catherine's parish near Chicago.

FELIX WILFRED was born in India. For the past fourteen years he has been teaching Systematic Theology in St. Paul's Seminary, Tiruchirapalli. He is a member of the Vatican's International Theological Commission and acting Executive Secretary of the Theological Advisory Committee to the Federation of Asian Bishops' Conferences.

PART II

EMILIO CASTRO is Director of the World Council of Churches' Commission on World Mission and Evangelism.

THOMAS CULLINAN, OSB, is a monk of Ampleforth Abbey and currently based near Liverpool. He is a noted speaker and author of *The Passion of Political Love*.

HELOISE DA CUNHA, RSCJ, works with basic Christian communities in Compira Gronde, Brazil.

EUGENIA D'COSTA is from Bangladesh and a member of the Congregation of Our Lady of the Missions. She attended the Pontifical Institute for Islamic and Arabic Studies in Rome.

GRACIELLA ESTRADA, MB, is a member of the Congregation Missioneria di Berriz and a community leader in the church of Guatemala.

ARMAND GARON, MAfr., was Director of the Pontifical Institute for Islamic and Arabic Studies in Rome. He is recently deceased.

CATHARINA HALKES is Professor of Feminist Theology at the Catholic University of Nijmegen where she is also engaged in research.

DESMOND HARTFORD is a member of the Society of St. Columban working in a largely Muslim area in the southern Philippines. For several years he lived with Muslim families.

ARCHBISHOP DENIS HURLEY is Archbishop of Durban, South Africa, and former President of the Southern African Bishops' Conference. He is the acknowledged leader of the Catholic church's opposition to apartheid.

RONALD LARKIN, MSC, is assistant to the Superior General of the Missionaries of the Sacred Heart.

SARA CASANOVA LOZADA, MMI, is a member of the Congregation Missionaria di Maria Immaculata. She has responsibility for a parish of Native American people in Ecuador.

BOB McCAHILL is a Maryknoll Father who has worked for many years in Bangladesh.

BISHOP BASIL MEEKING is Bishop of Christchurch, New Zealand. He was the former Secretary of the Vatican Secretariate for Promoting Christian Unity.

ALBERT NOLAN, OP, was born in South Africa and entered the Dominican Order in 1954. He has been engaged in pastoral work among the poor and was for many years a university chaplain. He now works for the Institute for Contextual Theology in Johannesburg.

DAVID POWER, OMI, is a Professor of Systematic Theology in the Department of Theology of the Catholic University, Washington, D.C.

BERNARD PRZEWOZNY is a tenured member of the Pontifical Theological Faculty of St. Bonaventure. Since 1981 he has been following the ecological crisis and environmental degradation in the name of the Franciscan group of Ministers General. He was instrumental in having the Franciscan Center for Environmental Studies in Rome.

MARIA ARLINDA RODRIGUEZ is a member of the Congregation of the Missionary Sisters of the Immaculate Conception in Joao Ressoa, Brazil. She and other members of her Congregation have made dialogue with the poor and the insertion of Religious life a priority in the Congregation.

ROBERT SCHREITER, CPPS, is a professor at the Catholic Theological Union in Chicago where he teaches Systematic Theology and History of Religions. He is Codirector of the Chicago Institute of Theology and Culture and author of *Constructing Local Theologies.*

JULIENNE DE WOLF, ICM, cooperates with the Farm Workers' Legal Services in North Carolina, USA.

MARCELLO ZAGO, OMI, was Secretary of the Vatican Secretariat for Non-Christian Religions. He is presently Superior General of the Oblates of Mary Immaculate.

ARCHBISHOP JEAN ZOA is Archbishop of Yaoundé in Cameroon, past President of the Episcopal Conference of Cameroon, and Vice-President of SECAM, the Federation of Episcopal Conferences of East Africa and Madagascar. He has encouraged the formation of basic ecclesial communities and the formation of lay leaders.

PART III

SEAN FAGAN, SM, held the position of Professor of Ethics and Lecturer in Moral Theology at the Pontifical Athenaeum in Ireland. Fr. Fagan is well known in Ireland for his interviews on radio and television. He has conducted retreats and renewal courses for priests and religious on four continents. He is a frequent contributor to theological and pastoral journals in Ireland and author of the much-discussed *Has Sin Changed?* which has gone through four editions. He is currently Secretary General of his congregation.

MATILDA HANDL, OSB, was born in Czechoslovakia and entered the Missionary Benedictines in 1952 in Tutzing. She was sent to the USA to complete her formation. She has worked in the Winnebago Indian Reservation in northeastern Nebraska. She was elected Prioress in Norfolk, Nebraska, and re-elected in 1987. For six years just prior to being elected to the General Council of her Congregation in Rome she served on the Archdiocesan Pastoral Council as an Executive Member.

DEIRDRE McLOUGHLIN was born in Zimbabwe and raised in Dublin. She qualified as a physiotherapist and practiced in Ireland, Nigeria, and Canada. Deirdre has served as the Executive Director of the Institute of Concern for Public Health in Toronto and made a permanent commitment to the Spiritan Congregation in 1984.

DERMOT McLOUGHLIN was born in Dublin where he later qualified as a physician. He was in charge of the leprosy unit at Abakaliki, Nigeria, and presently is Chief of Service at Chedoke Hospital, Hamilton, Ontario. He made a permanent commitment to the Spiritan Congregation in 1984.

DONALD NICHOLL was born in England and educated at Oxford University. During World War II he served with the British Army in the Far East. He has taught at Oxford and Edinburgh Universities as well as being Rector of the Ecumenical Institute for Theological Research, Tantur, Jerusalem. He has been a visiting Professor at the University of California, Santa Cruz, and the Multi-Faith Resource Unit, Selly Oak, Birmingham.

PAUL VAN PARIJS, CICM, was born in Belgium and joined CICM in 1956. He studied philosophy, theology, and scripture at Louvain, Lyons, and Rome. He taught for two years at the major seminary of Namur, Belgium before leaving for the Philippines in 1970. Paul was Dean and Old Testament Professor at Maryhill School of Theology and also taught at the Sisters' Formation Institute and the East Asian Pastoral Institute in Manila until 1987. He is presently Vicar General of his congregation.

ANA MARIA TEPEDINO is a Roman Catholic laywoman and has a Licentiate in Philosophy. The mother of four, she teaches Theology at the Catholic University and at St. Ursula's University, both located in Rio de Janeiro, Brazil.

PART IV

MICHAEL AMALADOSS, SJ, is a liturgist and theologian. He taught Theology at the Institute of Religious Studies, Delhi, India, and was editor of *Vidyajyoti*. At present, he is Assistant to the Superior General of the Jesuits in Rome. He is Vice-President of the International Association of Mission Studies and past member of the SEDOS Executive Committee. He is also a member of the editorial board of *Spiritus*.

DATE DUE

DEC 31 '98			